2000

Economic portrait of the European Union 1999

eurostat

THEME 2
Economy and finance

.... Immediate access to harmonized statistical data

Eurostat Data Shops:

A personalised data retrieval service

In order to provide the greatest possible number of people with access to high-quality statistical information, Eurostat has developed an extensive network of Data Shops (1).

Data Shops provide a wide range of **tailor-made services**:

- ★ immediate information searches undertaken by a team of experts in European statistics;
- ★ rapid and personalised response that takes account of the specified search requirements and intended use;
- ★ a choice of data carrier depending on the type of information required.

Information can be requested by phone, mail, fax or e-mail.

(1) See list of Eurostat Data Shops at the end of the publication.

Internet:

Essentials on Community statistical news

- ★ Euro indicators: more than 100 indicators on the euro-zone; harmonized, comparable, and free of charge;
- ★ About Eurostat: what it does and how it works;
- ★ Products and databases: a detailed description of what Eurostat has to offer;
- ★ Indicators on the European Union: convergence criteria; euro yield curve and further main indicators on the European Union at your disposal;
- ★ Press releases: direct access to all Eurostat press releases.

For further information, visit us on the Internet at: www.europa.eu.int/comm/eurostat/

A great deal of additional information on the European Union is available on the Internet.
It can be accessed through the Europa server (http://europa.eu.int).

Cataloguing data can be found at the end of this publication.

Luxembourg: Office for Official Publications of the European Communities, 2000

ISBN 92-828-9913-6

Printed in France

PRINTED ON WHITE CHLORINE-FREE PAPER

PREFACE

As with similar publications produced by a number of statistical institutes at national level, this document is designed to bring together in a single volume wide-ranging macroeconomic data on the European Union and the Member States and to provide statistical analysis of those data. As well as short-term aspects, this report looks at structural differences between Member States and how they develop.

Although the statistical analysis makes reference to specific national situations in the Member States, this report endeavours to use the main economic variables to draw a profile of the Fifteen and the euro zone. The comparison is extended, where possible, to the various economic areas of the world, as well as to the main economic partners of the Union. Great importance is given to the macroeconomic data of the candidate countries.

Unlike the economic analyses and forecasts made by other services of the European Commission, this report only provides a descriptive analysis of the facts. While the emphasis is primarily on 1999, retrospective series also figure prominently.

In an age where up-to-date information is crucial to our understanding of socioeconomic events, it may seem inappropriate to publish and comment on relatively old data. However, these data have certain advantages:

— they have been compiled, for the great majority, using the uniform definitions and methodologies of the European system of accounts (ESA 95);

— the data come mainly from the national statistical institutes of the Member States;

— a knowledge of recent trends helps in gathering information about the present.

Certainly, one of the major problems in producing a report of this kind concerns the availability of recent data for all the countries when the report is being drafted. Some countries do not transmit any data at all for some variables, or else the data become available only one or even more years after the reference year.

Eurostat nevertheless believes that, by presenting and commenting in one single volume the main macroeconomic data of the Union and the Member States, this report will render these data more accessible to users and will contribute significantly to a better understanding of the economic phenomena of our time.

Yves Franchet

Director-General

Eurostat

Under the responsibility of Marco De March, Eurostat Unit B.2 'Economic accounts and international markets: production and analysis' benefited for the production of this summary report from the precious expertise of UnIts B.3, B.4, B.5, C.4, E.1, E.2 and E.4. Unit C.1 and the Translation Service of the Commission also provided their essential logistic support.

Overall coordination

Claude Hublart

Economic coordination

Gabriella Manganelli

Writing team

Roberto Barcellan, Wayne Codd, Peter Degerstedt, Marco De March, Claude Hublart, Gabriella Manganelli and Silke Stapel (Economic accounts), Tim Allen (External trade), Paolo Paserini, Nikolaos Chryssanthou and Javier Llordén-Rodriguez (Balance of payments), Axel Behrens and Volker Stabernak (Regions), Harry Bierings and Karin Winqvist (Household budgets), Aarno Laihonen (Population), Alois Van Bastelaere (Labour market), Giuliano Amerini and Flavio Bianconi (Social protection), Sheldon Warton-Woods and Olivier Delobbe (Interest rates, euro and exchange rates), Patricia Klees (Prices).

File preparation for publishing

Cindy Brockly and Madeleine Larue

Manuscript completed in August 2000

For further information or any suggestions, please contact:

Eurostat — Unit B.2
5, rue Alphonse Weicker
L-2721 Luxembourg
Tel. (352) 43 01-33207
Fax (352) 43 01-33879
marco.demarch@cec.eu.int

All data requests should be addressed to:

Data Shop Luxembourg
4, rue Alphonse Weicker
L-2721 Luxembourg
(PO Box 453 L-2014 Luxembourg)
Tel. (352) 43 35-2251
Fax (352) 43 35-22221
dslux@eurostat.datashop.lu

CONTENTS

Introduction

In terms of economic performance, 1999 was a relatively good year for the European Union, whose gross domestic product (GDP) rose by 2.4 %. This overall assessment is strengthened by the data available for the first quarter of 2000, which show a 3.3 % growth compared with the corresponding period of last year. When comparing the four major European economies in 1999, somewhat varying trends are apparent. France and the United Kingdom enjoyed growth rates of + 2.9 % and + 2.1 % respectively, whereas Germany and Italy came in lower at + 1.5 % and + 1.4 % respectively.

However, to measure economic performance simply on the basis of GDP growth is rather a short-sighted approach. Reality is certainly more complex. This publication gives a series of macroeconomic indicators which are required to understand the economy of the Union and its Member States, presenting data, wherever appropriate, in a wider geographic context including in particular the United States, Japan and the candidate countries.

At the end of 1999, several indicators attest to the relatively healthy situation within the European economy. For the Fifteen as a whole, investment appears to be particularly dynamic (+ 4.9 %) and employment has risen by 1.4 %, bringing unemployment down to 9.2 %. In addition, average annual inflation remains low (+ 1.2 %). The general improvement in public finances also continues. The average general government deficit of the Fifteen reduced from – 1.5 % in 1998 to – 0.7 % in 1999. No country now exceeds – 2.0 %, and indeed seven record a budget surplus.

These data at the Union level sometimes disguise significant differences which exist among Member States. If we exclude Luxembourg due to its rather atypical nature, GDP growth ranges from 9.8 % in Ireland, one of the highest rates in the world, to 1.4 % in Italy. GDP per head varies from 25 000 PPS in Denmark to 14 200 PPS in Greece while the unemployment rate stands at 15.8 % in Spain as against just 3.3 % in the Netherlands. Moreover, three countries — Italy, Belgium and Greece — still have a public debt which exceeds 100 % of GDP, while all others are under 70 %. Obviously, the European economy is still divided between convergence and diversity, integration and individuality.

The goal of this publication is to give the reader, mainly in the form of simple and easily understandable tables and graphs, the basic information necessary for a better understanding of the European economy. Confronted with the figures, certainties can quickly waver, intuitions be confirmed or invalidated, judgments be revised. More than ever, an understanding of the fine nuances coupled with appropriate caution are absolutely necessary.

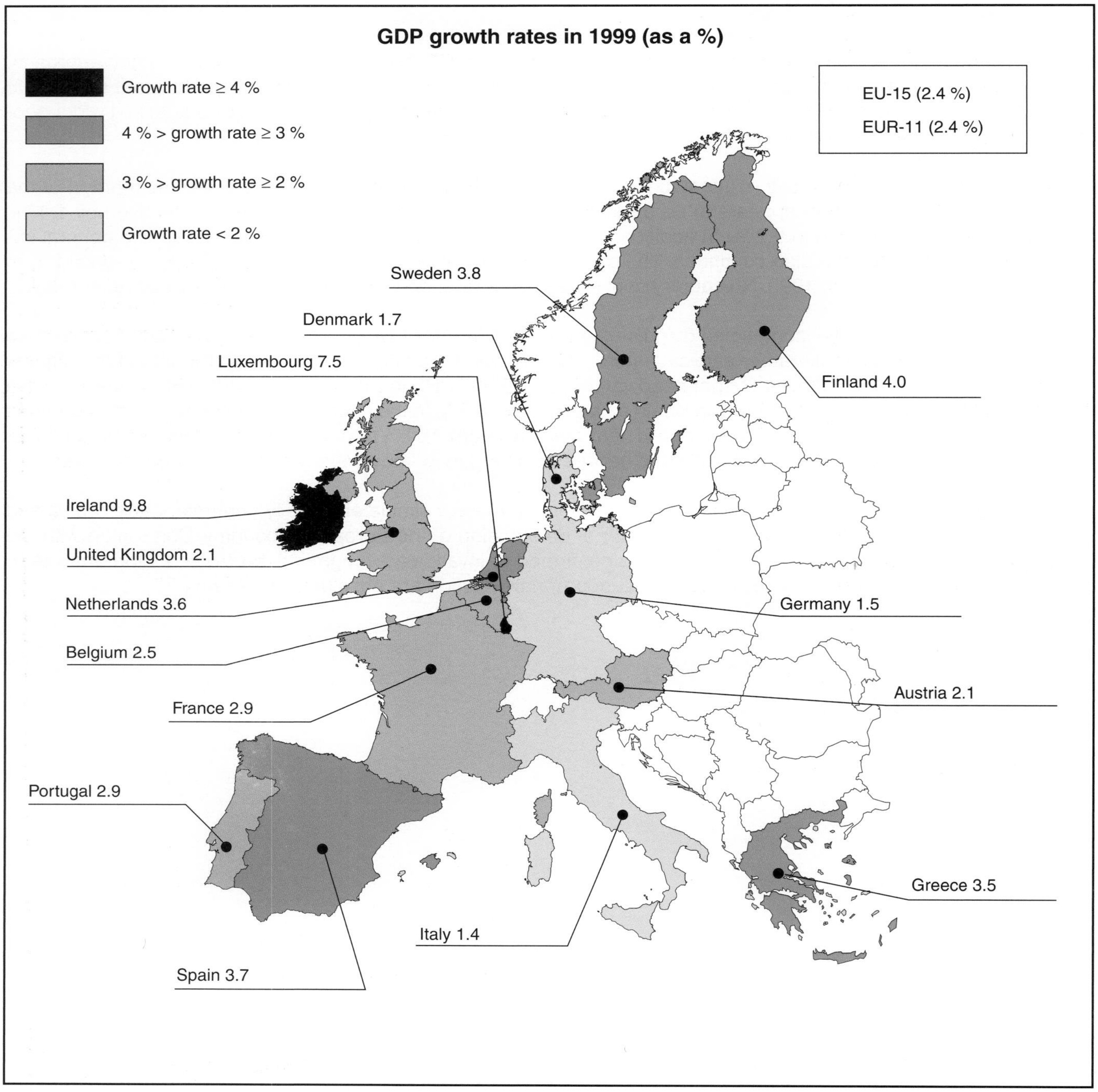

GDP growth rates in 1999 (as a %)

Growth rate ≥ 4 %

4 % > growth rate ≥ 3 %

3 % > growth rate ≥ 2 %

Growth rate < 2 %

EU-15 (2.4 %)

EUR-11 (2.4 %)

Sweden 3.8

Denmark 1.7

Luxembourg 7.5

Finland 4.0

Ireland 9.8

United Kingdom 2.1

Netherlands 3.6

Germany 1.5

Belgium 2.5

Austria 2.1

France 2.9

Portugal 2.9

Greece 3.5

Italy 1.4

Spain 3.7

Corrigendum

This page replaces page 9

Economic portrait of the European Union 1999

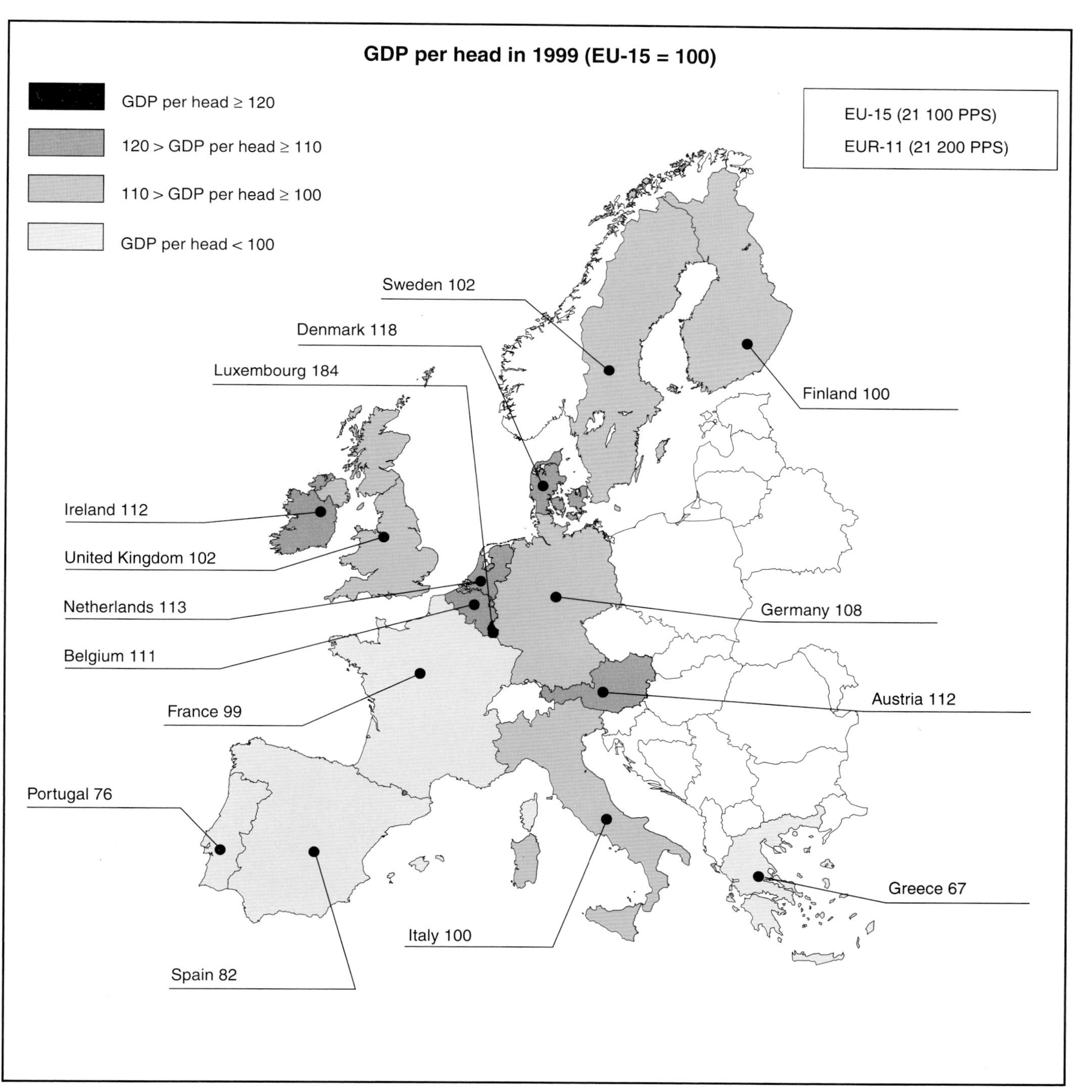

KS-31-00-336-EN-K

PIB par tête, 1999 (EU-15 = 100)

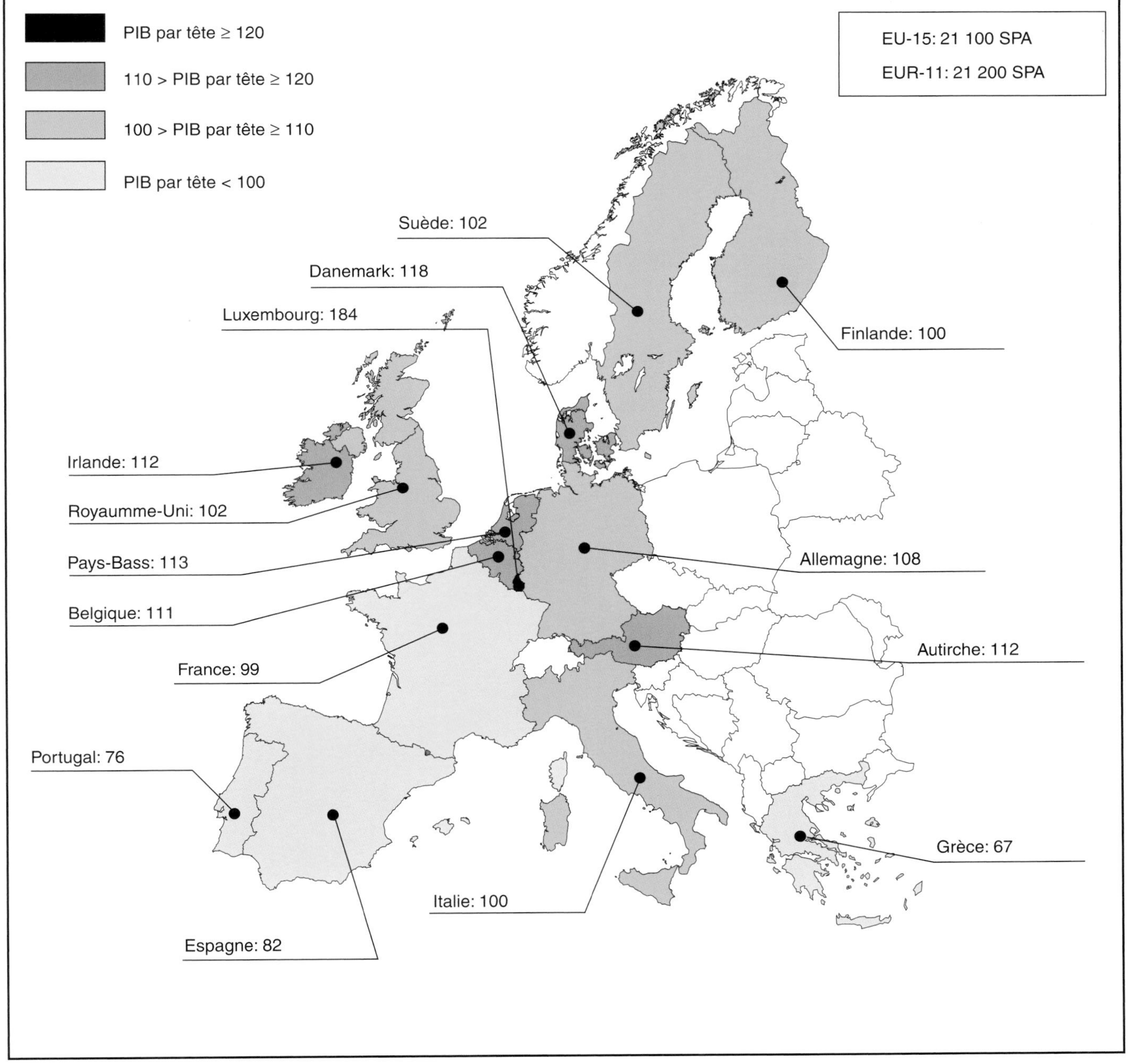

- PIB par tête ≥ 120
- 110 > PIB par tête ≥ 120
- 100 > PIB par tête ≥ 110
- PIB par tête < 100

EU-15: 21 100 SPA

EUR-11: 21 200 SPA

Suède: 102

Danemark: 118

Luxembourg: 184

Finlande: 100

Irlande: 112

Royaumme-Uni: 102

Pays-Bass: 113

Allemagne: 108

Belgique: 111

Autirche: 112

France: 99

Portugal: 76

Grèce: 67

Italie: 100

Espagne: 82

1. ECONOMY OF THE UNION

1.1. Gross domestic product

In 1999, the gross domestic product of the European Union was EUR 7 974 billion ([1]); GDP in the euro zone was EUR 6 116 billion, which is 23 % less than the EU total. If we compare the result for the European Union with the figures for its main trading partners, we see that the GDP of the United States (EUR 8 725 billion) exceeds that of the EU (albeit by just 11 %), whereas Japan's (EUR 4 081 billion) is about half that of EU-15.

Germany alone (EUR 1 982.3 billion) accounts for about one quarter of the EU's GDP; it is followed by the United Kingdom (EUR 1 352.7 billion in 1999, about 17 % of EU-15 GDP), which itself is closely followed by France (EUR 1 344.4 billion, or 16.9 % of the total). In 1999, Italy's GDP was EUR 1 099.1 billion, or 13.8 % of the total for EU-15. These four countries together account for 72.5 % of the Union's gross domestic product. If we add Spain, whose EUR 559.4 billion GDP contributes to 7.0 % of the EU total, and the Netherlands, which, at EUR 369.5 billion, accounts for 4.6 %, we see that just six countries account for 84.2 % of the European Union's GDP, the other nine Member States making up the remaining 15.8 %.

Figure 1.1.1. Gross domestic product at current prices, 1999 (billion EUR)

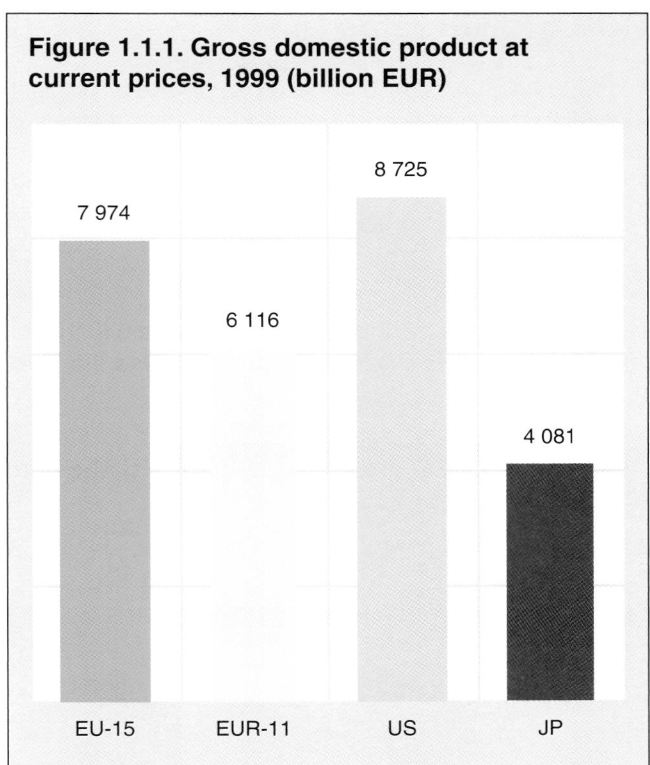

Source: Eurostat.

Figure 1.1.2. Gross domestic product, 1999

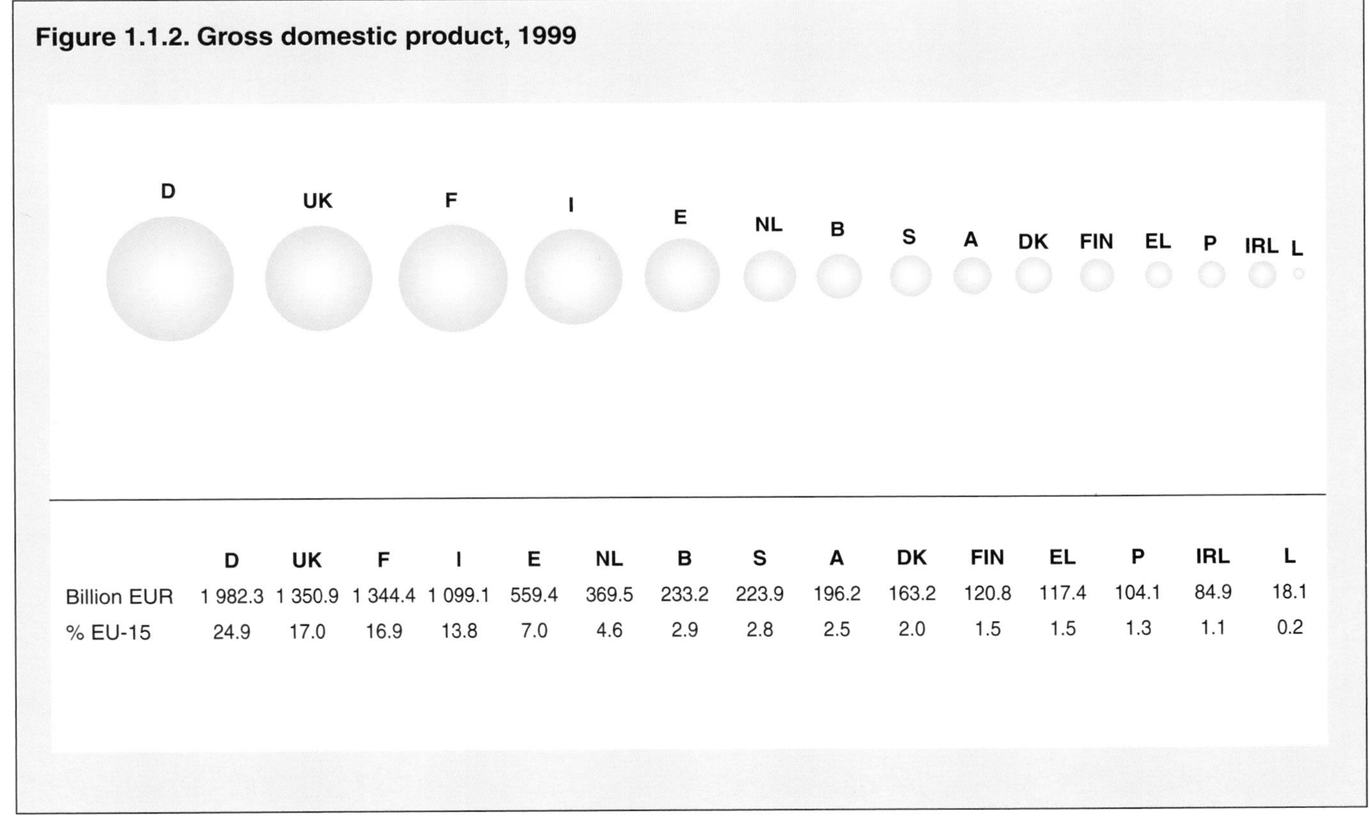

	D	UK	F	I	E	NL	B	S	A	DK	FIN	EL	P	IRL	L
Billion EUR	1 982.3	1 350.9	1 344.4	1 099.1	559.4	369.5	233.2	223.9	196.2	163.2	120.8	117.4	104.1	84.9	18.1
% EU-15	24.9	17.0	16.9	13.8	7.0	4.6	2.9	2.8	2.5	2.0	1.5	1.5	1.3	1.1	0.2

Source: Eurostat.

([1]) GDP at current prices.

GDP growth rates ([2])

In 1999, the European Union's gross domestic product rose by 2.4 %, which represents a slowdown compared with the two previous years (2.5 % in 1997 and 2.7 % in 1998). Compared with its main trading partners, the EU's economy grew much more slowly than that of the United States (+ 4.2 %) but much faster than Japan's (+ 0.2 %) (see Section 2.1).

The growth rate in the euro zone was identical to that in the Union as a whole (+ 2.4 %), just as it was the year before (+ 2.7 % in both the euro zone and EU-15). France recorded the highest rate of growth (2.9 %) of the EU's four biggest Member States, followed by the United Kingdom (+ 2.1 %) and, somewhat further behind, Germany (+ 1.5 %) and Italy (+ 1.4 %). This was broadly in line with the situation in 1998, when France (+ 3.1 %) achieved the highest growth rate of the 'Big four', followed by the United Kingdom (+ 2.6 %). France, the United Kingdom and Italy all saw slight declines in their GDP growth rates in 1999; in Germany, growth declined much more markedly, from 2.2 % in 1998 to just 1.5 % in 1999.

Figure 1.1.3. GDP growth rates in the EU, the euro zone and the 'Big four EU countries' (as a %)

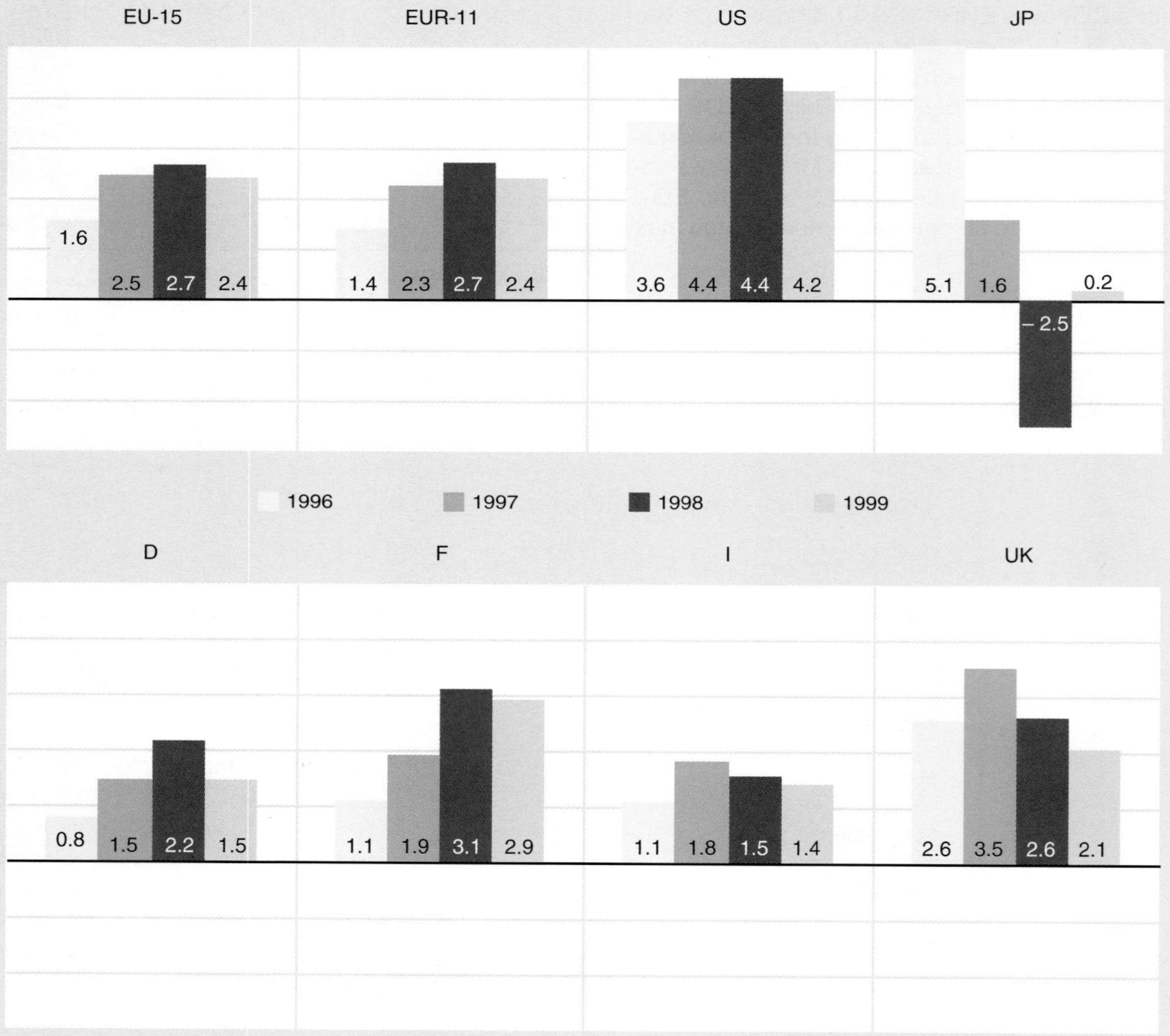

	1996	1997	1998	1999
EU-15	1.6	2.5	2.7	2.4
EUR-11	1.4	2.3	2.7	2.4
US	3.6	4.4	4.4	4.2
JP	5.1	1.6	– 2.5	0.2
D	0.8	1.5	2.2	1.5
F	1.1	1.9	3.1	2.9
I	1.1	1.8	1.5	1.4
UK	2.6	3.5	2.6	2.1

Source: Eurostat.

([2]) The GDP data used throughout this publication are those available on 15 June 2000. Nevertheless, after the revision of their figures by some countries during July, it has been decided, for this section only, to publish the data as available on 31 July 2000.

Ireland and Luxembourg are again remarkable for growth rates well above those in the other Member States: in 1999, Ireland's GDP expanded by 9.8 %, while Luxembourg's grew at a robust 7.5 %. More than four percentage points behind Ireland and Luxembourg came Sweden (+ 3.8 %) and Spain (+ 3.7 %). Apart from Luxembourg, only Sweden had a higher rate of growth than in the previous year. All the other EU Member States recorded stable or slightly lower growth rates: the biggest declines were recorded in Denmark (from + 2.5 % in 1998 to + 1.7 %) and Finland (from + 5.0 % to + 4.0 %).

Table 1.1.1. GDP growth rates (as a %)

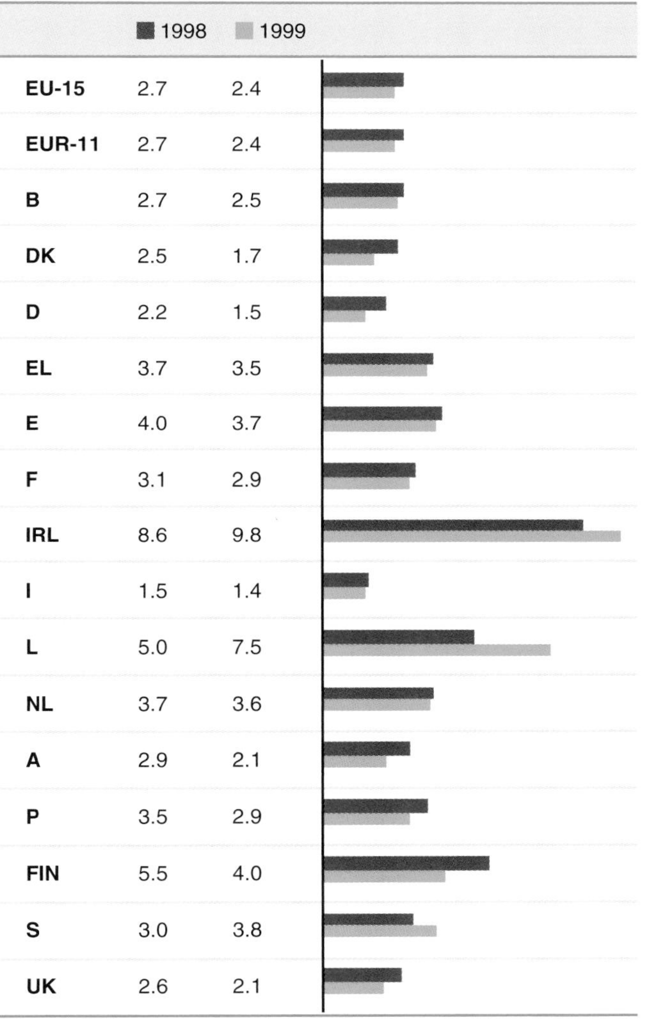

	1998	1999
EU-15	2.7	2.4
EUR-11	2.7	2.4
B	2.7	2.5
DK	2.5	1.7
D	2.2	1.5
EL	3.7	3.5
E	4.0	3.7
F	3.1	2.9
IRL	8.6	9.8
I	1.5	1.4
L	5.0	7.5
NL	3.7	3.6
A	2.9	2.1
P	3.5	2.9
FIN	5.5	4.0
S	3.0	3.8
UK	2.6	2.1

Source: Eurostat.

Contributions to GDP growth

The 2.4 % growth recorded by the European Union in 1999 was mainly due to household final consumption expenditure and investments (gross fixed capital formation (GFCF)): their respective contributions, calculated as percentages of GDP growth, were 66.5 % and 42.5 %. Government final consumption expenditure accounted for 15.4 %, whereas the trade balance (exports less imports) (3) slowed growth by 22.3 %. Compared to the previous year, household consumption and investments both made bigger contributions to GDP growth, as did public consumption; the impact of the trade balance declined, but was still negative (see Figure 1.1.4 and Table 1.1.2).

In the euro zone, the contribution of household consumption was smaller than in EU-15, but still came out at 59.9 %; the contribution of investments was in line with that in the EU as a whole (42.8 % of GDP growth). Public consumption (12.5 %) and the trade balance (– 19.1 %) had a smaller impact.

The 2.1 % GDP growth recorded in the United Kingdom in 1999 was the net result of contrasting developments: on the one hand, household consumption provided a major boost (+ 123.6 %), whereas a deteriorating trade balance situation acted as a brake (– 79.7 %). In Germany and Italy too (albeit to a lesser extent), the main factor behind GDP growth in 1999 was household consumption (which accounted for 81.9 % of growth in Germany and 72.8 % in Italy), followed by investments (34.5 % in Germany and 58.6 % in Italy); the trade balance, however, acted as a brake on economic growth in those two countries. In France, there was a fairly even balance between the impact of investments (which accounted for 45.6 % of the country's 2.9 % economic growth in 1999) and household consumption, which accounted for 39.2 %; the trade balance had only a negligible impact.

In most Member States, the main factor in GDP growth in 1999 was household consumption, the exceptions being Belgium and France, where the biggest boost came from investments, and Denmark and Finland, where the trade balance was the main factor. Luxembourg is a special case because of the small size of its economy and because stockbuilding was the main component of GDP growth.

(3) Note that a negative contribution does not mean that the variable itself or its rate of growth is negative. For example, where the trade balance is concerned, a negative contribution does not indicate a deficit: it indicates merely that growth in that variable was slower than that of the other components, with the result that it slowed the rate of GDP growth.

Figure 1.1.4. Component's contribution to GDP growth in 1999 (as a % of total GDP growth)

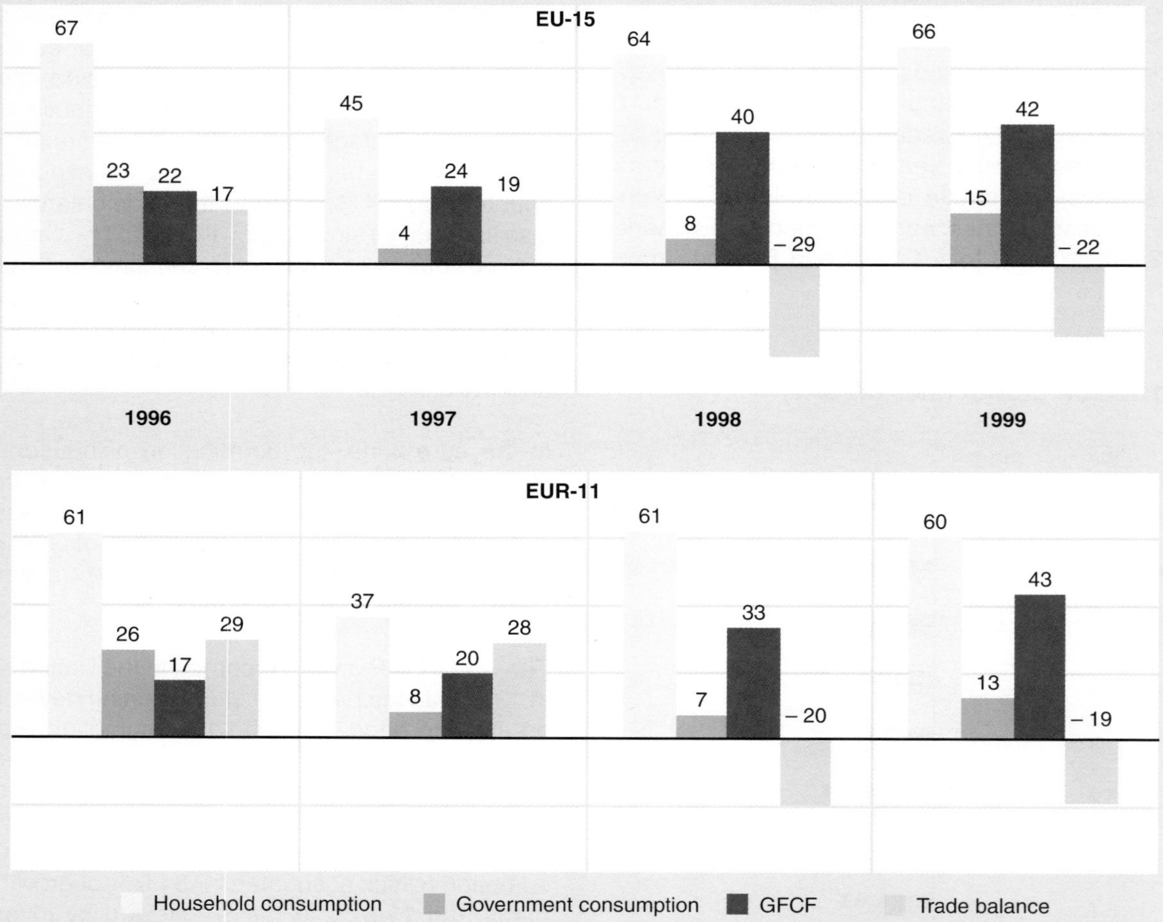

NB: To make reading easier, the changes in stocks have not been included.
Source: Eurostat.

Table 1.1.2. Component's contribution to GDP growth in 1999 (as a % of total GDP growth)

	Household consumption	Government consumption	Gross fixed capital formation	Trade balance	Stock	GDP growth rate
EU-15	66.5	15.4	42.5	– 22.3	– 2.0 ➔	**2.4**
EUR-11	59.9	12.5	42.8	– 19.1	3.9 ➔	**2.4**
B	41.2	23.1	44.7	31.8	– 40.7 ➔	**2.5**
DK	23.2	17.3	– 9.2	133.3	– 64.5 ➔	**1.7**
D	81.9	2.8	34.5	– 49.9	30.7 ➔	**1.5**
EL	56.0	2.1	53.3	– 10.7	– 0.7 ➔	**3.5**
E	70.0	8.3	51.6	– 31.3	1.4 ➔	**3.7**
F	39.2	20.6	45.6	3.9	– 9.3 ➔	**2.9**
IRL	49.0	6.6	32.1	13.4	– 1.1 ➔	**9.8**
I	72.8	7.6	58.6	– 70.3	31.3 ➔	**1.4**
L	25.3	28.6	27.3	– 25.6	44.5 ➔	**7.5**
NL	57.9	16.7	34.4	0.5	– 9.5 ➔	**3.6**
A	57.9	19.7	36.6	– 7.6	– 6.6 ➔	**2.1**
P	96.9	25.1	58.4	– 81.9	1.4 ➔	**2.9**
FIN	41.6	1.7	25.1	57.0	– 25.3 ➔	**4.0**
S	54.6	11.9	35.3	13.5	– 15.4 ➔	**3.8**
UK	123.6	38.7	47.4	– 79.7	– 29.9 ➔	**2.1**

NB: Negative contributions do not indicate a slowdown in the component growth.
Source: Eurostat.

Figure 1.1.5. Component's contribution to GDP growth in 1999 (as a % of total GDP growth)

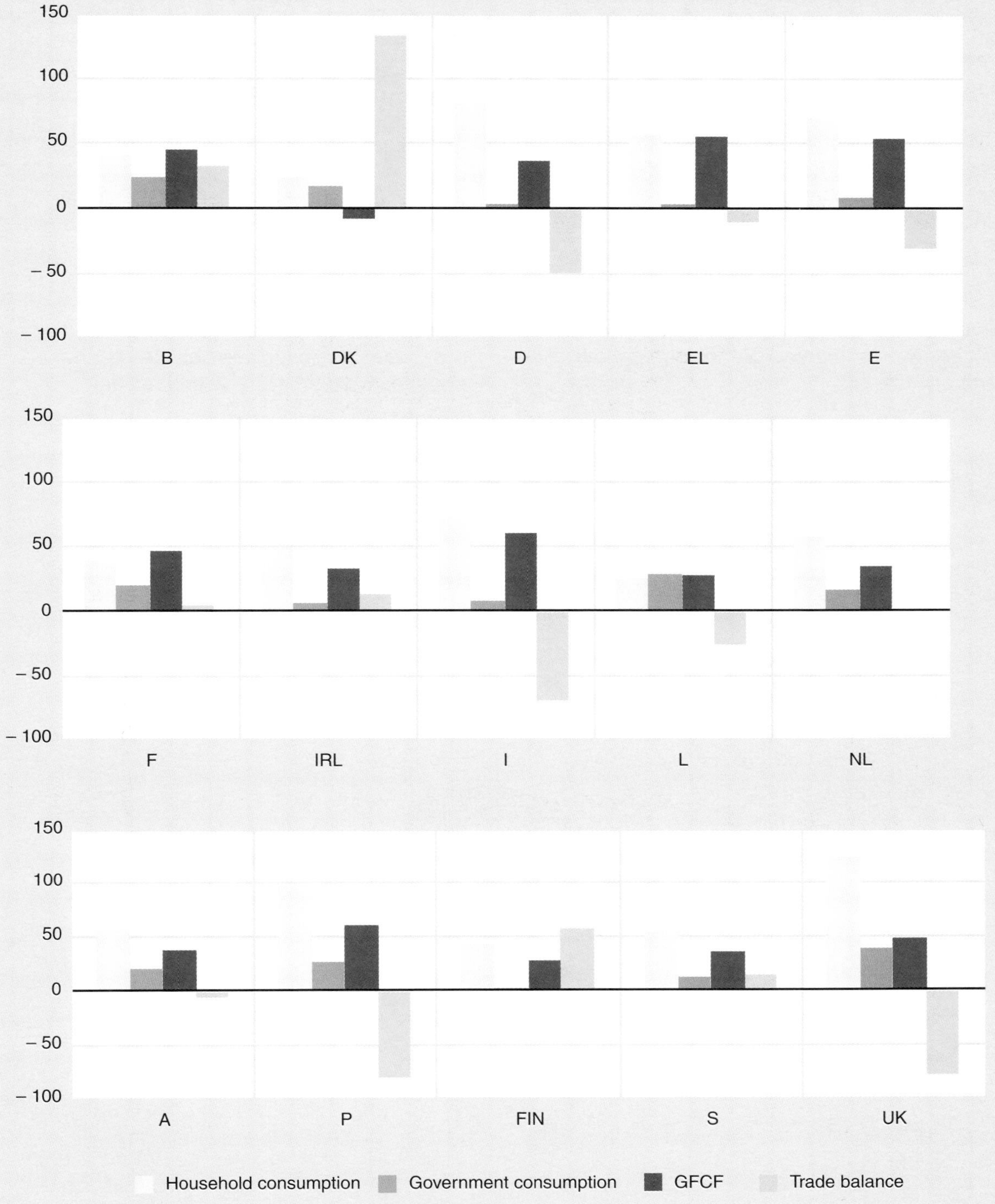

NB: To make reading easier, the changes in stocks have not been included.
Source: Eurostat.

1.2. GDP per head

If gross domestic product indicates the size of a country's economy in absolute terms, calculating per capita GDP (in relation to the population) provides an indication, albeit somewhat simplistic ([4]), of a country's wealth. To make comparison easier and precisely because we are referring to the concept of wealth, the data presented in this chapter have been calculated in purchasing power standards (PPS). The advantage of using PPS is that they eliminate distortions arising from the different price levels in the EU countries: they are conversion factors calculated as a weighted average of the price ratios of a basket of goods and services that are homogeneous, comparable and representative in each Member State.

In 1999, the per capita figure for each citizen in the European Union amounted to 21 100 PPS, only 100 PPS lower than the figure for the euro zone. The highest figures occurred in Luxembourg (38 800 PPS) and Denmark (25 000 PPS). Germany was the first of the four larger countries in terms of GDP per head, ranking seventh out of the Fifteen with 22 700 PPS, with the United Kingdom following in ninth place with 21 600 PPS, while Italy was tenth (21 200 PPS) and France (20 900 PPS) came only twelfth.

Figure 1.2.1 shows per capita GDP for all the EU countries. The web figure has the advantage of providing a visual overview of the distribution of the figures: if every country had the same figure, then the final shape would be a circle. The figures for 1995 are also shown, but it must be remembered that the PPS figures are at current prices and have been calculated primarily for comparison in terms of space and not time.

Figure 1.2.1. Gross domestic product per head, in PPS

	1995	1999
EU-15	17 600	21 100
EUR-11	17 900	21 200
B	19 800	23 400
DK	20 900	25 000
D	19 400	22 700
EL	11 600	14 200
E	13 800	17 300
F	18 300	20 900
IRL	16 300	23 600
I	18 300	21 200
L	30 500	38 800
NL	19 300	23 800
A	19 500	23 600
P	12 400	15 900
FIN	17 100	21 200
S	18 100	21 600
UK	16 900	21 600

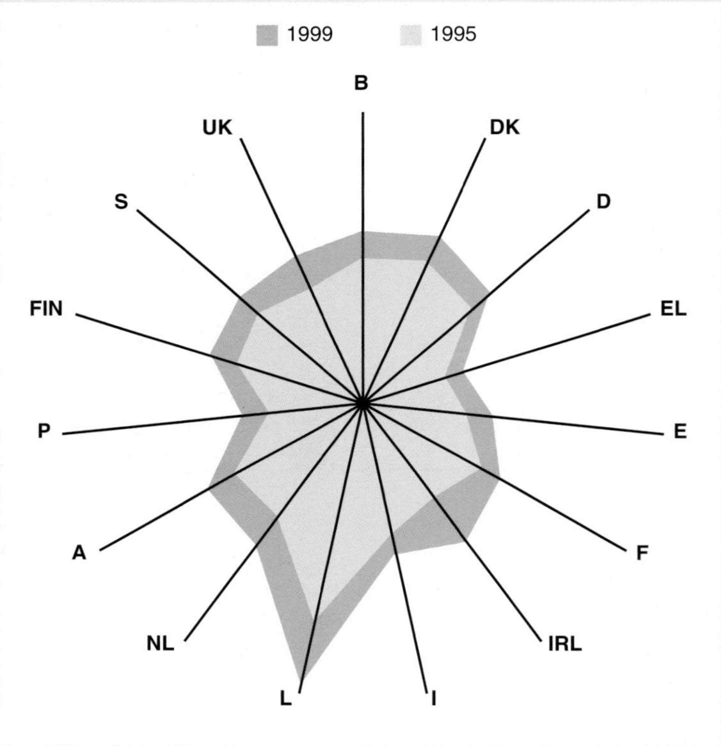

Source: Eurostat.

([4]) Per capita GDP provides no indication of the distribution of wealth.

Table 1.2.1. Gross domestic product per head, 1999

	PPS	Value growth index 1995 = 100
EU-15	21 100	119.9
EUR-11	21 200	118.3
B	23 400	118.4
DK	25 000	119.9
D	22 700	116.9
EL	14 200	122.0
E	17 300	125.4
F	20 900	114.2
IRL	23 600	145.1
I	21 200	115.9
L	38 800	127.6
NL	23 800	123.6
A	23 600	120.9
P	15 900	128.9
FIN	21 200	123.7
S	21 600	119.5
UK	21 600	127.9

Source: Eurostat.

However, in order to show how per capita GDP has developed over time, Table 1.2.1 shows the value growth index (1995 = 100). It is apparent from this that per capita GDP in the EU in 1999 was 19.3 % higher than in the reference year; the corresponding figure for the euro zone was a percentage point lower, at + 18.3 %. Among the four largest countries, the United Kingdom stands out with the biggest change (+ 27.9 %), while lower figures were recorded for Germany (+ 16.9 %), Italy (+ 15.9 %) and France (+ 14.2 %). Indeed, it was these three countries that recorded the smallest changes in per capita GDP among all the Member States. The biggest changes among the Fifteen were recorded in Ireland, where per capita GDP was 45.1 % higher than in 1995, and Portugal (+ 28.9 %).

To make it easier to compare the Member States, Figure 1.2.2 shows the GDP per capita figures in relation to the EU average (EU-15 = 100). It is thus easier to observe and measure the big gap between the EU average and the figure for Luxembourg, which is 84 % above the EU average. The second highest figure is for Denmark, but here the difference is only 18 %. The biggest differences for figures below the EU average are in Greece (33 % below average), Portugal (– 24 %) and Spain (– 18 %). Figure 1.2.2 also shows the situation in 1995, and it can be seen that the positions at the extremes remain unchanged. The most obvious change was for Ireland, which recorded a figure for per capita GDP that was lower than the EU average at the beginning of the period under review (1995–99), while in 1999 it was 12 % above average, placing Ireland fourth among the EU countries. The same type of change took place in the United Kingdom and Finland, which were both — slightly — above the EU average in 1999.

Figure 1.2.3 shows a set of data intended to show the similarities, or differences, between the Member State figures. Firstly, the top figure shows the highest figures (Luxembourg again first, followed by Denmark), the lowest figure (always Greece) and the EU average. The line that links these points shows the range, or the distance between the highest and lowest figures and their position in relation to the average (in this case EU-15). In 1999, the range between the highest and lowest per capita GDP recorded in the Union was 24 600 PPS; expressed differently, per capita GDP in Luxembourg was 2.6 times the figure for Greece. If we exclude Luxembourg, the gap between the figures for Denmark (second highest) and Greece was 10 800 PPS, meaning that the per capita GDP of the Danes was 1.8 times that of the Greeks.

To give a more summary indication of the range of values for all the EU countries, the relative standard deviation has been calculated, that is, the average standard deviation of the figures from the average ([5]). Thus, in 1999, per capita GDP figures for the 15 Member States had a range of deviation of 23.8 % around the average, a figure that was very similar to the 1995 figure but which had gone down by approximately one point in the intervening period. If Luxembourg is again excluded, however, the range of deviation shows a considerable drop to 14.7 % and the figures are more clearly and consistently aligned throughout the period in question.

([5]) In this case, the simple arithmetic average and not the EU value, which is a weighted average.

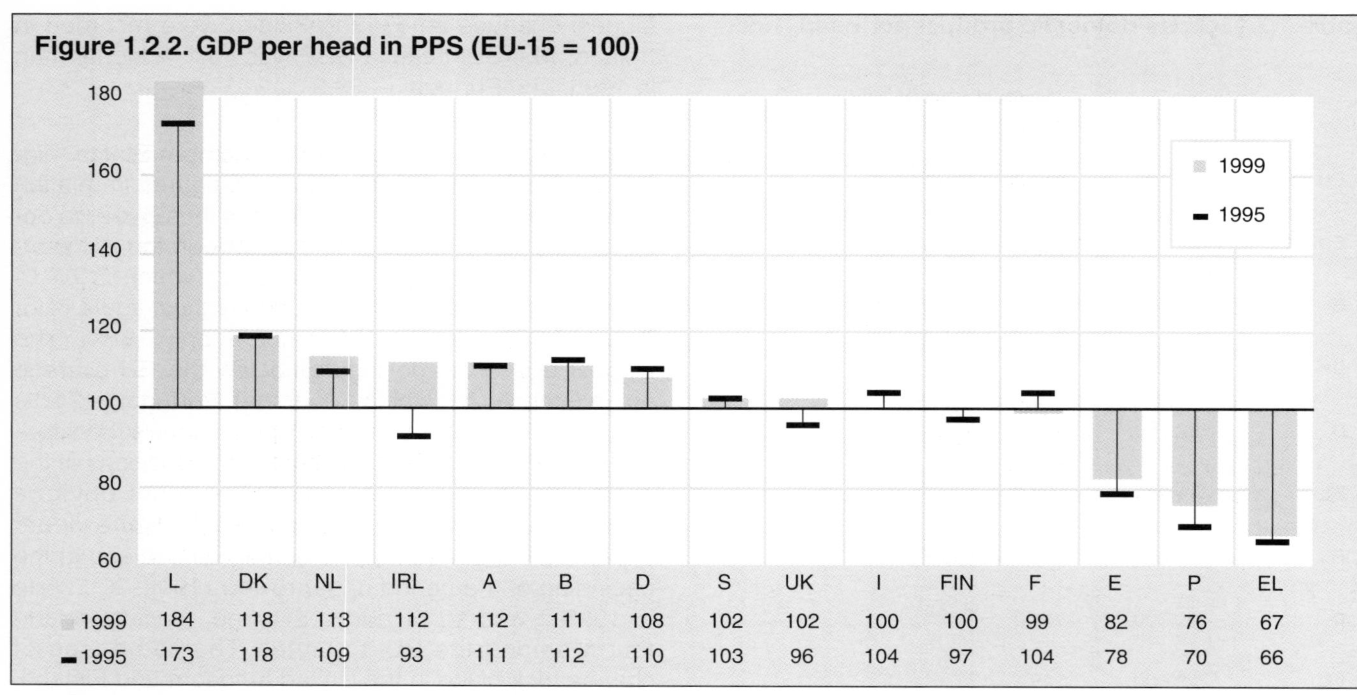

	L	DK	NL	IRL	A	B	D	S	UK	I	FIN	F	E	P	EL
1999	184	118	113	112	112	111	108	102	102	100	100	99	82	76	67
1995	173	118	109	93	111	112	110	103	96	104	97	104	78	70	66

Source: Eurostat.

Figure 1.2.3. GDP per head

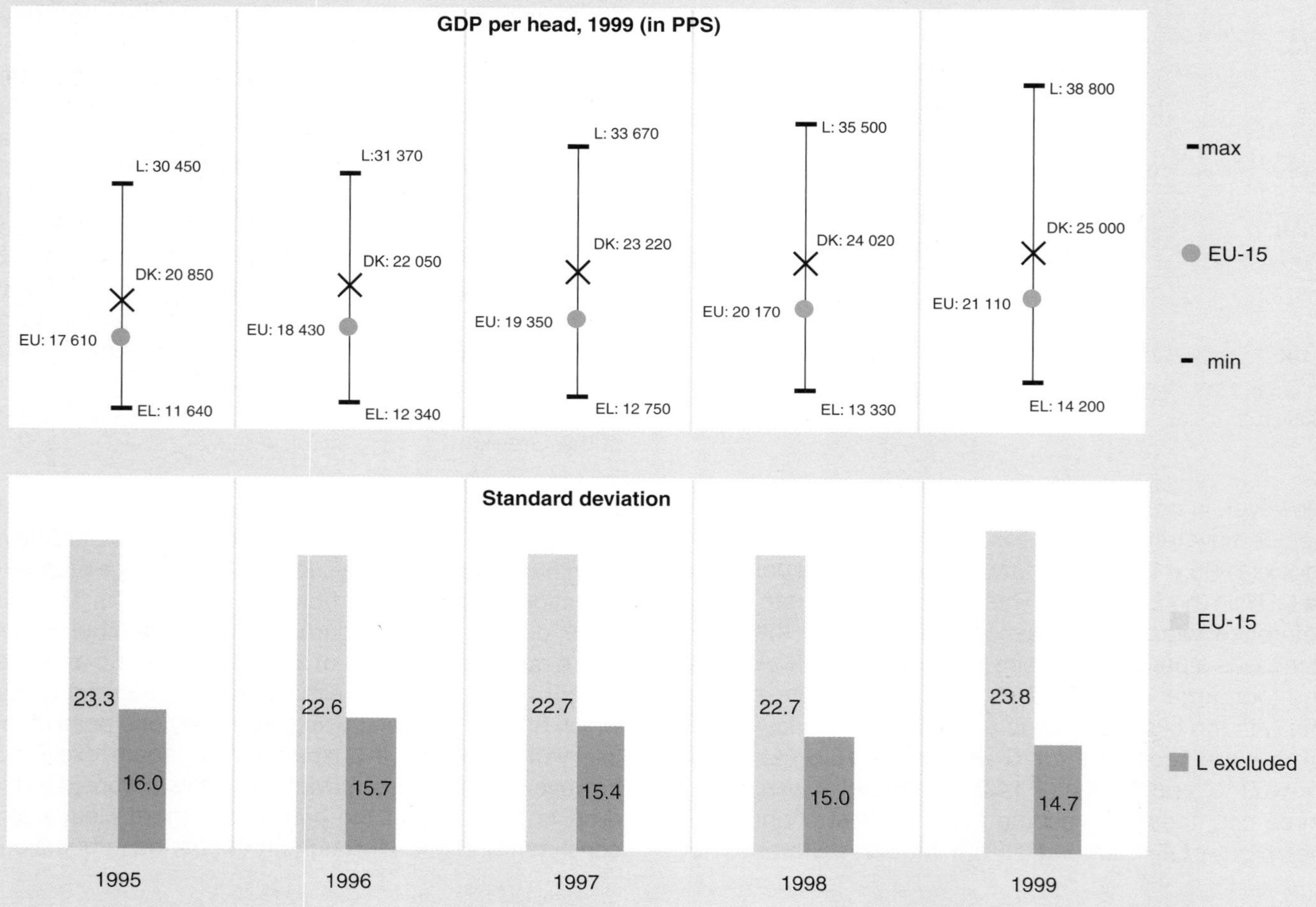

GDP per head, 1999 (in PPS)

	1995	1996	1997	1998	1999
max	L: 30 450	L:31 370	L: 33 670	L: 35 500	L: 38 800
X	DK: 20 850	DK: 22 050	DK: 23 220	DK: 24 020	DK: 25 000
EU-15	EU: 17 610	EU: 18 430	EU: 19 350	EU: 20 170	EU: 21 110
min	EL: 11 640	EL: 12 340	EL: 12 750	EL: 13 330	EL: 14 200

Standard deviation

	1995	1996	1997	1998	1999
EU-15	23.3	22.6	22.7	22.7	23.8
L excluded	16.0	15.7	15.4	15.0	14.7

NB: As all maximum figures have been recorded for Luxembourg, we also added the preceding values(X): Denmark, during the considered period.
Source: Eurostat.

1.3. GDP components

Table 1.3.1 shows the absolute values ([6]) of the main components of GDP: household final consumption expenditure, government final consumption expenditure and gross fixed capital formation. Other components of GDP are imports and exports ([7]) and changes in stocks, but these are left out of consideration in this chapter, for the sake of simplicity.

In 1999, household final consumption in the European Union amounted to EUR 4 632 billion, a level well above those recorded for investments (EUR 1 606 billion) and government final consumption (EUR 1 592 billion). An interesting situation has come about between two of the larger European countries, France and the United Kingdom: France has the higher figures for government consumption (EUR 318 billion) and investments (EUR 256 billion), whereas household consumption in the United Kingdom is greater than in France (EUR 883 billion in the UK and EUR 737 billion in France).

Consumption per head

To permit comparisons between countries, the per capita values for household consumption and government consumption ([8]) have been calculated and expressed in terms of the EU value (EU-15 = 100) (see Table 1.3.2 and Figure 1.3.1). As with GDP, Luxembourg stands out from the other Member States by having much higher household consumption (37 % higher than the EU as a whole) as well as government consumption (+ 64 %). This is in contrast with Denmark, the Member State with the second-highest per capita GDP, where government consumption is well above the EU average (+ 54 %), but household consumption is close to the average of the other Member States (+ 3 %).

As regards household consumption, the United Kingdom, alongside Luxembourg, stands out as having per capita figure well above the average (+ 15 %) for the other Member States. The United Kingdom is the only country where household consumption is above the

Table 1.3.1. Main components of GDP, 1999 (billion EUR, current prices)

	Household consumption	Government consumption	GFCF
EU-15	4 632.0	1 592.0	1 606.3
EUR-11	3 465.8	1 225.5	1 267.2
B	125.0	49.4	49.1
DK	82.5	42.0	31.8
D	1 144.7	376.4	415.0
EL	86.9	16.8	27.1
E	332.6	95.7	133.6
F	736.6	318.3	256.1
IRL	43.3	11.8	20.5
I	654.5	199.1	208.0
L	7.9	3.2	3.6
NL	185.2	85.5	82.3
A	109.7	39.1	47.7
P	65.3	21.2	28.0
FIN	61.1	25.7	23.3
S	113.2	60.5	37.1
UK	883.5	247.2	243.1

Source: Eurostat.

Table 1.3.2. Consumption per head, 1999

	Household consumption		Government consumption	
	PPS	EU-15 = 100	PPS	EU-15 = 100
EU-15	12 270	*100*	4 220	*100*
EUR-11	12 010	*98*	4 250	*101*
B	12 530	*102*	5 010	*119*
DK	12 610	*103*	6 490	*154*
D	13 070	*107*	4 350	*103*
EL	10 480	*85*	2 050	*49*
E	10 270	*84*	2 990	*71*
F	11 390	*93*	4 980	*118*
IRL	12 030	*98*	3 320	*79*
I	12 560	*102*	3 860	*91*
L	16 800	*137*	6 940	*164*
NL	11 910	*97*	5 560	*132*
A	13 150	*107*	4 730	*112*
P	9 970	*81*	3 270	*77*
FIN	10 670	*87*	4 540	*108*
S	10 880	*89*	5 880	*139*
UK	14 060	*115*	3 980	*94*

Source: Eurostat.

([6]) The absolute values are measured at current prices, rates of growth are calculated at constant prices, and per capita PPS values are based on current prices.

([7]) A more detailed analysis of external trade is given in Section 2.3, using data obtained from Comext. The data reproduced in this section, however, were obtained from the national accounts, and do not include intra-Community trade.

([8]) Per capita gross fixed capital formation has not been calculated because the investors do not actually correspond to the population.

average for EU-15 and government consumption is below the EU average. The lowest figures are those for Portugal (19 % below the EU average), Spain (16 % below) and Greece (15 % below)

The countries with the lowest figures for government consumption are the same, albeit in a different order: Greece has the lowest figure (51 % below the EU average), while Spain is 29 % below the average and Portugal 23 % below. Next comes Ireland, where per capita government consumption is 21 % below the average. In addition to Luxembourg and Denmark, which, it has already been seen, have the highest figures, Sweden and the Netherlands recorded values which were much higher (39 % and 32 % respectively) than the EU average.

As with per capita GDP, by comparing the scatter around the average, using the relative standard deviation, we see that the scatter between the per capita values for household consumption in the Member States is well below that for government consumption: in the case of household consumption, the relative standard deviation in 1999 was 14.0 %, whereas the figures for government consumption displayed a scatter of 28.7 % with respect to the average. If we examine this indicator for the period 1995–99, we see that, whereas the scatter for household consumption was on a downward trend, the relative deviation for government consumption was broadly unchanged. It should be remembered that the relative standard deviation for per capita GDP was 23.8 % in 1999.

Figure 1.3.1. Household consumption (HC) and government consumption (GC) per capita, 1999 (in PPS — EU-15 = 100)

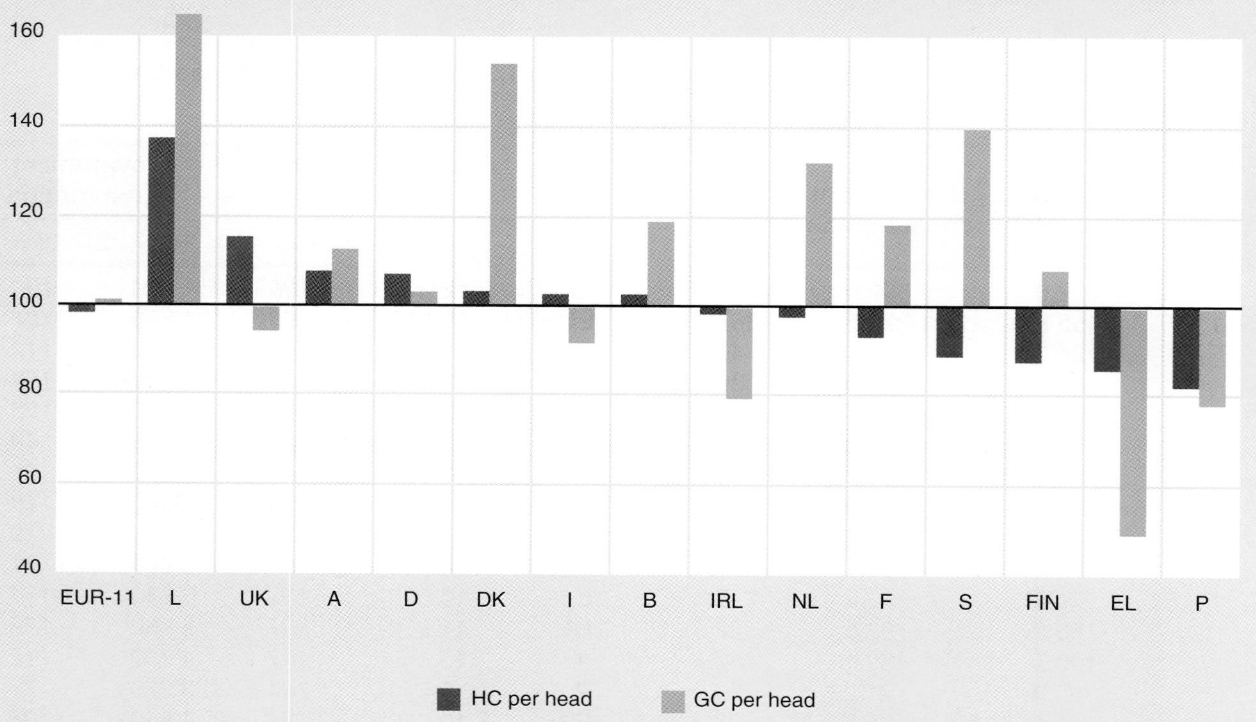

NB: In order to show the series in descending order, figures have been sorted by HC data — because of its major importance.
Source: Eurostat.

Growth rates of main GDP components

Turning now to rates of growth in 1999, investments (gross fixed capital formation) in the European Union had the fastest growth, increasing by 4.9 % compared with the previous year. Household consumption grew by 2.7 % and government consumption by 1.8 %. Over the last five years (1995–99), after two years of low growth (1996 and 1997), investments and household consumption grew very robustly in 1998 (+ 5.3 % in the case of investments and + 3.0 % for household consumption); the result for 1999 is therefore both a slight decline compared with the previous year's growth rate, but also confirms recent strength. In the case of government consumption, however, growth in 1999 was back to the level seen at the beginning of the reference period (+ 1.8 % in 1999 and in 1996). The trends in the euro zone ran in parallel, the only difference being that the increase in investments was more modest in 1998 (+ 4.3 %), with the result that the figure for 1999 represents an acceleration (see Figure 1.3.2 and Table 1.3.3).

Table 1.3.3. Growth of main GDP components, 1999 (as a %)

	Household consumption	Government consumption	GFCF
EU-15	2.7	1.8	4.9
EUR-11	2.5	1.5	4.8
B	2.0	2.8	5.4
DK	0.7	1.1	– 0.7
D	2.1	0.2	2.3
EL	2.6	0.5	8.3
E	4.4	1.8	8.3
F	2.1	2.6	7.1
IRL	7.7	3.8	12.5
I	1.7	0.6	4.4
L	4.1	12.8	10.1
NL	4.2	2.6	5.7
A	2.4	2.3	3.5
P	4.4	4.0	6.0
FIN	2.9	0.3	4.8
S	4.1	1.8	8.1
UK	3.9	4.4	5.2

Source: Eurostat.

Figure 1.3.2. Growth of main GDP components, 1999 (as a %)

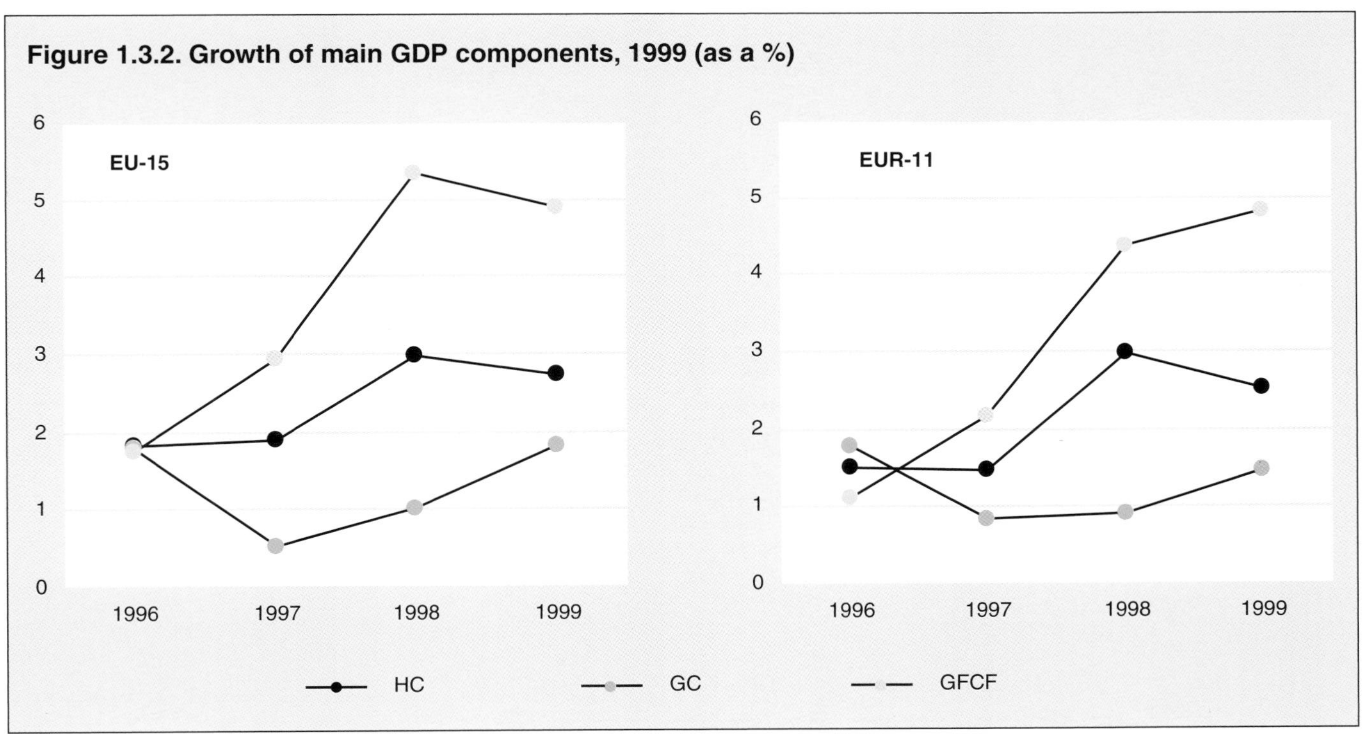

Source: Eurostat.

Household consumption grew the fastest in Ireland (+ 7.7 %) and in Spain and Portugal (by + 4.4 % in both countries), but was little changed in Denmark (+ 0.7 %) and Italy (+ 1.7 %).

Luxembourg stands out as having the fastest-growing government consumption (+ 12.8 % in 1999), followed by the United Kingdom (+ 4.4 %) and Portugal (+ 4.0 %). Government consumption grew only minimally in a number of Member States: the lowest rates of growth were recorded in Germany (+ 0.2 %), Finland (+ 0.3 %), Greece (+ 0.5 %) and Italy (+ 0.6 %).

In general, investments continued to grow rapidly, especially in Ireland (+ 12.5 %) and Luxembourg (+ 10.1 %), with significant growth rates also being recorded in Spain and Greece (+ 8.3 % in both countries), Sweden (+ 8.1 %) and France (+ 7.1 %). The only Member State to record negative growth for investments was Denmark (– 0.7 %).

Figure 1.3.3. Growth of main GDP components, 1999 (as a %)

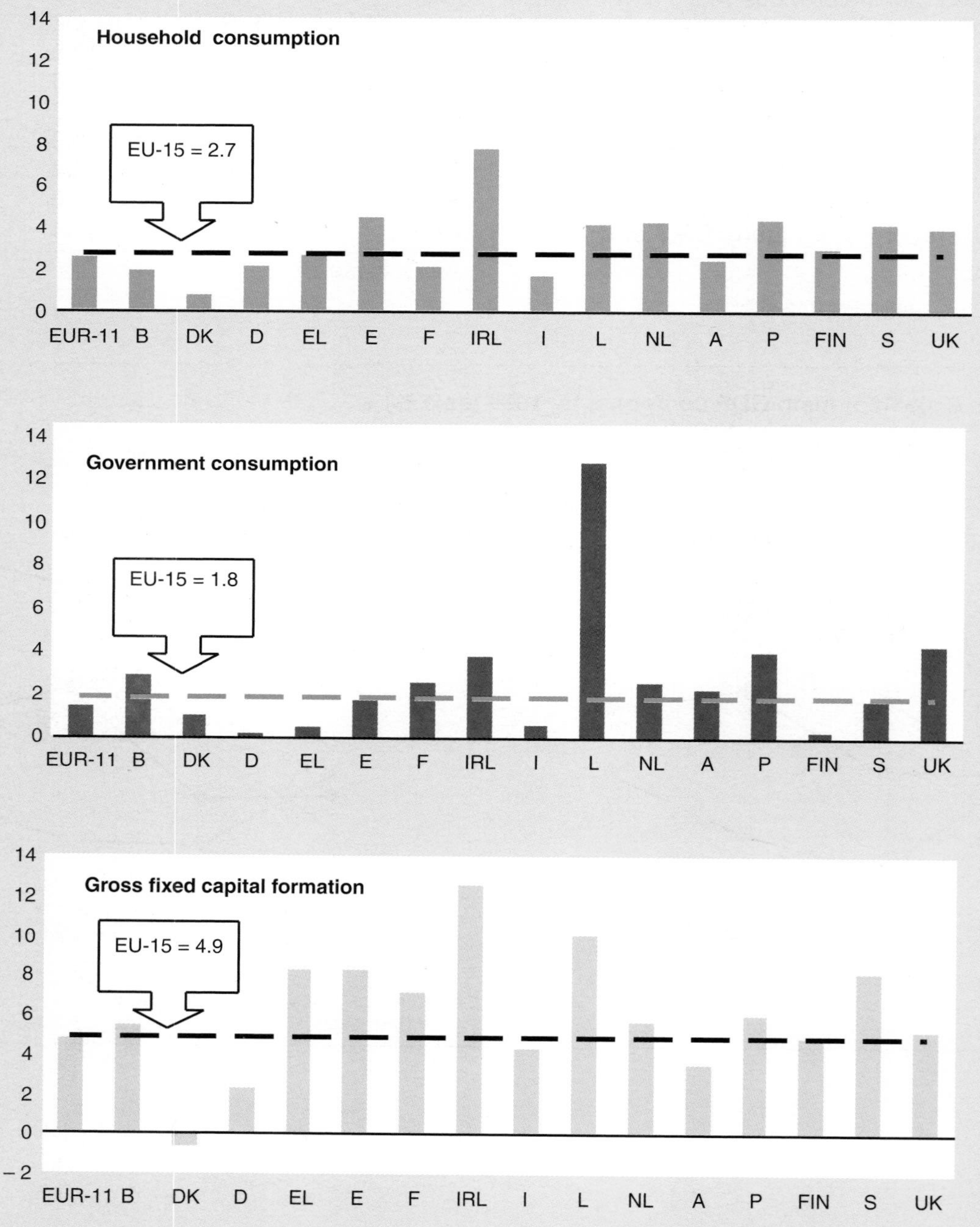

Household consumption

EU-15 = 2.7

EUR-11 B DK D EL E F IRL I L NL A P FIN S UK

Government consumption

EU-15 = 1.8

EUR-11 B DK D EL E F IRL I L NL A P FIN S UK

Gross fixed capital formation

EU-15 = 4.9

EUR-11 B DK D EL E F IRL I L NL A P FIN S UK

Source: Eurostat.

1.4. Structure of GDP

The main component ([9]) of gross domestic product (GDP) in the European Union is household final consumption expenditure, which in 1999 accounted for 58.2 % of GDP, followed by gross fixed capital formation and government final consumption expenditure with figures that were very similar: 20.2 % and 20.0 % respectively. Together, these three components accounted for practically all the Union's GDP (98.3 %).

The structure in the euro zone was basically the same as for the Union as a whole, although the percentage for investment was slightly higher (20.7 %, since the United Kingdom and Sweden had particularly low figures (see Table 1.4.1).

The structure of GDP in the United Kingdom was particularly dominated by household consumption, which, with a figure of 65.4 %, was among the highest in the Member States of the Union. The figures for government consumption and investment were similar: 18.3 % and 18.0 % respectively. The structure of GDP is similar in Germany and Italy, where household consumption was again the major component, albeit with slightly lower figures (57.7 % and 59.5 % respectively). The

Figure 1.4.1. Structure of gross domestic product in the EU, 1999 (as a % of GDP)

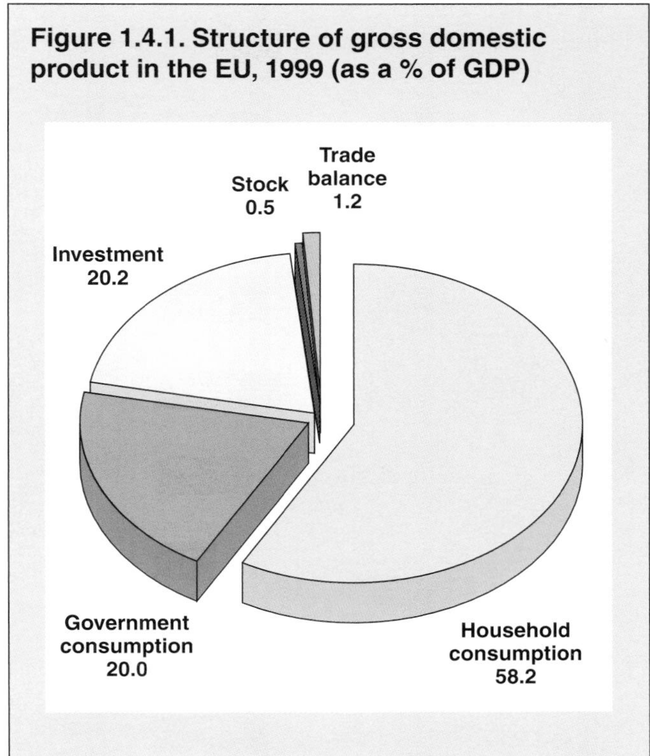

Source: Eurostat.

Table 1.4.1. Structure of gross domestic product, 1999 (as a % of GDP)

	Household consumption	Government consumption	GFCF	Stock change	Trade balance	Imports	Exports
EU-15	58.2	20.0	20.2	0.5	1.2 ➔	30.8	32.0
EUR-11	56.7	20.1	20.7	0.7	1.8 ➔	31.3	33.1
B	53.6	21.2	21.0	0.2	4.0 ➔	72.1	76.1
DK	50.6	25.8	19.5	0.0	4.2 ➔	32.4	36.6
D	57.7	19.0	20.9	1.2	1.1 ➔	28.1	29.2
EL	74.1	14.3	23.1	−4.0	−7.4 ➔	25.3	17.8
E	59.5	17.1	23.9	0.3	−0.8 ➔	28.4	27.6
F	54.8	23.7	19.1	0.0	2.5 ➔	23.6	26.1
IRL	51.9	14.2	24.5	−2.0	11.3 ➔	76.1	87.5
I	59.5	18.1	18.9	1.4	2.0 ➔	23.5	25.5
L	44.2	16.6	20.3	1.0	17.8 ➔	95.5	113.2
NL	50.1	23.2	22.3	−0.3	4.7 ➔	55.8	60.6
A	55.9	19.9	24.3	0.4	−0.5 ➔	46.3	45.8
P	62.7	20.3	26.9	0.9	−10.8 ➔	40.8	29.9
FIN	50.6	21.3	19.3	0.6	8.3 ➔	29.5	37.7
S	50.5	27.0	16.6	0.3	5.5 ➔	38.2	43.8
UK	65.4	18.3	18.0	0.0	−1.7 ➔	27.5	25.7

Source: Eurostat.

([9]) The figures for the components of GDP have been calculated in euro at current prices.

Figure 1.4.2. GDP structure, 1999 (as a % of GDP)

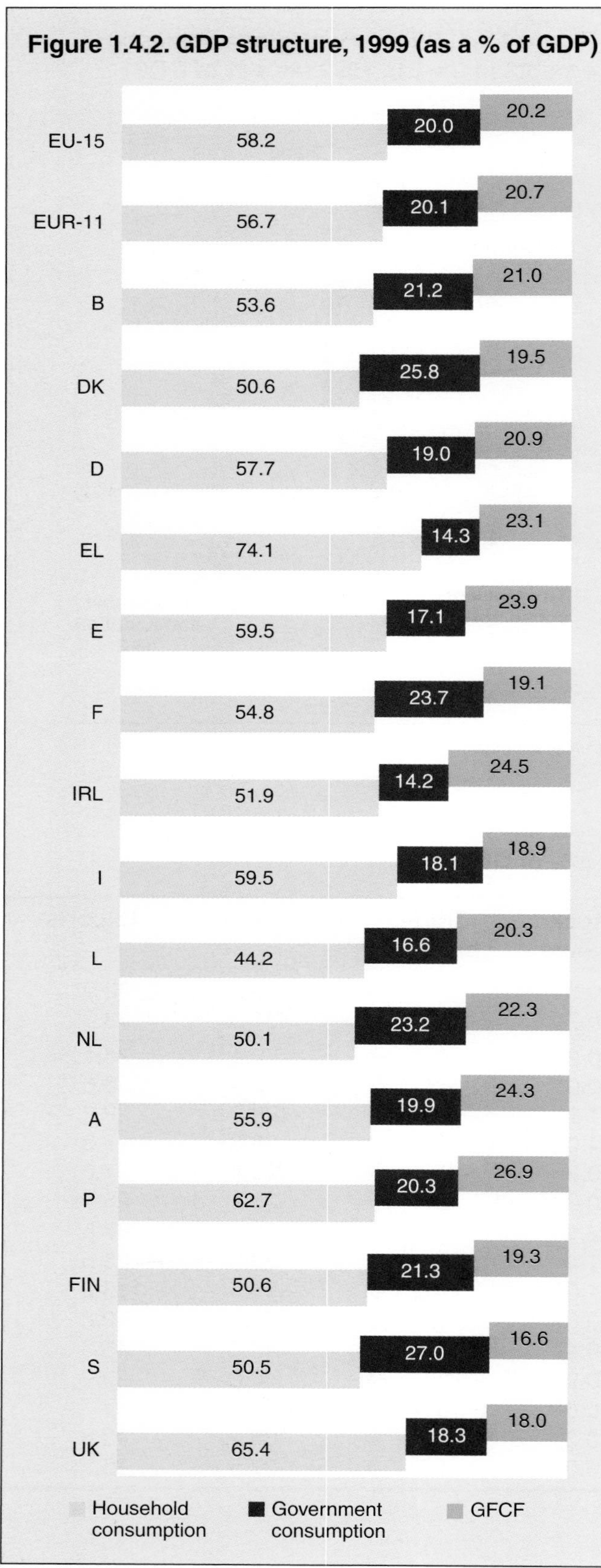

Source: Eurostat.

breakdown between government consumption and investment was again fairly even. In France, however, while household consumption accounted for the largest share of GDP (54.8 %), government consumption (23.7 %) was ahead of investment (19.1 %).

Household final consumption expenditure was the leading component of GDP in every Member State, with figures ranging from 74.1 % in Greece to 44.2 % in Luxembourg. In the case of the other two main components, investment ranked second in most Member States, the exceptions being Denmark and Sweden, where government consumption expenditure figured significantly. In Finland and the Netherlands, the figures for government expenditure and investment were identical.

Changes in GDP structure during 1995–99

A look at the breakdown of GDP into its components in 1995 and 1999 shows that GDP structure in the European Union remained essentially stable, with fluctuations all below one percentage point. Household consumption (+ 0.8 percentage points) and investment (+ 0.3 points) went up, while government consumption (– 0.7 points) and the trade balance (– 0.4 points) declined. As for trade ([10]) in particular, the figures for imports and exports recorded very similar changes: up by 2.8 percentage points for imports and by 2.4 points for exports (see Figure 1.4.3).

The structure of GDP also remained stable in the euro zone over the five-year period under review. There were modest increases in the case of household consumption expenditure (+ 0.3 points) and investment (+ 0.1 points), offset by a slight fall in government consumption expenditure (– 0.6 points). The was no change in the contribution of the trade balance to GDP, although the import/export figures were marked by significant but virtually matching increases: + 3.7 points for imports and + 3.6 for exports. The size of these variations was more than a percentage point more than for the Union as a whole; the reason for this was primarily the lost of weight of the trade balance in both the United Kingdom and Sweden (– 1.3 points for both).

The part of the trade balance on GDP increased in the United Kingdom in particular — but in a negative sense. The UK trade balance was negative throughout the period, but while its share of GDP was only – 0.4 % in 1995, by 1999 it had slipped to – 1.7 %. This change in

([10]) Trade balance figures in this section refer to national accounts and therefore do not include intra-Community trade. They might differ from figures shown in Chapter 2.3.

Figure 1.4.3. GDP structure in the EU, 1999 (as a % of GDP)

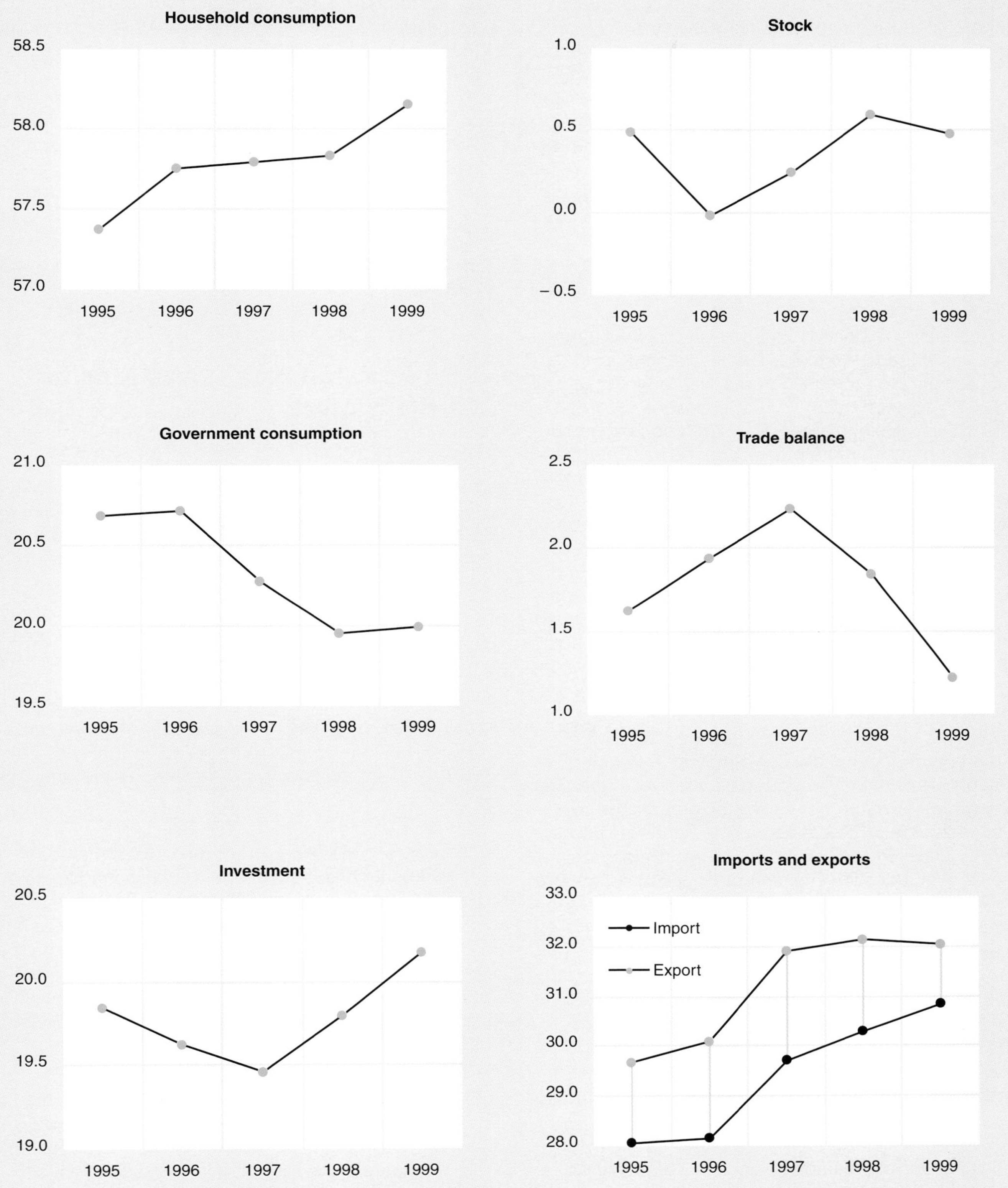

Household consumption

58.5
58.0
57.5
57.0
1995 1996 1997 1998 1999

Stock

1.0
0.5
0.0
– 0.5
1995 1996 1997 1998 1999

Government consumption

21.0
20.5
20.0
19.5
1995 1996 1997 1998 1999

Trade balance

2.5
2.0
1.5
1.0
1995 1996 1997 1998 1999

Investment

20.5
20.0
19.5
19.0
1995 1996 1997 1998 1999

Imports and exports

33.0
32.0
31.0
30.0
29.0
28.0
Import
Export
1995 1996 1997 1998 1999

Source: Eurostat.

the contribution of the trade balance to GDP can be ascribed essentially to decline in exports, which fell by 2.7 percentage points as a share of GDP during the period in question (1995–99). The changes in GDP structure in the United Kingdom were fairly significant: government consumption fell by 1.4 points, while household consumption expenditure and investment went up by 1.7 points. In Germany, the biggest change was the drop of 1.5 percentage points for investment, although this was offset by the increase of 0.9 points for household consumption. In France, on the other hand, household consumption went down while the trade balance increased its share of GDP by 1.1 percentage points. The opposite occurred in Italy: household consumption went up by 0.8 points and the trade balance fell by 2.1 points from 4.1 % in 1995 to 2.0 % in 1999.

Apart from in the United Kingdom — which has already been mentioned — the share of household consumption expenditure increased in the Netherlands as well (+ 1.1 percentage points). The reductions recorded in Ireland (– 4.0 points), Greece (– 2.8) and Luxembourg (– 3.6) were much more marked. In the case of Ireland and Greece, the reduction in household consumption, as well as in government consumption, was almost entirely offset by an increase in the percentage share of investment: + 7.1 points in Ireland and + 4.5 in Greece. In Luxembourg, on the other hand, the reduction in private consumption was accompanied by similar reductions in government consumption and investment, but the contribution of the trade balance to GDP went up by 4.6 points. In the other Member States, private consumption in 1999 generally maintained the level recorded five years earlier.

The share of government consumption in the Member States increased only in Portugal, where over the five-year period the figure went up by 1.6 percentage points. In the rest of the Member States the trend was towards stability, or even to a slight downturn in many cases. The biggest reduction in government consumption as a share of GDP occurred in Ireland (– 2.3 percentage points), Finland (– 1.6) and the United Kingdom (– 1.4). Investment (gross fixed capital formation) was the component that recorded the biggest changes during the five-year period: apart from the increases in Ireland (+ 7.1 points) and Greece (+ 4.5), there were also significant increases in Finland (+ 3.0) and Portugal (+ 2.9). The only countries where this component declined were Germany (– 1.5 points) and Luxembourg (– 1.3).

The variations in the trade balance call for some explanation: if the balance is negative, a change with a 'minus' sign does not indicate a lower percentage but an increase in the share. For our purposes, this means an increase in the significance of the trade balance as a component of GDP, regardless of whether the effect is positive (surplus) or negative (deficit). This applies in the case of the United Kingdom, Portugal, Austria and Greece. With particular regard to the large variations for Portugal (+ 4.0 percentage points) and the United Kingdom (+ 1.3 points), these indicate a worsening of the trade deficit but a bigger significance of trade as a component of GDP. In the case of Italy (– 2.1 points), Sweden (– 1.3) and the Netherlands (– 1.2), the figures moved in the opposite direction. The result was that the trade balance, although running a surplus, declined as a component of overall GDP.

More detailed information about the trade balance and how it was formed can be found in Table 1.4.2, which also shows variations in GDP percentages for imports and exports.

ESA 95: 'statistical' variations in GDP structure

The new ESA 95 system of national accounts was already used last year to calculate the data contained in this publication. Last year's edition included a fuller explanation of the new features introduced by the new methodology and of the impact of the new system on GDP and its components.

Although we are not going to cover the same ground again in this year's edition, it is nevertheless interesting to provide a comparison between GDP structure according to the former ESA 79 system and the structure resulting from the use of the new ESA 95 methodology. Figure 1.4.4 shows the components of GDP according to the two methodologies, with 1995 as the reference year.

There is a generalised trend towards an increase in government consumption and a reduction in final consumption of households. This translates in the case of many countries, therefore, as a reduction in household consumption with regard to housing allocations and reimbursements for health care and medicines, counterbalanced by a substantial increase in consumption by general government and non-profit institutions serving households.

The biggest drops in household consumption expenditure as a percentage of GDP occurred in the Netherlands (– 10 percentage points for household consumption, compared with + 9.1 for government consumption), Belgium (– 8.9 for household consumption and + 6.8 for government consumption) and Germany (– 8.2 for household consumption and + 7.5 for government consumption). The net effect on final consumption expenditure was generally quite small.

Table 1.4.2. Change in GDP structure during 1995-99 (in percentage points)

	Household consumption	Government consumption	GFCF	Trade balance	Imports	Exports
EU-15	0.8 ↑	– 0.7 ↓	0.3 ↗	– 0.4 ↙	2.8 ⬆	2.4 ⬆
EUR-11	0.3 ↗	– 0.6 ↓	0.1 ↗	0.0 ↙	3.7 ⬆	3.6 ⬆
B	– 0.3 ↙	– 0.3 ↙	0.7 ↑	– 0.1 ↙	6.0 ⬆	5.9 ⬆
DK	0.1 ↗	0.0 ↙	0.9 ↑	0.1 ↗	1.1 ↑	1.2 ↑
D	0.9 ↑	– 0.8 ↓	– 1.5 ↓	0.4 ↗	4.3 ⬆	4.7 ⬆
EL	– 2.8 ⬇	– 1.0 ↓	4.5 ⬆	0.1 ↗	0.3 ↗	0.2 ↗
E	– 0.3 ↙	– 1.0 ↓	1.9 ⇧	– 0.6 ↓	5.6 ⬆	5.0 ⬆
F	– 0.7 ↓	– 0.2 ↙	0.3 ↗	1.1 ↑	2.5 ⬆	3.6 ⬆
IRL	– 4.0 ⬇	– 2.3 ⇩	7.1 ⬆	0.5 ↗	11.9 ⬆	12.3 ⬆
I	0.8 ↑	0.3 ↗	0.6 ↑	– 2.1 ⬇	0.5 ↗	– 1.5 ↓
L	– 3.6 ⬇	– 1.0 ↓	– 1.3 ↓	4.6 ⬆	2.4 ⬆	7.1 ⬆
NL	1.1 ↑	– 0.9 ↓	2.0 ⇧	– 1.2 ↓	4.3 ⬆	3.1 ⬆
A	– 0.2 ↙	– 0.5 ↙	1.1 ↑	– 0.3 ↙	7.5 ⬆	7.7 ⬆
P	– 0.1 ↙	1.6 ⇧	2.9 ⬆	4.0 ⬆	4.1 ⬆	0.0 ↗
FIN	– 1.2 ↓	– 1.6 ⇩	3.0 ⬆	0.4 ↗	0.3 ↗	0.7 ↑
S	0.4 ↗	0.7 ↗	1.1 ↑	– 1.3 ↓	4.6 ⬆	3.3 ⬆
UK	1.7 ↑	– 1.4 ↓	1.7 ⇧	1.3 ↑	– 1.3 ↓	– 2.7 ⬇

NB:

Stable:	0 < x < 0.5 = ↗ – 0.5 < x < 0 = ↙	Low growth:	0.5 < x < 1.5 = ↑ – 1.5 < x < – 0.5 = ↓
Medium growth:	1.5 < x < 2.5 = ⇧ – 2.5 < x < 1.5 = ⇩	Strong growth:	x > 2.5 = ⬆ x < – 2.5 = ⬇

Source: Eurostat.

There was a general increase in gross fixed capital formation on account of the treatment of intangible assets (computer software, videotape, etc.), valuables and mineral exploration. The biggest increases were recorded in Belgium, where the GFCF as a component of GDP was 2.6 points higher in ESA 95, Germany and the Netherlands (both + 1.1). Reductions were recorded for Luxembourg (– 0.9 points), Austria (– 0.6) and Denmark (– 0.1).

The trade balance as a component of GDP was generally not affected by the changeover to ESA 95. The only significant changes affected Ireland, where the balance fell by 4.0 percentage points as a share of GDP, Greece (– 1.8) and France (– 1.0). France represents an exception, owing to the inclusion of its overseas *départements* into the economic territory. This reduces imports, and especially exports, from metropolitan France, since the overseas *départements* have a structural trade deficit with it. When calculated according to ESA 95, the percentage share of France's exports in 1995 came to 22.5 %. The same calculation, based on ESA 79, produced a figure of 23.5 %. Exports as well as imports are now computed 'fob'. Changes in recording also affect transport and insurance services.

Figure 1.4.4. Comparison of components' shares on GDP between ESA 95 and ESA 79 (as a % of GDP)

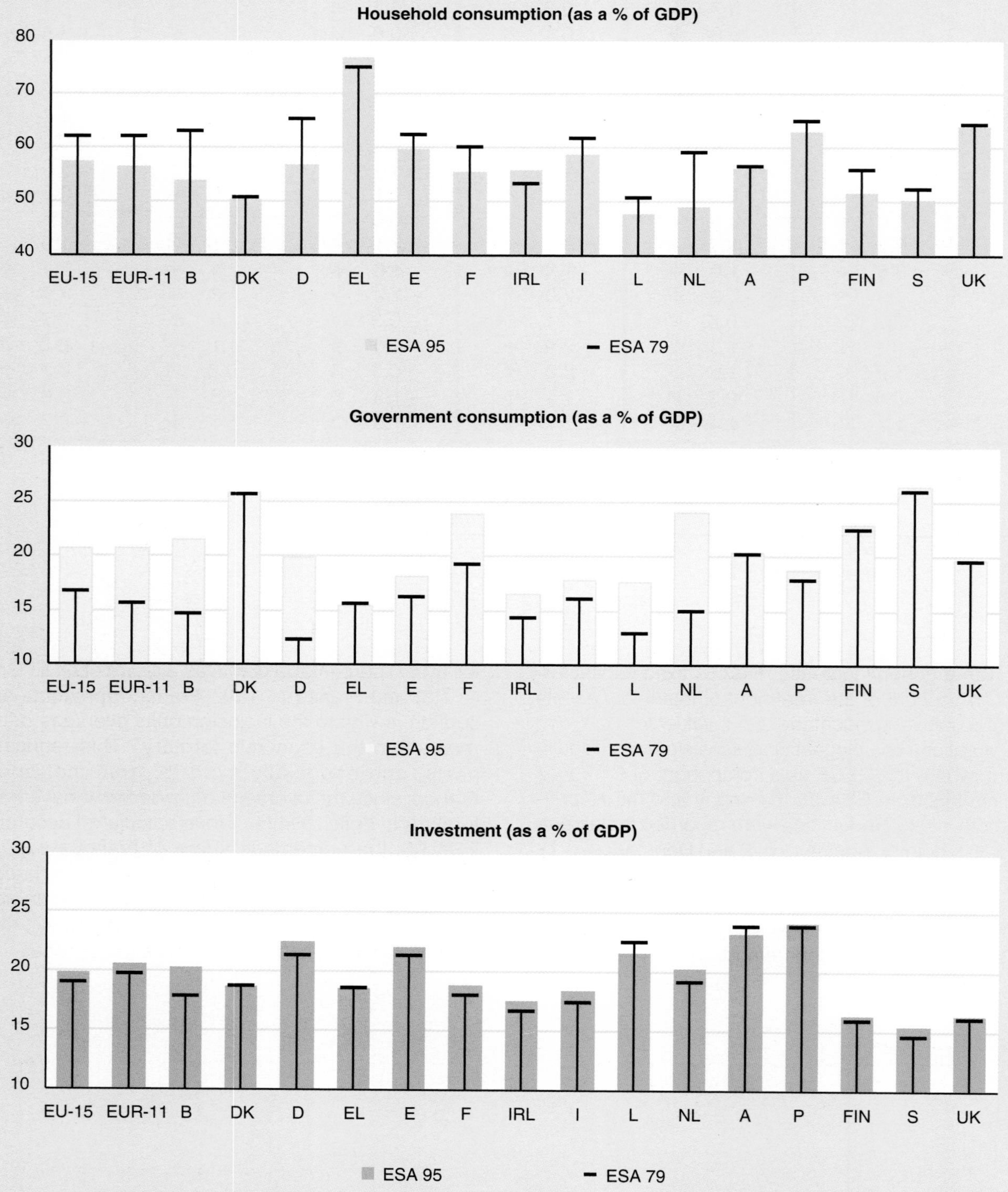

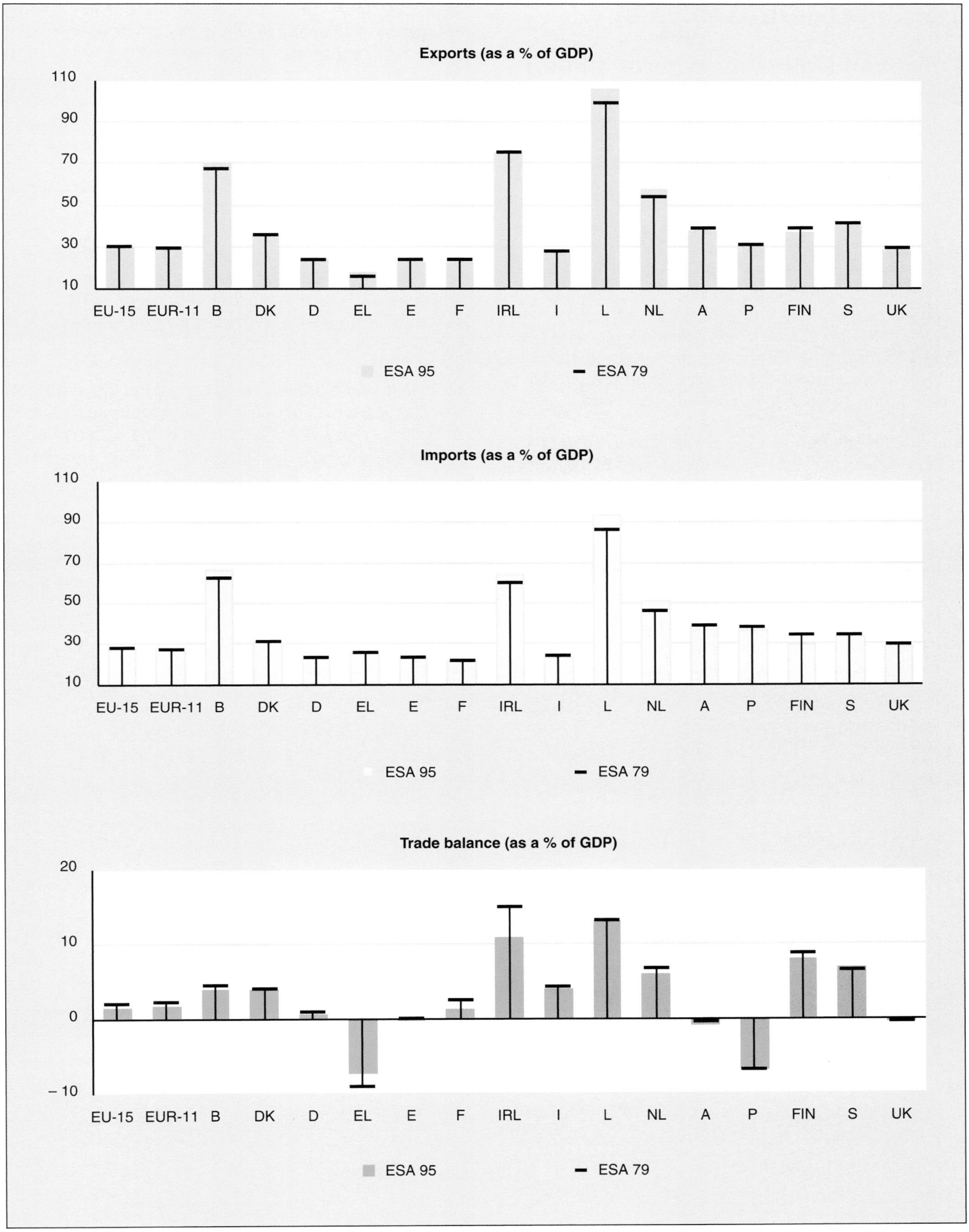

Exports (as a % of GDP)

Imports (as a % of GDP)

Trade balance (as a % of GDP)

NB: The histograms show the figures according to ESA 95 and the bars according to ESA 79.
Source: Eurostat.

1.5. Short-term analysis

European Union, euro zone, United States and Japan

The economies of the European Union and the euro zone were marked by faster growth in 1999, especially during the second half of the year. At the same time, the US economy maintained steady growth throughout the year, particularly from July onwards. In the case of Japan, however, the positive start to the year — which was a reversal of the trend that had been a feature of 1998 — gave way to a marked downturn in the second half of the year.

Growth in the European Union and the euro zone continued at the same rate in the first quarter of 2000. There was a slowdown in the United States, contrasting with a strong surge in the Japanese economy.

After the last quarter of 1998, which saw the end of the gradual slowdown that had been a feature of the whole year, the economy of the European Union steadily picked up throughout 1999. GDP recorded quarterly growth rates ([11]) that ranged between 0.6 % and 1.0 %.

Domestic demand was a major factor in the short-term pattern of GDP growth:

- household consumption expenditure grew steadily during the year, with rates varying between 0.9 % in the first quarter and 0.7 % in the last quarter;
- investments produced a more vigorous performance, especially in the first (+ 1.8 %) and third (+ 1.4 %) quarters.

External trade performed particularly well during the second half of 1999. The main reason for this was the boost in exports in the latter half of the year (+ 2.7 % and + 3.8 % in the third and fourth quarters) in conjunction with a less marked increase in imports, especially between July and September (+ 2.8 %).

The economy of the euro zone matched that of the EU as a whole in 1999, but with sharper increases during the year. GDP growth fluctuated between 0.7 % in the first quarter and 0.9 % in the last quarter, with a peak of + 1.0 % in the third quarter.

Domestic demand fuelled the growth in GDP, especially in the first and third quarters, while international trade was the primary factor for growth in the second half of the year:

- private consumption showed solid growth in the first and third quarters (+ 0.8 % in both cases);
- investments followed a similar pattern, albeit with generally higher rates of growth (+ 1.8 % in the first quarter, + 1.0 % in the second and + 1.5 % in the third).

There was a surge in exports (+ 3.6 %) during the summer. On the other hand, imports rose steadily from March onwards at a quarterly rate of close to 2.4 %.

Figure 1.5.1. GDP growth, volume index, 1995 = 100

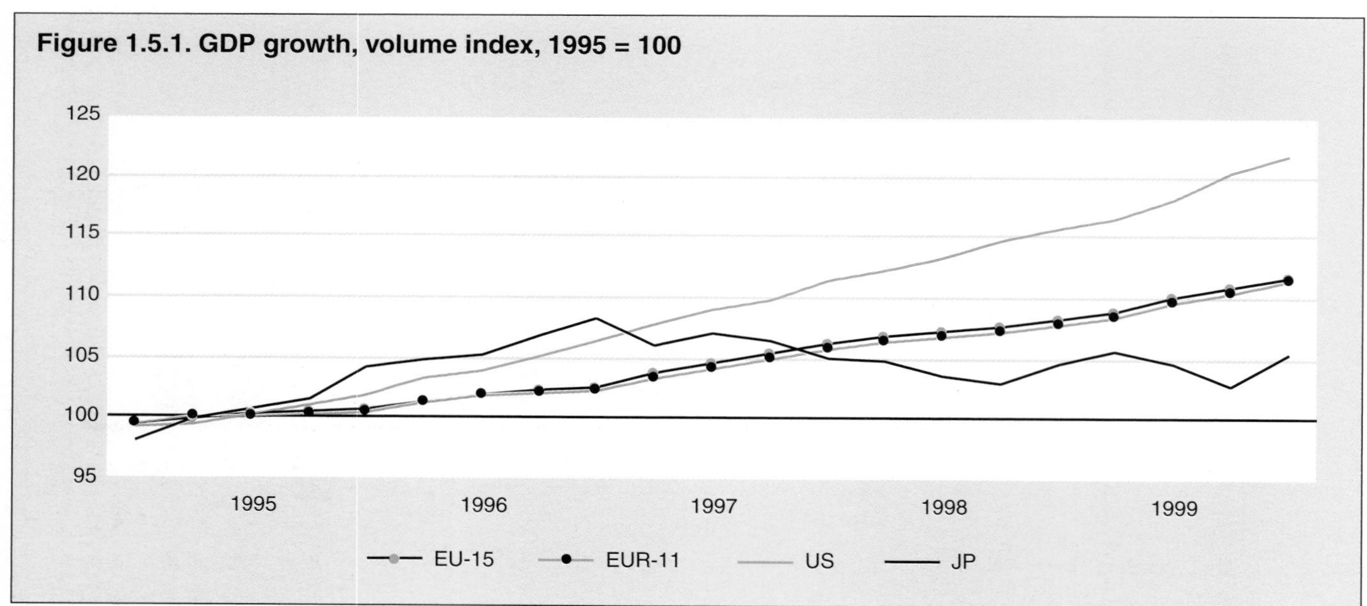

Source: Eurostat.

([11]) The growth rates referred to in this section are the rates in relation to the previous quarter. They are calculated using data at constant prices for 1995, expressed in euro. The quarterly data are seasonally adjusted and, in the case of some countries (France, Germany, Netherlands, Spain and United Kingdom), adjusted for working days.

Table 1.5.1. GDP, growth rate compared to the previous quarter (q/q-1) and the corresponding quarter of the previous year (q/q-4) (as a %)

	GDP growth with respect to the previous quarter					GDP growth with respect to the same quarter of the previous year				
	1999				2000	1999				2000
	Q1	Q2	Q3	Q4	Q1	Q1	Q2	Q3	Q4	Q1
EU-15	0.6	0.6	1.0	0.8	0.8	1.9	2.0	2.5	3.1	3.3
EUR-11	0.7	0.6	1.0	0.9	0.9	1.8	2.0	2.5	3.1	3.4
B	0.8	1.0	1.5	1.1	1.3	1.0	1.3	3.2	4.6	5.1
DK	0.1	0.3	1.1	0.9	– 0.6	0.7	2.3	1.3	2.4	1.7
D	0.7	0.1	0.8	0.7	0.7	0.7	0.9	1.4	2.3	2.3
E	0.9	0.9	1.2	0.7	1.4	3.5	3.9	3.8	3.7	4.2
F	0.5	0.8	1.0	0.9	0.7	2.7	2.6	3.1	3.2	3.4
I	0.3	0.6	0.8	0.6	1.0	1.1	1.1	1.3	2.3	3.0
NL	0.7	0.9	1.0	1.4	1.0	3.0	3.3	3.8	4.2	4.4
A	0.5	0.5	1.3	1.1	1.1	1.0	1.4	2.5	3.3	3.9
P	:	:	:	:	:	:	:	:	:	:
FIN	0.5	1.1	0.8	1.5	1.6	4.2	4.3	3.6	4.0	5.2
S	1.0	0.8	0.8	0.8	0.7	3.7	3.4	3.6	3.5	3.2
UK	0.3	0.8	1.0	0.7	0.5	1.6	1.7	2.3	2.8	3.0
US	0.9	0.6	1.4	2.0	1.2	3.9	3.8	4.3	5.0	5.3
JP	1.5	1.0	– 1.0	– 1.6	2.4	– 0.4	0.7	1.0	– 0.2	0.7

Source: Eurostat.

This confirmed a revival of external trade, which was particularly apparent in the second half of the year.

Among the Union's major trading partners, the United States maintained its phase of economic expansion in 1999, with figures for GDP growth that were even better in the second half of the year: + 1.4 % and + 2.0 % in the third and fourth quarters. Consumption and especially investments were the main factors fuelling the expansion of the US economy:

- household consumption expenditure recorded steady growth of about + 1.4 %;
- investments, after strong growth in the first quarter (+ 2.6 %), settled down to rates of + 1.8 % and + 2.2 % in the third and fourth quarters.

The trade deficit continued to grow (+ 4.1 % of GDP in the final quarter of 1999). Exports and especially imports rose sharply during the second half of the year, with imports recording a rise of + 4.0 % between October and December.

The Japanese economy failed to come out of recession in 1999. There were two distinct periods during the year: an initial phase of growth between January and June, when GDP grew by + 1.5 % and + 1.0 % in the first and second quarters, followed by a downturn in the next two quarters (– 1.0 % and – 1.6 %). Domestic demand remained shaky throughout the year:

- household consumption expenditure grew in the first half of the year (+ 0.9 % and + 1.1 % in the first and second quarters) before gradually slowing down in the last six months (– 0.2 % and – 1.6 % in the third and fourth quarters);
- investments also fluctuated, with a significant drop of – 1.3 % between April and June followed by a rise of + 0.9 % in the next three months.

There were also strong fluctuations in the pattern of external trade, with growth in exports peaking at + 5.0 % in the third quarter of the year and a similar rise in imports in the final quarter.

Short-term patterns and trends

In order to get an idea of how GDP performed in 1999, it is helpful to compare the data that were actually recorded and those relating to a linear evolution of the economy. The linear trend provides a simple and effective picture of the progress and direction of the economy. The figures for each quarter of 1999 can thus be compared with the general trend for 1995–99, by highlighting how the economy performed during the period under review. In technical terms, the linear trend is calculated on the basis of a linear regression.

Figure 1.5.4 shows the GDP trend as a volume index for 1995Q1–2000Q1, with 1995 = 100. Also shown, for each country, are the GDP trend for the Union as a whole and the linear trend for the period under review. It can be seen that in 1999 almost every country achieved growth that bettered the linear trend. Denmark and especially Japan were the only countries which bucked this trend.

The angle of the linear trend also provides information about the pace of growth in the period under review. The United States and Finland are the countries which showed the most rapid growth between 1995 and 2000. Japan, on the other hand, achieved the weakest growth during this period, mainly because of its performance in the last two years.

Figure 1.5.2. GDP, growth rate compared to the previous quarter (q/q-1) and to the corresponding quarter of the previous year (q/q-4) (as a %)

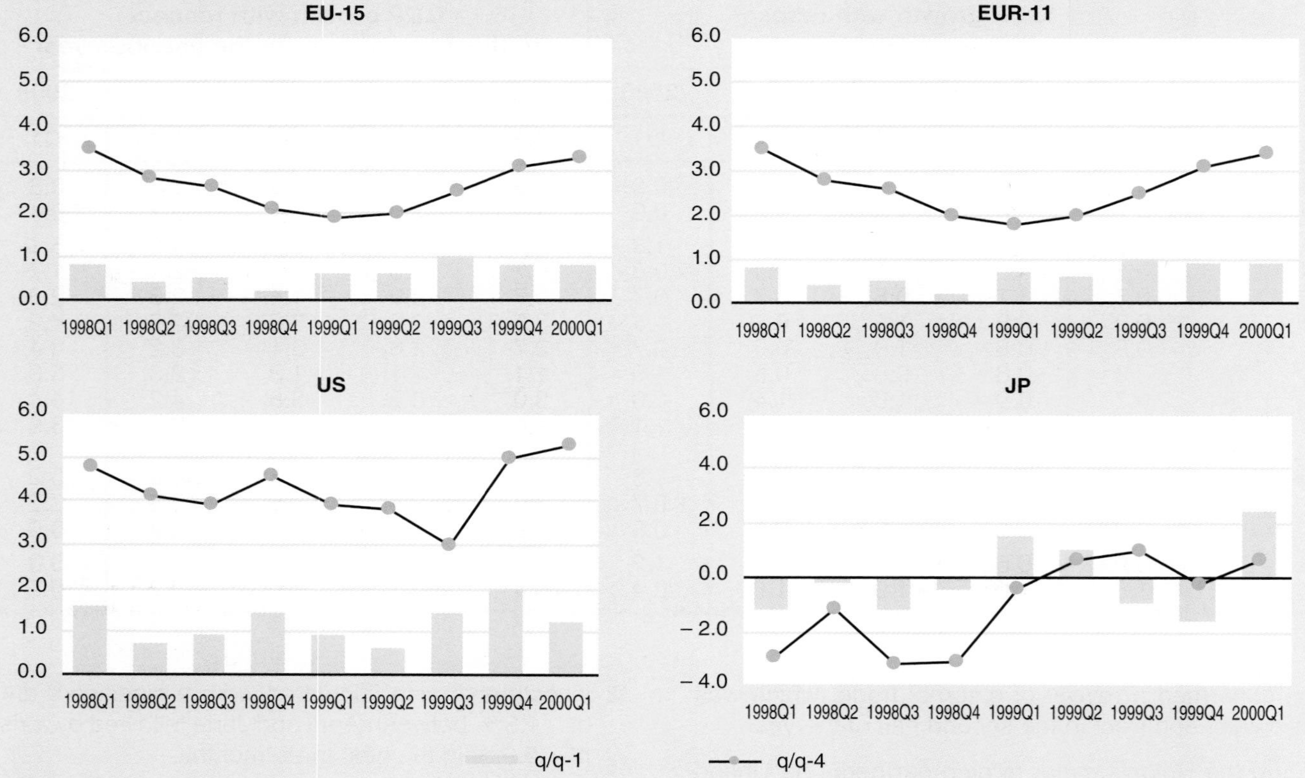

EU-15

EUR-11

US

JP

q/q-1

q/q-4

Source: Eurostat.

Figure 1.5.3. Household final consumption expenditure and gross fixed capital formation, growth rate compared to the previous quarter (as a %)

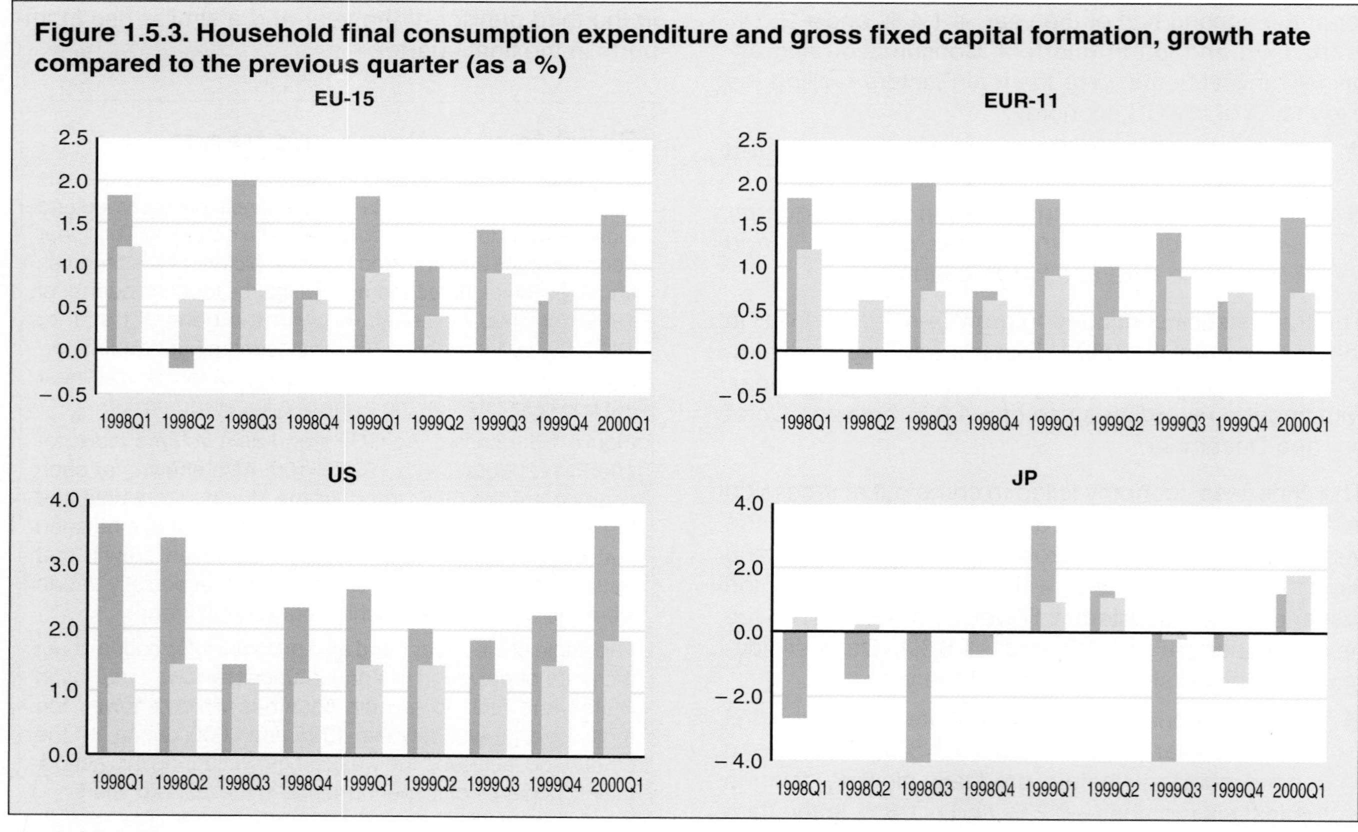

Source: Eurostat.

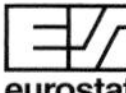

Figure 1.5.4. GDP, volume index and linear trend (1995 = 100)

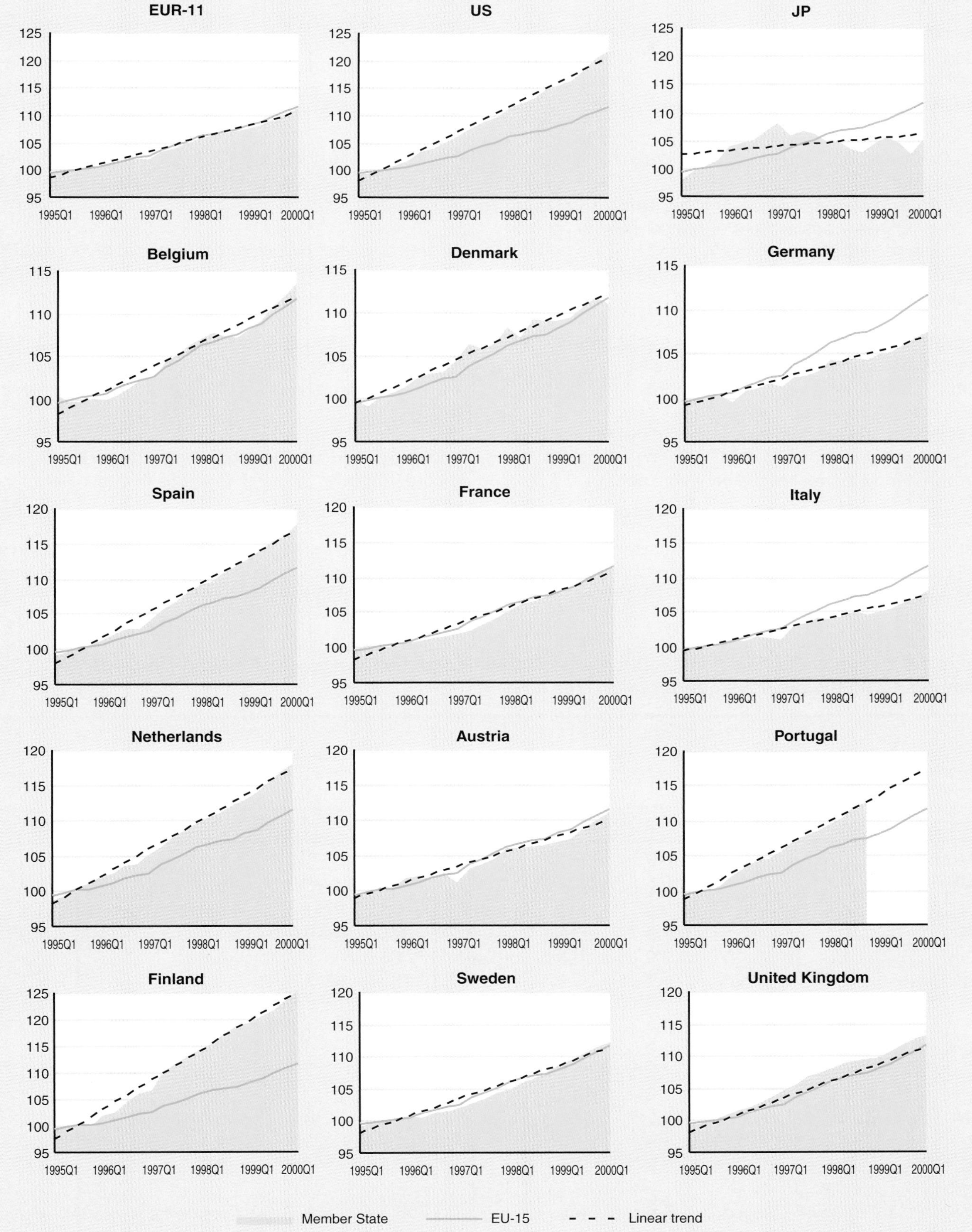
EUR-11
US
JP
Belgium
Denmark
Germany
Spain
France
Italy
Netherlands
Austria
Portugal
Finland
Sweden
United Kingdom
95
100
105
110
115
120
125
1995Q1
1996Q1
1997Q1
1998Q1
1999Q1
2000Q1
Member State
EU-15
Linear trend

Source: Eurostat.

Short-term economic situation in the Member States

For most of the Member States, 1999 was marked by economic growth. The pace of growth differed, however, depending on the country. They can be divided into three groups:

- Belgium, the Netherlands, Finland and Spain maintained a pattern of growth over all four quarters of the year;
- Austria, Sweden, France and the United Kingdom also posted a positive performance, but the growth in their economies was less marked;
- Germany, Italy and Denmark achieved more delayed and/or sluggish growth.

Growth picked up between April and September in almost every Member State, before slowing down slightly at the end of the year.

In Germany, the economy was affected by the results of the second quarter, when GDP grew by only + 0.1 %. Growth during the rest of the year was about + 0.7 %.

Domestic demand, expressed in terms of household final consumption expenditure and investments, stood still between April and June (– 0.1 % and 0.0 % respectively) before picking up again — especially in the case of consumption — in the last six months of the year.

External trade enjoyed a strong rise in exports in the second quarter (+ 3.6 %), which then continued at a slower pace in the second half of the year. Imports followed a similar pattern, peaking at + 3.2 % between March and June.

France experienced fairly stable growth in the last three quarters of the year, with figures ranging between + 0.8 % and + 1.0 %.

Growth in household consumption expenditure (+ 0.9 %) and a strong rise in exports (+ 4.5 %) meant that the third quarter showed the biggest increase in GDP.

Although investments grew throughout the year, the pace steadily slackened, with the rate slipping from + 2.3 % in the first quarter to + 1.3 % in the fourth quarter.

Imports picked up from April onwards (+ 2.5 %) and recorded growth of + 3.3 % in the final quarter of the year.

For the United Kingdom, economic growth achieved its best performance in the last three quarters of the year, especially during the summer (+ 1.0 %).

Table 1.5.2. Household final consumption expenditure and gross fixed capital formation, growth rate compared with the previous quarter (q/q-1) (as a %)

	Household final consumption expenditure					Gross fixed capital formation				
	1999				2000	1999				2000
	Q1	Q2	Q3	Q4	Q1	Q1	Q2	Q3	Q4	Q1
EU-15	0.9	0.4	0.9	0.7	0.7	1.8	1.0	1.4	0.6	1.6
EUR-11	0.8	0.3	0.8	0.5	0.7	1.8	1.0	1.5	0.5	1.9
B	0.6	– 0.3	1.2	1.0	1.3	1.6	1.4	2.2	– 2.2	3.1
DK	0.1	– 2.1	1.9	0.3	– 0.8	– 0.5	– 0.8	– 1.8	– 0.1	7.9
D	1.2	– 0.1	0.6	0.5	– 0.6	1.8	0.0	1.4	– 0.8	2.0
E	1.2	0.9	1.7	0.2	3.0	1.0	2.4	1.0	1.0	1.8
F	0.3	0.5	0.9	0.6	0.9	2.3	1.5	1.4	1.3	1.7
I	0.6	0.1	0.4	0.2	1.2	1.5	1.7	1.2	1.7	1.2
NL	0.6	1.3	0.8	0.8	2.1	2.3	– 0.7	2.9	2.5	1.6
A	0.9	0.7	1.3	0.6	0.5	0.6	1.1	1.5	1.2	2.2
P	:	:	:	:	:	:	:	:	:	:
FIN	– 0.6	0.8	1.2	1.1	1.2	– 2.5	2.6	0.8	0.1	0.8
S	0.9	0.9	1.5	1.3	1.1	2.7	0.8	2.7	1.7	0.6
UK	1.6	1.0	0.8	1.5	0.7	2.5	1.2	0.6	1.1	– 1.1
US	1.4	1.4	1.2	1.4	1.8	2.6	2.0	1.8	2.2	3.6
JP	0.9	1.1	– 0.2	– 1.6	1.8	3.3	1.3	– 4.0	– 0.6	1.2

Source: Eurostat.

Table 1.5.3. Government final consumption expenditure, growth rate compared with the previous quarter (as a %), and changes in inventories (as a % of GDP)

	Government final consumption expenditure, growth					Changes in inventories, percentage of GDP				
	1999				2000	1999				2000
	Q1	Q2	Q3	Q4	Q1	Q1	Q2	Q3	Q4	Q1
EU-15	1.0	0.1	0.3	0.2	0.3	0.6	0.5	0.3	0.6	0.6
EUR-11	0.9	0.1	0.3	0.2	0.8	0.8	0.8	0.5	0.9	0.7
B	1.0	0.3	1.2	0.5	0.4	– 1.7	– 0.7	– 0.1	1.3	– 0.8
DK	0.1	0.3	0.5	0.1	0.1	– 0.7	0.1	0.3	– 0.2	0.1
D	1.4	– 0.6	0.0	– 0.4	1.9	1.4	1.5	1.3	1.6	1.8
E	0.7	0.3	– 0.1	– 0.3	0.3	0.5	– 0.1	0.0	0.9	0.3
F	1.0	0.7	0.5	0.7	0.2	0.3	0.3	– 0.2	0.3	0.2
I	0.0	0.1	0.2	0.5	0.6	1.9	1.7	0.9	1.5	0.7
NL	0.3	0.6	0.9	1.0	0.1	– 0.2	– 0.2	0.2	– 0.5	– 1.0
A	0.2	0.7	– 0.1	0.3	0.0	0.0	– 0.2	– 0.9	– 0.7	0.6
P	:	:	:	:	:	:	:	:	:	:
FIN	– 0.5	1.1	0.8	0.3	– 1.8	1.0	0.0	– 1.1	– 1.4	– 0.1
S	0.4	0.5	0.3	0.6	– 6.0	0.5	0.1	– 0.3	– 2.8	0.7
UK	1.8	0.0	0.2	0.3	– 0.6	0.1	– 0.7	– 0.4	0.2	0.4
US	0.0	0.0	1.2	1.5	– 0.9	0.7	0.4	0.7	1.1	0.7
JP	0.8	– 1.3	0.9	– 0.1	0.8	0.2	0.3	0.2	0.0	0.3

Source: Eurostat.

The relatively poor performance of household consumption expenditure between April and September (+ 1.0 % and + 0.8 % in the second and third quarters) was accompanied by a gradual slowdown in investments, especially in the third quarter (+ 0.6 %).

On the other hand, exports rose substantially during the same period (+ 5.6 %), before declining in the fourth quarter (– 1.4 %). In addition, imports also rose sharply in the third quarter (+ 4.8 %), following a period between April and June when there was virtually no change (+ 0.2 %).

After recording a lacklustre performance in the first quarter (+ 0.3 %), the economy in Italy picked up from April onwards. This trend continued in the second half of the year, with figures of + 0.8 % and + 0.6 % for the third and fourth quarters.

Domestic demand was weak throughout the year. The primary reason for this was the sluggish performance of household consumption expenditure, especially in the second and third quarters (+ 0.1 % and + 0.2 %). This was only partially offset by growth in investments.

Italian exports had slumped at the end of 1998 and in the first quarter of 1999 (– 1.5 %) but then recovered strongly, in line with other European countries, in the third quarter of the year (+ 3.5 %). Imports, however, produced a patchy performance, rising noticeably only from October onwards (+ 3.1 %).

GDP in Spain, the Netherlands, Finland and Belgium grew steadily in 1999. In the case of Spain and the Netherlands, the main reason was the solid performance of investments together with the relative stability of household consumption expenditure, which showed more vigorous growth in Spain. In the case of Finland and Belgium, however, exports were the major factor, thanks in particular to the strong rise in the third quarter.

Austria and Sweden produced similar overall results during the year, but the quarterly pattern was different. In Austria, the moderate growth of the first six months of 1999 quickened in the second half of the year, thanks primarily to solid domestic demand and increased exports. In Sweden, on the other hand, growth was stable throughout the year thanks to the steady pace of consumption and the consistent performance of investments. There was also a noticeable rise in Swedish exports and imports during the second half of the year.

The economy in Denmark turned round only in the second half of 1999. The slump in household consumption between April and June and the decline of investments throughout the year severely curbed the positive effects of the external trade figures.

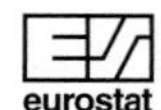

Figure 1.5.5. GDP, growth rate compared to the previous quarter (q/q-1) and to the corresponding quarter of the previous year (q/q-4) as a %

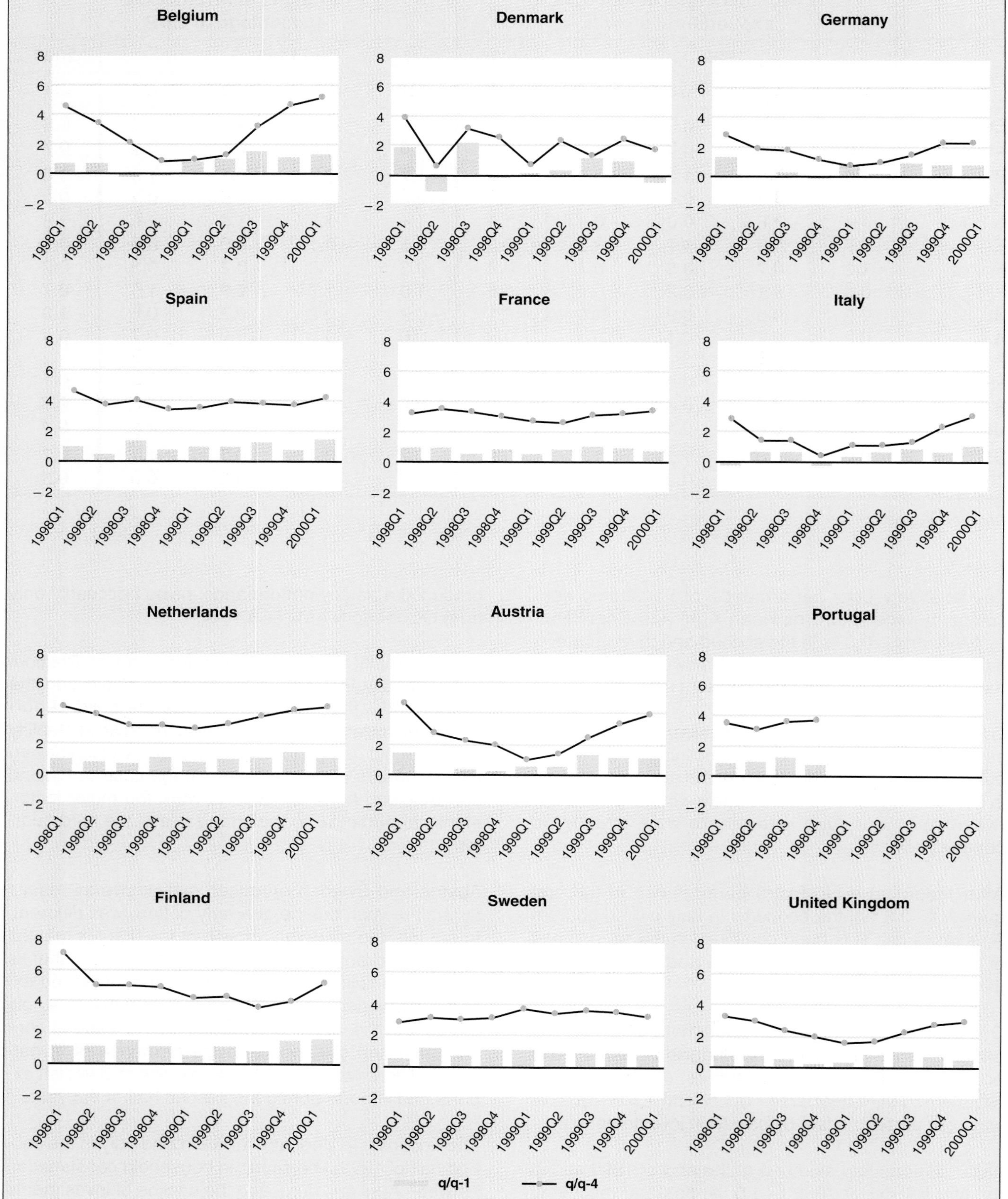
Belgium
Denmark
Germany
Spain
France
Italy
Netherlands
Austria
Portugal
Finland
Sweden
United Kingdom
8
6
4
2
0
– 2
1998Q1
1998Q2
1998Q3
1998Q4
1999Q1
1999Q2
1999Q3
1999Q4
2000Q1
q/q-1
q/q-4

Source: Eurostat.

Table 1.5.4. Exports and imports, growth rate compared to the previous quarter (q/q-1) (as a %)

	Exports					Imports				
	1999				2000	1999				2000
	Q1	Q2	Q3	Q4	Q1	Q1	Q2	Q3	Q4	Q1
EU-15	0.1	2.8	3.6	2.2	2.7	1.0	2.3	2.4	2.4	2.5
EUR-11	0.1	2.7	3.8	1.9	2.4	1.1	1.8	2.8	2.1	2.4
B	1.6	0.0	6.6	2.3	5.1	0.4	0.2	7.7	3.0	2.7
DK	3.4	2.2	1.6	3.5	− 2.5	− 1.9	0.6	1.3	0.2	2.9
D	0.2	3.6	3.1	1.9	3.9	1.8	3.2	1.8	0.6	4.0
E	2.0	5.7	1.9	3.5	− 0.4	3.7	4.3	2.2	5.0	0.8
F	− 0.2	2.7	4.5	1.6	2.6	− 1.1	2.5	2.4	3.3	2.8
I	− 1.5	2.6	3.5	1.2	3.6	0.2	1.2	− 0.3	3.1	1.2
NL	− 0.3	1.6	1.3	3.7	0.6	0.6	1.2	2.6	2.4	0.6
A	− 1.6	0.6	3.6	1.3	− 0.3	1.6	0.8	1.5	0.9	2.0
P	:	:	:	:	:	:	:	:	:	:
FIN	2.3	2.3	5.7	4.6	− 1.0	2.3	− 0.2	4.0	2.5	− 0.9
S	1.0	− 0.1	3.9	3.6	− 0.6	2.5	− 1.3	5.0	− 1.3	4.1
UK	− 0.8	2.7	5.6	− 1.4	2.4	2.0	0.2	4.8	2.0	1.4
US	− 2.0	1.4	2.5	2.5	1.5	1.1	3.8	4.0	2.6	2.9
JP	0.0	1.5	5.0	0.7	5.4	2.4	2.6	2.8	5.0	− 0.6

Source: Eurostat.

1.6. Distribution of GDP, disposable income, saving and net lending/borrowing

Distribution of GDP — income side

The previous sections looked at GDP as the sum of the end uses of goods and services, i.e. from the demand side. Another definition, and another way of calculating GDP, is to look at the income produced and how that income is divided among the various recipients. To use the terminology of ESA 95, this is the primary distribution of income, i.e. distribution among the factors of production and among general government. For the factors of production, labour is remunerated by compensation of employees and capital by operating surplus and mixed income (in the case of households). General government, however, receives income in the form of taxes.

GDP as the sum of uses of the primary income that is generated is thus broken down in ESA 95 as follows:

1. compensation of employees;
2. operating surplus or mixed income;
3. net taxes (taxes less subsidies) on production and imports.

In 1999, compensation of employees in the European Union accounted for about half (50.6 %) of all generated income, with operating surplus and taxes accounting for 36.7 % and 12.7 % respectively. The structure of income distribution has not changed much over time: compared with 1995, compensation of employees accounted for a smaller share of GDP in 1999, with a figure that was – 0.9 percentage points down on the earlier year. Operating surplus was also down (– 0.4 points), while taxes increased by 1.3 points (see Figure 1.6.2). When the changes are considered in absolute terms (value growth index), again with 1995 as the benchmark year (1995 = 100), incomes in 1999 showed a similar rise for both compensation of employees (+ 19.0 %) and for gross operating surplus and mixed income (+ 19.7 %). Taxes, on the other hand, showed a rise of 35.3 %, spread fairly evenly over the period, with increases of about 10 % per year from 1996 onwards (see Figure 1.6.1).

Figure 1.6.1. Gross domestic product: income side

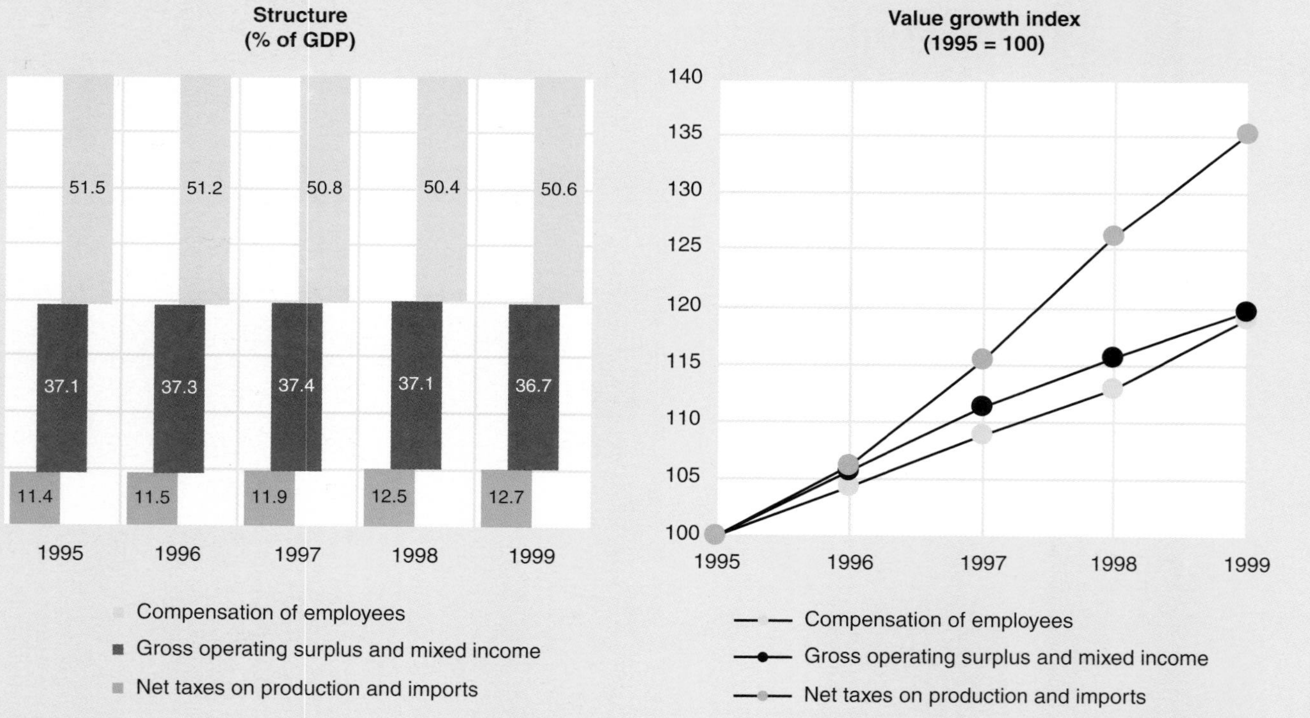

Structure (% of GDP)

51.5
51.2
50.8
50.4
50.6
37.1
37.3
37.4
37.1
36.7
11.4
11.5
11.9
12.5
12.7
1995
1996
1997
1998
1999
Compensation of employees
Gross operating surplus and mixed income
Net taxes on production and imports

Value growth index (1995 = 100)

140
135
130
125
120
115
110
105
100
1995
1996
1997
1998
1999
Compensation of employees
Gross operating surplus and mixed income
Net taxes on production and imports

NB: Growth index is in value terms, since data are available only at current prices.
Source: Eurostat.

With regard to the structure of GDP in the euro zone, the reduction in the percentage share of compensation of employees was more noticeable (– 1.7 points). Although this component went up by + 1.3 points in the United Kingdom, this was offset by reductions in the other 'big' countries: Germany (– 2.4), Italy (– 1.6) and France (– 0.4). There was a small increase in the share of gross operating surplus and mixed income (+ 0.4 points), while the rise in taxes on production and imports (+ 1.2) matched the EU-15 figure (see Table 1.6.2). A look at the value growth index (1995 = 100) shows that the variations in the figures for the components were less marked in the euro zone than in the Community as a whole: + 11.4 % for compensation of employees, + 16.5 % for gross operating surplus and mixed income and + 28.1 % for taxes. Here, again, a major factor in these changes was the performance of the United Kingdom, where growth figures for every variable were among the highest in the Union.

In short, the structure of GDP in the 'big four' followed quite distinct patterns. As we have seen, compensation of employees showed a downward trend as a component of GDP in Germany, France and Italy, while in the United Kingdom this particular component increased its percentage share. For gross operating surplus, however, it was Germany that ran counter to the trend, increasing this component's share of GDP by + 1.6 points, whereas the figure went down in the other three countries. Lastly, taxes increased their percentage share in all four countries, with Italy showing a particularly strong increase (+ 3.2 points). As for the absolute variation (value growth index), the United Kingdom stood out in 1999 for the size of its increases for every component of income: + 61.0 % for compensation of employees, + 47.7 % for gross operating surplus and mixed income and + 64.8 % for net taxes on production and imports. The increases were noticeable in Italy as well, especially for taxes, which showed an increase of + 69.5 % compared with 1995. In Germany and France the variations were more contained.

Table 1.6.1. Structure of GDP — income side, 1999 (as a % of GDP)

	Compensation of employees	Gross operating surplus and mixed income	Net taxes on production and imports	Compensation … / Gross operating … / Net taxes …
EU-15	50.6	36.7	12.7	
EUR-11	49.6	38.1	12.3	
B	51.0	36.8	12.2	
DK	53.9	31.3	14.8	
D	52.8	36.6	10.7	
EL (¹)	32.7	54.8	12.5	
E	50.0	39.8	10.2	
F (¹)	51.7	33.7	14.5	
IRL (¹)	40.8	48.1	11.1	
I	40.9	45.0	14.1	
L	50.0	34.2	15.7	
NL	51.2	37.7	11.1	
A (¹)	52.3	34.9	12.8	
P (¹)	43.2	43.4	13.4	
FIN	49.1	38.4	12.5	
S	56.2	28.4	15.3	
UK	55.4	30.8	13.8	

(¹) Eurostat estimation.
Source: Eurostat.

A more detailed look at the structure of GDP shows that compensation of employees was the major component in most Member States in 1999, with the highest figures occurring in Sweden (56.2 %), the United Kingdom (55.4 %) and Denmark (53.9 %). In Greece, Ireland and Italy, however, it was gross operating surplus that was the major contributor to GDP. In Portugal, the two components were equal. Greece clearly stood out from the other Member States in having the lowest percentage share for compensation of employees (32.7 %) and the highest for gross operating surplus and mixed income (54.8 %) (see Table 1.6.1).

When the situation in 1999 is compared with that of four years earlier in 1995, the general trend in the Member States is revealed as a declining share of compensation of employees as a component of GDP. The only exceptions were Sweden (+ 1.5 points), the United Kingdom (+ 1.3) and Denmark (+ 1.0), which now have the highest shares in the Union. In the case of gross operating surplus and mixed income, the trend was also towards a smaller share of GDP, the exceptions here being Ireland (with a significant increase of + 4.4 percentage points), Germany (+ 1.6) and Portugal (+ 1.2). The share in GDP of taxes on production and imports went up in practically every Member State, the sole exception being Portugal, where the figure remained virtually unchanged. The biggest increases in the percentage share of taxes as a component were recorded in Sweden (+ 4.9 points), Luxembourg (+ 3.8) and Italy (+ 3.2) (see Figure 1.6.2).

Figure 1.6.2. GDP components — income side — in 1995 and 1999 (as a % of GDP)

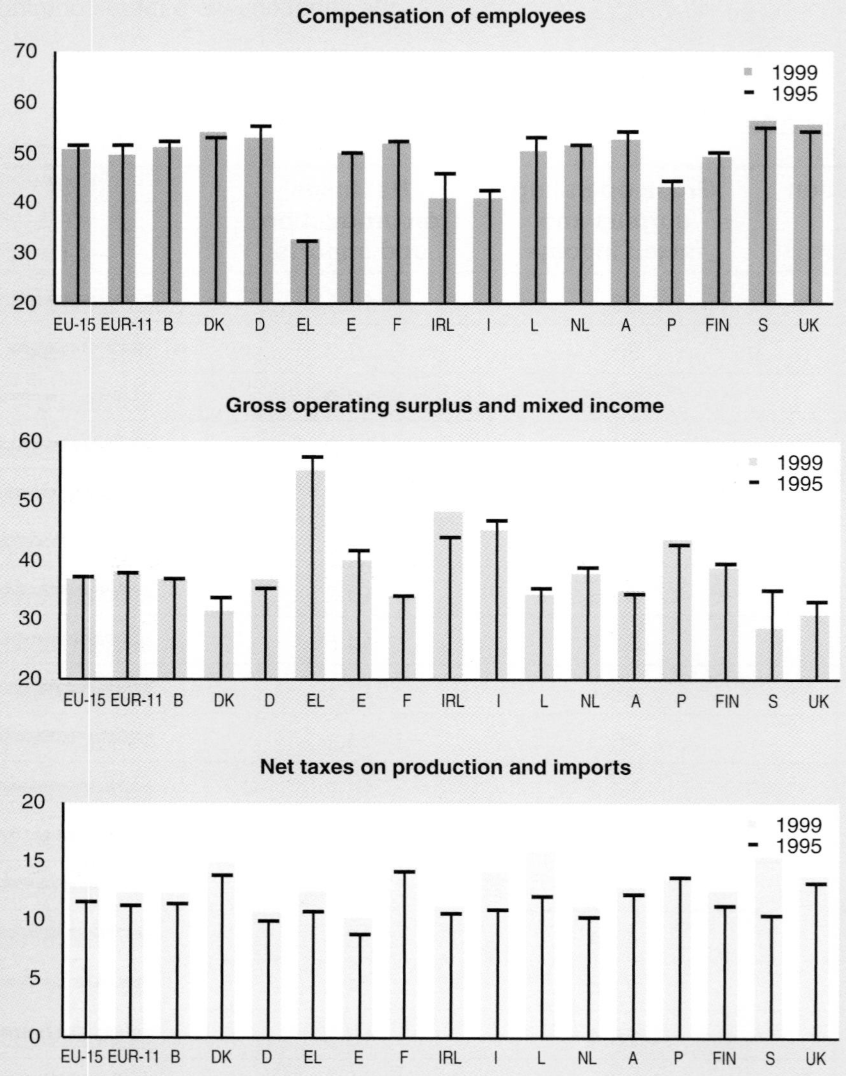

Compensation of employees

Gross operating surplus and mixed income

Net taxes on production and imports

NB: Eurostat estimation for Greece, France, Ireland, Austria and Portugal.
Source: Eurostat.

A look at the absolute variation (value growth index: 1995 = 100) shows that the Member States which recorded the biggest variations for every component were the United Kingdom — as has already been mentioned — and Ireland. Compensation of employees showed modest increases only in Austria (+ 5.9 %) and Belgium (+ 8.4 %). In Germany, as already indicated, the figures were unchanged. Gross operating surplus and mixed income almost doubled in Ireland (+ 85.6 %) over the period under review, while at the other extreme there was almost no change in Sweden. The component that produced the biggest variations was taxes on products and imports: apart from the United Kingdom (+ 64.8 %) and Ireland (+ 77.6 %), there were also significant increases in Italy (+ 69.5 %), Greece (+ 52.7 %) and Spain (+ 46.5 %) (see Table 1.6.2).

Table 1.6.2. Value growth index of GDP components — income side, 1999 (1995 = 100)

	Compensation of employees	Gross operating surplus and mixed income	Net taxes on production and imports	■ Compensation … ■ Gross operating … ■ Net taxes …
EU-15	119.0	119.7	135.3	
EUR-11	111.4	116.5	128.1	
B	108.4	110.9	119.6	
DK	120.6	110.8	128.8	
D	100.9	110.1	114.0	
EL (1)	132.4	125.5	152.7	
E	125.4	120.4	146.5	
F (1)	112.4	112.5	117.6	
IRL (1)	150.6	185.6	177.6	
I	125.9	126.6	169.5	
L	122.8	126.4	171.2	
NL	116.5	113.8	126.7	
A (1)	105.9	111.6	114.6	
P (1)	123.8	130.3	125.7	
FIN	120.3	120.1	137.2	
S	125.3	99.5	179.8	
UK	161.0	147.7	164.8	

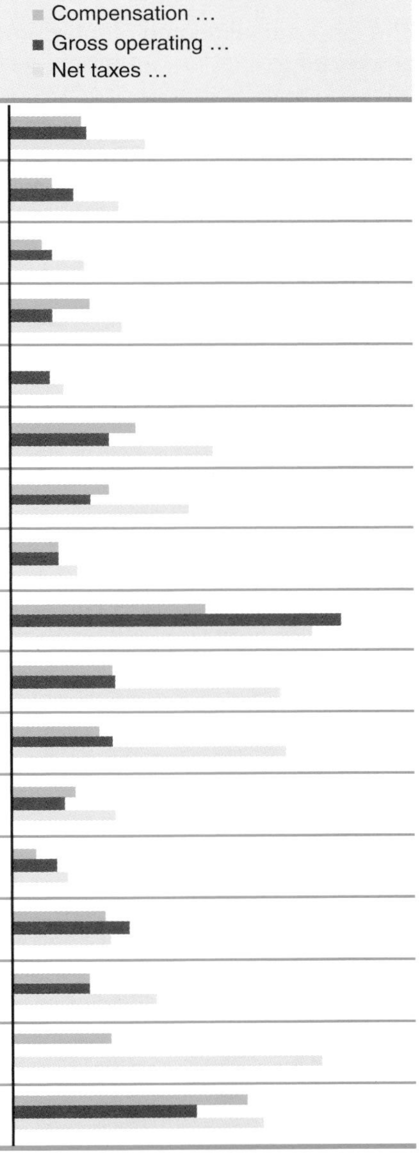

(1) Eurostat estimation.
Source: Eurostat.

Disposable income: breakdown between consumption and saving

Still on the income side, when net income abroad (i.e. the balance between transfers to and from other countries) is deducted from GDP, the result is a figure for national income. When current transfers ([12]) are excluded from national income, what is left is national disposable income, or the resources that a country has at its disposal. These resources are divided between consumption and saving.

The disposable income of the European Union in 1999 amounted to EUR 7 754 billion, with EUR 6 135 billion going on both private and public consumption and EUR 1 619 billion earmarked for saving. In percentage terms, consumption accounted for 79.1 % of disposable income, and saving for the remaining 20.9 %. In absolute growth terms, disposable income in 1999 was 20.8 % more than in the reference year (1995). The figure for consumption was 21.2 % higher, with saving showing a slightly smaller increase of 19.3 % (see Figure 1.6.3).

In the euro zone the division between consumption and saving is marked by a higher proportion devoted to saving; at 21.9 %, it is one percentage point higher than for the Union as a whole. The main reason for this is the situation in the United Kingdom, which stands out from all the other Member States with the lowest percentage of disposable income earmarked for saving (16.6 % in 1999). There is a much greater propensity for saving in Italy (21.0 %), France (21.5 %) and Germany (21.7 %) (see Table 1.6.3). When these figures are compared with the benchmark figures for 1995, it shows that there was no great change in the United Kingdom, Germany and Italy; in France, on the other hand, saving as a percentage of disposable income went up by 1.3 points (see Table 1.6.4). As for the absolute variation in value

Figure 1.6.3. Gross disposable income: redistribution

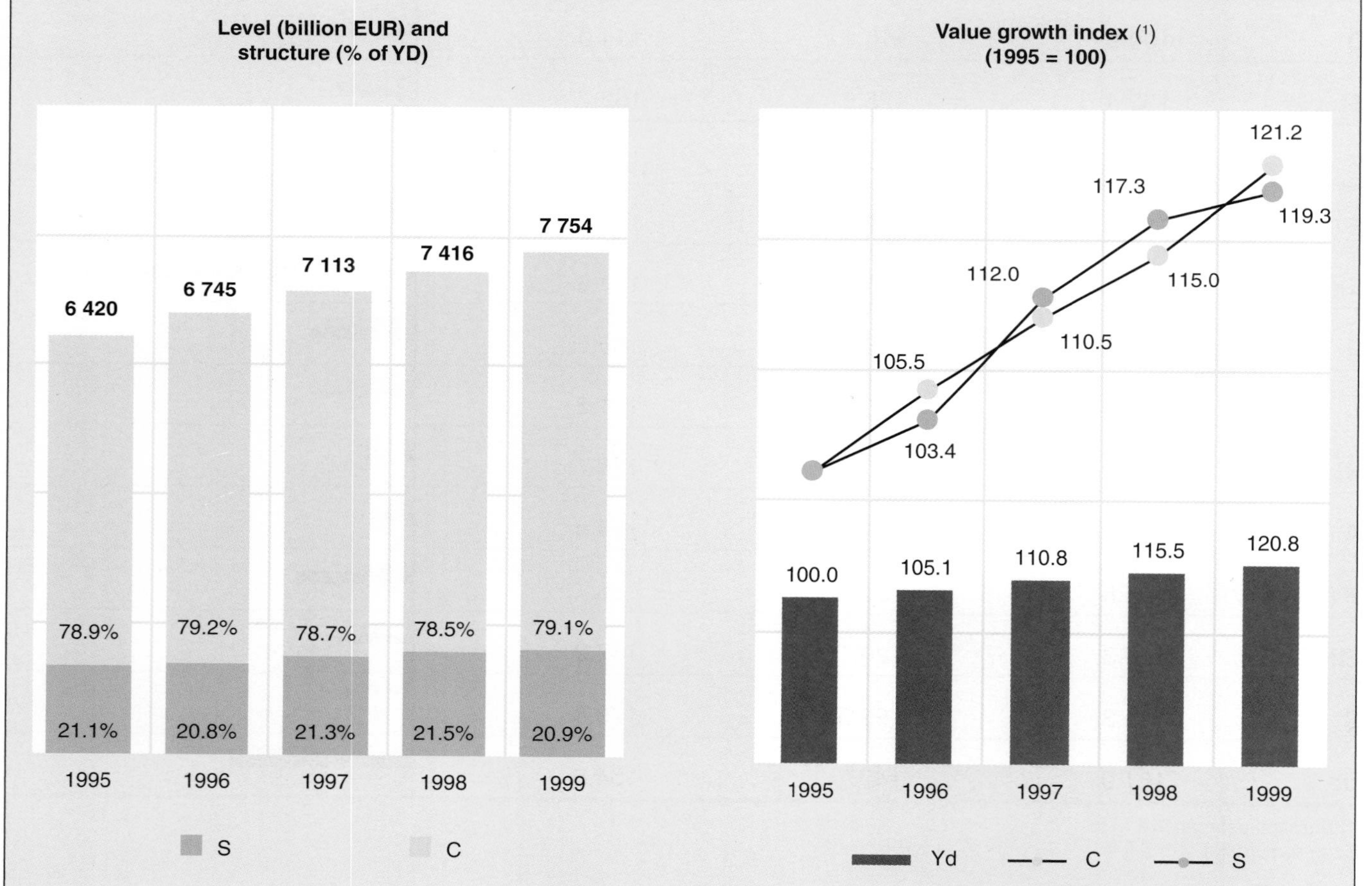

Level (billion EUR) and structure (% of YD)

	1995	1996	1997	1998	1999
Total	6 420	6 745	7 113	7 416	7 754
C	78.9%	79.2%	78.7%	78.5%	79.1%
S	21.1%	20.8%	21.3%	21.5%	20.9%

Value growth index ([1]) (1995 = 100)

	1995	1996	1997	1998	1999
Yd	100.0	105.1	110.8	115.5	120.8
C		105.5	110.5	115.0	121.2
S		103.4	112.0	117.3	119.3

([1]) Growth index is in value terms, since data are available only at current prices.
NB: Yd = disposable income
Source: Eurostat.

([12]) Current taxes on income, capital, etc., social contributions, social benefits and other current transfers.

terms, saving in France increased by 21.5 %, compared with + 12.1 % for consumption, whereas the changes in Germany were fairly contained (+ 2.5 % for saving and + 5.6 % for consumption). The variations in Italy were much larger in scale, with consumption (+ 32.8 %) ahead of saving (+ 28.8 %). The biggest increases occurred in the United Kingdom, however, where saving increased in absolute terms between 1995 and 1999 by 58.8 % and consumption by 57.6 % (see Table 1.6.5).

Among the Member States, those that are most inclined to save rather than consume are Luxembourg (32.8 %) and Ireland (28.4 %). At the other extreme, consumption is highest — and saving lowest, of course — in the United Kingdom (83.4 %) and Spain (81.5 %) (see Table 1.6.3).

Table 1.6.3. Disposable income and redistribution, 1999

Disposable income (billion EUR)		Redistribution C	S
EU-15 (1)	7 754	79.1%	20.9%
EUR-11 (1)	5 899	78.1%	21.9%
B	233	74.8%	25.2%
DK	158	78.9%	21.1%
D	1 944	78.3%	21.7%
EL (3)	125	80.3%	19.7%
E (2)	525	81.5%	18.5%
F (3)	1 339	79.0%	21.0%
IRL (3)	76	71.6%	28.4%
I	1 087	78.5%	21.5%
L (2)	16	67.2%	32.8%
NL (3)	371	73.0%	27.0%
A (3)	192	77.7%	22.3%
P	:	:	:
FIN	117	74.1%	25.9%
S	217	80.1%	19.9%
UK (3)	1 355	83.4%	16.6%

(1) Portugal is not included.
(2) Eurostat estimation.
(3) The disposable income distribution account has been corrected. to include the adjustment for the change in net equity of households in pension funds reserves.
Source: Eurostat

When the data for 1995 and 1999 are compared, the biggest changes appear in Luxembourg, Ireland and Finland, albeit with the trend running in opposite directions. While the propensity to save declined by no less than 6.0 percentage points in Luxembourg, saving as a percentage of disposable income increased by 5.8 points in Ireland and by 3.4 points in Finland over the same period (see Table 1.6.4).

Table 1.6.4. Variation in redistribution of disposable income between 1995 and 1999 (in % points)

	C		change in % points		S
EU-15	↗	+	0.3	–	↙
EUR-11	↗	+	0.1	–	↙
B	↓	–	0.3	+	↑
DK	:	:	0.0	:	:
D	↗	+	0.5	–	↙
EL	↓	–	2.8	+	↑
E	↑	+	2.5	–	↓
F	↓	–	1.3	+	↑
IRL	↓	–	5.8	+	↑
I	↗	+	0.5	–	↙
L	↑	+	6.0	–	↓
NL	↗	+	0.3	–	↙
A	↗	+	0.1	–	↙
P	:		:		:
FIN	↓	–	3.4	+	↑
S	↗	+	0.7	–	↙
UK	↙	–	0.1	+	↗

NB:
↗ ↙ slight variation: below 1 percentage point
↑ ↓ moderate variation: 1–3 percentage points
↑ ↓ strong variation: over 3 percentage points
Source: Eurostat.

As for the absolute variation (value growth index), saving in Ireland more than doubled over the period under review. There were also considerable increases in Greece (+ 51.1 %) and Finland (+ 42.0 %). Luxembourg was the only country where the nominal value of saving declined (– 6.7 %) in relation to the reference year (see Table 1.6.5).

Table 1.6.5. Value growth index of disposable income components, 1999 (1995 = 100)

	Saving	Consumption
EU-15	119.3	121.2
EUR-11	114.0	114.5
B	111.5	109.7
DK	118.5	118.6
D	102.5	105.6
EL	151.5	125.8
E	105.3	123.1
F	121.5	112.1
IRL	206.1	151.7
I	128.8	132.8
L	93.3	121.1
NL	115.2	116.7
A	107.3	108.0
P	:	129.0
FIN	142.0	117.6
S	118.3	123.6
UK	158.8	157.6

Source: Eurostat.

Net lending/borrowing

In the final analysis, a country's resources that are not consumed are either saved or invested or transferred to or from the country. The balance between saving, investment (capital formation) and net capital transactions with other countries therefore provides a summary of the country's lending/borrowing in relation to the rest of the world.

In 1999, the European Union's lending position amounted to about EUR 46 billion. This position remained steadily in the black in the period under review, with the figure peaking in 1997, when EUR 126.5 billion was lent to the rest of the world. The figures for the euro zone were a little below the EU-15 figures until 1999, when the EUR-11 figure of EUR 59.8 billion exceeded the figure for the Union as a whole. The main reason for this was the increased borrowing by the United Kingdom, where in 1999 the net borrowing figure reached EUR 18.2 billion. France and Italy produced steady net lending figures throughout the period under review (1995–99). Germany generated EUR 16.3 billion of borrowing in 1999; this followed a five-year period in which the figures had fluctuated somewhat, even resulting in net lending in 1997 (see Table 1.6.6).

Apart from the United Kingdom and Germany — which have just been mentioned — Spain was the only other Member State in a position of net borrowing in 1999. Austria and Portugal were also in the red, but the figures here refer to 1998, the last year for which data are available.

Table 1.6.6. Net lending and borrowing (billion EUR, current prices)

	1995	1996	1997	1998	1999
EU-15 (1)	48.3	78.5	129.5	91.9	45.9
EUR-11 (1)	0.0	0.1	0.1	86.8	59.8
B	9.1	9.5	10.4	9.1	9.4
DK	0.9	2.1	0.5	– 2.1	1.6
D	– 16.2	– 7.1	0.1	– 2.5	– 16.3
EL	– 0.1	– 1.0	– 0.6	0.2	:
E	4.4	5.7	7.7	3.9	– 3.2
F	3.1	11.0	31.5	29.3	30.7
IRL (2)	2.8	3.3	3.5	:	:
I	20.0	31.2	31.7	20.9	11.9
L (2)	3.3	3.7	3.5	:	:
NL	19.2	15.8	21.9	20.3	17.9
A	– 3.9	– 4.0	– 2.6	– 4.2	:
P	– 0.1	– 0.9	– 1.9	– 3.6	:
FIN	4.1	3.9	6.2	6.1	6.5
S	5.6	5.1	6.8	7.2	2.6
UK	– 3.9	0.2	10.7	– 0.3	– 18.2

(1) Eurostat estimation.
(2) Only ESA 79 data available for Ireland and Luxembourg.
Source: Eurostat.

Figure 1.6.4. Net lending and borrowing

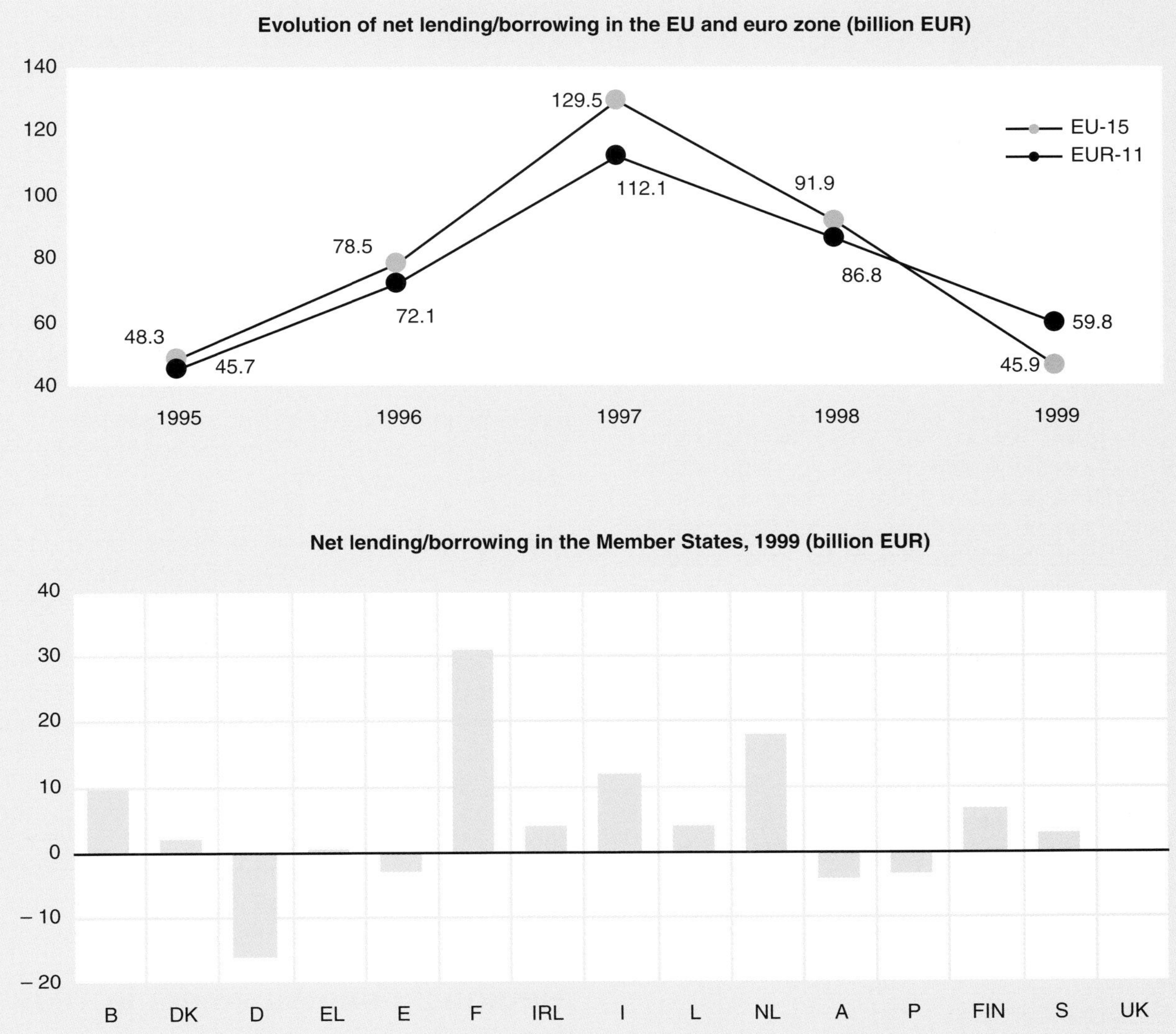

NB: Data refer to 1998 for Greece, Austria and Portugal; to 1997 for Ireland and Luxembourg.
Source: Eurostat.

1.7. The economic situation in the regions

Per capita GDP of the regions of the Union in 1997

Per capita gross domestic product at market prices, one of the key indicators for the structural and regional policies of the EU, varied in 1997 between 8 200 PPS in the Greek region of Ipeiros and 45 000 in Inner London. The figures thus ranged from 43 to 233 % of the overall EU average (19 300 PPS).

Table 1.7.1 shows that, in 1997, these two regions differed markedly from the other regions with high and low per capita GDP values. The figure for Hamburg, the region with the second highest value, was more than 35 percentage points below the figure for Inner London. The other regions with relatively high values also lie more or less in the centre of the EU. The situation is quite different for the regions with the lowest per capita GDP figures. They are exclusively in the Mediterranean area — four of them in Greece, three in Portugal, two in Spain and one in Italy.

Table 1.7.1. The regions of the EU with the highest/lowest per capita GDP in PPS (EU-15 = 100)

Regions	1996	1997
Inner London	227	233
Hamburg	199	197
Région Bruxelles-Capitale	171	169
Luxembourg	170	174
Vienna	167	164
Darmstadt	167	165
Oberbayern	167	165
Île-de-France	156	153
Bremen	146	145
Antwerp	136	139
EU-15 = 100	**100**	**100**
Centro (P)	60	63
Calabria	60	59
Andalusia	58	58
Peloponissos	58	57
Dytiki Ellada	57	56
Extremadura	54	55
Madeira	54	56
Voreio Aigaio	51	51
Azores	49	51
Ipeiros	43	43

Source: Eurostat.

It is striking that all regions with high per capita GDP values in PPS are relatively small. A key underlying factor here is net commuter inflow, which takes regional production activity beyond the level possible with working residents alone. Table 1.7.1 additionally gives the per capita GDP values (as a percentage of the EU average) for 1996.

Comparison between 1995 and 1997 per capita GDP values

A comparison of the situations in 1995 and 1997 highlights distinct shifts between the regions of the European Union. In 82 out of 208 regions for which basically comparable data are available, per capita GDP as a percentage of the EU average fell between 1995 and 1997. In 49 regions the figure hardly changed; however, it rose in as many as 77.

The sharpest relative rise in the reference period occurred in Hampshire and Isle of Wight, where per capita GDP rose over this period by 14.3 percentage points from 92 to 107 % of the EU average. Table 1.7.2 shows further regions, which recorded particularly sharp increases or decreases in per capita GDP in PPS. It is remarkable that all regions with particularly strong rises are exclusively in the United Kingdom. All regions with the strongest falls are situated in Germany and France. However, the relative changes reflect not only developments within the production activities, but reflect also changes in the size and structure of the population and in the purchasing power parities.

Regional unemployment in 1999

In April 1999, the unemployment rate — i.e. the ratio of unemployed persons to the labour force — varied across the regions under consideration from 2.1 % in Åland in Denmark to 28.7 % in the Italian region of Calabria. Related in each case to 100 members of the labour force, Calabria thus had around 14 times more jobless people than Åland in Denmark.

Of all regions taken into account, as many as 43 achieved an unemployment rate in April 1999 of less than 4.7 % — lower than half the EU average. These 43 NUTS 2 regions were spread over nine Member States, and concentrated in the United Kingdom, the Netherlands, Austria and Portugal. At the other end of the scale were 11 regions in Spain, Germany and Italy where the rate stood at more than 18.8 % and was thus at least twice as high again as the overall European Union average. Table 1.7.3 lists the regions with the lowest and the highest unemployment rates in April 1999.

Table 1.7.2. The regions of the EU with the highest increase/decrease of per capita GDP in PPS, 1995–97 (relative to EU-15 per capita GDP)

Regions	Relative increase/ decrease
EU-15	0,0
Hampshire and Isle of Wight	14.3
Gloucestershire, Wiltshire and North Somerset	11.6
Berkshire, Buckinghamshire and Oxfordshire	10.5
Surrey, East and West Sussex	10.0
Bedfordshire and Hertfordshire	9.0
Cheshire	8.0
Derbyshire and Nottinghamshire	7.9
Cornwall and Isles of Scilly	7.8
Shropshire and Staffordshire	7.6
Essex	7.4
Haute-Normandie	– 4.5
Languedoc-Roussillon	– 4.8
Berlin	– 4.8
Centre (F)	– 4.8
Provence-Alpes-Côte d'Azur	– 5.0
Saarland	– 5.1
Rheinhessen-Pfalz	– 5.1
Alsace	– 5.4
Rhône-Alpes	– 5.5
Île-de-France	– 6.8

Source: Eurostat.

Table 1.7.3. The regions of the EU with the highest/lowest unemployment rates, April 1999 (as a %)

Regions	Unemployment rate
Åland	2.1
Berkshire, Buckinghamshire and Oxfordshire	2.2
Utrecht	2.3
Luxembourg (Grand Duchy)	2.4
Centro (P)	2.4
Oberösterreich	2.7
North Brabant	2.8
Gelderland	3.0
Surrey, East and West Sussex	3.0
Niederösterreich	3.1
Puglia	19.8
Halle	20.6
Dessau	20.9
Sardinia	21.9
Campania	23.7
Sicily	24.8
Ceuta y Melilla	25.5
Extremadura	25.5
Andalusia	26.8
Calabria	28.7

Source: Eurostat.

Change in unemployment rate from 1994 to 1999

From April 1994 to April 1999, the unemployment rate at EU level fell by 1.8 percentage points. 131 of the 188 regions under consideration, where data are available, recorded an increase over this period. As many as 55 regions enjoyed a marked decrease — of up to 13.9 percentage points in the Canaries.

Table 1.7.4 shows that, of the 10 regions in which the unemployment rate fell by the most between April 1994 and April 1999, as many as 8 are in Spain. There is also one is in Ireland, as well as one in Finland. Moreover, all regions of Spain, the Netherlands, Portugal, Finland and the United Kingdom taken into account recorded a fall in the rate of unemployment over the period under review.

In a total of 10 regions, in which the unemployment rate rose by the most between April 1994 and April 1999, Greece and Italy account for all of these regions.

Table 1.7.4. The regions in the EU with the highest increase/decrease of unemployment rates, from 1994 to 1999 (% points)

Regions	Decrease/ Increase
Canarias	– 13.9
La Rioja	– 11.2
Región de Murcia	– 10.7
Cataluña	– 10.6
Pais Vasco	– 10.5
Comunidad Valenciana	– 10.4
Islas Baleares	– 9.8
Väli-Suomi	– 9.1
Ireland	– 8.8
Cantabria	– 8.7
EU-15	**– 1.8**
Kentriki Makedonia	3.5
Sterea Ellada	3.6
Notio Aigaio	3.8
Voreio Aigaio	4.3
Puglia	5.1
Anatoliki Makedonia, Thraki	5.4
Dytiki Makedonia	5.5
Ipeiros	5.8
Thessalia	5.9
Calabria	6.9

Source: Eurostat.

2. THE UNION IN THE INTERNATIONAL FRAMEWORK

2.1. The EU in the world

In 1999, the US economy continued to expand rapidly, as it has done for the last four years: GDP rose by an annual rate of 4.2 % (see Table 2.1.1). Domestic demand accounted for most of the strong economic growth: + 6.9 % for investment, + 5.2 % for private consumption and + 2.6 % for government consumption. In view of its large share of GDP, private consumption was the principal driving force behind GDP growth, accounting for 81.7 % of the total 4.2 % rate (see Table 2.1.2).

Canada also maintained robust growth, with a 1999 annual rate of GDP growth of 4.2 %, the same as for the United States. Investment recorded the strongest increase, with a 9.5 % rate, and contributed to more than half of GDP growth (see Table 2.1.2). Private consumption increased by 3.1 %, and government consumption had a modest + 0.9 % growth.

The Japanese economy continued to suffer from recession. 1999 GDP growth, at 0.3 %, was nevertheless a recovery from the – 2.5 % recorded in the previous year. With an annual rate of 1.3 %, government consumption was the most buoyant component. Private consumption reversed the negative result of 1998 (– 0.6 %) and grew by 1.2 %. Investment continued to fall, with a – 0.6 % rate of growth, which is still an improvement when compared with the – 9.3 % recorded in 1998.

Overall, GDP in the G7 countries grew at a rate of 2.6 %, with economic performance differing widely: the United States and Canada accounted for the strongest growth, Japan is not yet emerging from recession, and the European Union [13] is still recording modest growth.

In Asia, the NICs made a full economic recovery, and in 1999 the group of most developed Asian countries achieved GDP growth of + 6.7 %, which is an impressive result when compared with the – 3.3 % recorded the previous year. Most NICs reversed the sign of economic performance: the strongest pick-up was in South Korea, where the GDP growth rate made a turnaround of 16.4 percentage points from – 5.8 % in 1998 to + 10.6 % in 1999, the highest rate of all NICs. Strong recovery was also recorded for Thailand (+ 4.2 % in 1999 and – 10.2 % in 1998) and Malaysia (+ 4.9 % in 1999 and – 7.5 % in 1998). The driving force behind recovery in those countries was mostly private consumption, which increased in all the Asian NICs. The strongest growth was recorded for private consumption in Malaysia (+ 7.3 %) and Taiwan (+ 6.0 %). Public consumption continued to support economic activity in all

Table 2.1.1. Real GDP growth rates (as a %)

	1998	1999	Average 1995–99
EU-15	2.7	2.4	2.3
EUR-11	2.7	2.4	2.2
US	4.3	4.2	3.8
Canada	3.1	4.2	3.2
JP	– 2.5	0.3	1.2
G7 countries	2.2	2.6	2.6
Australia	4.8	4.4	4.3
Russia	– 3.1	2.9	– 1.5
NICs LA	2.1	0.9	2.5
Argentina	3.9	– 3.3	2.3
Brazil	– 0.1	0.8	2.2
Chile	3.4	– 1.1	5.5
Mexico	4.8	3.6	2.8
NICs Asia	– 3.3	6.7	4.5
Hong Kong	– 5.1	2.9	2.2
Taiwan	4.8	5.3	5.7
South Korea	– 5.8	10.6	5.1
Singapore	1.5	4.9	6.1
Malaysia	– 7.5	4.9	4.9
Philippines	– 0.5	3.2	3.7
Thailand	– 10.2	4.2	1.4
China	7.8	7.1	8.4
India	4.6	6.0	6.1
Middle East	0.6	2.5	2.4
Israel	2.2	2.0	3.8
Africa	4.0	3.6	4.0
South Africa	0.6	1.3	2.3

Source: Eurostat.

the countries considered, while investment had contrasting results in 1999. Investment growth was particularly high in Malaysia, where it was responsible for most of the GDP growth. Investment growth was also dynamic in Taiwan (+ 7.0 %) and Hong Kong (+ 2.5 %). By contrast, investment dropped in Singapore (– 9.9 %), Thailand (– 9.4 %) and the Philippines (– 1.6 %).

With growth of 7.1 % in 1999, China confirmed the pace of expansion of economic activity already experienced in recent years. The GDP result in 1999 was fuelled mainly by investment growth (+ 7.1 %), but in conjunction with a + 4.6 % increase in both private and public consumption. India accelerated GDP growth by + 6.0 % in 1999. Private consumption was the less dynamic

(13) The EU countries which are also G7 countries are Germany, France, the United Kingdom and Italy — those countries account for 72.5 % of total EU GDP.

component, but still rose by + 4.8 %, while government consumption (+ 6.9 %) and investment (+ 6.1 %) grew faster.

The newly industrialised countries in Latin America (NICs LA) had rather a difficult year in 1999: the NICs LA overall GDP growth rate was only 0.9 %. Argentina (– 3.3 %) and Chile (– 1.1 %) recorded falls in output; Brazil's GDP remained stable for the second year running (+ 0.8 % in 1999 and – 0.1 % in 1998), and only in Mexico did GDP expand at a rate of + 3.6 %. Negative results for Argentina and Chile mainly reflect contractions in both private consumption and investment, but much more so for the latter. Again in Brazil, investment dropped by – 0.7 %, but private consumption grew by + 1.2 %. In Mexico, healthy growth was recorded for both investment (+ 6.4 %) and private consumption (+ 3.1 %).

In order to give a full picture of economic results in 1999, in addition to Table 2.1.2, illustrating GDP growth, Table 2.1.2 indicates the main components ([14]) of GDP, the components' growth rates, their contribution to GDP growth and their share of GDP.

Table 2.1.2. GDP main components, 1999

	Growth rates (as a %)			Contribution to GDP growth (as a % of GDP growth rate)			Structure (as a % of GDP)		
	PC	GC	I	PC	GC	I	PC	GC	I
EU-15	2.7	1.8	4.9	66.5	15.4	42.5	58.2	20.0	20.2
EUR-11	2.5	1.5	4.8	59.9	12.5	42.8	56.7	20.1	20.7
US	5.2	2.6	6.9	81.7	0.1	38.2	67.2	13.7	24.0
Canada	3.1	0.9	9.5	42.4	0.9	50.2	56.2	21.6	23.3
JP	1.2	1.3	– 0.6	228.7	97.3	– 55.7	59.3	9.6	28.9
G7	:	:	:	:	:	:	:	:	:
Australia	4.5	5.1	6.7	57.4	9.1	40.6	56.2	17.2	27.3
Russia	:	:	:	:	:	:	:	:	:
NICs LA	***0.4***	***– 0.5***	***– 1.3***	***32.0***	***12.6***	***– 32.0***	***64.9***	***13.9***	***21.6***
Argentina	– 4.3	1.2	– 7.7	93.9	– 3.1	60.0	70.9	12.9	24.3
Brazil	1.2	– 0.3	– 0.7	91.4	28.3	– 17.4	63.3	18.0	20.9
Chile	– 3.8	– 17.1	– 17.4	232.2	– 33.2	481.1	64.6	6.3	25.5
Mexico	3.1	– 0.3	6.4	55.0	– 3.3	35.8	64.3	8.9	20.8
NICs Asia	***4.8***	***– 1.5***	***4.9***	***38.5***	***11.7***	***18.7***	***53.2***	***12.1***	***25.3***
Hong Kong	1.2	– 12.1	2.5	23.9	191.2	6.8	58.4	29.4	7.9
Taiwan	6.0	5.9	7.0	67.9	2.9	33.2	59.9	13.7	25.4
South Korea	5.2	– 7.8	0.4	25.1	0.7	1.2	48.3	7.5	27.3
Singapore	4.4	11.1	– 9.9	37.3	15.5	– 80.8	41.5	11.6	34.4
Malaysia	7.3	13.8	70.0	61.0	16.6	368.8	42.0	13.9	41.8
Philippines	5.0	7.3	– 1.6	120.2	17.2	– 11.4	78.2	10.5	22.2
Thailand	2.5	1.7	– 9.4	31.6	11.9	– 49.4	52.7	9.7	19.3
China	4.6	4.6	7.1	8.2	1.5	43.8	12.2	12.2	43.8
India	4.8	6.9	6.1	8.1	52.8	60.5	10.0	26.4	59.4
Middle East	***2.5***	***– 4.4***	***4.6***	***61.2***	***2.7***	***40.3***	***62.0***	***15.3***	***22.3***
Israel	3.8	2.9	1.6	129.5	19.4	19.4	70.1	22.2	24.1
Africa	***4.3***	***4.3***	***3.6***	***18.4***	***3.1***	***64.2***	***15.6***	***19.2***	***64.6***
South Africa	1.2	– 1.6	– 0.9	62.2	– 87.7	– 14.0	66.6	18.5	20.0

NB: PC: private consumption; GC: government consumption; I: investment, that is gross fixed capital formation.
Source: Eurostat.

([14]) The trade balance was not included, since an extensive description of world trade is given in Section 2.3.

In order to compare different countries and regions, the population and GNP have been selected to give an indication of size, whilst per capita GNP gives a measure of wealth; unfortunately, the last available data in PPS relate to 1998 ([15]).

When compared with major countries and regions, the population of the EU (6.4 %) as a share of the world's is comparable to that of the United States (4.6 %) and nearly three times Japan's (2.2 %). In all, it is roughly equivalent to one tenth of the total population of Asia, a third of China's or roughly 40 % of India's.

If we consider its importance in world GNP, the EU's share (20.2 %) is more than three times its share of the population. The GNP generated in the 15 European countries is similar to that produced in the United States (20.8 %), and more than twice Japan's (8.0 %). Compared with Asia, although in population terms the imbalance is great, the EU's GNP is four percentage points higher. It is roughly twice that of Latin America, and more than six times the GNP produced in the entire African continent.

Figure 2.1.1. Size of world's main economies (as a % of world total)

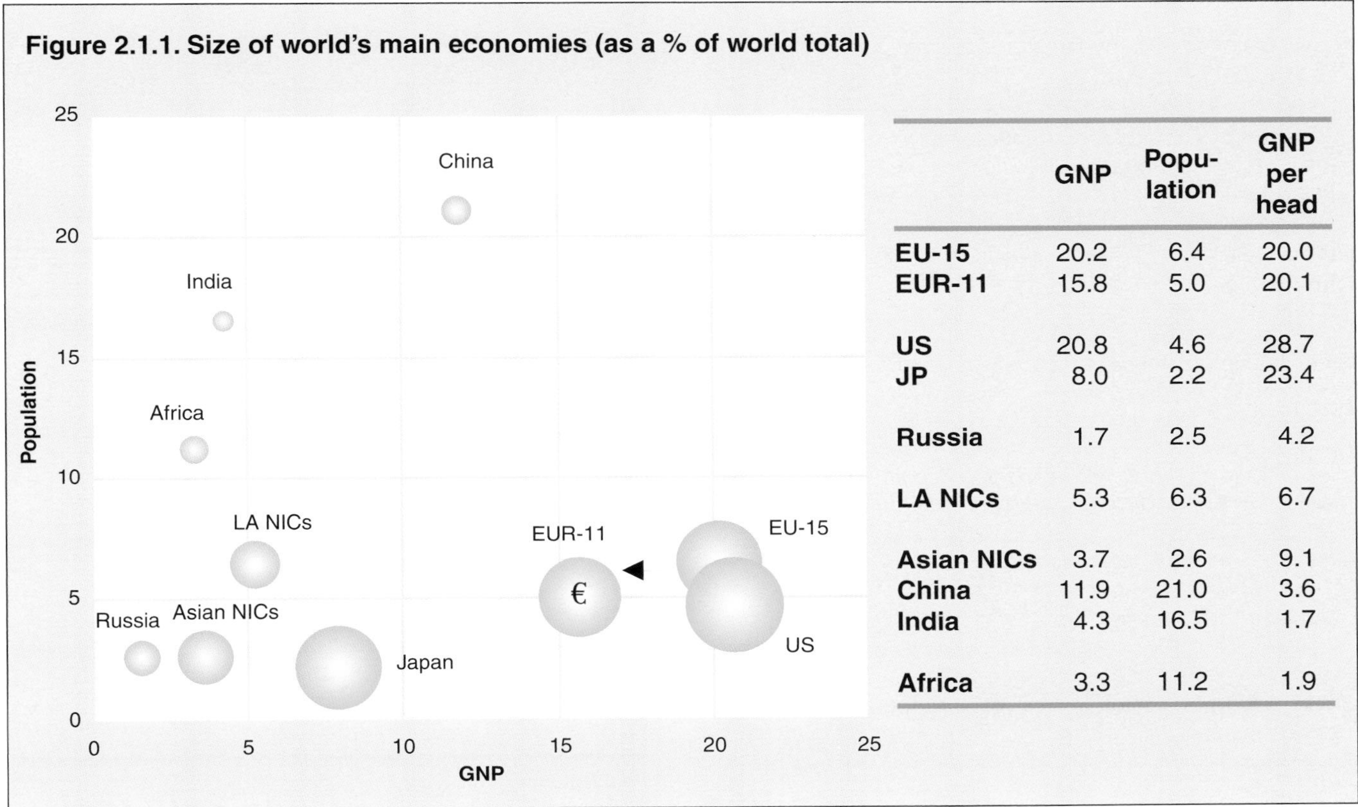

	GNP	Population	GNP per head
EU-15	20.2	6.4	20.0
EUR-11	15.8	5.0	20.1
US	20.8	4.6	28.7
JP	8.0	2.2	23.4
Russia	1.7	2.5	4.2
LA NICs	5.3	6.3	6.7
Asian NICs	3.7	2.6	9.1
China	11.9	21.0	3.6
India	4.3	16.5	1.7
Africa	3.3	11.2	1.9

NB: X axis shows the GNP (in PPS) shares in total for world while the Y axis indicates the share in world population.
The size of the bubbles is proportional to GNP per capita, in PPS.
Source: Eurostat, World Bank, *World development indicators 2000.*

([15]) For non EU-countries, source: World Bank, *World development indicators 2000.*

2.2. Candidate countries

This section sets out the principal macroeconomic developments of the candidate countries (CCs) for membership of the European Union. This group comprises Bulgaria (BG), Cyprus (CY), the Czech Republic (CZ), Estonia (EE), Hungary (HU), Latvia (LV), Lithuania (LT), Malta (MT), Poland (PL), Romania (RO), the Slovak Republic (SK), Slovenia (SI) and Turkey (TR). The following sections highlight the main trends in GDP, including quarterly analysis, its main components, employment and productivity data, regional differences and comparisons with the European Union. Monetary issues such as exchange rates, interest rates and public debt and deficit are also explored.

Data compatibility

The NA data of the CCs are not yet fully compliant with the ESA 95 standard and should therefore continue to be treated with some caution; comparability with EU Member States cannot be guaranteed. However, the CCs have generally made significant progress in improving the quality of their estimates over the past couple of years. This was supported by a series of EU-sponsored projects and workshops, which helped to improve the sources and methods used to compile national accounts and heightened the exhaustiveness and consistency of the different national accounting systems. However, not all the changes have yet been implemented in the accounts for all years and the problem of consistent time series, in particular, remains to be solved in most CCs. In future, revisions of the level and growth rates of GDP may therefore be expected.

Turkey and Malta have not, as yet, participated in this work. However, Turkey bases its accounts on SNA 1993 (according to its Statistical Office website). Malta, however, still uses a dated system established in 1954 with some elements of SNA 1968.

GDP growth

With nine of the CCs experiencing a decline in growth in 1999 and Estonia, Lithuania and Turkey joining Romania and the Czech Republic in negative growth, the CC-13 group as a whole has plummeted from a growth rate of 2.8 % in 1998 to – 0.2 % in 1999. Turkey, because of its economic size, has a high weighting in the average, and its growth rate of – 5.0 % is reflected in this. Cyprus, Hungary, Malta, and Slovenia, however, all enjoyed rates of at least 4.5 %. Only 7 of the 13 bettered the slowest-growing EU Member State, compared to 12, 10 and 11 countries in the 1996 to 1998 period.

Figure 2.2.1. GDP growth rates (as a %)

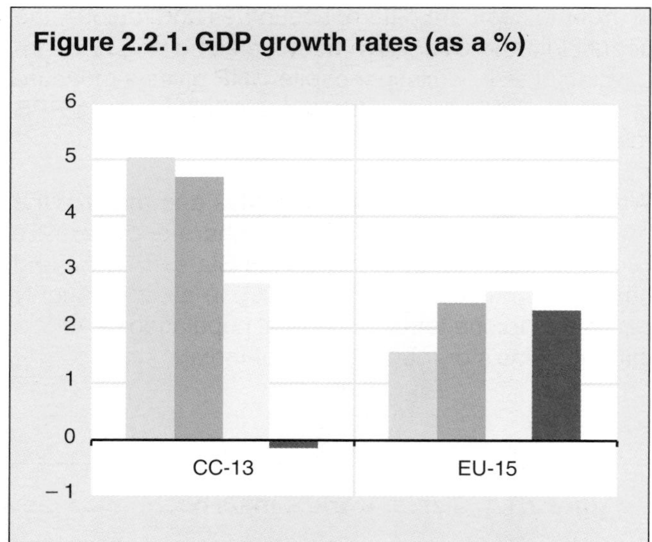

Source: Eurostat.

Table 2.2.1. GDP growth rates (as a %)

	1996	1997	1998	1999
CC-13	**5.0**	**4.7**	**2.8**	**– 0.2**
BG	– 10.1	– 7.0	3.5	2.4
CY	1.9	2.4	5.0	4.5
CZ	4.8	– 1.0	– 2.2	– 0.2
EE	3.9	10.6	4.7	– 1.1
HU	1.3	4.6	4.9	4.5
LV	3.3	8.6	3.9	0.1
LT	4.7	7.3	5.1	– 4.1
MT	4.0	4.9	3.4	4.6
PL	6.0	6.8	4.8	4.1
RO	3.9	– 6.1	– 5.4	– 3.2
SK	6.6	6.5	4.4	1.9
SI	3.5	4.6	3.8	4.9
TR	7.0	7.5	3.1	– 5.0
Memorandum				
EU-15	1.6	2.5	2.7	2.4
EU-min	0.8	1.2	1.5	1.4
	D	**A**	**I**	**I**
EU-max	7.7	10.7	8.9	9.8
	IRL	**IRL**	**IRL**	**IRL**

Source: Eurostat.

Figure 2.2.2. Annual growth in the CCs (as a %)

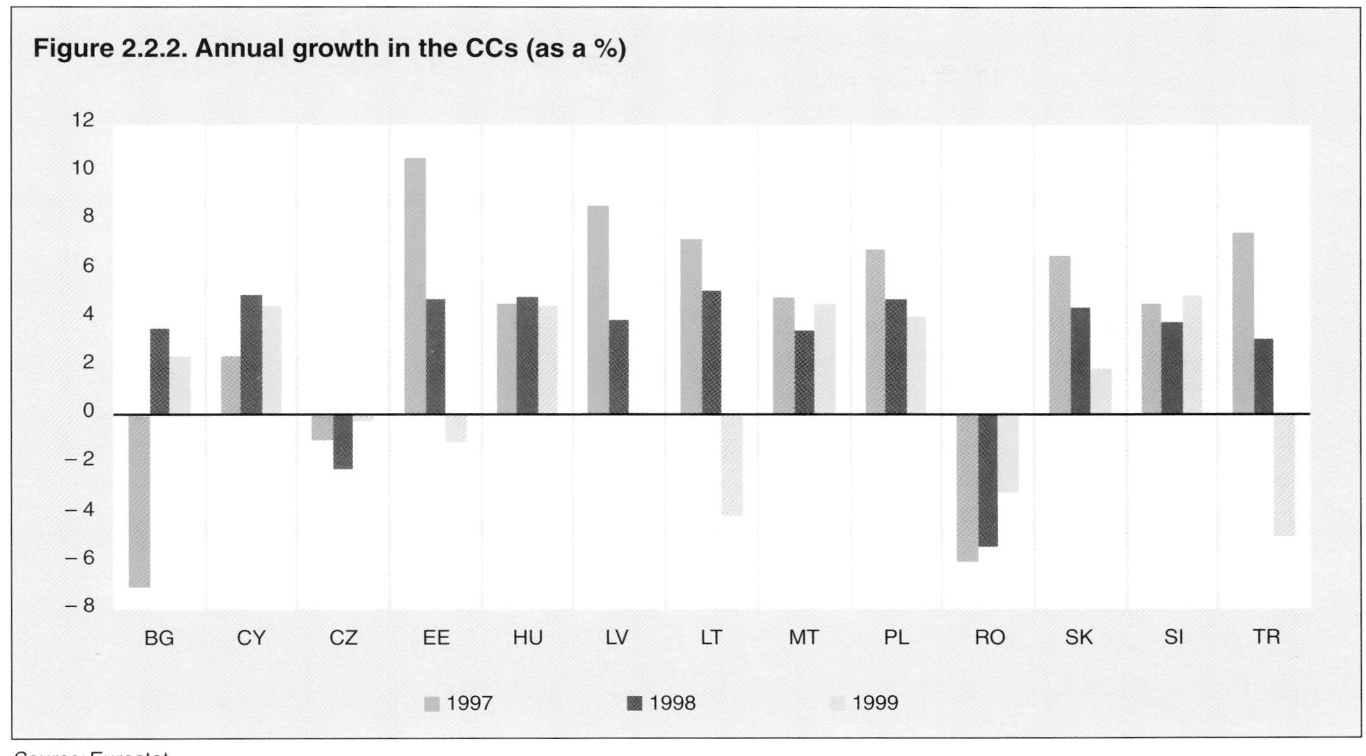

Source: Eurostat.

GDP in current prices and euro

In simple euro terms, the CC-13 group, even with the inclusion of Turkey, amounts to a very small economic area compared to the European Union. The total GDP in euro of the CC-13 represents just 6.6 % of EU-15 GDP. Before 1999, this ratio had been increasing, but the downturn of the CCs average in this year reversed this trend.

As in the EU-15, the CC economies are very diverse in size. Turkey is by far the largest CC in euro terms, representing 33 % of the CC-13 total. Only the Polish economy is even vaguely comparable in size, with 28 % of CC-13 GDP. Malta has the smallest economy with a GDP of only EUR 3.4 billion (51 times smaller than Turkey, five times smaller than Luxembourg). Even grouping Malta with the five other smallest CCs (Bulgaria, Cyprus, Estonia, Latvia and Lithuania) gives a total of only EUR 44 billion, or 8 % of the CC-13 total, barely 0.5 % of the EU-15 figure.

Table 2.2.3. GDP at current prices and exchange rate (billion EUR)

	1996	1997	1998	1999
CC-13	425.5	482.3	523.9	525.3
EU-15	6 906.6	7 269.7	7 593.6	7 965.3
CC-13 as a % of EU-15	6.2	6.6	6.9	6.6

Source: Eurostat.

Table 2.2.4. GDP at current prices, 1999

	Billion EUR	As a % of CC-13	Billion PPS	As a % of CC-13
CC-13	**525.3**	**100**	**1 222.3** (¹)	**100**
TR	173.0	32.9	378.3	30.9
PL	144.7	27.5	299.1	24.5
CZ	49.8	9.5	128.5	10.5
HU	45.4	8.7	107.8	8.8
RO	31.9	6.1	127.6	10.4
SI	18.7	3.6	29.7	2.4
SK	17.7	3.4	53.0	4.3
BG	11.6	2.2	39.0	3.2
LT	10.0	1.9	22.8	1.9
CY	8.5	1.6	11.4	0.9
LV	5.7	1.1	14.1	1.2
EE	4.8	0.9	11.1	0.9
MT	3.4	0.6	:	:
Memorandum				
CC-13 as a % of EU-15		**6.6**		**15.3** (¹)

(¹) Not including Malta.
Source: Eurostat.

When making comparisons between the GDP of different countries, it is informative to express figures in PPS (purchasing power standard). This makes allowances for the varying price levels at a given point in time in different countries and makes the comparisons of GDP, both in absolute terms and 'per head', more meaningful.

Looking at Table 2.2.4 we see that the CC-13 group is not as small compared to the EU-15 as it appeared in euro terms. Without Malta, which does not yet provide PPS figures, it amounts to 15.3 % of the EU total in 1999, compared to just 6.6 % when using the euro figures.

The individual CCs and EU Member States are ranked in Table 2.2.4 by their GDP in 1999. Turkey and Poland can be seen to be significant players.

GDP per head: there are massive differences in per head figures across the CCs

Measured in per head terms, countries can be more meaningfully compared using PPS figures which take into consideration the price differences between countries: in 1999 the CC figures are very wide-ranging, stretching from 4 700 PPS in Bulgaria (22.5 % of the EU-15 figure) to 17 100 PPS in Cyprus (80.9 % of the EU-15 figure).

Cyprus has only very recently supplied data in PPS and we are now able to see from Table 2.2.5 that its GDP per head is significantly above that of both Portugal and Greece. Slovenia has managed, in the last four years, to move from a GDP per head which was 66.1 % of the EU-15 figure to one of 70.9 %, overtaking Greece in the process. The Czech Republic and Romania, on the other hand, fell further behind the EU-15 and the CC-13 group, dropping by 6 percentage points their GDP per head.

Table 2.2.5. GDP per head at current prices in PPS

	In PPS				EU-15 = 100			
	1996	1997	1998	1999	1996	1997	1998	1999
CC-13	6 500	7 000	7 200	7 200	35.4	35.9	35.5	34.1
CY	14 500	15 300	16 000	17 100	78.8	78.9	79.2	81.0
SI	12 200	13 200	13 900	15 000	66.3	68.0	68.8	71.1
CZ	12 000	12 300	12 200	12 500	65.2	63.4	60.4	59.2
HU	8 600	9 300	9 900	10 700	46.7	47.9	49.0	50.7
SK	8 100	8 900	9 400	9 800	44.0	45.9	46.5	46.4
PL	6 200	6 800	7 200	7 700	33.7	35.1	35.6	36.5
EE	6 100	7 100	7 500	7 700	33.2	36.6	37.1	36.5
LT	5 300	5 900	6 300	6 200	28.8	30.4	31.2	29.4
TR	5 600	6 100	6 400	5 900	30.4	31.4	31.7	28.0
LV	4 700	5 300	5 600	5 800	25.5	27.3	27.7	27.5
RO	6 100	6 000	5 700	5 700	33.2	30.9	28.2	27.0
BG	4 600	4 400	4 500	4 700	25.0	22.7	22.3	22.3
MT	:	:	:	:	:	:	:	:
EU-15	18 400	19 400	20 200	21 100	100	100	100	100
Memorandum								
EU	12 300	12 800	13 300	14 200	69.9	73.2	74.7	67.3
min.	P	P	P	EL	P	P	P	EL

NB: For the calculation of per capita GDP, the data for the total population is taken from the national accounts: it may be different from that obtained via demographic statistics.
Source: Eurostat, OECD, ÖSTAT (Austrian Statistical Office).

Figure 2.2.3. GDP per head in PPS, 1999 (EU-15 = 100)

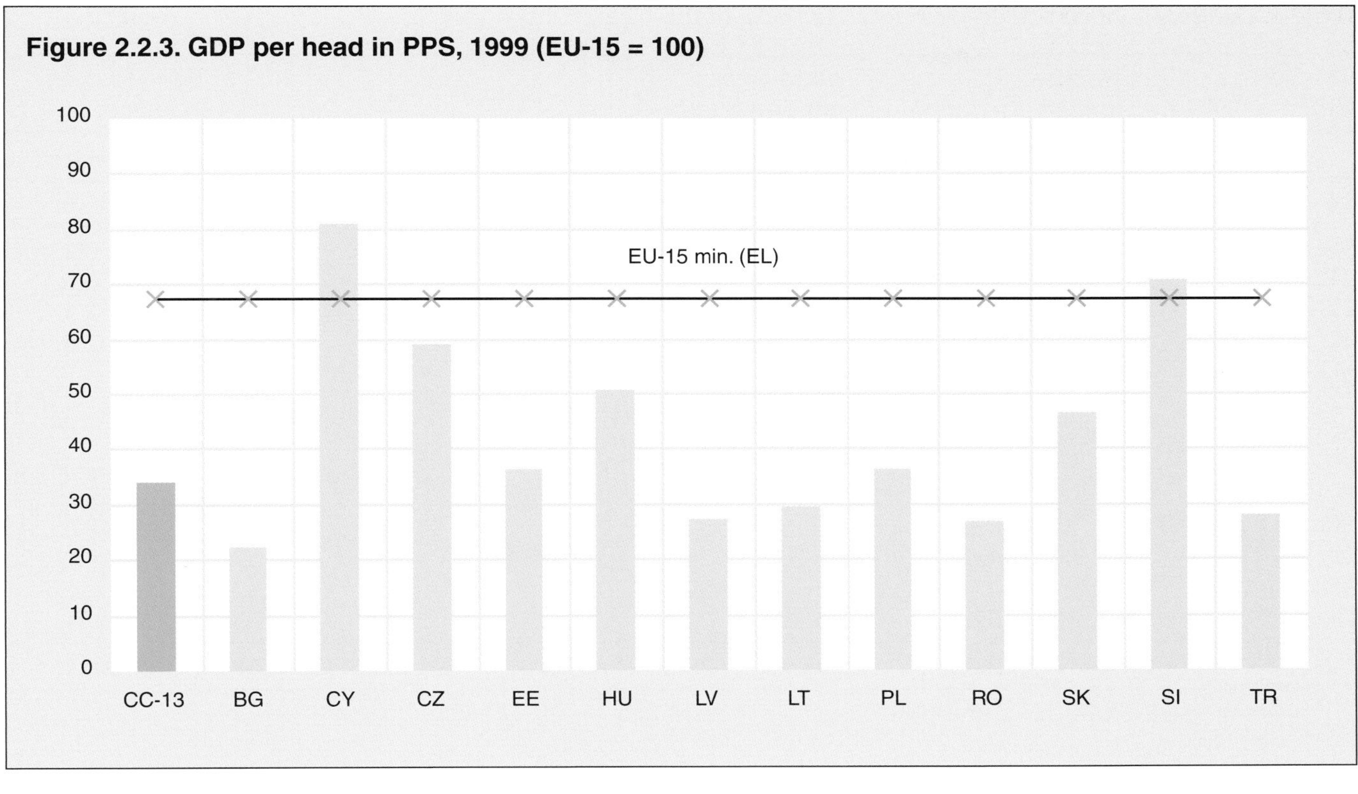

Source: Eurostat.

Main aggregates: GDP components

In 1999, the share of GDP accounted for by final consumption of households and NPISH varied amongst the CCs from 51.1 % in the Slovak Republic to 74.8 % in Bulgaria, Table 2.2.6 shows. EU-15 figures, however, are even more wide-ranging, from 44.2 % in Luxembourg to 74.1 % in Greece. With the exception of Cyprus (whose share rose steeply between 1995 and 1999), there is a tendency for the low-performing countries to use a higher share of their GDP for this component, satisfying basic needs from limited incomes.

Concerning final consumption of general government, CC figures range from just 14.1 % in Turkey to 23.7 % in Estonia. Most of the CCs fall within the EU-range, however, which begins with 14.2 % in Ireland and ends with the high Scandinavian rates of 25.8 % and 27.0 % in Denmark and Sweden.

In terms of GFCF, the Slovak Republic far exceeds the other CCs with 33.0 % of its GDP being attributed to this, though this is lower than the 38.6 % of 1997. This is far above the highest Member State, Portugal, on 26.9 %. At the other end of the scale, Bulgaria records 15.9 % compared to the EU-minimum of 16.6 % in Sweden.

New data for Malta shows them to be by far the most prolific foreign traders, relative to their economic size. Exports in 1999 were worth 91.9 % of their GDP, with imports slightly higher at 96.8 %. Turkey's exports, on the other hand, amounted to 21.6 % of its GDP, whilst it imports 25.0 %. Trade for EU Member States varies even more greatly, with imports ranging from 17.8 % to 113.2 % of GDP (Greece and Luxembourg) and exports stretching from 23.5 % to 95.5 % (Italy and Luxembourg). On average, the economies of the CC-13 group are far more foreign trade-oriented than the EU-15 economies.

In 1999, all CCs exhibited a trade deficit with Bulgaria and Hungary slipping from positions of surplus and balance in 1997. The Baltic States of Latvia and Lithuania had the highest trade deficits in 1999, exceeding 10 % of their GDP.

Table 2.2.6. Gross value added by branch (as a % of the total)

	Agriculture, fishing ...		Industry, including energy		Construction		Service activities	
	1995	1998	1995	1998	1995	1998	1995	1998
CC-13	**10.5**	**10.1**	**29.0**	**26.2**	**6.3**	**6.7**	**54.2**	**57.0**
BG (1)	15.4	21.1	25.9	24.9	4.3	3.7	54.5	50.2
CY	5.3	4.4	15.0	13.8	8.9	8.1	70.7	73.8
CZ	4.7	4.6	33.3	35.3	8.7	8.0	53.4	52.1
EE	7.9	6.3	23.1	21.2	5.9	6.4	63.1	66.0
HU	6.7	5.5	26.3	28.2	4.6	4.6	62.3	61.7
LV	10.8	4.3	28.1	23.4	5.1	6.9	56.0	65.4
LT	11.7	10.3	26.1	23.9	7.1	8.6	55.0	57.3
MT	2.9	2.7	25.5	25.0	3.3	2.8	68.3	69.5
PL	6.9	4.8	31.7	27.6	7.3	8.7	54.1	59.0
RO	20.7	16.1	34.5	30.4	6.9	5.9	37.9	47.6
SK	5.7	4.6	31.6	28.1	7.6	7.1	55.2	60.2
SI	4.5	4.1	32.6	32.0	5.0	5.6	57.9	58.3
TR	15.0	16.9	25.8	21.4	5.4	5.6	53.8	56.1
EU-15	**2.7**	**2.6**	**23.9**	**23.8**	**5.8**	**5.4**	**67.6**	**68.1**

(1) 1995 data are not available. 1996 shown instead.
Source: Eurostat.

Production: GVA and employment by branch

Gross value added (GVA) figures broken down by branch (Table 2.2.7) are now available for all CCs up to and including 1998.

In 1998, it is in agriculture where the differences between the CCs are most obvious, ranging from 2.7 % in Malta to 21.1 % in Bulgaria.

Concerning differences between 1995 and 1998, Bulgaria's increased agriculture share of almost five percentage points in GVA stands out (though actually from 1996), while it dropped significantly in Latvia, Poland and Romania. In these three countries this was concurrent with a considerable increase in the share of service activities in GVA.

Service activities, a broad category taking the largest share of GVA (amongst other things, it includes trade, hotels and restaurants, financial services, public administration, defence, education and health), varies between 62.7 % and 78.7 % in the EU Member States (Portugal and Luxembourg) and between 47.6 % and 73.8 % (Romania and Cyprus) in the CCs, with a great deal of overlap. Industry and construction occupy slightly higher shares in the CCs than in the available EU Member States.

Table 2.2.7. Main GDP aggregates (as a % of total GDP)

	Final consumption								
	of households and NPISH			of general government			GFCF		
	1995	1997	1999	1995	1997	1999	1995	1997	1999
BG	70.7	70.3	74.8	15.3	12.8	15.8	15.3	10.8	15.9
CY	63.7	66.1	66.9	16.1	18.8	18.0	19.2	19.0	17.8
CZ	50.8	53.3	53.4	19.9	19.9	19.7	32.0	30.8	26.4
EE	58.9	59.0	58.6	25.4	22.1	23.7	26.0	27.9	25.1
HU	53.7	50.3	51.8	23.6	21.9	21.9	20.0	22.2	23.9
LV	62.6	66.6	64.5 (¹)	22.2	19.1	19.0	15.1	18.7	25.0
LT	67.4	65.1	64.9	19.7	19.0	22.5	23.0	24.4	22.5
MT	61.1	62.4	62.8	20.5	20.5	18.7	31.9	25.3	22.7
PL	61.2	63.5	63.2	16.6	16.1	16.5	18.7	23.6	26.5
RO	67.6	74.1	72.7 (¹)	13.7	12.3	14.0 (¹)	21.4	21.2	18.5
SK	51.4	49.7	51.1	19.5	21.9	20.9	26.4	38.6	33.0
SI	58.1	56.5	55.4	20.2	20.5	20.6	21.4	23.5	26.9
TR	68.9	68.3	67.6	10.6	12.3	14.1	23.3	26.5	20.3
CC-13	62.4	63.2	62.9	15.7	15.9	16.9	22.4	25.3	23.5
EU-15	57.4	57.8	58.2	20.7	20.3	20.0	19.8	19.5	20.2

	Exports			Imports			External trade balance		
	1995	1997	1999	1995	1997	1999	1995	1997	1999
BG	44.7	61.9	44.1	46.3	56.4	51.9	– 1.6	5.5	– 7.8
CY	46.6	47.0	44.6	49.9	52.1	49.3	– 3.3	– 5.1	– 4.7
CZ	53.6	56.9	63.6	58.4	62.9	65.2	– 4.8	– 6.0	– 1.6
EE	72.4	78.1	76.9	80.4	89.6	82.6	– 8.0	– 11.5	– 5.7
HU	36.9	45.5	52.6	38.2	45.5	55.0	– 1.3	0.0	– 2.4
LV	46.9	51.0	46.7	49.3	59.5	57.6	– 2.4	– 8.5	– 10.9
LT	53.0	54.5	39.8	64.8	65.1	50.1	– 11.8	– 10.6	– 10.3
MT	93.8	85.1	91.9	107.5	93.5	96.8	– 13.7	– 8.4	– 4.9
PL	25.5	25.7	25.7	23.2	30.0	32.9	2.3	– 4.3	– 7.2
RO	27.6	29.2	30.1	33.2	36.2	34.3	– 5.6	– 7.0	– 4.2
SK	59.8	60.7	64.8	58.0	71.0	69.8	1.8	– 10.3	– 5.0
SI	55.2	57.1	52.7	56.8	58.3	56.7	– 1.6	– 1.2	– 4.0
TR	19.5	24.7	21.6	19.6	30.5	25.0	– 0.1	– 5.8	– 3.4
CC-13	32.0	35.1	34.9	32.9	40.1	39.6	– 0.9	– 5.0	– 4.7
EU-15	29.7	31.9	32.0	28.0	29.7	30.8	1.7	2.2	1.2

(¹) 1998 data.
Source: Eurostat.

Structure of employment

Table 2.2.8 shows employment by branch for the years 1995 and 1998. Romania (the highest at 38.1 %), Poland, Lithuania and Cyprus are the countries with labour forces most heavily dominated by agriculture, but the CCs are very diverse in this branch with shares as low as 5.5 % in the Czech Republic. Between 1995 and 1998, all countries (of those available) oversaw a decrease in the proportion of employment involved in this branch, except for Romania, rising by almost four percentage points. A smaller percentage of people in the CCs are also being employed in industry, though the Czech Republic and Hungary posted modest increases.

There are vast differences in the employment patterns between the CCs and the EU, centred around agriculture and service activities. In agriculture, the share is more than four times higher in the CCs, while in service activities, the CCs share is lower, at around two thirds of the EU figure.

Table 2.2.8. Employment by branch (as a % of the total)

	Agriculture, fishing ...		Industry, including energy		Construction		Service activities	
	1995	**1998**	**1995**	**1998**	**1995**	**1998**	**1995**	**1998**
CC-13	**22.0**	**22.0**	**27.4**	**26.0**	**6.2**	**6.2**	**44.4**	**45.8**
BG	:	:	:	:	:	:	:	:
CY	23.5	:	13.6	:	7.5	:	55.4	:
CZ	6.2	5.5	32.5	32.8	9.0	8.2	52.3	53.6
EE	10.5	9.1	28.6	25.9	5.4	7.3	55.4	57.7
HU	8.0	7.5	26.7	28.0	5.9	6.2	59.4	58.3
LV	18.5	17.6	20.4	18.4	5.4	6.1	55.7	57.9
LT	23.8	21.5	21.2	20.0	7.0	7.1	48.0	51.4
MT	:	:	:	:	:	:	:	:
PL	26.1	25.2	25.5	23.4	5.7	6.1	42.7	45.3
RO	34.4	38.1	28.6	26.3	5.0	4.4	31.9	31.2
SK	9.2	8.3	30.3	30.1	8.6	9.3	51.8	52.3
SI	6.4	5.6	36.7	33.6	6.2	6.9	50.7	53.9
TR	:	:	:	:	:	:	:	:
EU-15	**5.2**	**4.8**	**20.9**	**20.2**	**7.0**	**6.8**	**67.0**	**68.2**

Source: Eurostat.

Productivity in the CCs

Looking at the productivity figures for the whole economy in Table 2.2.9, Cyprus and Slovenia display figures far above any of the other CCs. These productivity levels are generally mirrored in the individual branches, though agriculture is an exception. Industry, construction and service activities all have broadly similar overall productivity levels in the CC-13 group, but agriculture is around 50 % lower.

Turning to the changes in productivity between 1995 and 1998, also shown in Figure 2.2.4, the CCs as a group have improved by around 10 %. Estonia is the most dynamic, with its total economy becoming more productive by 23 %, closely followed by the other Baltic States of Latvia and Lithuania. All three, however, grew from very low levels of productivity in 1995. Across, the CCs, growth in industrial productivity was the main driving force behind the improvements, increasing by 20 %, while construction and service activities increased by 3 %.

Romania was the only country to see its productivity fall, of those which are able to provide figures.

Figure 2.2.4. Productivity 1995 and 1998 (1 000 EUR, constant prices)

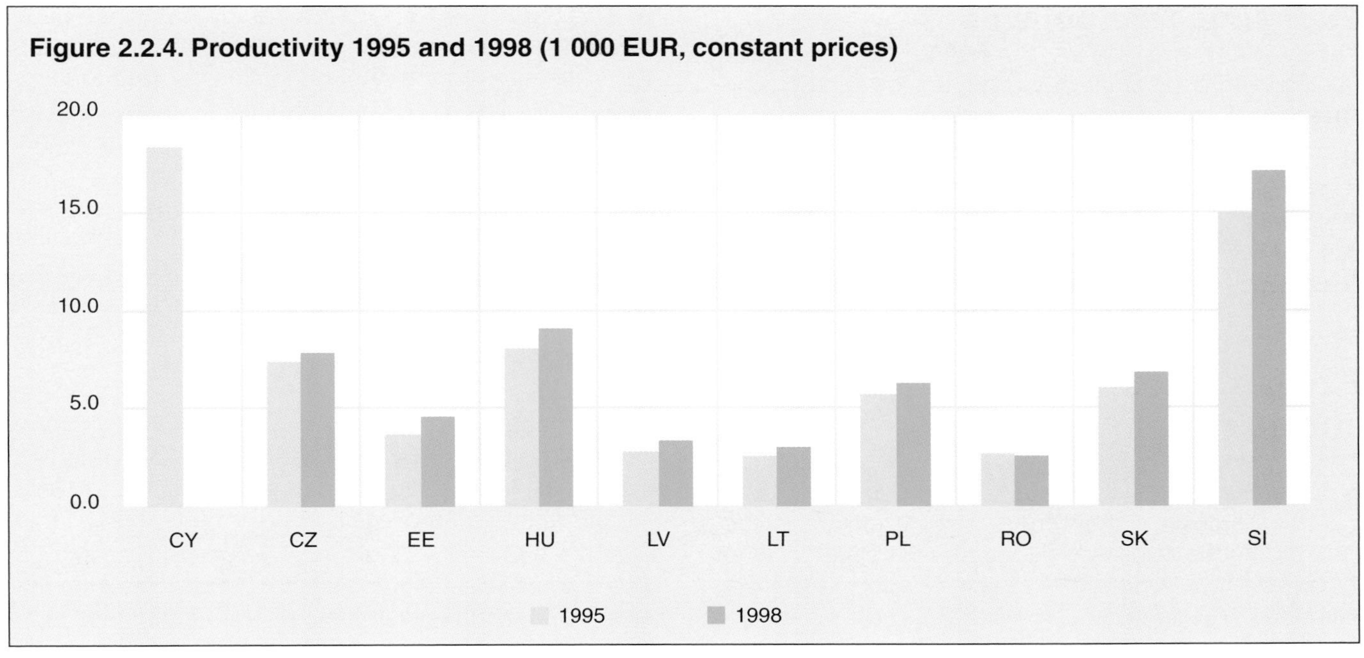

Source: Eurostat.

Table 2.2.9. Productivity by branch, 1998 (GVA per person employed)

	Agriculture, fishing ...		Industry, including energy		Construction		Service activities		Total	
	EUR	1995 = 100	EUR	1995 = 100	EUR	1995 = 100	EUR	1995 = 100	EUR	1995 = 100
CC-13 (¹)	3 200	*110*	7 300	*120*	6 100	*102*	6 500	*103*	5 900	*109*
BG	:	:	:	:	:	:	:	:	:	:
CY	:	:	:	:	:	:	:	:	:	:
CZ	7 100	*127*	9 000	*118*	5 100	*71*	7 500	*99*	7 800	*105*
EE	3 400	*121*	4 100	*137*	4 700	*118*	4 900	*117*	4 600	*124*
HU	7 400	*107*	9 500	*119*	6 400	*100*	9 400	*109*	9 100	*112*
LV	1 600	*100*	5 200	*133*	3 100	*119*	3 200	*114*	3 300	*118*
LT	1 700	*131*	3 900	*122*	3 300	*127*	3 100	*107*	3 000	*115*
MT	:	:	:	:	:	:	:	:	:	:
PL	1 600	*107*	9 000	*127*	8 200	*112*	7 300	*100*	6 300	*111*
RO (²)	1 400	*88*	2 900	*88*	3 700	*100*	3 200	*100*	2 600	*96*
SK	4 200	*111*	6 700	*106*	4 500	*85*	7 700	*120*	6 800	*113*
SI	12 500	*117*	16 600	*125*	14 000	*117*	18 200	*106*	17 100	*114*
TR	:	:	:	:	:	:	:	:	:	:
EU-15	45 700	*112*	48 900	*107*	32 800	*98*	41 900	*104*	42 700	*104*

(¹) To achieve comparability over time, Cyprus is not included in the CC-13 total.
(²) Eurostat estimate for service activities.
Source: Eurostat.

Exchange rate policies

The candidate countries have adopted the following exchange rate policies:

- managed floating exchange rate (Romania, Slovakia, Slovenia, the Czech Republic and Turkey);
- crawling peg (Hungary and Poland);
- fixed rate peg (Cyprus, Latvia and Malta);
- currency board (Bulgaria, Estonia and Lithuania).

Exchange rate trends between 1994 and 1999

In general, the monetary authorities of the candidate countries stabilised their currencies in relation to the euro during the reference period, the exceptions being those countries which were unable to adopt restrictive exchange rate policies.

In Bulgaria, after a period of turbulence, the lev stabilised in July 1997 following the introduction of a currency board. The Bulgarian currency has since been pegged to the German mark. In July 1999, following further monetary reform, the authorities decided to introduce a new lev (worth 1 000 old leva). The positive effects of this exchange rate policy have fed through into interest rates.

The Cyprus pound fluctuated within a band of 1 % of its central rate (CYP 0.5853 = ECU 1), apart from a dip in January 1996, when it touched 0.6006 to the ecu. Since January 1999, the Cypriot currency has been linked to the euro, with a fluctuation band of 2.25 %.

In the Czech Republic, after having lost almost 18 % of its value at the beginning of 1998, the Czech koruna clawed its way back to its pre-crisis level. During 1999, the currency became less volatile.

The Estonian kroon remained stable throughout the reference period, thanks to the monetary authorities' policy of pegging the currency rate to the German mark. In January 1999, this link with the mark became a *de facto* link with the euro.

Table 2.2.10. Interest rates as a % (interbank average)

	1993	1994	1995	1996	1997	1998	1999
BG	:	97.4	69.6	287.7	134.8	2.4	2.6
CY (1)	6.5	6.5	6.5	7.5	7.0	7.0	7.0
CZ	9.6	7.9	10.6	11.6	19.0	13.6	6.8
EE	:	5.7	4.9	3.5	6.5	11.6	3.3
HU	15.4	25.6	31.3	23.8	20.8	18.0	14.8
LV	51.4	37.2	22.4	13.1	3.7	4.4	4.7
LT	:	69.5	26.8	18.9	10.7	6.1	6.3
MT	:	:	:	:	5.15	5.45	4.98
PL	17.5	18.7	26.4	21.2	22.7	21.1	14.1
RO	:	:	48.5	53.4	85.9	80.7	94.7
SK	:	13.1	5.7	11.6	24.7	14.5	12.6
SI	34.7	29.1	12.1	14.0	9.7	7.4	6.9
TR	62.8	136.5	72.3	76.2	70.3	74.6	73.5

(1) Discount end year.
Source: Eurostat.

Hungary's currency, the forint, lost more than 80 % of its value against the ecu between 1994 and 1998. Its value was stable in 1999, however, fluctuating by no more than about 1 % from the average for the year.

In Latvia, the exchange rate policy adopted by the monetary authorities made it possible to cope with the monetary turbulence caused by the financial crises in Asia and Russia. In 1999, the lat appreciated by about 12 % against the euro, dragged upwards by the rising US dollar and yen, the two main components of the SDR, the lat's reference currency.

Lithuania, like the two other Baltic States, benefited from considerable monetary stability following the introduction of a currency board. Since 1994, the Lithuanian currency has been linked to the US dollar at a rate of 4 litas to the dollar. 1999 was marked by changes in the euro/US dollar exchange rate, which caused the litas to appreciate by 14 % against the euro.

The Maltese lira fluctuated within a band of 5 % around its average value in the reference period. In 1999, Malta saw its currency appreciate by 5.8 % against the euro, pulled upwards by the appreciation of the US dollar and pound sterling in relation to the euro: the Maltese lira's reference basket comprises the euro (with a weighting of 56.8 %), pound sterling (21.6 %) and US dollar (21.6 %).

In Poland, the zloty lost more than 50 % of its value during the reference period. This was in line with the devaluation policy pursued by the country's monetary authorities. Interestingly, the zloty stabilised somewhat towards the end of the reference period. Since 1 January 1999, the zloty has been linked to the euro (55 %) and the US dollar (45 %).

Romania, whose exchange rate policies have been the least restrictive, saw its currency decline from 1 972 lei to the ecu in 1994 to more than 16 345 on average in 1999. In that year alone, the leu lost more than 40 % of its value.

During the period under review, the Slovak koruna went through three distinct phases. In the first phase up to August 1998, the Slovak Republic enjoyed a relatively stable exchange rate of between 38 and 39 koruny to the ecu, with the currency linked to a basket of German marks and US dollars. On 2 October 1998, the Slovak monetary authorities switched to a managed floating exchange rate. From then on, the value of the koruna fell considerably, to SKK 45.5 to the euro in May 1999. In the second half of 1999 the koruna appreciated by 6.8 %.

The Slovenian tolar depreciated continuously from 1994 to 1997, from 152 to 194 tolars to the ecu. In other words, the Slovenian currency depreciated by an annual average of about 5 %, apart from in 1998, when it was stable.

Turkey has adopted a managed floating exchange rate, but one which is firmly linked to a crawling peg, with a reference basket made up of the euro and US dollar. The monetary policy adopted by the Turkish authorities is aimed at minimising fluctuations in the real effective exchange rate.

Public deficit and debt

Reliable and comparable national accounts statistics on government deficit (surplus) and government debt of the candidate countries are not yet available. Information is not complete and the methodology not sufficiently harmonised. However, with the help of technical assistance from the EU, countries are starting to report to Eurostat data on general government net borrowing (lending) and debt, which in due course will be consistent with the European system of accounts (ESA 95).

The following table is based on the IMF's GFS (government finance statistics) methodology. With some exceptions, the government financial position during 1993–98 does not compare unfavourably with that of EU countries. However, apart from the problem of data quality, the large structural changes which have taken place in these economies have resulted, at least for some countries, in sharp swings in the deficit/surplus.

Table 2.2.11. Exchange rates of candidate countries: annual averages 1 ECU/EUR (¹) = ...

			1993	1994	1995	1996	1997	1998	1999
BG	Lev	BGN	0.032	0.064	0.088	0.225	1.902	1.969	1.956
CY	Pound	CYP	0.583	0.584	0.592	0.592	0.583	0.577	0.579
CZ	Koruna	CZK	34.17	34.15	34.70	34.46	35.93	36.32	36.89
EE	Kroon	EEK	15.49	15.40	14.99	15.28	15.72	15.75	15.65
HU	Forint	HUF	107.61	125.03	164.55	193.74	211.65	240.57	252.77
LV	Lat	LVL	0.794	0.664	0.690	0.700	0.659	0.660	0.624
LT	Litas	LTL	5.087	4.732	5.232	5.079	4.536	4.484	4.263
MT	Pound	MTL	0.447	0.449	0.461	0.458	0.437	0.435	0.426
PL	Zloty	PLN	2.122	2.702	3.170	3.422	3.715	3.918	4.227
RO	Leu	ROL	886	1 972	2 662	3 922	8 112	9 985	16 345
SK	Koruna	SKK	36.03	38.12	38.86	38.92	38.11	39.54	44.12
SI	Tolar	SIT	132.49	152.77	154.88	171.78	181.00	185.96	194.47
TR	Lira	TRL	12 879	35 535	59 912	103 214	171 848	293 736	447 230

(¹) Euro from 1999/ecu up to 1998.
Source: Eurostat.

Interest rates

The link between interest rates and inflation has been apparent among the candidate countries: rates have tended to be higher in those countries suffering from relatively high inflation, most notably Romania, Turkey, and (until 1998) Bulgaria. As the general trend in inflation in 1993–99 has been downwards, interest rates have fallen. This trend has been particularly evident in Latvia, Lithuania, Slovenia, Hungary, and more recently Bulgaria (following the establishment of a currency board in July 1997).

During 1999, interest rates tended to fall, the main exception being Romania. In the Czech Republic, the steep decline in interest rates reflected the low level of economic activity and inflation, and renewed currency stability. Foreign capital flows into Estonia, following a return to economic stability, caused a sharp fall in interest rates there. Lower interest rates in the Slovak Republic also reflected foreign capital inflows.

Rates in Lithuania were slightly higher on average in 1999 compared with 1998, but moved much higher in real terms because of inflation falling towards zero. Polish rates fell considerably in 1999 on an annual average basis, but remained high in real terms.

For Romania and Turkey, the persistently high interest rates should be seen not only in the context of high inflation, but the domestic adjustment programme in Romania and economic stabilisation programme in Turkey as well.

Table 2.2.12. General government deficit (–) or surplus (+) (as a % of GDP)

	1993	1994	1995	1996	1997	1998
BG	– 11.3	– 5.2	– 5.1	– 15.3	– 0.3	1.3
CY (¹)	– 1.9	– 1.3	– 0.9	– 3.4	– 5.3	– 5.5
CZ	0.4	– 1.3	– 1.2	– 1.7	– 2.1	– 2.4
EE	2.5	3.3	0.0	– 1.6	2.6	– 0.2
MT (¹)	– 3.4	– 4.3	– 3.5	– 7.7	– 6.6	:
HU	– 9.3	– 9.2	– 6.6	– 3.2	– 5.4	– 7.1
LV	:	– 1.9	– 2.9	– 1.3	1.8	0.1
LT	2.1	– 1.7	– 1.6	– 2.8	– 0.7	– 3.4
PL	:	– 2.4	– 2.1	– 2.4	– 2.6	– 2.1
RO	0.5	– 2.0	– 2.1	– 3.5	– 4.4	:
SK	– 7.0	– 0.5	1.0	– 1.7	– 3.6	– 4.8
SI (¹)	0.4	– 0.3	– 0.3	0.1	– 1.5	– 0.8
TR (¹)	– 6.7	– 3.9	– 4.1	– 8.4	– 7.9	:

(¹) Excluding local government.
Source: Eurostat.

2.3. External trade

Extra-EU trade

Figure 2.3.1. Extra-EU trade flows 1990–99 (billion EUR)

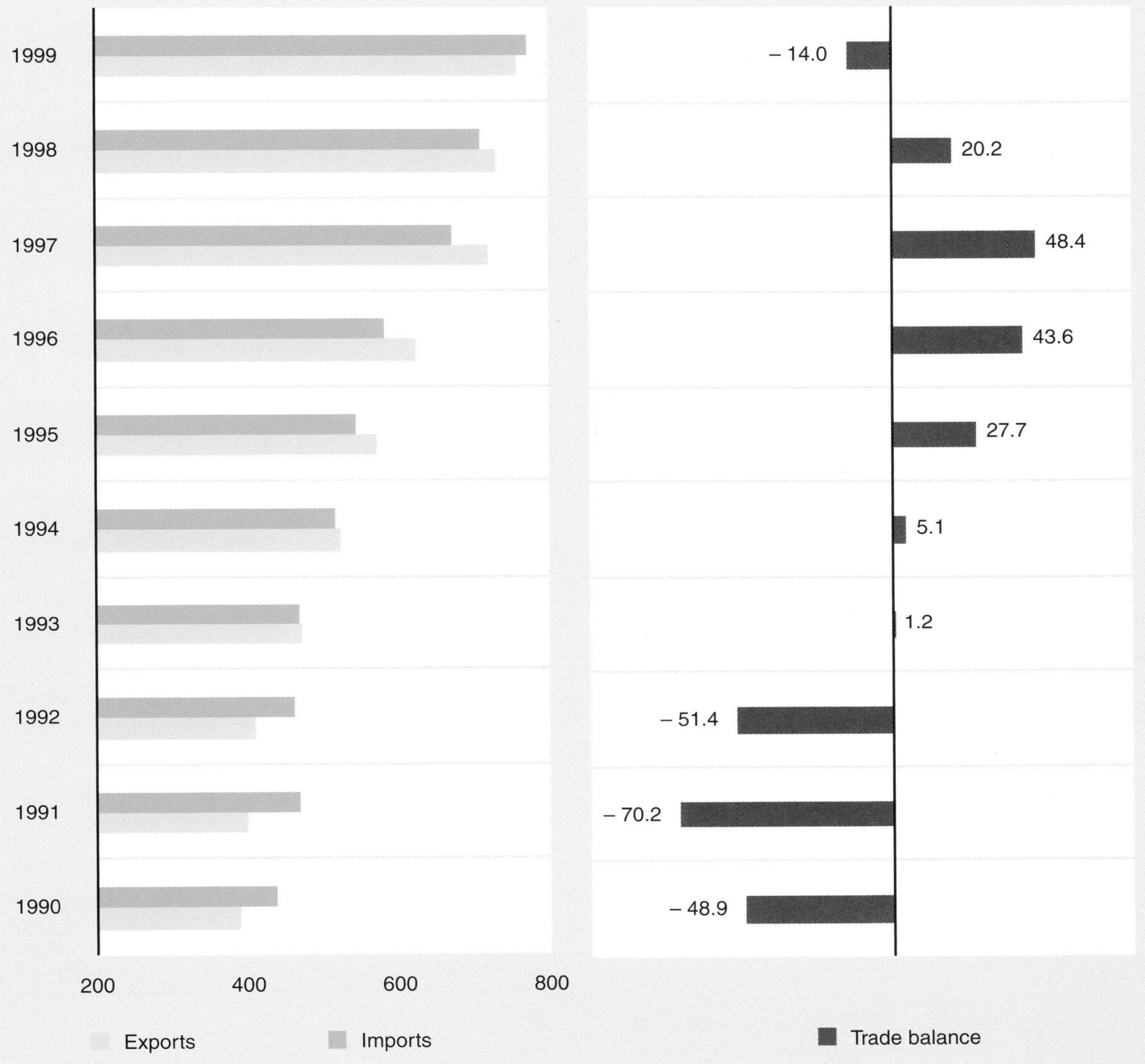

Source: Eurostat, Comext.

Total extra-EU trade flows

Graph 2.3.1 shows that extra-EU trade increased up to 1999: only in 1986 and 1987 (partly due to exchange rate movements and the drop in the price of raw materials) did the volume of trade decrease. However, as the figures are measured in nominal terms, it is sometimes difficult to assess the actual size of the increase, especially when there has been high inflation as in the 1970s.

In 1999, the EU again recorded a deficit.

During the 1990s the average growth rate has been 7.7 %, due to the combination of sluggish growth during the early 1990s followed by a sharp upturn in EU sales to non-member countries, starting in 1993. In 1998, extra-EU exports were weak, but recovered a little in 1999, with a growth rate of 4.0 % over the previous year.

Table 2.3.1. Extra-EU trade

	1990	1997	1998	1999	1990	1997	1998	1999
	EU-15 exports (billion EUR)				EU-15 imports (billion EUR)			
	390.6	720.7	729.6	758.5	439.4	672.4	709.4	772.5
	Exports as a % of EU-15				Imports as a % of EU-15			
B/L	5.0	5.4	5.3	5.3	5.8	6.1	6.1	5.9
DK	2.3	2.0	1.9	2.0	1.8	1.8	1.7	1.6
D	28.8	27.9	28.9	28.6	23.2	23.9	24.3	24.3
EL	0.5	0.7	0.6	0.6	1.1	1.2	1.2	1.1
E	3.8	3.9	3.8	3.7	5.7	5.1	5.0	5.1
F	15.5	14.0	14.7	15.1	13.9	12.7	12.6	12.7
IRL	1.0	2.0	2.4	3.0	1.0	1.8	2.1	2.1
I	12.7	13.2	12.9	12.2	12.3	10.8	10.4	10.3
NL	5.2	5.3	5.4	5.6	8.8	10.4	10.4	10.9
A	2.7	2.8	2.8	2.9	2.6	2.3	2.3	2.4
P	0.6	0.6	0.5	0.5	1.2	1.1	1.1	1.1
FIN	2.0	2.4	2.3	2.2	1.9	1.5	1.4	1.3
S	4.3	4.5	4.4	4.4	3.5	2.8	2.6	2.7
UK	15.6	15.3	14.0	13.9	17.3	18.7	18.8	18.5

Source: Eurostat, Comext.

Among the Member States, Germany has always been the main extra-EU exporter, accounting for 28.6 % of the total in 1999. France, the United Kingdom and Italy follow with shares of 15.1 %, 13.9 % and 12.2 % respectively. During the 1990s, the total share of the four leaders has remained almost stable at about 70 %. Ireland, whose export share has trebled since 1990, has recorded the most spectacular increase.

The general trend in extra-EU imports has been similar to that for exports. After declining in 1992, EU purchases from non-member countries started rising slightly in 1993 and registered a sharp increase in 1994. In 1999, extra-EU imports grew by 8.9 %, above the average annual growth rate for the 1990s (6.5 %).

Germany was the main outlet for exports from non-member countries to the Union, with around a quarter of the total in 1999, followed by the United Kingdom (18.5 %), France (12.7 %), the Netherlands (10.9 %), and Italy (10.3 %). The total share of these five countries together was stable during the 1990s, representing over three quarters of total extra-EU imports.

Between 1991 and 1997 the extra-EU trade balance had improved each year, and a surplus of ECU 48.4 billion was reached in 1997. In 1998 the surplus fell to ECU 20.2 billion, and in 1999 the EU recorded a trade deficit of EUR 14.0 billion.

While the total extra-EU trade flows are in surplus, the balances of individual Member States are widely divergent. Germany has usually recorded the greatest surplus among the Member States. During recent years, after absorbing the shock of reunification in the early 90s, it has again produced the greatest extra-EU surplus, reaching EUR 29.2 billion in 1999. France ranked in second place (EUR 16.3 billion) and Italy was third (EUR 12.5 billion). Sweden also had a substantial surplus, at EUR 12.3 billion.

Table 2.3.2. Extra-EU trade growth rates (as a %)

	Exports		Imports	
	1999–98	1999–90	1999–98	1999–90
EU-15	4.0	7.7	8.9	6.5
B/L	5.1	8.5	4.7	6.7
DK	7.2	6.3	2.8	5.5
D	3.1	7.6	8.9	7.1
EL	– 0.2	10.1	– 3.0	5.6
E	1.5	7.3	13.2	5.3
F	6.4	7.3	10.3	5.4
IRL	27.8	21.3	9.9	16.0
I	– 2.3	7.1	7.8	4.4
NL	7.1	8.5	13.6	9.0
A	10.0	8.4	13.4	5.4
P	– 3.1	5.6	9.1	4.7
FIN	– 2.9	8.7	3.1	2.5
S	4.3	7.8	11.3	3.5
UK	3.7	6.3	6.9	7.3

Source: Eurostat, Comext.

By contrast, the Netherlands and the United Kingdom registered, as almost always, the highest deficits totalling EUR 41.8 billion and EUR 37.1 billion respectively in 1999. Nevertheless, the Dutch deficit should be seen in the light of its intra-EU surplus and its transit role in EU trade.

Extra-EU trade by main partner

In the period under review, the group of industrialised countries made up of the United States, Japan and EFTA represented the main market for the EU as a whole. The United States is the main individual partner for extra-EU exports with a 23.8 % share in 1999. Japan's share of extra-EU exports has fallen from its 1996 peak to 4.6 %, while the share of exports to EFTA was stable at 11.4 %.

The central and east European countries (CEECs) and the Commonwealth of Independent States (CIS) together received 15.8 % of extra-EU exports in 1999, and have steadily increased their share of EU exports over recent years.

African markets dramatically reduced their share, partly due to the fall in primary goods prices and the loosening of colonial economic ties in this period.

Latin America's share of extra-EU exports went down to 5.9 % in 1999. In fact thanks to the economic recovery, the EU export share to these countries has begun to increase from the beginning of the 1990s.

The export share of the dynamic Asian economies (DAE) had reached 10.8 % in 1997, but fell back to 7.9 % in 1999 as a result of the financial crisis in the region.

The relatively low share of extra-EU exports to China in comparison to other partners (2.5 % in 1999) should be noted.

EU exports to Near and Middle Eastern countries have fallen back to below 7 % in considered years.

Oceania's extra-EU export share has remained at around 2.2 % since 1991.

Table 2.3.3. Extra-EU trade balance

	1990	1997	1998	1999	99/98
	Billion EUR				Absolute variation
EU-15	– 48.9	48.4	20.2	– 14.0	– 34.2
B/L	– 6.0	– 1.9	– 4.7	– 4.8	– 0.1
DK	1.0	2.8	1.9	2.6	0.7
D	10.9	40.6	38.1	29.2	– 8.9
EL	– 3.0	– 3.3	– 3.7	– 3.5	0.2
E	– 10.2	– 6.6	– 7.7	– 11.9	– 4.2
F	– 0.5	15.5	18.6	16.3	– 2.3
IRL	– 0.3	2.7	3.0	6.4	3.5
I	– 4.6	23.2	20.5	12.5	– 7.9
NL	– 18.4	– 31.3	– 34.5	– 41.8	– 7.2
A	– 0.7	4.4	4.0	3.8	– 0.1
P	– 3.0	– 3.3	– 3.5	– 4.3	– 0.8
FIN	– 0.5	7.2	7.1	6.2	– 0.8
S	1.5	13.7	13.0	12.3	– 0.8
UK	– 15.2	– 15.4	– 31.7	– 37.1	– 5.3

Source: Eurostat, Comext.

Imports

The group of industrialised countries constituted by the United States, Japan and EFTA are by far the most important suppliers of the European Union. The United States is also the main individual partner for extra-EU imports, with a share of 20.3 % in 1999. Japan's share has declined, from a peak of 12.2 % in 1992 to 9.1 % in 1999. The share of imports from EFTA has also declined in the last three years, to 10.5 % in 1999.

The CEECs and CIS, which accounted for 9.0 % in 1992, accounted together for 13.9 % of total extra-EU imports in 1999. This trend reflects the economic changes that occurred in these countries during these years. After the crisis that followed the dissolution of Comecon, the CEECs quickly redirected their trade towards the EU markets.

Africa, Latin America and Oceania all saw a decrease in their shares during the period under review.

The DAE and China have become very important suppliers to the European Union in recent times. Their shares of total EU imports went up to 10.7 % and 6.4 % in 1999.

Table 2.3.4. Extra-EU trade, by partner

	1990	1997	1998	1999	1990	1997	1998	1999
	Extra EU exports (billion EUR)				Extra imports EU (billion EUR)			
	390.6	720.7	729.6	758.5	439.4	672.4	709.4	772.5
	Exports as a % of EU-15				Imports as a % of EU-15			
US	21.2	19.6	21.9	23.8	20.8	20.5	21.3	20.3
JP	6.3	5.0	4.3	4.6	11.7	8.9	9.2	9.1
EFTA	15.3	10.8	11.5	11.4	13.3	12.0	11.3	10.5
CEECs	6.2	12.1	13.5	13.1	5.4	9.0	10.1	10.3
CIS	:	4.7	4.0	2.7	:	4.7	3.9	3.6
Africa	11.9	7.2	8.0	7.4	11.6	8.4	7.4	7.0
Latin America	4.3	6.3	6.7	5.9	6.2	5.2	4.9	4.7
DAE	7.9	10.8	8.2	7.9	8.2	10.1	10.8	10.7
China	1.5	2.3	2.4	2.5	2.6	5.6	5.9	6.4
Near-Middle East	7.9	7.1	6.8	6.3	6.0	4.5	3.7	4.0
Oceania	2.6	2.3	2.2	2.2	1.6	1.4	1.5	1.3
ACP	4.5	2.8	3.1	2.8	4.8	3.4	3.0	2.8
Mediterranean basin	12.4	11.6	11.9	11.2	10.1	8.5	8.0	7.9
ASEAN	4.4	6.3	4.2	3.8	4.0	6.9	7.2	6.3
OPEC	9.6	7.2	6.6	5.9	10.6	7.8	6.1	6.2
NAFTA	24.9	22.6	25.2	27.3	23.8	22.9	23.6	22.7

Source: Eurostat, Comext and IMF, DOTS.

Trade balance

The EU's trade balance with the group of countries made up by the United States and EFTA have moved into surplus.

Trade with Japan still registered the biggest deficit in 1999 at EUR 35.4 billion. However, in relative terms (as a percentage of trade with each country), it was bilateral trade with China which recorded the biggest deficit in 1999 (44.2 %), whereas Japan ranked in second place for the same year (33.8 %).

The European Union has registered remarkable improvements in its trading positions with the CEECs and CIS. Taken together, their deficit of ECU 0.6 billion in 1992 shifted to a surplus of ECU 27.7 billion in 1998. In 1999, the surplus fell back to EUR 13 billion, as a result of the financial difficulties in the region.

The EU balance with Latin America and Near and Middle Eastern countries declined in 1999, reaching surpluses of EUR 8.6 billion and EUR 17.1 billion (10.6 % and 21.7 % in relative terms).

The trade position with the DAE continued to worsen in 1999, with the surplus of the last few years turning into a EUR 22.1 billion deficit.

Table 2.3.5. Extra-EU trade balance, by partner

	1990	1997	1998	1999	1990	1997	1998	1999
	Billion EUR				As a % of total trade (1)			
Extra EU-15	−48.9	48.4	20.2	−14.0	−5.9	3.5	1.4	−0.9
US	−8.7	3.4	9.3	23.5	−5.0	1.2	3.0	7.0
JP	−26.9	−23.7	−34.1	−35.4	−35.5	−24.7	−35.2	−33.8
EFTA	1.1	−2.4	3.6	4.9	0.9	−1.5	2.2	2.9
CEEC	0.5	26.7	26.7	20.4	1.0	18.1	15.7	11.4
CIS	:	1.7	1.0	−7.4	:	2.6	1.8	−15.2
Africa	−4.5	−4.7	5.4	1.6	−4.6	−4.3	4.9	1.5
Latin America	−10.1	10.5	13.6	8.6	−23.0	13.2	16.2	10.6
DAE	−5.2	9.5	−16.9	−22.1	−7.8	6.5	−12.3	−15.5
China	−5.6	−21.0	−24.4	−30.2	−32.4	−38.9	−41.3	−44.2
Near-Middle East	4.5	21.1	22.8	17.1	7.9	26.0	30.1	21.7
Oceania	2.9	7.3	5.3	7.1	16.7	28.5	20.1	26.4
ACP	−3.6	−2.6	1.2	0.2	−9.3	−6.0	2.7	0.5
Mediterranean Basin	4.3	26.4	29.5	24.2	4.6	18.7	20.5	16.6
ASEAN	−0.4	−0.7	−20.7	−19.6	−1.1	−0.8	−25.5	−25.2
OPEC	−9.1	0.0	4.2	−3.0	−10.8	0.0	4.6	−3.3
NAFTA	−7.1	8.6	16.6	32.2	−3.5	2.7	4.7	8.4

(1) Imports and exports.
Source: Eurostat, Comext and IMF, DOTS.

Extra-EU trade by main product

The European Union is a traditional exporter of manufactured products in 1999, the share of manufactured products in total extra-EU exports reached 87.5 %.

Among manufactured products, the biggest share of extra-EU exports was accounted for by machinery and transport equipment (46.4 % of total extra-EU exports in 1999). During the period under consideration, the share of chemical products also grew while the group 'Other manufactures' remained stable at around 27 %.

Table 2.3.6. Extra-EU trade, by product

	1997	1998	1999	1997	1998	1999
	Exports (billion EUR)			Imports (billion EUR)		
Total	720.7	729.6	758.5	672.4	709.4	772.5
	Exports as a %			Imports as a %		
Raw material	**10.9**	**9.8**	**9.9**	**26.2**	**22.0**	**21.5**
Food, beverages, tobacco	6.4	5.9	5.7	7.2	6.9	6.4
Crude material	2.2	1.9	2.0	6.3	5.9	5.2
Energy	2.4	1.9	2.2	12.7	9.1	10.0
Manufactured goods	**87.1**	**87.3**	**87.5**	**71.0**	**74.2**	**75.6**
Chemicals	12.9	12.9	14.0	7.7	7.7	7.6
Machinery, transport	45.9	46.8	46.4	34.1	37.0	39.1
Other manufactured goods	28.2	27.6	27.1	29.2	29.5	28.9
Not classified elsewhere	**2.0**	**2.9**	**2.6**	**2.8**	**3.8**	**2.9**

Source: Eurostat, Comext.

The corresponding reduction in the share of raw materials was mainly due to the declining importance of extra-EU exports of fuel products (2.2 % in 1999) and of agri-food products (5.7 % in 1999). Meanwhile exports of crude materials were fairly stable at around 2 %.

The trend in extra-EU imports clearly shows the growing role of manufactured products. Raw materials accounted for only 21.5 % in 1999. During the last two decades, various factors substantially modified the EU import structure and consequently the share of manufactured imports increased, 75.6 % in 1999.

Transport equipment increased their shares and it became the most important group of products imported, reaching 39.1 % in 1999 compared with 10.0 % for fuel products in the same year. Other manufactured products achieved a remarkable increase, 28.9 % in 1999.

The European Union economy, based on manufacturing industry, has a structural deficit in the primary sector. For manufactured products the relative surplus is by 6.4 % in 1999.

Table 2.3.7. Extra-EU trade balance, by product

	1997	1998	1999	1997	1998	1999
	Billion EUR			As a % of total trade ([1])		
Total	48.4	20.2	– 14.0	3.5	1.4	– 0.9
Raw material	**– 97.6**	**– 84.8**	**– 91.1**	**– 38.3**	**– 37.3**	**– 37.8**
Food, beverages, tobacco	– 2.5	– 5.9	– 6.0	– 2.6	– 6.4	– 6.5
Crude material	– 27.0	– 28.0	– 24.6	– 46.3	– 49.7	– 44.7
Energy	– 68.1	– 50.8	– 60.5	– 66.6	– 65.0	– 64.9
Manufactured goods	**150.2**	**110.5**	**79.4**	**13.6**	**9.5**	**6.4**
Chemicals	41.6	39.1	47.6	28.8	26.3	28.9
Machinery, transport	101.7	79.5	49.6	18.1	13.2	7.6
Other manufactured goods	7.0	– 8.1	– 17.8	1.7	– 2.0	– 4.1
Not classified elsewhere	**– 4.3**	**– 5.6**	**– 2.3**	**– 12.7**	**– 11.4**	**– 5.4**

([1]) Intra and extra.
Source: Eurostat, Comext.

Intra-EU trade

The Intrastat system was introduced on 1 January 1993 due to the abolition of customs formalities within the EU. Since that date, data have been collected directly from firms. As the Intrastat system for collecting data is different from the system used in previous years, the change in the figures between 1992 and 1993 should be interpreted with caution.

Share of intra-EU trade in total EU trade flows

Intra-EU trade has always represented more than 50 % of the EU's total trade, and at present it is almost 60 %.

Since 1970, there have been three periods when intra-EU trade declined as a percentage of total EU trade. During the periods 1973–75 and 1979–81, the relative importance of intra-EU trade fell sharply due to increases in primary goods prices. The total value of extra-EU imports went up, raising total extra-EU trade figures in comparison with intra-EU trade. In 1993, in spite of implementation of the internal market, another decline in the relative importance of intra-EU trade occurred. At this time the collection of intra-EU data was reorganised. A substantial drop in intra-EU figures, implying a certain degree of underestimation of flows, corresponded with the introduction of Intrastat. In particular, arrivals are underestimated, and dispatches are considered the most reliable figure of intra-EU trade. However, it is difficult to assess to what extent the shift in 1993 is a statistical phenomenon.

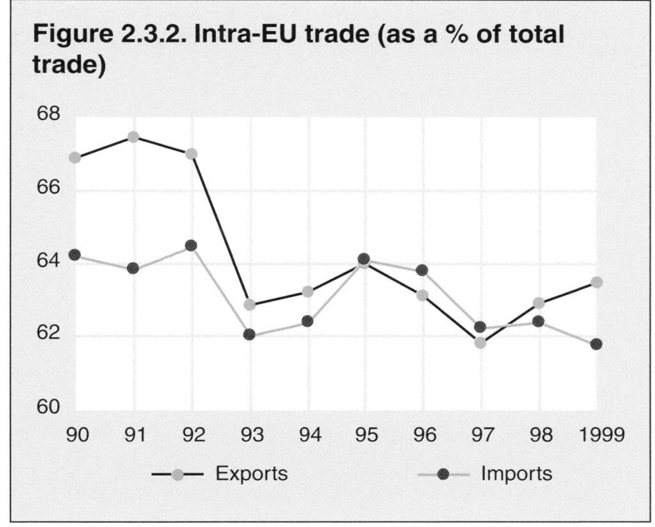

Figure 2.3.2. Intra-EU trade (as a % of total trade)

Source: Eurostat, Comext.

The volume of intra-EU trade did in fact increase significantly with the enlargement of the EU in 1995, since the trade of Austria, Sweden and Finland is strongly geared to the EU market. Thus, the intra-EU share of total EU trade before the three new Member States joined the EU was 58 % in 1994. One year later, in 1995, when the enlargement took place, the share of intra-EU trade reached around 64 %. The EU time series presented in this statistical yearbook do not show this shift, because they are calculated as if all 15 Member States had belonged to the EU since the beginning in order to keep the time series stable. Nevertheless, the time series reflects the increasing importance of intra-EU trade within total EU trade. This has become possible because the links among Member States' economies have become stronger over the last few decades.

Table 2.3.8. Intra-EU dispatches/arrivals

	1990	1997	1998	1999	1990	1997	1998	1999
	Dispatches (billion EUR)				Arrivals (billion EUR)			
	787.3	1 166.4	1 237.1	1 317.2	786.6	1 107.6	1 175.8	1 248.0
	As a % of total exports (1)				As a % of total imports (2)			
EU-15	66.8	61.8	62.9	63.5	64.2	62.2	62.4	61.8
B/L	79.9	74.6	75.8	76.5	74.2	71.3	70.9	71.7
DK	68.4	66.4	67.3	67.5	69.4	70.2	70.2	70.5
D	64.0	55.5	56.4	56.9	62.1	58.7	58.3	56.9
EL	68.0	51.0	49.5	48.8	67.7	65.4	63.4	65.7
E	67.6	68.4	70.5	71.4	62.3	66.1	68.5	68.7
F	65.3	62.0	62.3	62.3	68.1	65.9	67.5	66.5
IRL	78.6	68.9	69.9	65.9	73.9	64.0	61.5	62.4
I	62.8	54.9	56.2	57.3	61.9	60.9	61.6	60.8
NL	81.4	79.0	78.8	79.3	63.7	58.6	57.7	55.8
A	67.2	62.2	62.8	63.6	70.7	73.4	73.2	72.6
P	81.2	80.8	81.5	82.8	72.0	76.3	77.2	77.4
FIN	62.2	53.2	55.9	57.9	60.5	64.3	65.6	65.4
S	62.3	55.6	58.0	58.3	63.4	67.7	69.1	67.6
UK	57.3	55.6	57.9	58.3	56.5	53.7	53.0	52.9

(1) Dispatches and exports.
(2) Arrivals and imports.
Source: Eurostat, Comext.

The share of intra-EU trade varies widely from one Member State to another. As a general rule, for relatively small countries such as Portugal, Belgium, Luxembourg, the Netherlands and Austria, the shares are higher, while Germany and the United Kingdom have lower ratios. Some countries like France are in an intermediate position.

As mentioned above, dispatches are considered the most reliable figure for analysing intra-EU trade. Manufactured goods registered the highest share of total intra-EU trade with 75.0 % in 1990. As in the case of extra-EU trade, the most dynamic product category in the last 10 years has been machinery and transport equipment, which grew from 35.7 % in 1989 to 38.8 % in 1999, while chemical products increased less than one percentage point during the same period.

Table 2.3.9. Intra-EU dispatches, by product (as a %)

	1990	1997	1998	1999
Total (billion EUR)	**787.3**	**1 166.4**	**1 237.1**	**1 317.2**
	Shares (as a %)			
Raw material	**17.3**	**16.6**	**14.6**	**13.7**
Food, beverages, tobacco	9.9	9.8	9.2	8.6
Crude material	4.0	3.5	3.1	2.6
Energy	3.5	3.3	2.3	2.5
Manufactured goods	**78.6**	**79.9**	**79.7**	**75.0**
Chemicals	10.7	12.5	12.5	11.4
Machinery, transport	36.2	38.7	39.7	38.8
Other manufactured goods	31.7	28.7	27.5	24.9
Not classified elsewhere	**4.1**	**3.5**	**5.7**	**11.3**

Source: Eurostat, Comext.

The intra-EU share for raw materials decreased from 17.9 % in 1989 to 13.7 % in 1999. In 1999, intra-EU trade as a percentage of total EU trade in raw materials and manufactured products was fairly similar (around 60 % and 61 %), although from 1989 until 1992 the ratio for manufactured products was always significantly higher. This reflects the fact that extra-EU trade in manufactured goods is becoming more important. Major differences can be found between product categories. In the case of raw materials the intra-EU ratios for food products were conspicuously higher (71 % in 1999) than those for fuel products and crude material (around 41 % and 56 % respectively), which are more oriented to extra-EU trade. As for manufactured products, the intra-EU ratios for chemicals were higher (65 %) than those for machinery and transport equipment (61 %).

Intra-EU trade balance

Since 1993 and the introduction of the Intrastat system (see note above), the sums of the intra-EU arrivals and dispatches recorded by the Member States do not tally as they should have done theoretically. Before 1993, although divergences existed, they were relatively small, but from 1993 new statistical problems occurred, mainly because of non-response from firms and the threshold system introduced.

As far as the threshold system is concerned, the import (arrival) flow is in principle less concentrated than the export (dispatch) flow and this could partially explain the underestimation of arrivals: with Intrastat, the smaller companies are no longer obliged to make a statistical declaration. Only a few Member States produce 'corrected' figures which take account of the threshold effect.

The statistical discrepancies in intra-EU trade flows make it difficult to assess the development of intra-EU trade balances by Member States. This applies particularly to the transition from 1992 to 1993. However, the following can be concluded:

Figure 2.3.3. Total Intra-EU dispatches and arrivals (billion EUR)

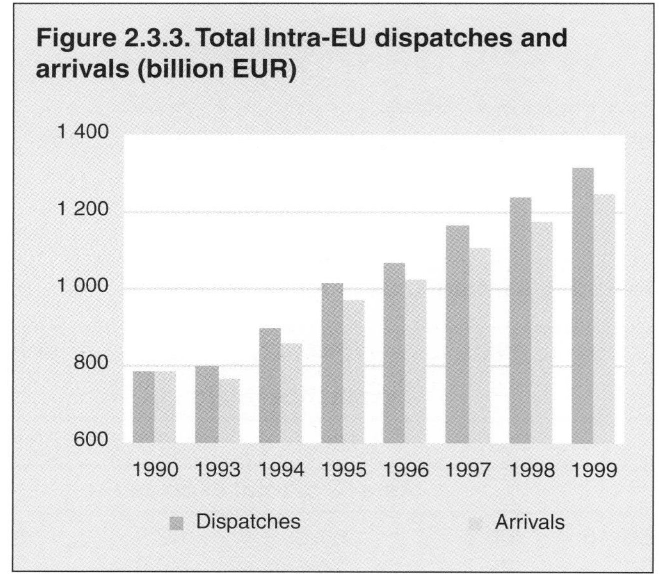

Source: Eurostat, Comext.

Table 2.3.10. Intra-EU share of total trade ([1]) by product (as a %)

	1990	1997	1998	1999
Total	**65.5**	**62.6**	**63.2**	**63.2**
Raw material	**58.4**	**60.3**	**61.4**	**59.9**
Food, beverages, tobacco	70.1	70.9	71.0	70.8
Crude material	59.3	58.1	57.6	55.9
Energy	39.0	43.0	42.3	41.0
Manufactured goods	**67.5**	**62.8**	**62.9**	**61.3**
Chemicals	69.6	66.9	67.6	64.5
Machinery, transport	66.7	61.7	61.9	61.0
Other manufactured goods	67.7	62.6	62.4	60.5
Not classified elsewhere	**62.3**	**70.8**	**74.3**	**87.5**

([1]) Intra and extra.
Source: Eurostat, Comext.

Since 1985, the Netherlands have almost always recorded the largest intra-EU surplus. In 1999, it reached EUR 56.6 billion, followed by Germany (EUR 37.8 billion), Ireland (EUR 16.8 billion) and Belgium and Luxembourg (EUR 16.7 billion). Nevertheless, the Netherlands is a special case, as an important part of its trade is 'in transit' (i.e. coming from outside the EU and going to another Member State). This is consistent with its large extra-EU deficit. As for Germany, the fall in its intra-EU surplus in 1991 after reunification had taken place is evident. The growth in the Irish surplus during the 1990s is particularly impressive.

Spain, the United Kingdom, Greece, Austria and Portugal recorded the largest intra-EU deficits, totalling EUR 17.4 billion, EUR 12.7 billion, EUR 11.2 billion, EUR 9.8 billion and EUR 9.5 billion respectively in 1999.

For some countries at different periods, their global deficits (their extra-EU deficits must be added) have shown a dramatic increase in comparison with the size of their economies (e.g. Italy in the early 1980s and Spain in the early 1990s).

Table 2.3.11. Intra-EU trade balance (billion EUR)

	1990	1997	1998	1999
B/L	4.2	13.0	15.4	16.7
DK	1.4	1.0	0.2	1.4
D	33.9	22.3	31.0	37.8
EL	– 6.3	– 10.4	– 10.0	– 11.2
E	– 10.4	– 6.6	– 10.6	– 17.4
F	– 16.2	– 0.4	– 7.0	– 5.8
IRL	2.6	11.1	17.4	16.8
I	– 4.6	3.7	2.7	0.2
NL	20.7	46.3	45.9	56.6
A	– 5.5	– 9.9	– 10.0	– 9.8
P	– 3.6	– 6.5	– 7.8	– 9.5
FIN	0.2	1.5	2.5	3.2
S	1.2	1.4	2.0	2.8
UK	– 16.9	– 7.7	– 10.3	– 12.7

Source: Eurostat, Comext.

Figure 2.3.4. Intra-EU trade balance (billion EUR)

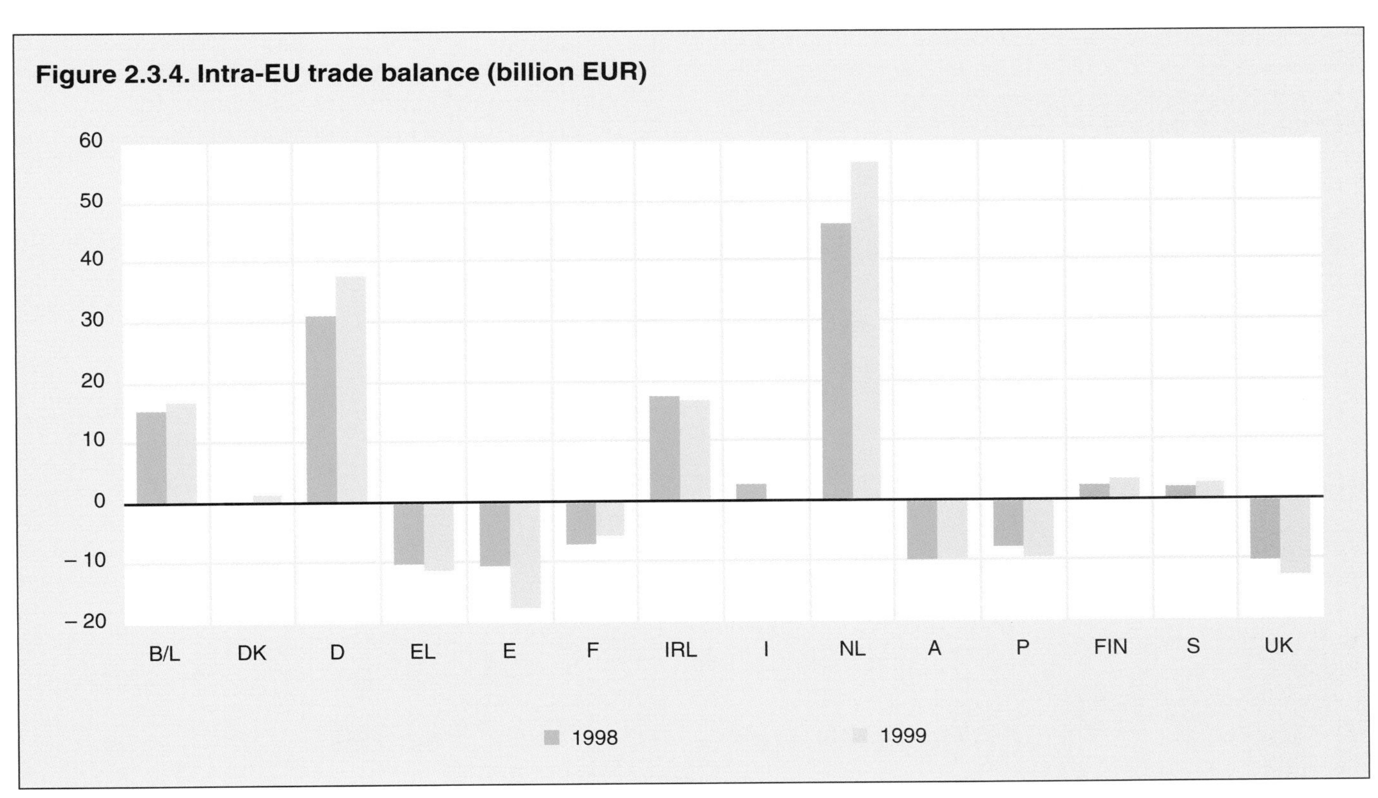

Source: Eurostat, Comext.

2.4. International trade in services

Balance of payments

A country's external trade in services is registered in its balance of payments (BOP).

The balance of payments records all economic transactions undertaken between the residents and non-residents of a country during a given period of time.

The balance of payments of the European Union is compiled as the sum of harmonised balance of payments accounts of the 15 Member States.

The methodological framework is that of the fifth edition of the *International Monetary Fund (IMF) balance of payments manual.*

In 1998, the EU was the largest trader in services in the world in value terms, representing 24.6 % (EUR 458.9 billion) of total services transactions (exports and imports), followed by the United States with a 21.2 % share and Japan with a 8.3 % share.

The annual growth rate of the EU total transactions in services slowed down to 3 % in 1998, after an average 7 % growth in the previous five years. EU imports of services from the rest of the world climbed by 5 % to EUR 223.2 billion in 1998. On the other hand, EU exports of services to third parties reached EUR 235.8 billion, recording a modest 1 % growth from the year before. The EU external surplus in trade in services was then cut from EUR 20 billion in 1997 to EUR 12.6 billion in 1998.

Figure 2.4.1. Evolution of the EU trade in services with the rest of the world (billion EUR)

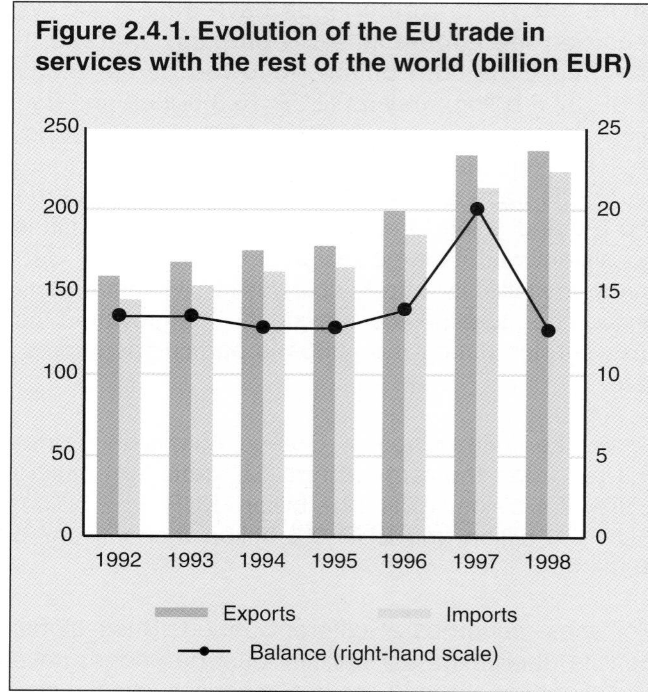

Source: Eurostat.

Figure 2.4.2. EU total transactions in services, 1998 (as a %)

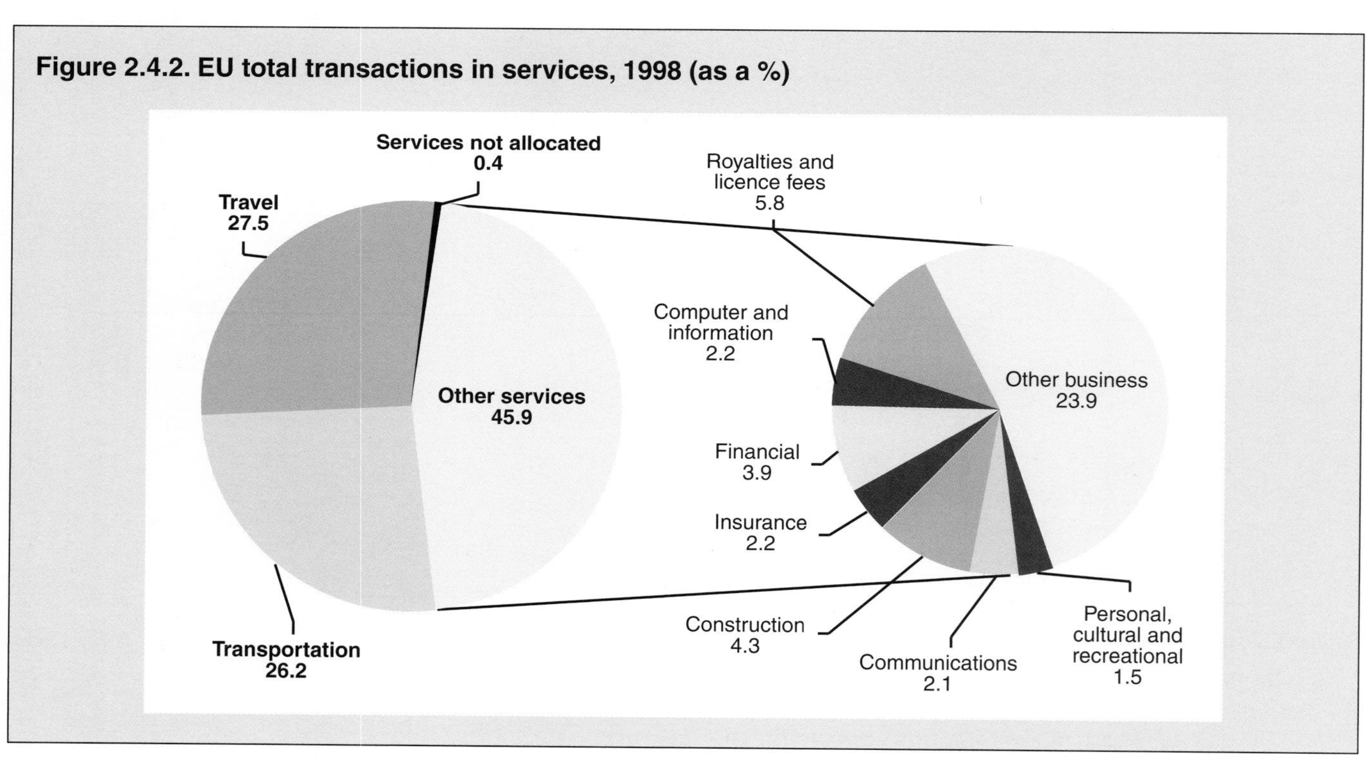

Source: Eurostat.

Breakdown of the EU trade in services

The fall of EU imports of transportation services from the rest of the world, from EUR 60.9 billion to EUR 56.8 billion in 1998 (down by 7 %), offset the 2 % drop of EU exports (from EUR 62.3 billion to EUR 60.7 billion), leaving an external surplus of EUR 4 billion.

Trade in air transport services represented 45 % of the EU total transactions in transportation services (exports and imports) in 1998, followed by sea transport with 40 % of the total and other types of transport with the remaining 15 %.

EU exports of sea transport services to the rest of the world shrank by 13 % to EUR 22.4 billion in 1998. The EU exports of freight transport services on sea to the rest of the world fell by 23 % in 1998, falling from EUR 21 billion to EUR 16.2 billion. EU imports of sea transport services from third parties also registered a 17 % decline in 1998, dropping from EUR 30.3 billion to EUR 25.1 billion in 1998. The external surplus of the EU air transport services in 1998 (EUR 6 billion) broadly offset the EUR 2.7 billion deficit in the sea transport services for the EU.

Figure 2.4.3. Evolution of the EU total transactions in transportation services with the rest of the world (billion EUR)

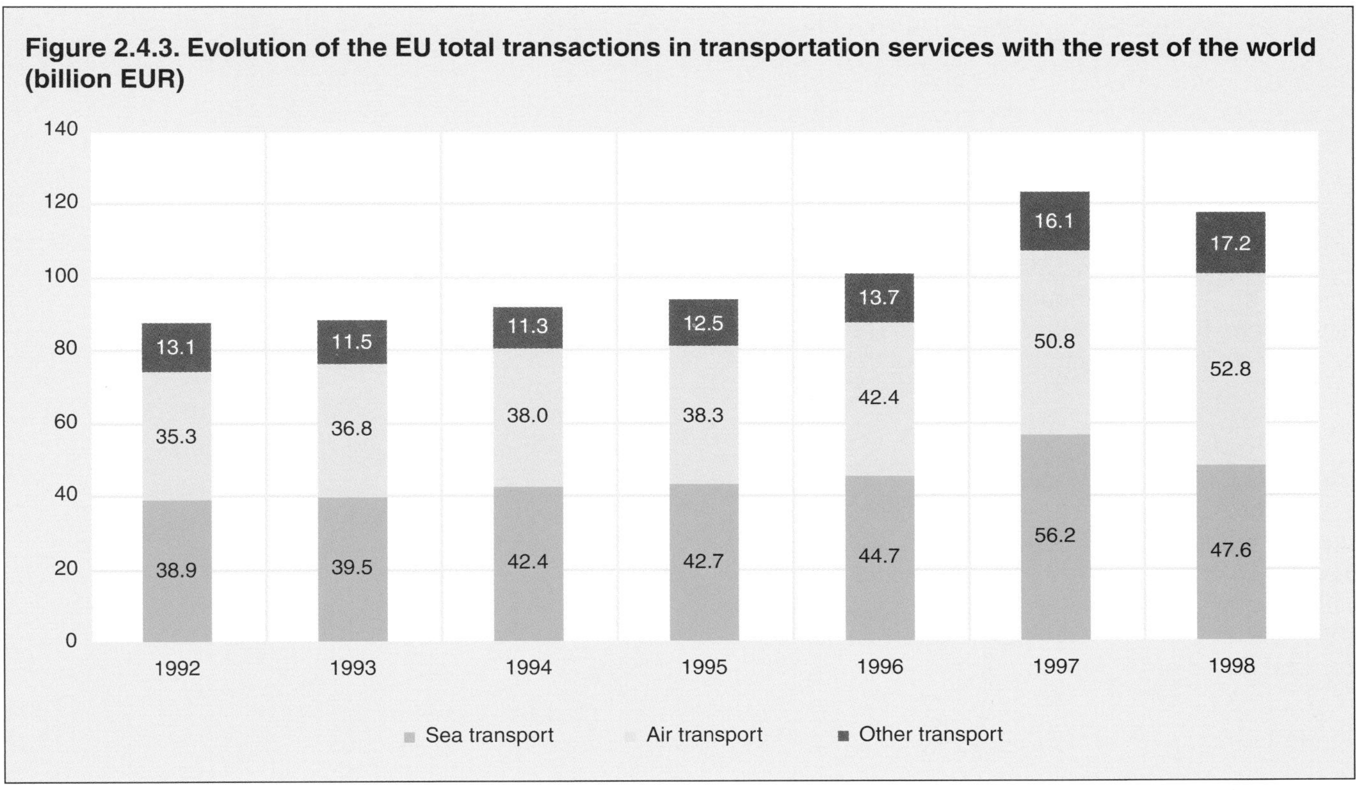

Source: Eurostat.

Travel covers the goods and services acquired from an economy by travellers during visits of less than one year in that economy. Therefore, EU travel exports represent the amount of goods and services that were sold or provided by European Union residents to foreign travellers in visits of less than one year. Travel exports only grew by 2 % in 1998, compared to the 9 % increase of the European Union purchases of goods and services abroad. The solid expansion of EU travel imports, reaching EUR 62.3 billion in 1998, generated the first deficit for the European Union in the provision of travel services. In 1998, the European Union residents spent EUR 1.3 billion more abroad than received from non EU-resident travellers.

The United States was the top travel destination outside of the European Union, representing 29 % of the total extra-EU trade. Other European countries (including Turkey and Russia) came in as second top destination, with a share of 15 % of the total extra-EU trade. Mediterranean basin countries appeared as third, followed by Asia, the European Free Trade Association (Switzerland, Iceland, Liechtenstein and Norway), and Africa as a whole. The United States was also the first partner for receipts on travel for the European Union. The EFTA Member States ranked second, followed by Asia and other European countries.

EU exports of computer and information services increased by 26 % to a value of EUR 5.7 billion directed mainly towards the United States (representing 41 % of the total EU external trade), EFTA (27 %) and other Asian countries (8 %). Imports amounted to EUR 4.3 billion, in particular from the United States (59 % of the total), EFTA (16 %) and other Asian countries (10 %).

Royalties and licence fees comprise the exchange of payments and receipts between residents and non-residents for the authorised use of intangible, non-produced, non-financial assets and proprietary rights and with the use, through licensing agreements, of produced originals or prototypes. The EU increased the payments of royalties and licence fees to the rest of the world in 1998 by 13 % and reached EUR 16.8 billion, while receipts shrank to EUR 9.2 billion in 1998.

Other business services cover highly varied services such as trade earnings, legal, accounting, management, consulting, advertising, market research, public opinion polling, research and development, architectural, engineering, agricultural, mining, etc. The EU exported these services to the rest of the world for a value of EUR 55.8 billion in 1998 (6 % more than the year before), and imports amounted to EUR 51.2 billion (a remarkable 12 % more than in 1997). The difference between exports and imports narrowed from EUR 7.2 billion in 1997 to EUR 4.6 billion in 1998. EU imports, again, grew faster than exports.

Trade in personal, cultural and recreational services (including audiovisual services) decreased in 1998. EU exports fell by 8 % to EUR 2 billion, while imports dropped by 4 % to EUR 4.9 billion. The European Union continued to be in deficit with the rest of the world in 1998, and in particular with the United States (70 % of the total EU external deficit).

Figure 2.4.4. EU trade in services by partner and geographic zone in 1998 (exports and imports)

EFTA 15 %
Other 3 %
Oceania 2 %
Japan 5 %
America 7 %
US 34 %
Canada 2 %
Asia 15 %
Africa 7 %
Europe 10 %

NB: Asia — excluding Japan; Europe — excluding EU and EFTA; America — excluding US.
Source: Eurostat.

2.5. Foreign direct investment

Foreign direct investment (FDI) statistics give information on one of the major aspects of globalisation. FDI is a supplement or an alternative to cross-border trade in goods and services.

Within the balance of payments statistics Eurostat maintains a FDI database that comprises harmonised and thus comparable data with a geographical breakdown of inward and outward FDI flows, positions and earnings for the European Union, its Member States and its major FDI partners.

Foreign direct investment (FDI) is the category of international investment that reflects the objective of obtaining a lasting interest by a resident entity in one economy in an enterprise resident in another economy. The lasting interest implies the existence of a long-term relationship between the direct investor and the enterprise, and a significant degree of influence by the investor on the management of the enterprise. Formally defined, a direct investment enterprise is an unincorporated or incorporated enterprise in which a direct investor owns 10 % or more of the ordinary shares or voting power (for an incorporated enterprise) or the equivalent (for an unincorporated enterprise).

FDI flows and positions

Through direct investment flows, an investor builds up a foreign direct investment position that features on his balance sheet. This FDI position (or FDI stock) differs from the accumulated flows because of revaluation (changes in prices or exchange rates) and other adjustments like rescheduling or cancellation of loans, debt forgiveness or debt-equity swaps.

This section first gives a brief overview by presenting the latest FDI flows figures (for 1999 and revised data for 1998) for individual EU Member States and for the EU as a whole. Secondly, we look at the geographical and sectoral breakdown of the EU FDI position at the end of 1997.

European Union direct investment: First results for 1999

The preliminary figures presented here cover equity capital and inter-company loans but exclude reinvested earnings.

Strong growth in FDI activities in 1999

The year 1999 was another one of strong growth for the EU's FDI accounts. At close to EUR 500 billion, total outflows rose more than 40 % in 1999. Direct investments into the European Union also progressed considerably reaching nearly EUR 300 billion, resulting in an EU net capital outflow of nearly EUR 200 billion, an absolute record level.

Figure 2.5.1. Total EU-15 FDI by major partner 1999 (billion EUR)

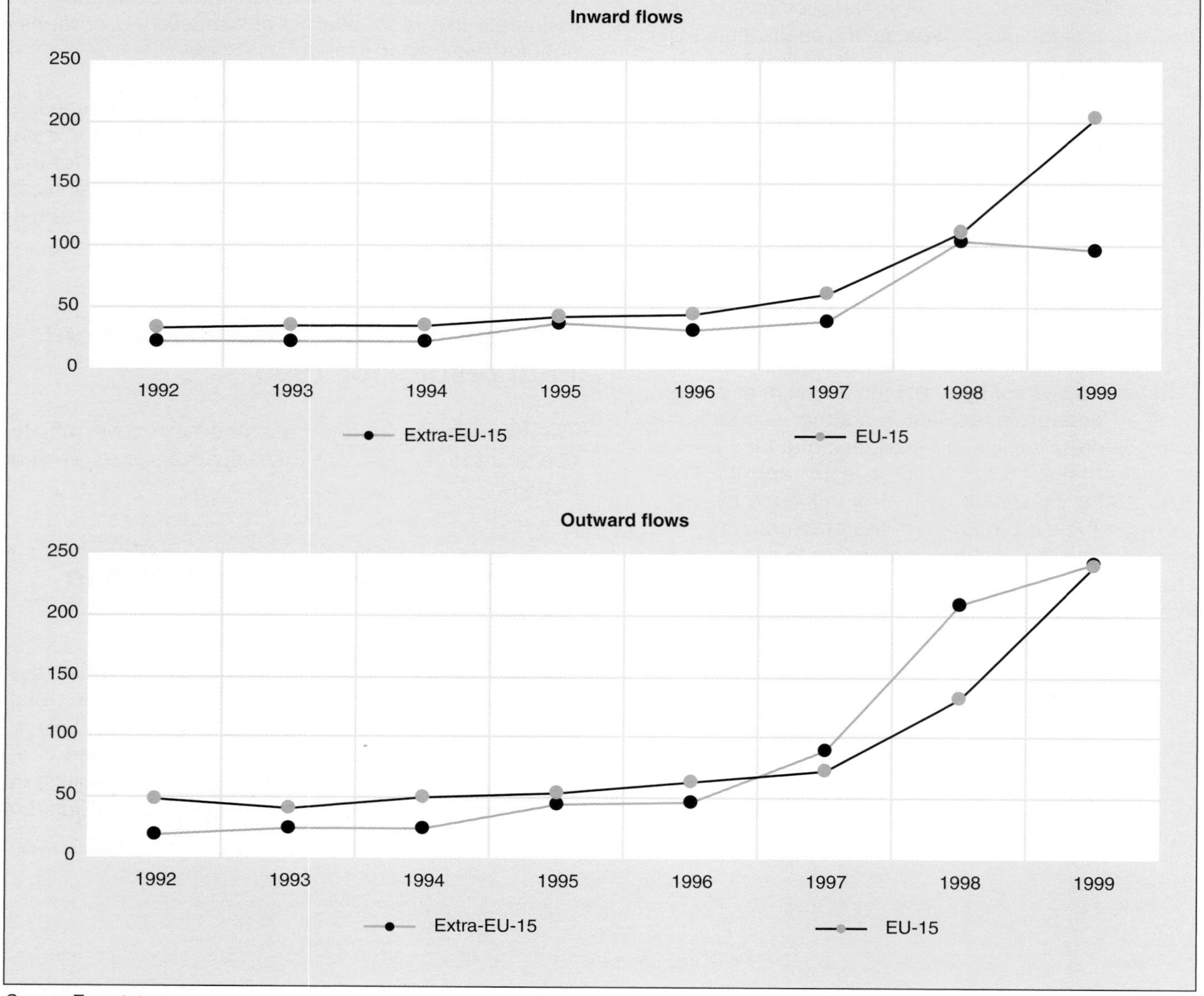

Inward flows

250
200
150
100
50
0
1992 1993 1994 1995 1996 1997 1998 1999
Extra-EU-15
EU-15

Outward flows

250
200
150
100
50
0
1992 1993 1994 1995 1996 1997 1998 1999
Extra-EU-15
EU-15

Source: Eurostat.

Intra-EU flows nearly doubled in 1999

As shown in Figure 2.5.1, an important characteristic of this development is that it was the intra-EU flows among the 15 Member States which pulled the weights. This phenomenon was particularly outspoken in the inward investments. Due to a 7 % drop in inflows from extra-EU countries combined with a 80 % growth in intra-EU flows, about two thirds of all inflows in 1999 came from the 15 Member States, a trend that was even more pronounced for the 11 countries of the euro zone (see Figure 2.5.2).

As for outward flows, extra-EU flows grew by 16 % compared to the 80 % increase in intra-EU flows, thereby also switching focus towards the 15 EU markets.

The 11 countries in the euro zone appear (at least in terms of outward flows) to be relatively more focused on markets within the Union compared to EU-15 as a whole (see Figure 2.5.2).

Figure 2.5.2. Breakdown of total flows into intra/extra for EU-15 and EUR-11

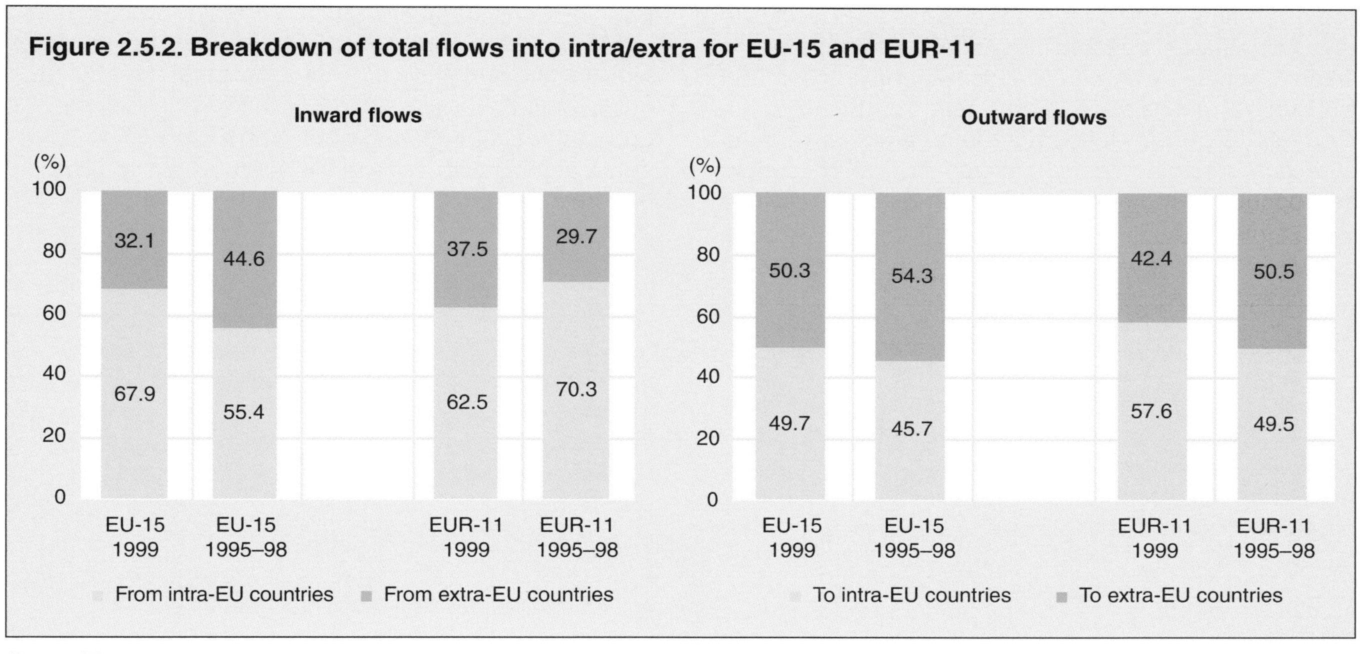

Source: Eurostat.

FDI was still more important in northern EU Member States

The United Kingdom, France, and Germany made up the main contributors of total EU outward flows in 1999. France and the United Kingdom increased their share in total outflows compared to previous years, while Germany and the Netherlands contributed less to overall outflows in 1999 compared to the years before.

As regards inward flows, particularly high FDI was made in Sweden and Ireland during 1999, but investments into the German market also rose significantly. On the other hand, the share in total inflows for France and the Netherlands fell during the course of last year.

Figure 2.5.3. Share of total 1999 EU-15 flows by reporter

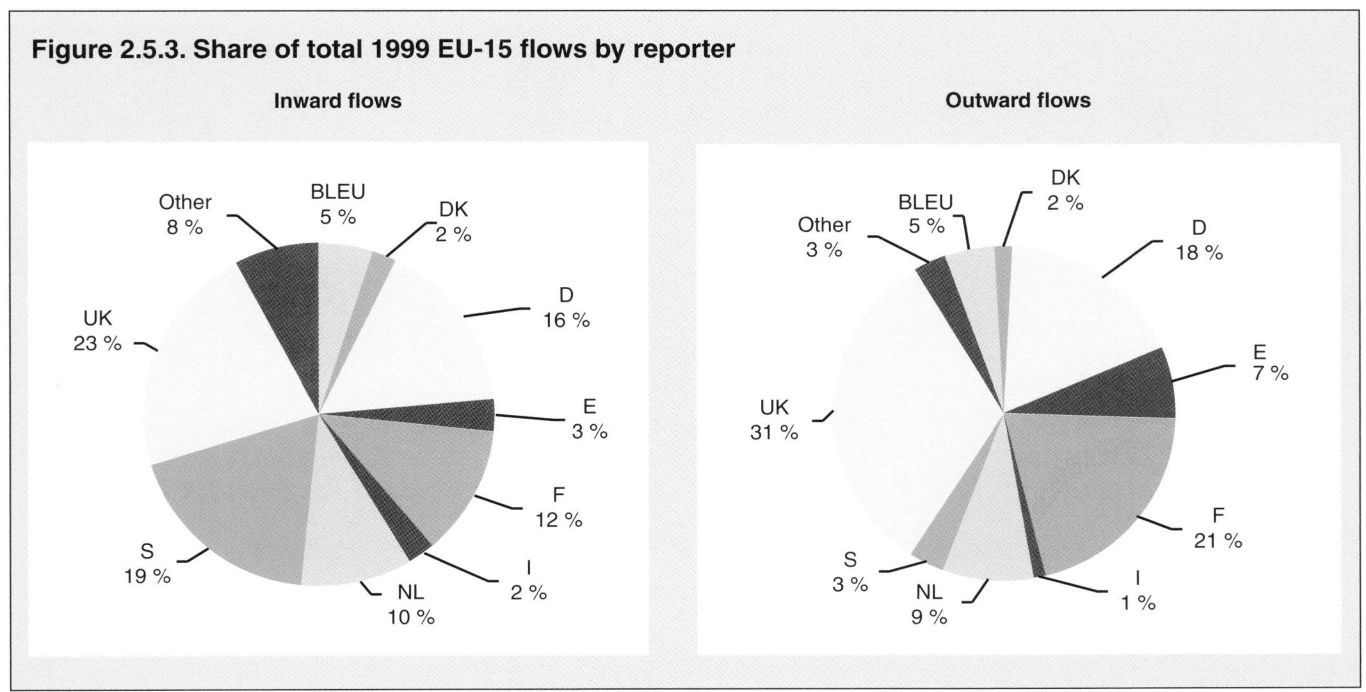

Source: Eurostat.

The 1999 figures also reflect the fact that FDI inflows have had different economic importance throughout the Union. Countries where FDI inflows appear to have had the highest economic weight includes the Benelux countries, Sweden, United Kingdom and Ireland, while especially incoming direct investments appear to have less economic momentum in countries such as Italy and Germany.

For almost all Member States (the major exception being Finland) the importance of direct investments grew significantly during recent years. In 1999, the ratio 'FDI outflows to GDP' reached 12 % in the United Kingdom and in the Netherlands and 8 % in France. The figure below highlights the size of the 1999-inflows to Sweden and Ireland.

Figure 2.5.4. FDI inflows in percentage of GDP (as a %)

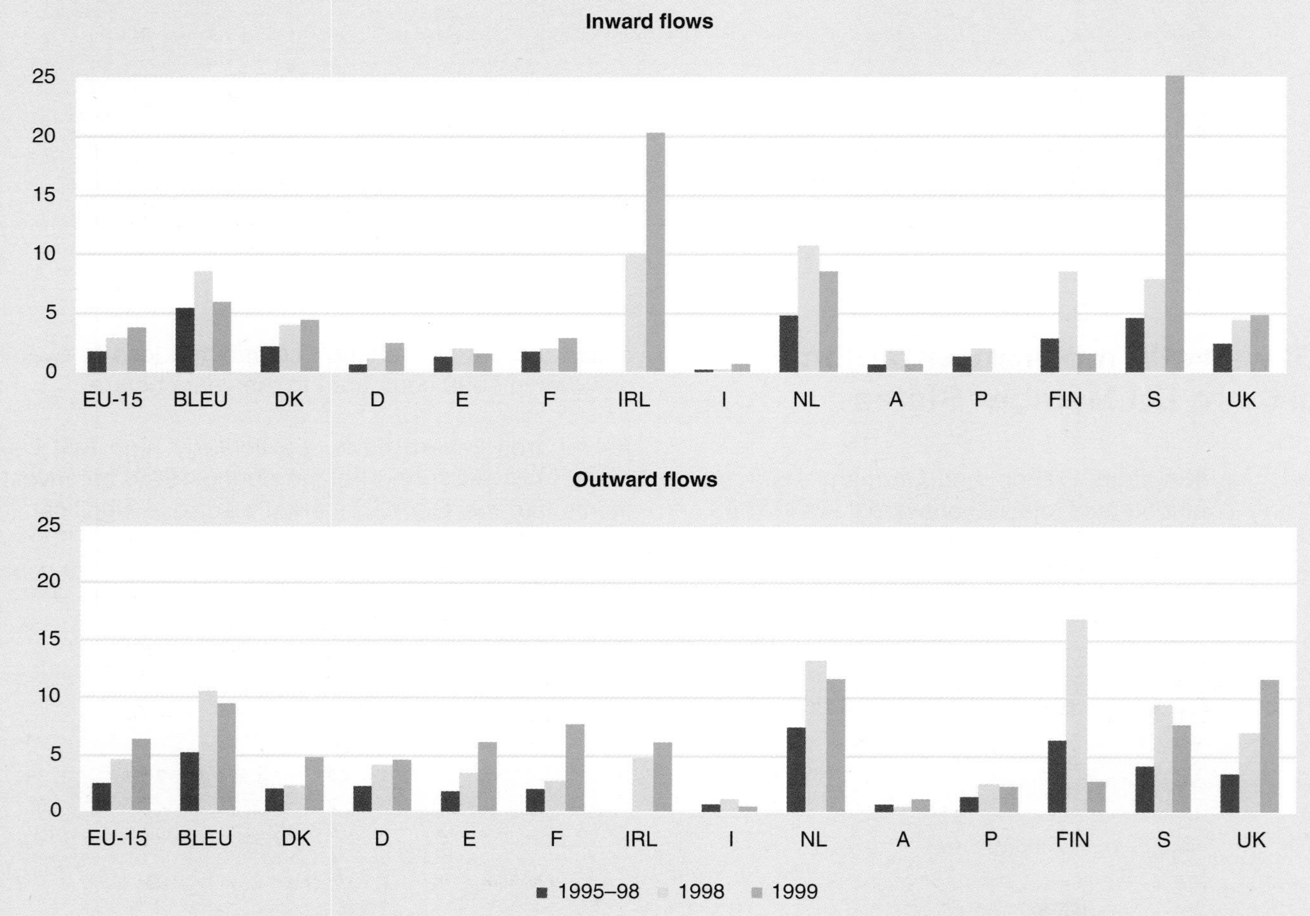

Inward flows

25
20
15
10
5
0
EU-15 BLEU DK D E F IRL I NL A P FIN S UK

Outward flows

25
20
15
10
5
0
EU-15 BLEU DK D E F IRL I NL A P FIN S UK

■ 1995–98 ■ 1998 ■ 1999

Source: Eurostat.

Table 2.5.1. Outward and inward FDI flows in 1999 and 1998, breakdown by major source and destination equity and other capital (million EUR)

	Outward flows to						Inward flows from					
1999	**World**	**EU**	**Non-EU**	**US**	**JP**	**CA**	**World**	**EU**	**Non-EU**	**US**	**JP**	**CA**
EU-15	490 260	240 037	243 180	160 850	3 206	777	299 737	203 824	95 664	68 354	2 613	2 337
BLEU	23 397	22 083	1 352	138	– 4	– 1 232	14 888	12 709	4 839	2 164	62	133
DK	7 706	4 707	2 999	525	0	27	6 993	4 721	2 273	1 574	27	0
D	87 769	54 928	32 841	21 211	535	1 215	49 238	37 113	12 125	8 930	525	– 40
EL	:	:	:	:	:	:	:	:	:	:	:	:
E	33 240	5 391	27 849	1 115	18	– 234	8 781	6 858	1 922	1 426	– 63	23
F	101 385	:	:	:	:	:	36 722	:	:	:	:	:
IRL	5 085	1 510	3 577	:	:	:	17 197	5 870	11 327	:	:	:
I	4 587	3 827	759	338	– 21	– 74	7 082	4 505	2 590	584	182	3
NL	42 788	24 538	18 250	9 960	6	317	31 326	19 303	12 023	10 209	– 76	88
A	1 997	485	1 512	174	– 1	21	1 125	683	442	98	27	92
P	2 346	– 1 954	4 301	37	0	13	– 45	– 94	50	81	7	16
FIN	3 178	2 589	589	336	0	34	1 832	1 798	34	– 219	0	0
S	17 074	5 312	4 710	3 078	– 6	– 127	55 937	47 132	5 885	5 874	– 145	93
UK	157 643	52 763	104 880	104 074	2 392	44	65 380	44 775	20 605	24 848	1 714	1 594

	Outward flows to						Inward flows from					
1998	**World**	**EU**	**Non-EU**	**US**	**JP**	**CA**	**World**	**EU**	**Non-EU**	**US**	**JP**	**CA**
EU-15	346 689	132 743	209 032	128 676	571	3 849	217 583	110 704	102 804	59 373	1 592	8 899
BLEU	25 426	18 324	7 236	1 765	61	1 819	20 307	13 691	4 731	4 180	– 87	144
DK	3 534	3 374	160	– 560	40	13	6 001	1 600	4 400	3 574	0	0
D	75 114	22 091	53 022	40 242	326	105	19 511	16 193	3 318	3 451	107	– 339
EL	:	:	:	:	:	:	:	:	:	:	:	:
E	16 921	5 241	11 679	608	– 2	625	10 541	9 493	1 049	612	– 46	7
F	34 334	15 753	18 581	6 417	60	212	24 577	19 684	4 894	3 882	103	290
IRL	3 489	1 126	2 363	1 785	0	9	7 663	4 382	3 280	3 988	17	36
I	10 787	5 667	5 120	1 777	70	118	2 332	2 125	200	– 258	69	7
NL	45 877	19 774	26 103	12 666	34	778	37 491	15 055	22 436	7 794	288	8 836
A	2 108	1 282	825	– 6	15	2	3 178	3 472	– 294	50	– 74	0
P	2 353	951	1 401	62	0	0	1 987	491	1 496	710	4	1
FIN	19 326	18 154	1 172	871	26	63	9 751	9 508	244	204	159	2
S	20 053	9 519	5 509	2 225	21	179	16 610	12 950	1 522	612	– 91	200
UK	85 909	10 928	74 981	60 290	– 81	– 90	55 252	849	54 403	29 969	1 126	– 378

NB: EU-15 aggregate includes estimations for Greece for 1998–99 and partly France and Ireland in 1999. Discrepancies between sums and totals are due to non-allocated transactions.
Source: Eurostat.

European Union foreign direct investment position at end 1997: overview

At the end of 1997, the European Union recorded FDI assets of EUR 659 billion, a value that was up by more than 20 % compared to 1996.

Foreign direct investors' engagements in the EU amounted to EUR 500 billion, resulting in a net FDI position of roughly EUR 158 billion.

Geographical breakdown of extra-EU FDI positions

The majority of the 15 Member States' FDI assets were located on the American continent where more than EUR 6–10 were placed.

Some 11 % of the FDI assets were placed in Asia, while 9 % were placed in the Swiss market. During 1997. a moderate shift in the distribution of EU FDI assets from most of the other continents towards the American continent took place. Around EUR 7 out of 10 of the FDI capital was placed in one of the non-EU OECD economies, which marked a moderate augmentation.

Direct investors from the American continent also represented the most important providers of FDI capital to the EU markets. More than EUR 6 out of 10 invested in the EU were owned by American investors. Investors from Switzerland were behind nearly 20 % of the FDI commitments while only 10 % of the liabilities were owed to Asian investors.

Nearly 90 % of the total FDI liabilities of the EU area were owned by an investor from one of the non-EU OECD countries.

Figure 2.5.5. EU FDI net position with major partners, 1997 (billion EUR)

Source: Eurostat.

Figure 2.5.6. EU FDI structure, 1997 (as a %)

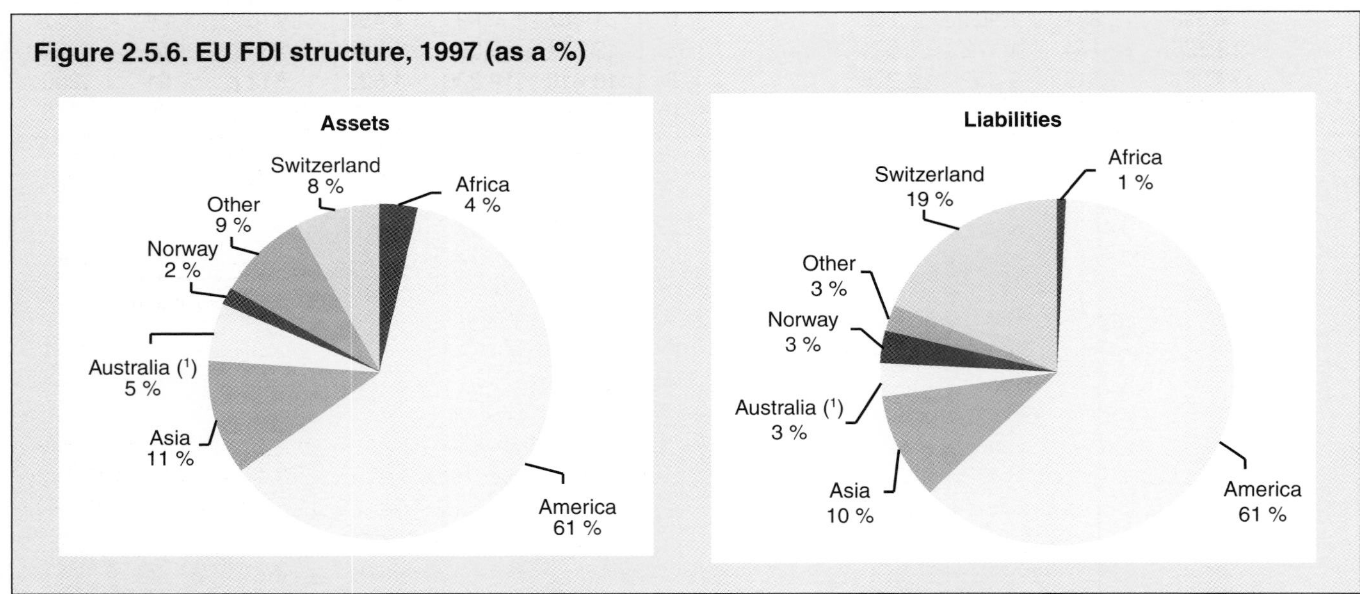

(1) Australia, Oceania and other territories.
Source: Eurostat.

Table 2.5.2. Extra EU FDI positions, 1997 (billion EUR)

	Assets	Liabilities
Europe	**107.2**	**119.3**
of which		
Switzerland	52.4	93.0
Norway	10.5	15.2
Russia	2.4	2.4
Asia	**74.4**	**50.1**
of which		
Japan	12.0	35.3
Singapore	15.5	2.9
Hong Kong	10.7	1.1
America	**403.7**	**310.4**
of which		
United States	298.2	270.1
Canada	24.4	12.5
Mexico	6.9	0.5
Brazil	24.2	1.2
Africa	**23.6**	**4.2**
of which		
North Africa	4.3	1.3
Rep. of South Africa	7.0	1.5
Australia and Pacific	**35.9**	**14.9**
of which		
Australia	29.5	12.2
New Zealand	4.4	2.6
Total Extra EU-15	**658.6**	**501.0**

Source: Eurostat.

Emerging markets — where do EU companies invest?

Data on the activity of European enterprises in the so-called emerging markets are often at the centre of attention from policy-makers and analysts, who consider that due to the high market potential of these economies, obtaining access is one of the keys to success in the globalisation process.

At the end of 1997 almost 21 % of the value of all EU direct investment assets were placed in one of the emerging markets, a figure that did not change significantly from 1996.

However, within the group of emerging economies, an interesting relative displacement of the FDI assets took place between 1996 and 1997.

Central and east European countries now host more than EUR 1 out of 5 invested in emerging markets, a share that increased significantly from the year before. It is first of all the three large economies under transition — the Czech Republic, Hungary and Poland — which have called for the attention of EU direct investors. Together they have attracted more than 75 % of all EU FDI capital which have been placed in this region until now.

Table 2.5.3. EU FDI assets in emerging markets, end 1997

	EU FDI assets	Expansion rate	Share of extra-EU assets
	Billion EUR	As a %	As a %
NICs1 Asia	**31.5**	**12.1**	**4.8**
of which			
Hong Kong	10.7	5.2	1.6
Rep. of Korea	2.4	40.9	0.4
Singapore	15.5	16.9	2.4
Taiwan	3.0	– 10.3	0.5
NICs2 Asia	**10.8**	**23.7**	**1.6**
of which			
Malaysia	5.6	12.9	0.9
Philippines	1.8	36.6	0.3
Thailand	3.4	34.6	0.5
NICs Latin America	**42.9**	**35.3**	**6.5**
of which			
Mexico	6.9	45.9	1.0
Brazil	24.2	27.8	3.7
Chile	3.0	60.0	0.5
Argentina	8.8	39.3	1.3
Other Asia	**15.2**	**42.2**	**2.3**
of which			
China	6.0	54.6	0.9
Other Latin America	**7.7**	**85.3**	**1.2**
of which			
Columbia	2.8	89.5	0.4
Venezuela	1.9	125.7	0.3
Other	3.0	55.9	0.5
Cental and eastern Europe	**29.5**	**55.4**	**4.5**
of which			
Czech Republic	7.7	40.5	1.2
Hungary	8.1	30.4	1.2
Poland	7.2	68.0	1.1
Russia	2.4	98.2	0.4
Other	4.1	110.5	0.6
Total emerging markets	**137.5**	**37.7**	**20.9**

NB: Expansion rate = 1996–97 FDI flows in percentage of 1997 FDI positions.
Source: Eurostat.

Fig. 2.5.7. EU FDI assets in emerging markets 1997

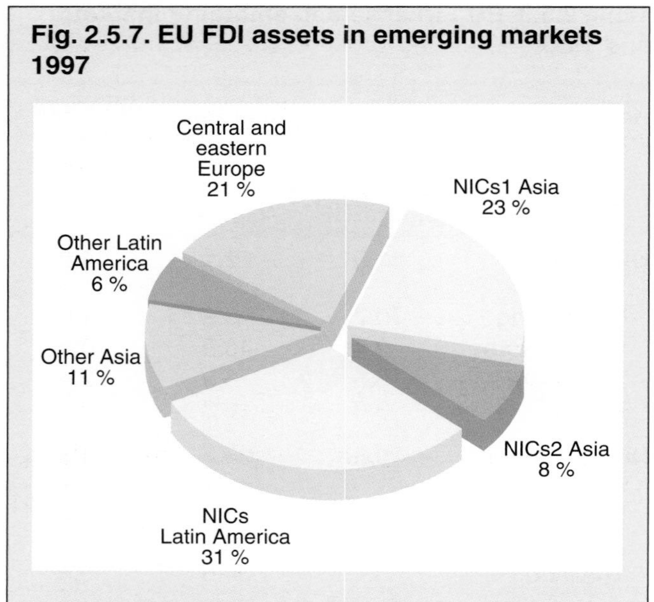

Source: Eurostat.

The traditional emerging markets NICs1 ([16]) now only hold about 23 % of EU direct investment capital in emerging economies. Here about half of FDI assets are still located in Singapore while Hong Kong also still plays an important role.

However, the most important group of emerging markets for EU direct investors is still the NICs LA where about 31 % of all assets are placed. Brazil holds more than half of these investments.

The group of other Asian countries holds now about 11 % of the EU emerging markets investments, which is significantly more than the year before. EU direct investors' increasing focus on China during 1997 explains an important part of this shift.

EU direct investors' FDI capital in Latin American countries other than NICs LA ([17]) has been reduced during 1997. This group of countries now holds only about 6 % of the emerging market investments.

Major investment sectors

The value of the EU FDI assets held by companies from the services sectors now exceeds the value of all EU FDI assets of the manufacturing industry. The shift in focus towards the services sectors is well known and has been on the way during the last decades.

By the end of 1997 the manufacturing sectors were behind some 43 % of the total EU FDI capital, a figure that has been slowly reducing over the last years. Compared to this, companies based in the financial intermediation sectors stood for 19 % of EU FDI equity, a level that did not unambiguously change over the last years.

Direct investors from the real estate and business activities are clearly gaining importance and now hold 15 % of all EU FDI assets.

Figure 2.5.8. FDI positions at end 1997 by sector, share in total activity (as a %)

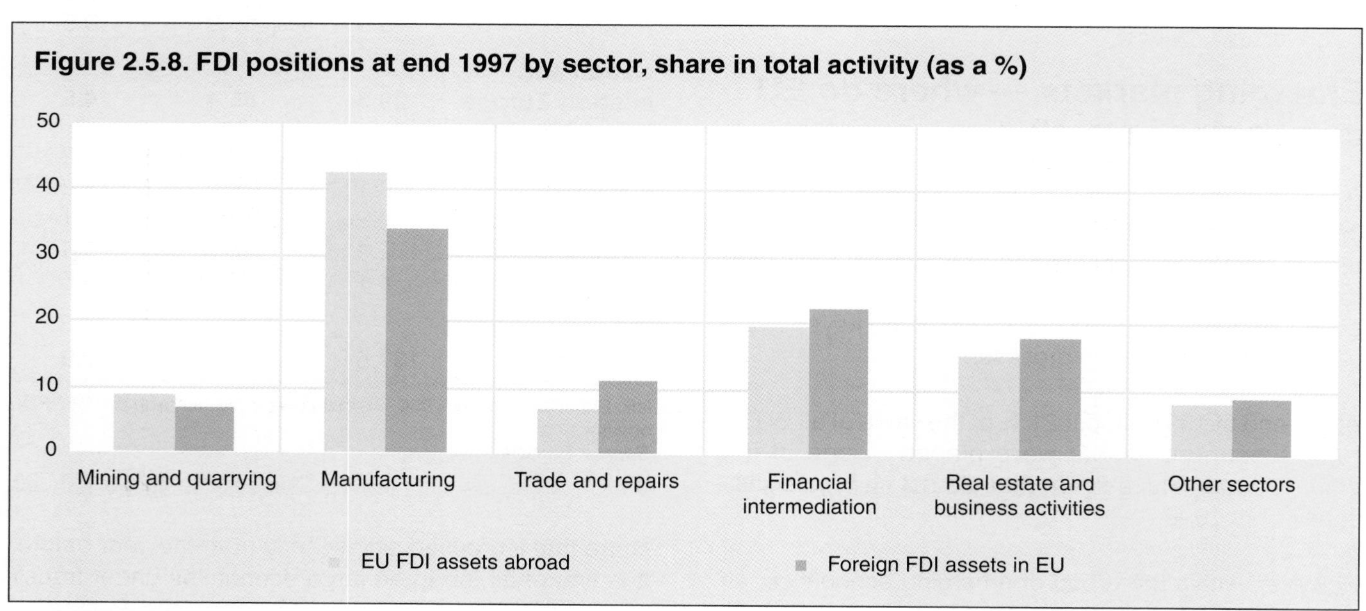

Source: Eurostat.

([16]) NICs1: Hong Kong, Singapore, Taiwan, Republic of Korea; NICs2: Malaysia, Philippines, Thailand.
([17]) NICs LA: Brazil, Argentina, Chile, Mexico.

EU services providers: major target for foreign capital

One of the main indications of the figure above, however, is the fact that the FDI capital of foreign direct investors in the EU area has a significant different sector profile. The dominant role of manufacturing is far less striking here, with a 34 % share.

Foreign investors' capital in the EU area has clearly been more focused on the services sectors in the past. At the end of 1997, EU services hosted more than 55 % of all FDI capital placed by foreigners in the European Union. This number is opposed to the fact that only about 46 % of the EU investors' FDI placements abroad was done by services sectors.

Table 2.5.4. EU FDI positions at end 1997 (million EUR)

	Assets				Liabilities			
	Extra-EU	US	JP	EFTA	Extra-EU	US	JP	EFTA
Agriculture and fishing	826	401	1	83	409	160	11	91
Mining and quarrying	53 591	18 926	325	2 245	33 283	28 517	51	1 204
Services ([1])	303 061	139 490	4 974	34 669	277 761	125 072	27 909	70 849
Manufacturing	280 448	132 991	6 615	25 364	169 480	100 901	7 596	36 977
Food products	46 541	18 590	1 063	3 679	22 982	12 167	212	7 411
Textiles and wood activities	20 149	11 772	156	2 547	18 295	5 970	787	2 521
Petroleum, chemical, rubber, plastic products	88 103	42 370	3 058	6 561	53 422	35 872	831	13 751
Metal and mechanical products	27 667	13 394	749	3 722	21 917	12 927	989	5 577
Machinery, computers, RTV, communication	29 234	11 941	986	4 876	22 670	13 370	2 957	3 504
Vehicles and other transport equipment	18 370	5 986	279	2 549	12 183	8 807	1 350	1 810
Electricity, gas and water	8 755	2 811	27	814	14 805	13 502	– 258	1 400
Construction	7 590	3 312	39	580	4 159	1 413	– 290	1 564
Trade and repairs	44 736	15 208	2 241	5 807	55 921	20 777	14 138	13 064
Hotels and restaurants	6 149	3 552	20	283	6 441	2 425	– 340	565
Transport and communication	15 699	5 124	20	920	7 723	4 025	100	1 823
Land, sea and air transport	5 741	1 549	– 18	513	2 561	966	3	784
Telecommunications	4 425	1 077	30	182	3 141	1 924	640	608
Financial intermediation	127 336	50 345	2 022	15 010	110 428	43 129	11 650	28 547
Monetary intermediation	45 192	10 239	1 298	6 000	56 244	19 556	6 549	12 510
Other financial intermediation	29 443	8 008	317	7 211	34 673	15 387	4 584	10 775
Insurance and activities auxiliary to insurance	52 663	32 019	178	2 755	19 073	7 858	702	6 921
Other financial intermediation and insurance	82 106	40 026	496	9 966	53 745	23 245	5 286	17 696
Real estate and business activities	98 398	57 445	518	11 713	88 390	48 652	2 030	25 781
Real estate	13 871	8 866	11	1 022	19 346	3 487	280	1 995
Computer activities	2 294	1 636	12	174	2 650	2 163	97	405
Research and development	469	171	13	91	1 117	1 001	7	93
Other business activities	74 889	44 883	391	10 357	74 891	41 469	1 619	23 214
Computer, research, other business activities	77 651	46 688	422	10 623	78 653	44 628	1 723	23 711
Other services	10 742	7 817	153	937	8 858	6 063	26	1 069
Not allocated	33	204	13	138	1 031	529	54	238
Total	658 570	298 167	12 005	64 265	500 955	270 100	35 334	112 323

([1]) Sum of trade and repairs, hotels and restaurants, transport and communication, financial intermediation, real estate and business activities, other services.
Source: Eurostat.

3. UNION'S ECONOMY BY MAIN BRANCHES

3.1. Gross value added

GVA growth by branch of production

The most vigorous growth in gross value added (GVA) in the European Union in 1999 occurred in trade, transport and communication (+ 3.3 % compared with the previous year) and financial services and business activities (+ 2.9 %). These were followed by agriculture (+ 2.2 %), construction (+ 2.0 %) and manufacturing (+ 1.6 %), with public services (+ 1.2 %) in last place (see Figure 3.1.1). A look at the results in relation to the average for the reference period (1995–99) shows that the figures are mostly in line: 1999 growth rates for financial services and business activities and trade, transport and communication were below average for the period, but only by about half a percentage point, while construction achieved its first positive result during the period under review (see Figure 3.1.2).

Branches of production

- Agriculture, hunting, forestry and fishing.
- Mining and quarrying; manufacturing; electricity, gas and water supply.
- Construction.
- Wholesale and retail trade, repair of motor vehicles, motorcycles and personal and household goods; hotels and restaurants; transport, storage and communication.
- Financial intermediation, real estate, renting and business activities.
- Public administration and defence; compulsory social security; education; health and social work; other community, social and personal service activities; private households with employed persons.

Figure 3.1.1. GVA growth rates by branch of production, 1999 (as a %)

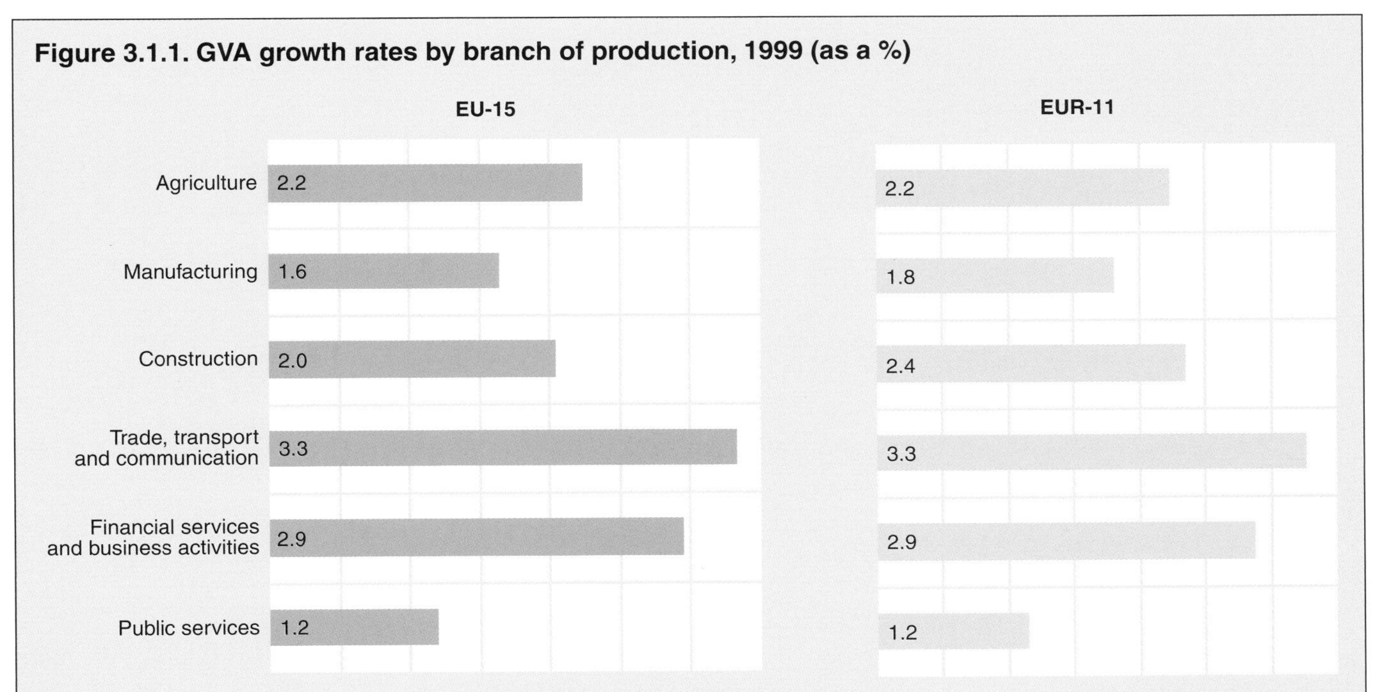

Source: Eurostat.

The euro zone figures generally matched those of the Union. Of the four larger EU countries in 1999, Germany and the United Kingdom recorded the highest growth rates in financial services and business activities and trade, transport and communication: + 3.6 % for financial services and business activities and + 2.8 % for trade in Germany, and + 2.7 % and + 3.0 % respectively in the United Kingdom. In France, trade, transport and communication (+ 3.9 %) and construction (+ 4.2 %) showed the most rapid growth. Italy, however, proved the exception in that financial services and business activities remained static (only + 0.1 growth); there was little growth in the other branches, with only agriculture (+ 5.1 %) achieving substantial growth.

Figure 3.1.2. GVA growth rates, 1999 and average 1995–99 (as a %)

Agriculture

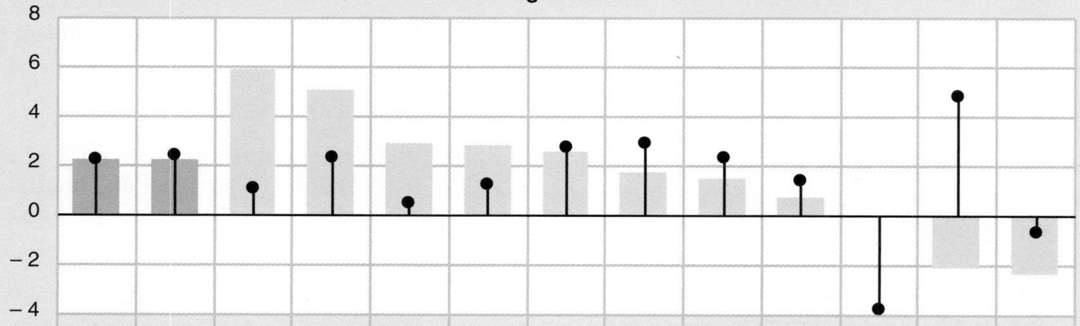

	EU-15	EUR-11	NL	I	B	UK	DK	D	F	FIN	L	E	S
1999	2.2	2.2	5.9	5.1	2.9	2.9	2.5	1.8	1.5	0.7	0.0	– 2.1	– 2.3
● Average 1995–99	2.3	2.4	1.0	2.3	0.5	1.2	2.8	2.9	2.4	1.4	– 3.8	4.8	– 0.6

Manufacturing

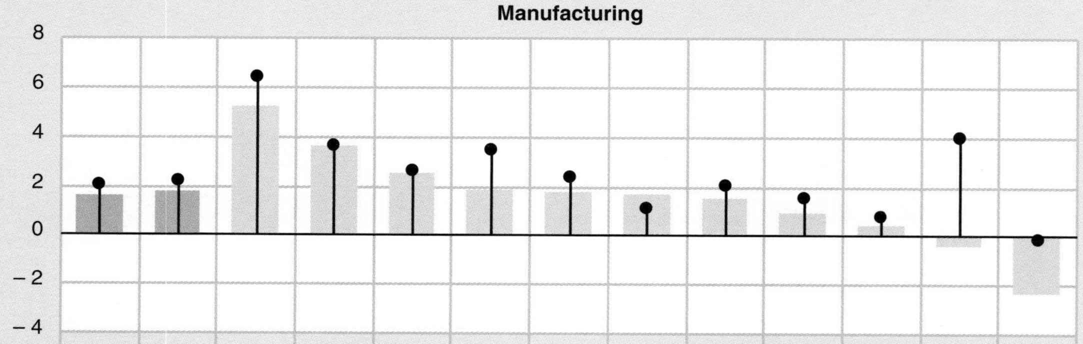

	EU-15	EUR-11	FIN	S	F	E	B	I	NL	D	UK	L	DK
1999	1.6	1.8	5.2	3.7	2.5	1.8	1.8	1.7	1.5	1.0	0.5	– 0.4	– 2.3
● Average 1995–99	2.0	2.2	6.4	3.6	2.6	3.5	2.4	1.2	2.0	1.6	0.8	4.0	– 0.2

Construction

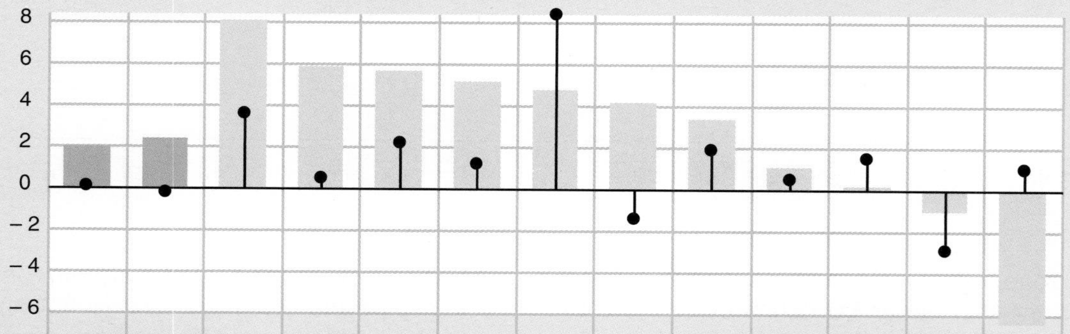

	EU-15	EUR-11	E	S	NL	B	FIN	F	L	I	UK	D	DK
1999	2.0	2.4	8.1	5.9	5.7	5.2	4.8	4.2	3.4	1.1	0.2	– 1.0	– 6.4
● Average 1995–99	0.1	– 0.2	3.6	0.5	2.2	1.2	8.4	– 1.4	1.9	0.5	1.5	– 2.9	1.0

Trade, transport and communication

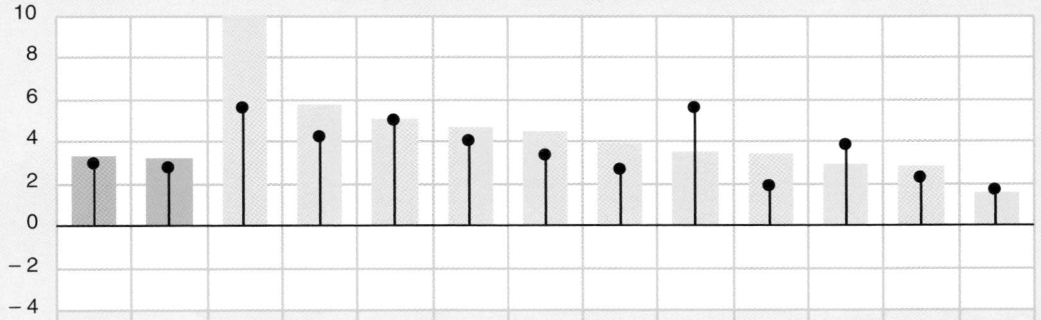

	EU-15	EUR-11	L	S	NL	DK	E	F	FIN	B	UK	D	I
1999	3.3	3.3	15.4	5.8	5.1	4.7	4.5	3.9	3.5	3.4	3.0	2.8	1.5
● Average 1995–99	3.0	2.7	5.6	4.2	5.0	4.1	3.3	2.6	5.6	1.9	3.8	2.3	1.7

Financial services and business activities

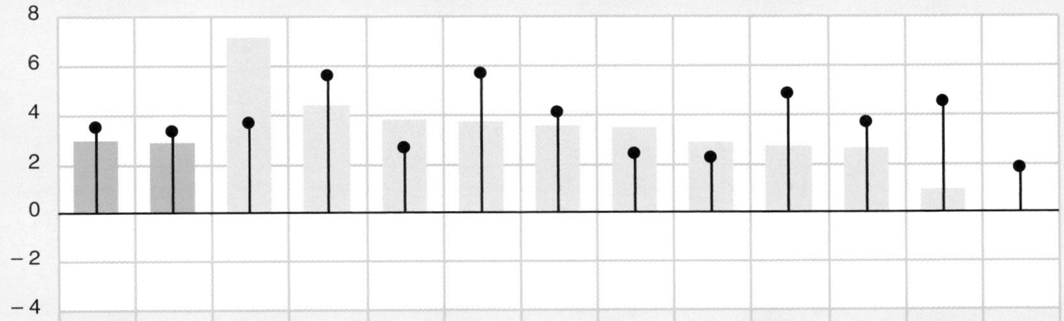

	EU-15	EUR-11	DK	NL	S	L	D	E	F	UK	B	FIN	I
1999	2.9	2.9	7.1	4.4	3.8	3.7	3.6	3.5	2.9	2.7	2.6	0.9	0.1
● Average 1995–99	3.5	3.3	3.7	5.6	2.6	5.6	4.0	2.4	2.2	4.8	3.6	4.5	1.8

Public services

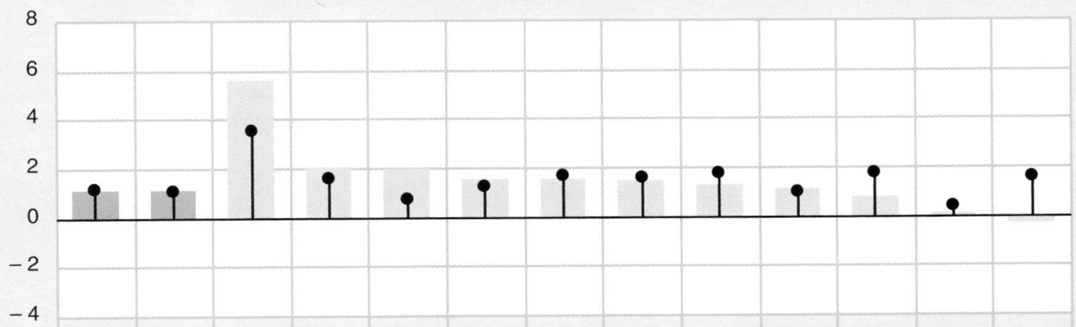

	EU-15	EUR-11	L	NL	S	B	E	F	UK	I	FIN	D	DK
1999	1.2	1.2	5.6	2.1	2.0	1.6	1.6	1.5	1.4	1.1	0.8	0.1	– 0.3
● Average 1995–99	1.2	1.1	3.5	1.6	0.7	1.2	1.7	1.6	1.7	1.0	1.8	0.4	1.6

NB: There are no data available at constant prices for 1999 for Greece and Austria and for Ireland and Portugal no data are available for all period under consideration.
Source: Eurostat.

For those Member States for which data are available ([18]), the majority showed relatively high GVA growth in financial services and business activities, with the highest levels being recorded in Denmark (+ 7.1 %) and the Netherlands (+ 4.4 %). Finland (+ 0.9 %) was the only EU country, apart from Italy (+ 0.1 %), where growth was modest.

In trade, transport and communication growth levels were also generally high. The best performance was in Luxembourg (+ 15.4 %), followed by Sweden (+ 5.8 %) and the Netherlands (+ 5.1 %). The 1999 growth levels recorded in public services were much lower, and Denmark even recorded a slight decrease in GVA (– 0.3 %).

The Member States achieved a variety of results for GVA in manufacturing, ranging from + 5.2 % in Finland to – 2.3 % in Denmark. The trends in construction were even more varied, with Spain recording strong growth (+ 8.1 %) and Denmark declining sharply (– 6.4 %). Lastly, in agriculture, the Netherlands (+ 5.9 %) and Italy (+ 5.1 %) produced a vigorous performance in 1999, whereas the trend in Spain (– 2.1 %) and Sweden (– 2.3 %) was in the opposite direction.

Figure 3.1.2 shows the growth rates per branch. Average growth rates for the period 1995–99 have also been included. Given the quantity of data, it has been presented graphically to allow comparisons both in time and between countries.

Figure 3.1.3. Structure of GVA in the EU, 1999 (as a % of total economy)

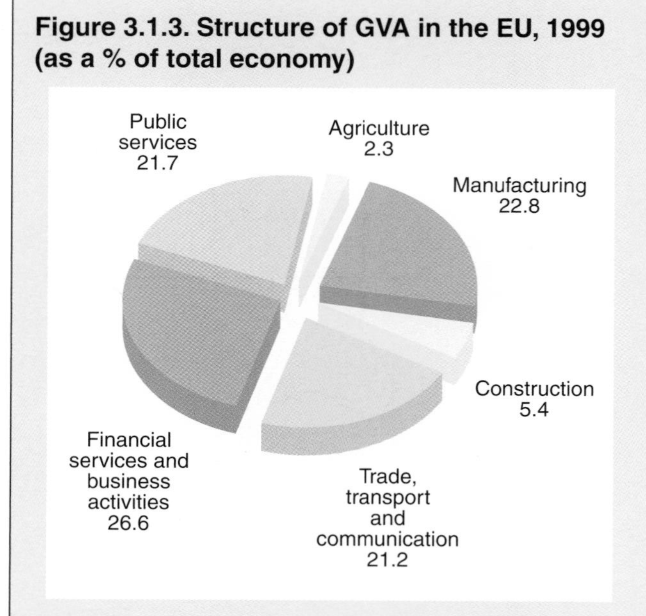

Source: Eurostat.

Structure of GVA in 1999

The structure of production in the European Union (see Figure 3.1.3) is based mainly on the three service sector headings. Financial services and business activities (26.6 %) accounted for the largest proportion of gross value added (GVA) produced by the 15 Member States in 1999, followed by the services for trade, transport and communication (21.2 %) and public services (21.7 %). Overall, these three branches accounted for almost 70 % of total GVA in the Union's economy. Manufacturing accounted for 22.8 % of total GVA. In fact, if the GVA produced by manufacturing and services is disregarded, the remaining contributions made by agriculture and construction are negligible: 2.3 % and 5.4 % respectively. In the euro zone, the structure of production was essentially the same as that in the Union as a whole.

As in the EU as a whole, in all four larger Member States financial services and business activities played a major role as a source of GVA. In Germany, GVA in this branch contributed to 29.8 % of the total economy, while in France the figure was 29.2 %, in the United Kingdom 27.1 % and in Italy 24.9 %. As for the other branches, Germany derived a particularly high contribution from manufacturing (25.1 %), as did France from public services (23.8 %) and the United Kingdom from trade, transport and communication (22.8 %). Italy's figures reveal a relatively balanced structure for financial services and business activities (24.9 %), manufacturing (24.4 %) and trade, transport and communication (23.6 %), but public services (19.4 %) were less important.

A closer look at the structures in individual Member States ([19]) (see Table 3.1.1) shows that in most cases production in the EU countries is concentrated in one of the service branches. There is a large group of countries where financial services and business activities make the biggest contribution to GVA. Public services play the main role in Denmark (26.7 %), Sweden (25.6 %) and Portugal (25.3 %), while trade, transport and communication is the branch that is the biggest contributor in Greece (27.9 %), Spain (27.5 %) and Austria (24.0 %). Ireland and Finland are exceptions, in that the biggest proportion of GVA comes from manufacturing (32.8 % and 26.9 % respectively).

Figure 3.1.4 shows the structure of GVA by branch, together with the structure of employment. GVA and employment are two fundamental indicators for analysing the branches of the economy, and the web diagrams allow the relations between these two factors to be seen at a glance, together with the results in terms of productivity.

([18]) There are no data available at constant prices for 1999 for Greece and Austria and no data are available for all the period under review for Ireland and Portugal.

([19]) The structure has been calculated at current prices. No data were available for 1999 for Greece, Austria, Ireland or Sweden; Eurostat estimates have therefore been used.

Figure 3.1.4. Structure of value added and employment by main branch, 1999 (as a % of total economy)

Financial services, business activities

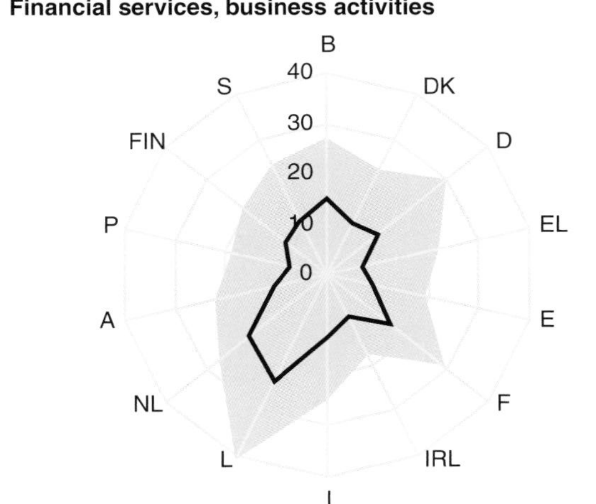

Public services

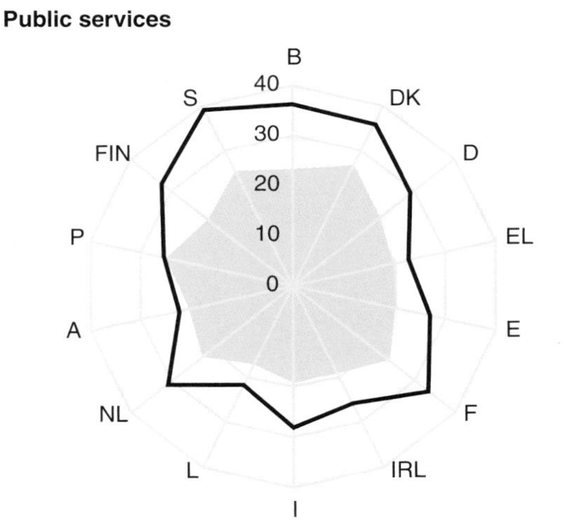

Manufacturing

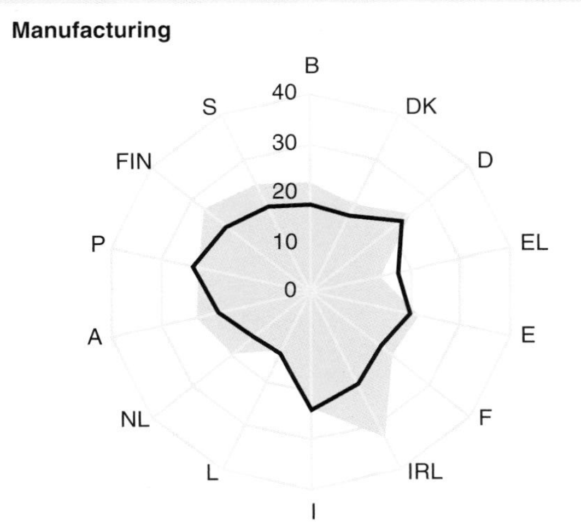

Trade, transport, communication

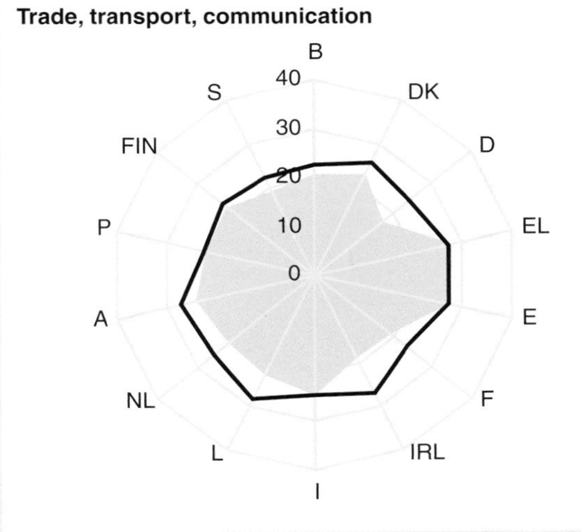

Agriculture

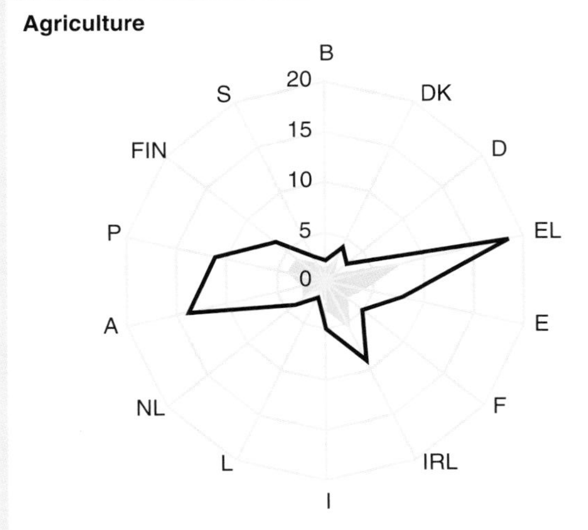

Construction

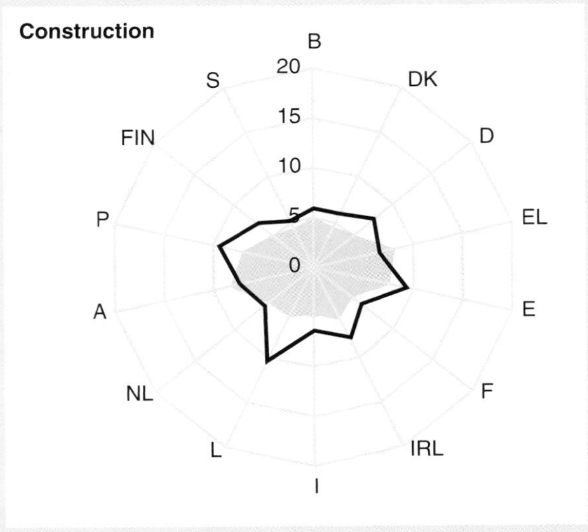

NB: Scales are different; only in this way is it possible to show differences among countries, although it is not possible to compare branches. No data are available on employment in the UK.
Source: Eurostat.

Table 3.1.1. Structure of gross value added in 1999 (as a % of total economy)

	Agriculture	Manufacturing	Construction	Trade, transport and communication	Financial services and business activities	Public services
EU-15	2.3	22.8	5.4	21.2	26.6	21.7
EUR-11	2.4	23.0	5.5	20.8	26.8	21.5
B	1.3	22.2	5.0	20.8	27.2	23.5
DK	2.8	19.7	4.7	23.1	23.1	26.7
D	1.2	25.1	5.2	17.4	29.8	21.3
EL	8.1	14.1	8.3	27.9	22.0	19.6
E	4.0	21.6	7.7	27.5	19.1	20.1
F	2.9	20.2	4.8	19.1	29.2	23.8
IRL	5.4	32.8	5.8	19.0	17.6	19.3
I	3.0	23.6	4.8	24.4	24.9	19.4
L	0.7	12.8	5.5	22.8	40.6	17.5
NL	2.9	20.1	5.7	22.0	26.8	22.5
A	2.3	23.0	8.4	24.0	22.0	20.3
P	3.9	22.6	7.2	22.1	18.9	25.3
FIN	3.6	26.9	5.2	22.2	20.9	21.2
S	2.1	24.5	4.3	19.2	24.2	25.6
UK	1.1	22.5	5.0	22.8	27.1	21.4

NB: Eurostat estimation for Greece, Ireland, Austria and Sweden.
Source: Eurostat.

3.2. Employment and productivity by branch

Structure of employment by branch

The number of people employed in each branch is another important factor in defining the importance of the branch in the economy. A look at the structure of employment in the European Union in 1999 shows that public services provided the most jobs (27.1 % of total employment), followed by trade, transport and communication (26.9 %), while only 14.4 % of the workforce was employed in financial services. The latter branch produced more than a quarter of the value added produced in the EU, while employing a much smaller proportion of the workforce.

Figure 3.2.1. Structure of employment in the EU, 1999 (as a % of total economy)

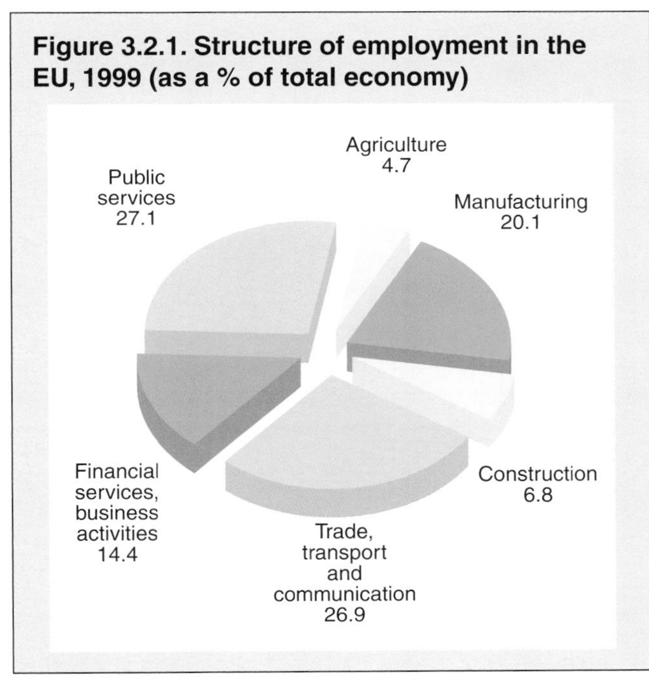

Source: Eurostat.

Among the Member States for which data are available ([20]), there is broad similarity in the structure of employment. Throughout the EU, public services and trade, transport and communication are the branches that provide most jobs. Public services account for the largest share in most countries, while trade, transport and communication is the largest provider of employment in Luxembourg, Greece, Ireland, Austria and Spain.

Sweden is the Member State which has the biggest share of employment in public services (39.1 %). Next comes Belgium (36.3 %), followed by Denmark (35.9 %). There were fewer jobs in this branch in Luxembourg (22.0 % of total employment) and Austria (22.5 %). As mentioned earlier, trade, transport and communication accounted for the largest share of employment in Luxembourg (28.2 %), followed by Greece (27.3 %), Austria (27.2 %) and Spain (27.1 %). In the case of employment in financial services, Luxembourg (23.5 %) and the Netherlands (19.2 %) stood out with figures higher than those recorded in other EU countries. Portugal (23.9 %) and Italy (23.7 %) were remarkable for the importance that employment in manufacturing has in their economies. Luxembourg (10.5 %) also had the highest percentage for employment in construction. Echoing the situation with regard to GVA, Greece (18.5 %) recorded the largest share of employment in agriculture. Austria (13.9 %) and Portugal (11.3 %) were also ahead of the other Member States.

Productivity

To give an overview of the relationship between production and employment in each branch, productivity has been calculated as a simple ratio between gross value added and total employment.

Productivity, or rather a general productivity indicator of output per unit of labour, allows the branches to be considered in terms of labour and employment and, obviously, also allows the comparison of data from different-sized productive systems. This indicator is, of course, very simplified. Firstly, the ratio should be based on hours actually worked ([21]) and not simply on the number of those employed. Secondly, no account is taken of the efficient use of resources and technical progress. The study therefore uses an unorthodox analytical method, which nevertheless allows a 'labour productivity' indicator to be calculated. This then makes it possible to illustrate, summarise and compare data relating to the branches of production

The highest productivity level in the European Union ([22]) in 1999 was achieved in financial services and business activities, where each worker produced EUR 84 300 of value added. Next came manufacturing with EUR 52 000, followed by public services, construction and trade, transport and communication (all about EUR 36 000). Productivity in agriculture, however, was much lower than in the other branches: EUR 22 100 in 1999 (see Figure 3.2.2).

([20]) For Greece, Spain and Portugal the structure illustrated refers to 1998 and for Ireland to 1997. There are no data available for the United Kingdom.

([21]) In quantifying the labour effectively employed in a productive process, hours worked would avoid distortions resulting from the inequality between the number of people employed and the number of jobs.

([22]) Productivity level has been calculated at current prices; opposite, in the calculation of growth index GVA is at constant prices.

Table 3.2.1. Structure of employment in 1999 (as a % of total economy)

	Agriculture	Manufacturing	Construction	Trade, transport and communication	Financial services and business activities	Public services
EU-15	4.7	20.1	6.8	26.9	14.4	27.1
EUR-11	5.0	20.8	7.2	24.6	12.9	29.5
B	2.1	17.8	5.9	22.8	15.1	36.3
DK	3.7	17.3	6.0	25.7	11.4	35.9
D	2.7	23.2	7.6	24.3	12.9	29.2
EL	18.5	17.5	6.7	27.3	7.0	23.0
E	7.7	19.8	9.3	27.1	9.1	27.0
F	4.7	17.3	6.1	23.2	15.4	33.2
IRL	9.1	20.7	8.0	26.8	9.4	26.0
I	4.9	23.7	6.4	24.7	12.3	28.0
L	1.9	13.9	10.5	28.2	23.5	22.0
NL	3.7	14.2	6.2	25.6	19.2	31.1
A	13.9	18.4	7.5	27.2	10.6	22.5
P	11.3	23.9	9.5	22.6	7.0	25.7
FIN	6.4	21.2	7.0	23.4	10.0	32.0
S	2.7	19.1	5.1	22.1	11.8	39.1
UK	:	:	:	:	:	:

NB: The structure illustrated refers to 1998 for Greece, Spain and Portugal, and to 1997 for Ireland.
Source: Eurostat.

Table 3.2.2. Productivity by branch in 1999 (EUR, current prices)

	Agriculture		Manufacturing		Construction		Trade, transport and communication		Financial services and business activities		Public services		Total	
	EUR	*EU = 100*	EUR	*EU = 100*	EUR	*EU = 100*	EUR	*EU = 100*	EUR	*EU = 100*	EUR	*EU = 100*	EUR	*EU = 100*
EU-15	22 100	*100*	52 000	*100*	36 400	*100*	36 100	*100*	84 300	*100*	36 600	*100*	45 800	*100*
EUR-11	22 400	*101*	51 500	*99*	35 000	*96*	39 100	*108*	96 000	*114*	33 800	*92*	46 300	*101*
B	34 800	*158*	70 500	*136*	48 200	*132*	51 900	*144*	102 300	*121*	36 700	*100*	56 700	*124*
DK	39 400	*179*	59 700	*115*	41 500	*114*	47 300	*131*	106 400	*126*	39 100	*107*	52 700	*115*
D	22 300	*101*	55 500	*107*	35 200	*97*	36 600	*101*	118 100	*140*	37 300	*102*	51 200	*112*
EL	11 800	*54*	21 700	*42*	33 300	*92*	27 600	*76*	85 300	*101*	22 900	*63*	27 000	*59*
E	18 000	*82*	38 000	*73*	28 900	*79*	35 200	*97*	73 100	*87*	25 700	*70*	34 700	*76*
F	32 200	*146*	61 000	*117*	40 600	*112*	42 900	*119*	99 100	*117*	37 400	*102*	52 200	*114*
IRL	28 700	*130*	76 100	*146*	35 000	*96*	34 000	*94*	89 900	*107*	35 800	*98*	48 100	*105*
I	27 100	*123*	44 500	*86*	33 800	*93*	44 100	*122*	90 400	*107*	31 000	*85*	44 700	*98*
L	25 300	*115*	67 300	*129*	38 700	*106*	59 100	*164*	126 600	*150*	58 300	*159*	73 200	*160*
NL	33 800	*153*	60 700	*117*	39 200	*108*	36 900	*102*	59 800	*71*	31 100	*85*	42 900	*94*
A	7 700	*35*	57 400	*110*	51 500	*141*	40 600	*112*	95 000	*113*	41 600	*114*	45 900	*100*
P	6 700	*30*	21 200	*41*	15 600	*43*	18 400	*51*	47 300	*56*	18 700	*51*	19 600	*43*
FIN	26 900	*122*	59 900	*115*	35 500	*97*	44 600	*124*	98 500	*117*	31 200	*85*	47 200	*103*
S	39 000	*177*	63 200	*121*	41 500	*114*	42 700	*118*	100 600	*119*	32 100	*88*	49 100	*107*
UK	:	:	:	:	:	:	:	:	:	:	:	:	44 800	*98*

Source: Eurostat.

Figure 3.2.2. Productivity by branch in 1999 (EUR, current prices)

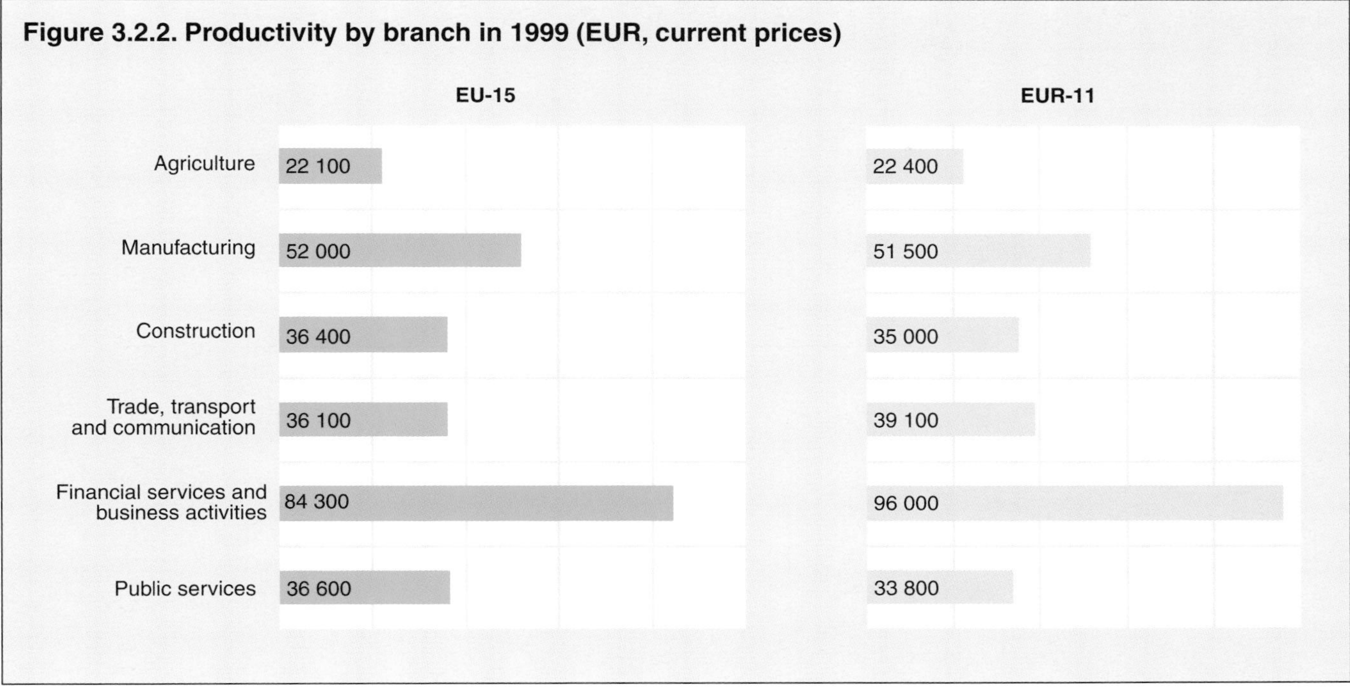

Source: Eurostat.

The figures for the euro zone were more or less in line with those of the EU, albeit a little higher for in financial services and business activities (EUR 96 000) and trade, transport and communication (EUR 39 100) and a little lower for public services (EUR 33 800).

Data are available for only three of the four larger Member States, since there are no data on employment in the United Kingdom. Productivity figures in the branches are essentially similar, with the highest figures being recorded for financial services and business activities in Germany (EUR 118 100), France (EUR 99 100) and Italy (EUR 90 400). In the case of Germany, the figure was among the highest for any branch in the Union. Manufacturing came next for all three countries: EUR 55 500 in Germany, EUR 61 000 in France and EUR 44 500 in Italy. The latter country stands out with a particularly low figure for public services (EUR 31 000), for which productivity was nearly as low as the figure for agriculture (EUR 27 100). France, on the other hand, achieved a relatively high level of productivity in agriculture in 1999 (EUR 32 200).

A clearer comparison of the Member States can be seen in Table 3.2.3, where the productivity figures for the six branches of the economy are shown in relation to the average for the Union as a whole (EU-15 = 100).

A closer look at the figures shows that the highest productivity in agriculture was achieved in Denmark (EUR 39 400) and Sweden (EUR 39 000), where the figures were almost 80 % above the EU average. The leaders in manufacturing were Belgium and Luxembourg, with figures (EUR 70 500 and EUR 67 300 respectively) that were 36 % and 29 % above the EU average. In addition to Greece, Spain and Portugal, where productivity was lower than the EU average in almost every branch, Italy was also below the EU-15 average for manufacturing, with a figure of EUR 44 500 in 1999.

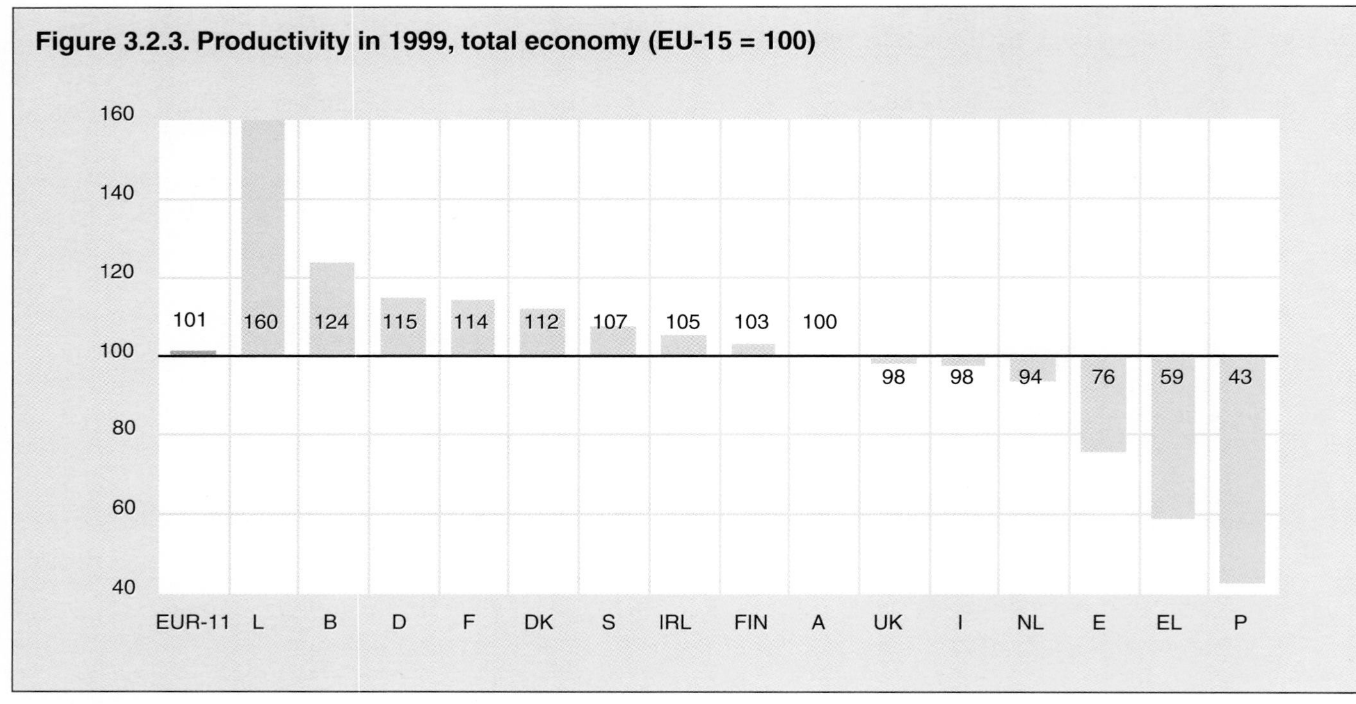

Source: Eurostat.

The Member States with the highest productivity in construction were Austria (EUR 51 100 per unit of labour) and Belgium (EUR 48 200), these figures exceeding the EU average by 32 % and 41 % respectively. In trade, transport and communication, Luxembourg (EUR 59 100) and Belgium (EUR 51 900) ranked at the top. Productivity in financial services and business activities was particularly high in Germany — 40 % better than the EU average — but still lagged behind the figure for Luxembourg (EUR 126 600). Lastly, Luxembourg with EUR 58 300 was the only country where productivity in public services differed greatly from the general trend. The figures for public services in the other Member States were much closer together than in other branches.

When the growth indices (see Figure 3.2.4) are considered, it must be remembered that productivity, however simple, is nevertheless a ratio that is the result of two components (value added and employment) that work in opposite directions: if value added goes up and employment goes down, productivity is increased, and vice versa. On the other hand, if both components go up — or down — the increase or reduction in productivity that this causes will depend on the difference in the variations. In the unlikely event that value added and employment show exactly the same variation, productivity would remain the same — even though the two components had increased or decreased.

In the European Union in 1999, the highest growth rate in terms of volume (1995 = 100) was in agriculture,

Table 3.2.3. Growth index of productivity in 1999, total economy (1995 = 100)

	Employment	GVA	Productivity
EU-15	110	105	104
EUR-11	109	105	104
B	109	106	103
DK	110	105	105
D	108	109	99
EL	113	109	104
E	112	101	111
F	109	104	104
IRL	121	140	116
I	106	102	103
L	120	103	116
NL	114	103	111
A	109	107	102
P	114	106	107
FIN	120	109	111
S	111	108	102
UK	106	111	105

Source: Eurostat

where productivity increased by 14 % in comparison with the reference year. This increase in productivity was a result of growth in GVA (+ 9 %), together with a decrease in employment in this branch (– 5 %). Productivity also increased in manufacturing (+ 8 % in 1999) and in trade, transport and communication (+ 7 %), but with different underlying causes. In manufacturing, the increase in productivity was due entirely to an increase in GVA accompanied by no change in employment; while in trade, transport and communication both GVA and employment increased, but primarily the former. In the other branches productivity remained essentially unchanged in comparison with the benchmark year: in financial services and business activities, GVA and employment both experienced large and matching variations (respectively + 14 % and + 15 %), with the result that productivity was unchanged. The same situation occurred in public services and construction, although the variations were on a smaller scale.

Variations in productivity in the larger EU countries — although for only three of them, since no data are available for the United Kingdom — showed a wide variety of trends. An analysis of the figures for the whole economy in 1999, shows that productivity rose most in Germany (+ 9 % in 1999, with 1995 = 100), resulting from an increase in GVA (+ 8 %) and a slight decrease in employment (– 1 %). In France, productivity in 1999 was higher than in the reference year by 4 %, due to a major rise in GVA (+ 9 %) coupled with a more modest increase in employment (+ 4 %). GVA (+ 6 %) also rose in Italy, but the figure for employment (+ 3 %) was much closer, with the result that productivity in 1999 was 2 % higher than in the reference year.

As observed, analysing variations in productivity is somewhat complex because it involves two factors and therefore two variations. Figure 3.2.4 illustrates the growth indices in terms of volume for productivity and its components (GVA and employment) both graphically and numerically. The data that are provided can thus be used to analyse variations in productivity in the six branches and the 15 Member States.

Figure 3.2.4. Growth index of productivity, 1999 (1995 = 100)

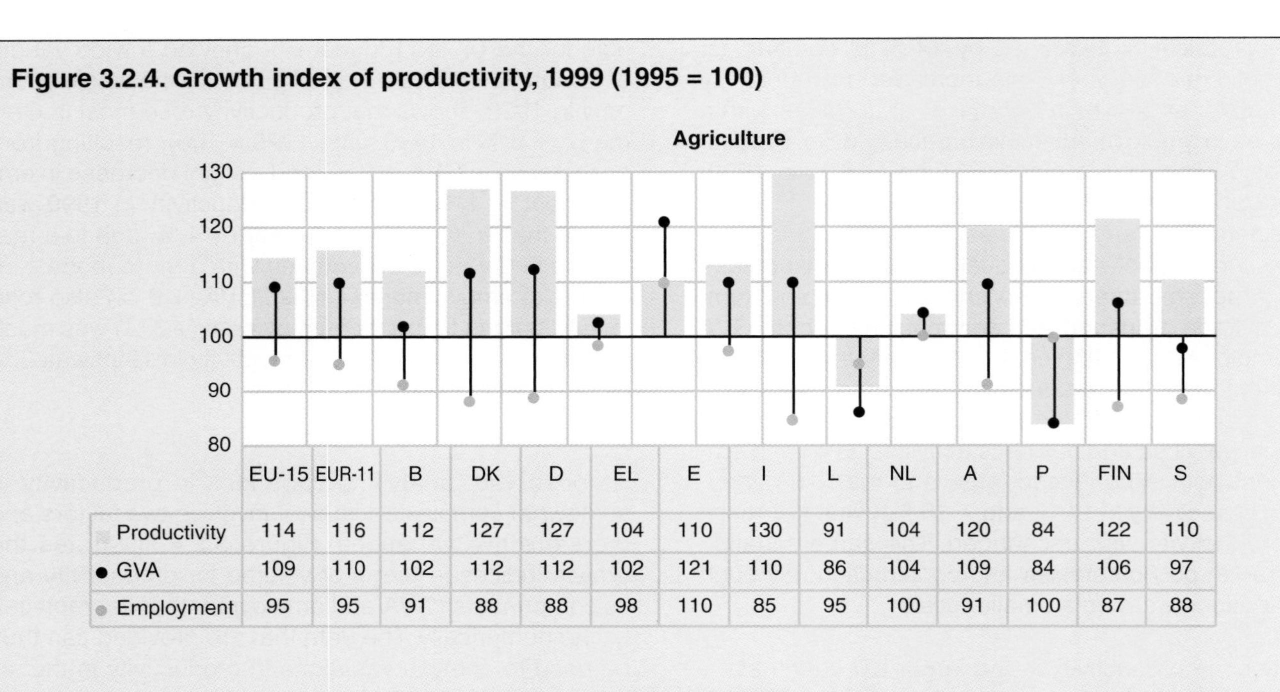

	EU-15	EUR-11	B	DK	D	EL	E	I	L	NL	A	P	FIN	S
Productivity	114	116	112	127	127	104	110	130	91	104	120	84	122	110
● GVA	109	110	102	112	112	102	121	110	86	104	109	84	106	97
● Employment	95	95	91	88	88	98	110	85	95	100	91	100	87	88

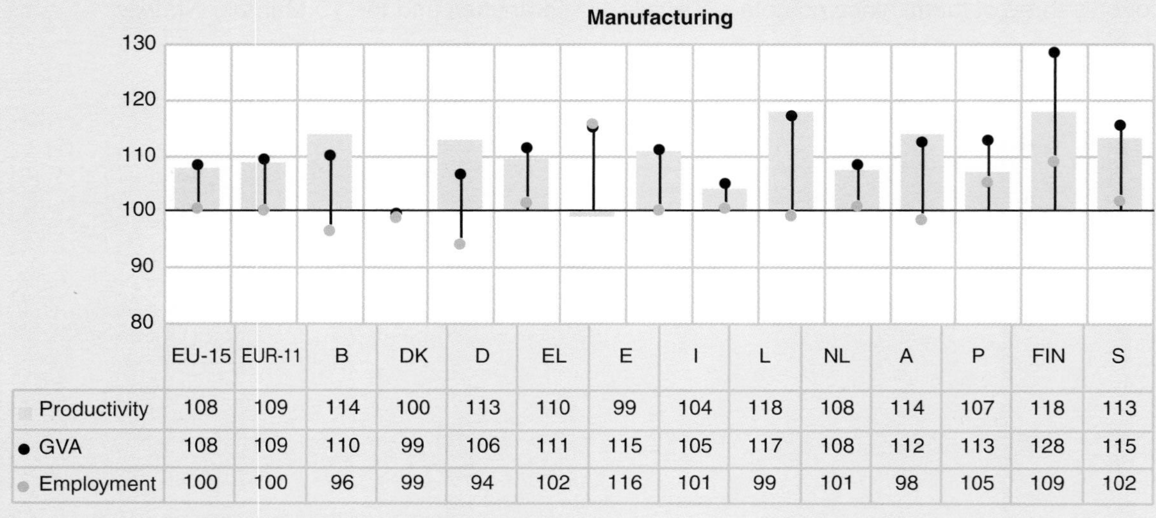

	EU-15	EUR-11	B	DK	D	EL	E	I	L	NL	A	P	FIN	S
Productivity	108	109	114	100	113	110	99	104	118	108	114	107	118	113
● GVA	108	109	110	99	106	111	115	105	117	108	112	113	128	115
● Employment	100	100	96	99	94	102	116	101	99	101	98	105	109	102

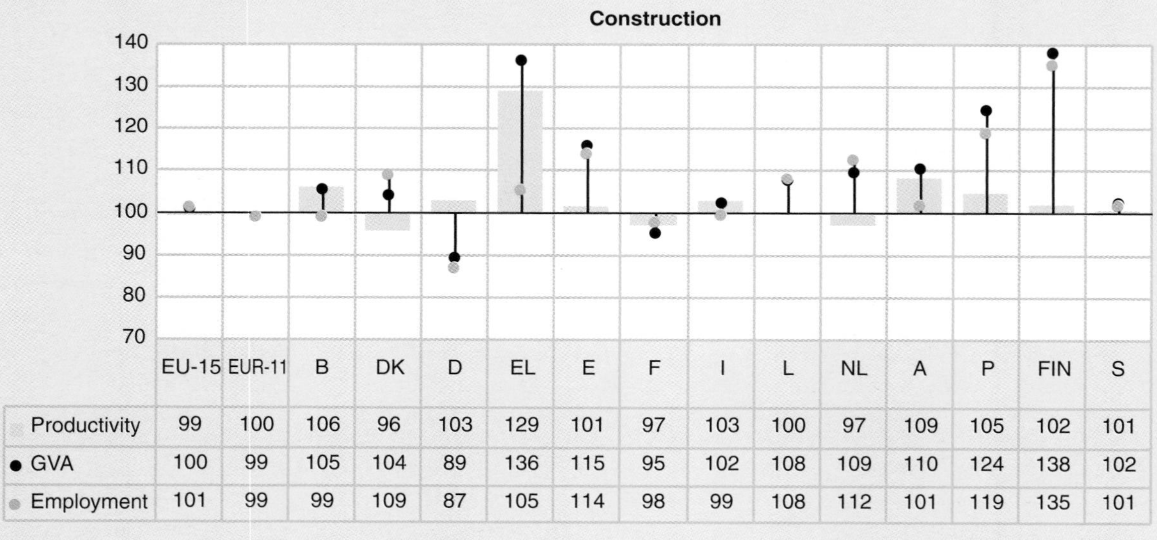

	EU-15	EUR-11	B	DK	D	EL	E	F	I	L	NL	A	P	FIN	S
Productivity	99	100	106	96	103	129	101	97	103	100	97	109	105	102	101
● GVA	100	99	105	104	89	136	115	95	102	108	109	110	124	138	102
● Employment	101	99	99	109	87	105	114	98	99	108	112	101	119	135	101

Trade, transport and communication

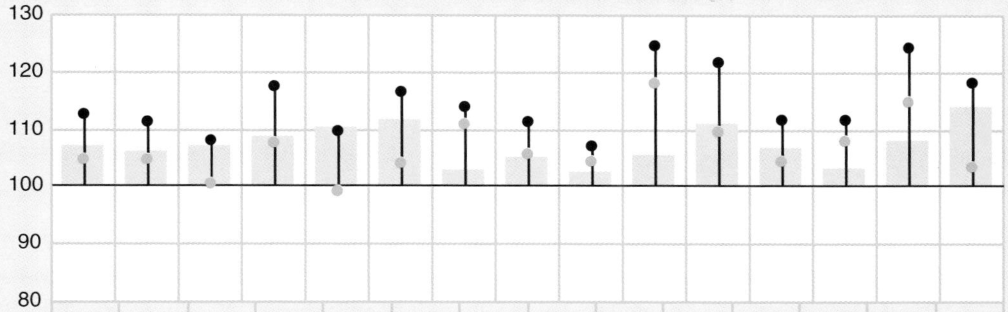

	EU-15	EUR-11	B	DK	D	EL	E	I	L	NL	A	P	FIN	S
Productivity	107	106	107	109	110	112	103	103	106	111	107	103	108	114
● GVA	112	111	108	117	109	116	114	107	124	122	112	112	124	118
● Employment	105	105	100	107	99	104	111	104	118	109	104	108	115	103

Financial services and business activities

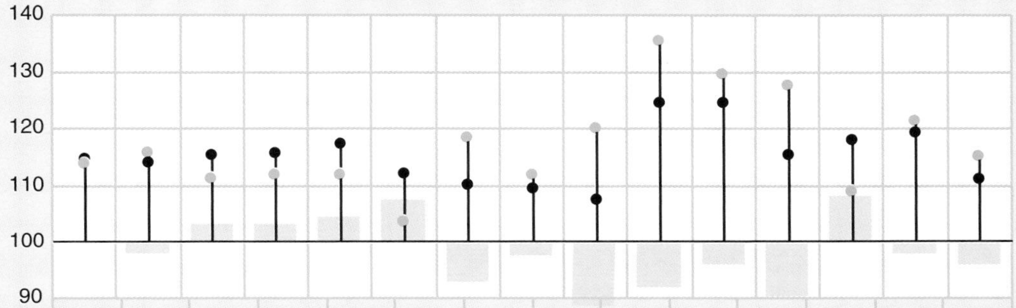

	EU-15	EUR-11	B	DK	D	EL	E	I	L	NL	A	P	FIN	S
Productivity	101	98	104	103	105	108	93	89	92	96	90	108	98	96
● GVA	115	114	115	116	117	112	110	107	124	124	115	118	119	111
● Employment	114	116	111	112	112	104	118	120	135	129	128	109	121	115

Public services

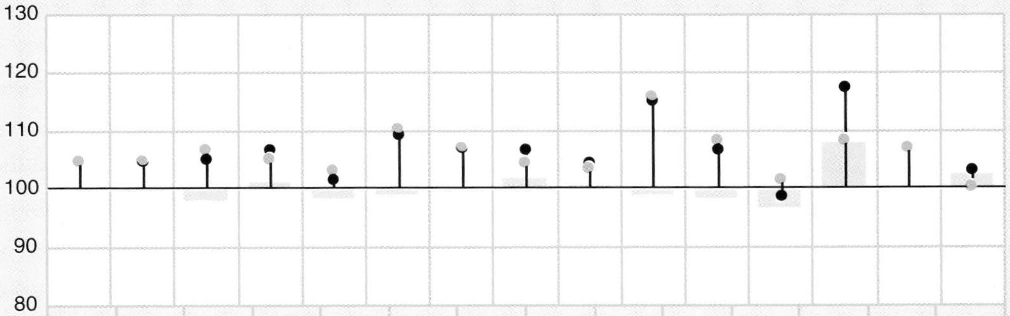

	EU-15	EUR-11	B	DK	D	EL	E	I	L	NL	A	P	FIN	S
Productivity	100	100	98	101	98	99	100	101	99	98	97	108	100	103
● GVA	105	105	105	107	101	109	107	104	115	106	98	117	107	103
● Employment	105	105	107	105	103	110	107	103	116	108	102	108	107	100

NB: It was not possible to calculate productivity growth for the United Kingdom and Ireland as no data are available on employment per branch in the United Kingdom or on GVA (constant prices) per branch in Ireland.
Source: Eurostat.

3.3. Compensation per employee and unit labour cost

Rate of remuneration

Having seen how much the branches produce in terms of GVA and how many workers they employ, we shall now look at how much each branch distributes in wages. However, the information provided by 'compensation of employees' refers only to salaried employment and as such does not provide any information for the self-employed. Furthermore, only data at current prices are available, which means that they cannot be compared over time. To allow comparisons to be drawn between branches and countries, the income distributed to employees by the branches of production (compensation of employees) is considered in relation to the number of those receiving such income. This ratio then provides the rate of remuneration (compensation per employee) for each branch of production.

The highest per capita wages in the European Union in 1999 were paid to employees in manufacturing (EUR 34 600) and public services (EUR 30 800), which both came above financial services and business activities (EUR 29 000). At the other end of the scale, by far the lowest wages were in agriculture, where compensation per employee (EUR 15 700) was about half the figure for the economy as a whole (EUR 29 800).

In Table 3.3.1 remuneration rates by branch are shown for all Member States. In order to compare data from different-sized productive systems, the cost of labour per unit of product has been calculated.

Figure 3.3.1. Remuneration rates in 1999 (EUR, current prices)

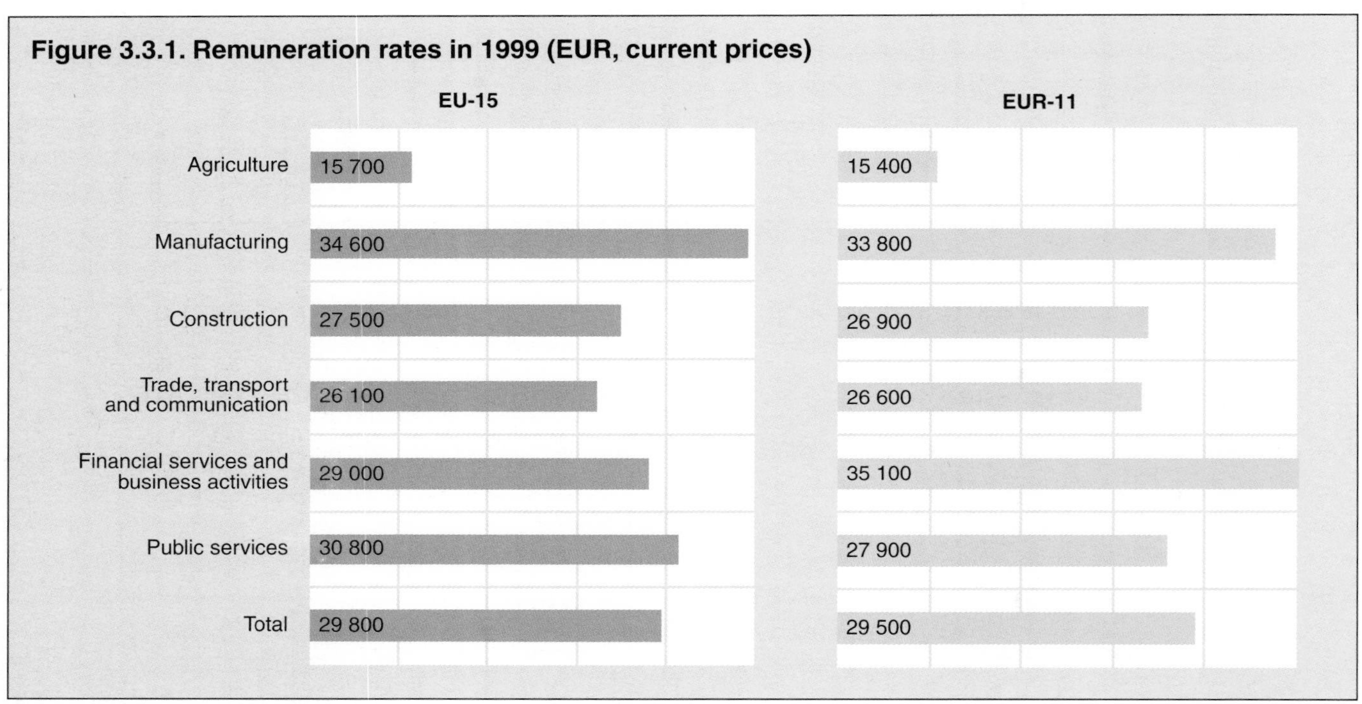

Source: Eurostat.

Table 3.3.1. Remuneration rates in 1999 (EUR, current prices)

	Agriculture		Manufacturing		Construction		Trade, transport and communication		Financial services and business activities		Public services		Total	
	EUR	*EU = 100*	EUR	*EU = 100*	EUR	*EU = 100*	EUR	*EU = 100*	EUR	*EU = 100*	EUR	*EU = 100*	EUR	*EU = 100*
EU-15	15 700	*100*	34 600	*100*	27 500	*100*	26 100	*100*	29 000	*100*	30 800	*100*	29 800	*100*
EUR-11	15 400	*98*	33 800	*98*	26 900	*98*	26 600	*102*	35 100	*121*	27 900	*91*	29 500	*99*
B	15 900	*101*	43 200	*125*	32 900	*120*	36 400	*139*	56 200	*194*	32 000	*104*	37 800	*127*
DK	24 700	*157*	36 500	*105*	37 300	*136*	32 000	*123*	41 700	*144*	33 600	*109*	34 700	*116*
D	20 800	*132*	39 900	*115*	28 400	*103*	27 900	*107*	36 100	*124*	30 400	*99*	32 600	*109*
EL	9 000	*57*	17 400	*50*	12 400	*45*	15 300	*59*	22 600	*78*	19 300	*63*	17 300	*58*
E	8 600	*55*	23 900	*69*	21 900	*80*	19 700	*75*	33 500	*116*	21 300	*69*	22 300	*75*
F	20 800	*132*	39 600	*114*	33 100	*120*	30 700	*118*	37 800	*130*	29 900	*97*	33 200	*111*
IRL	15 700	*100*	28 000	*81*	32 200	*117*	19 900	*76*	32 200	*111*	31 600	*103*	27 300	*92*
I	12 700	*81*	28 100	*81*	22 100	*80*	27 600	*106*	32 000	*110*	25 800	*84*	26 800	*90*
L	19 500	*124*	41 100	*119*	27 600	*100*	30 000	*115*	50 300	*173*	43 300	*141*	39 200	*132*
NL	19 900	*127*	32 600	*94*	31 900	*116*	24 100	*92*	29 500	*102*	28 000	*91*	28 100	*94*
A	21 300	*136*	34 500	*100*	28 700	*104*	24 900	*95*	28 300	*98*	32 900	*107*	29 900	*100*
P	7 100	*45*	10 300	*30*	9 000	*33*	11 500	*44*	21 100	*73*	16 300	*53*	13 000	*44*
FIN	22 200	*141*	34 600	*100*	30 500	*111*	26 100	*100*	33 300	*115*	27 700	*90*	29 500	*99*
S	16 000	*102*	27 500	*79*	28 900	*105*	21 200	*81*	32 400	*112*	40 500	*131*	31 800	*107*
UK	:	:	:	:	:	:	:	:	:	:	:	:	31 100	*104*

Source: Eurostat.

Cost of labour per unit of product

The cost of labour per unit of product (CLUP) is simply the ratio between remuneration and productivity — i.e. GVA/employment (productivity) and compensation/employee (remuneration) ([23]). More specifically, CLUP is the ratio between how much each worker is paid and how much each worker produces ([24]).

Given that CLUP is a ratio involving data that are already expressed 'per worker', the result is a simple numerical value, or ratio. The point of reference is one, which is the ratio obtained when each worker's output equals his or her remuneration ([25]).

The data for the European Union in 1999 show that in the economy as a whole each worker received compensation of EUR 29 800 and produced output valued at EUR 36 600 (productivity). This gives a CLUP figure of 0.65, indicating that the cost of labour (compensation) was 65 % of unit production per worker. In absolute terms, the figures are not very illuminating, but they do make for interesting comparisons between branches and countries. For example, a look at the branches in the Union shows that the figure is particularly low in financial services and business activities (0.34) but particularly high in public services (0.84).

In order to make it possible to compare the various countries, the CLUP figures for the Member States ([26]) in Table 3.3.2 have been calculated in relation to the figure for the Union as a whole (EU-15 = 100). In relation to the EU average, for example, unit labour cost was higher in Belgium (3 % above the EU average) and Portugal (+ 2 %). The Member States with the lowest cost of labour per unit of product in 1999 were Luxembourg (18 % below average) and Ireland (13 % below the EU figure).

The range of figures in the individual branches was much wider. In the case of financial services and business activities, the CLUP figure in Belgium was nearly 60 % higher than the EU average, while at the opposite extreme Greece was almost 23 % lower. In other words,

([23]) Given that compensation of employees is available only at current prices, gross value added has also been calculated at current prices.

([24]) It must be remembered that productivity is calculated for total employment, but remuneration is restricted to salaried employees.

([25]) In this extreme example, productivity in the case of self-employment would be exactly equal to productivity in the case of salaried employment.

([26]) For CLUP as well, it was not possible to calculate the figures for the United Kingdom.

Figure 3.3.2. Unit labour cost by branch in 1999, total economy (EU-15 = 100)

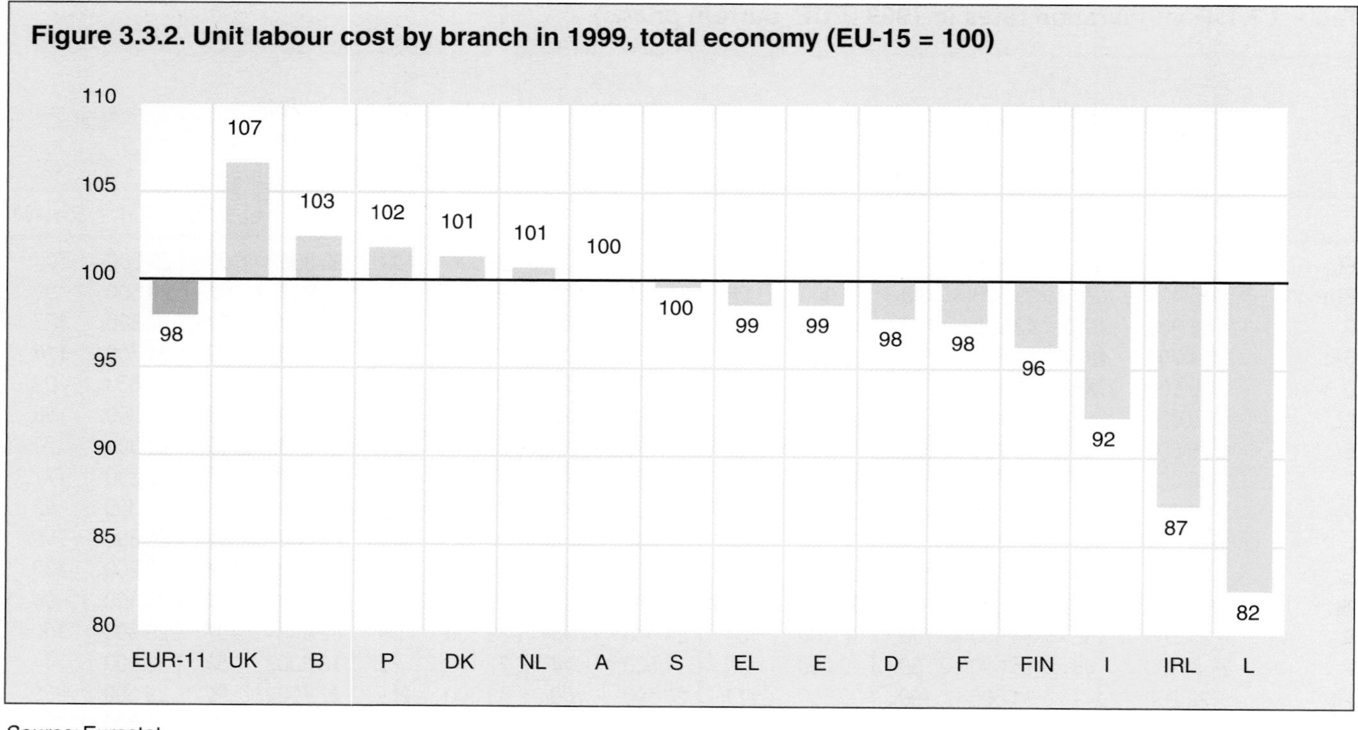

Source: Eurostat.

Table 3.3.2. Unit labour cost, 1999

	Agriculture	Manufacturing	Construction	Trade, transport and communication	Financial services and business activities	Public services	Total
EU-15	0.71	0.67	0.75	0.72	0.34	0.84	0.65
				EU-15 = 100			
EUR-11	97	98	102	94	106	98	98
B	64	92	90	97	160	104	103
DK	88	92	119	94	114	102	101
D	131	108	107	106	89	97	98
EL	107	120	49	77	77	100	99
E	67	95	101	77	133	98	99
F	91	97	108	99	111	95	98
IRL	77	55	122	81	104	105	87
I	66	95	87	87	103	99	92
L	108	92	94	70	116	88	82
NL	83	81	108	91	144	107	101
A	391	90	74	85	87	94	100
P	149	73	76	87	129	104	102
FIN	116	87	114	81	98	105	96
S	58	65	93	69	94	150	100
UK	:	:	:	:	:	:	107

Source: Eurostat.

the unit labour cost in Belgium for this branch was more than double the figure for Greece. In public services, Sweden stood out with a particularly high figure (50 % above EU average); CLUP in this country is even higher than one: this means that the unit cost of labour was higher than the unit production figure. In trade, transport and communication, however, Sweden had the lowest unit labour cost (– 31 % in relation to the EU average), while Germany recorded the highest figure (+ 6 %). In manufacturing, it was Greece that had the highest unit labour cost (+ 20 %); followed by Germany (+ 8 %). In construction, labour cost is the highest in Ireland and Denmark where it exceeds EU average by 22 % and 19 % respectively.

The CLUP figures in agriculture showed the widest range. Austria was well ahead of the other Member States, with a figure that was almost four times higher than the EU average, and even in absolute terms the Austrian figure was extremely high. This is due to the fact that remuneration (EUR 21 300 per employee) was far higher than productivity (EUR 7 700 per person employed). The same occurred in Portugal, but to a lesser extent. As has already been seen, a CLUP ratio exceeding one means that what is produced is worth less than the cost of producing it. However, in the case of agriculture certain facts make this comparison less meaningful. Most importantly, self-employment is not taken into account, so compensation only includes employees, while productivity is calculated for all workers. The fact is that there is a particularly high percentage of self-employment in agriculture.

To demonstrate the changes in CLUP figures over time — given that the figure has been calculated at current prices — 1995 was used as the reference year (1995 = 100) to calculate the growth index. Table 3.3.3 charts the evolution of CLUP and its components (remuneration and productivity) for the period 1995–99. It shows that remuneration increased more slowly than productivity, with the result that the unit cost of labour decreased.

In the European Union, 1999 CLUP was 2 % lower than in the reference year (1995), while productivity was 15 % higher and remuneration 13 % higher.

Table 3.3.3 shows the results for the EU economy as a whole. It can be seen that in the majority of the Member States for which data are available, productivity went up more than compensation and therefore caused the unit cost of labour to decrease. Sweden and Denmark were exceptions: in these countries productivity increased less than compensation and therefore the unit cost of labour was up in 1999, but by only 3 % and 2 % respectively.

Table 3.3.3. Unit labour cost in 1999, value growth index total economy (1995 = 100)

	Remuneration	Productivity	CLUP
EU-15	113	115	98
EUR-11	106	109	97
B	104	106	98
DK	114	112	102
D	103	106	97
EL	124	124	100
E	110	109	101
F	108	108	100
IRL	123	138	89
I	121	125	97
L	105	110	96
NL	104	104	100
A	91	106	86
P	113	118	97
FIN	106	109	98
S	122	119	103
UK	150	147	101

NB: CLUP = cost of labour per unit of product, i.e. unit labour cost.
Source: Eurostat.

To illustrate the growth of CLUP in each branch, its components (remuneration and productivity) must also be considered. In view of the complexity, the set of figures includes all the variables and also provide a summarised graphic overview (see Figure 3.3.4).

Table 3.3.4. Unit labour cost, 1999, value growth index (1995 = 100)

	EU-15			EUR-11		
	Remu-neration	Productivity	CLUP	Remu-neration	Productivity	CLUP
Agriculture	105	109	96	109	108	101
Manufacturing	108	110	98	113	114	100
Construction	105	104	102	110	109	101
Trade, transport and communication	104	109	95	112	116	96
Financial services and business activities	104	104	99	107	112	95
Public services	107	108	100	117	113	103

NB: CLUP = cost of labour per unit of product, i.e. unit labour cost.
Source: Eurostat.

Figure 3.3.3. Unit labour cost in 1999, value growth index (1995 = 100)

Agriculture

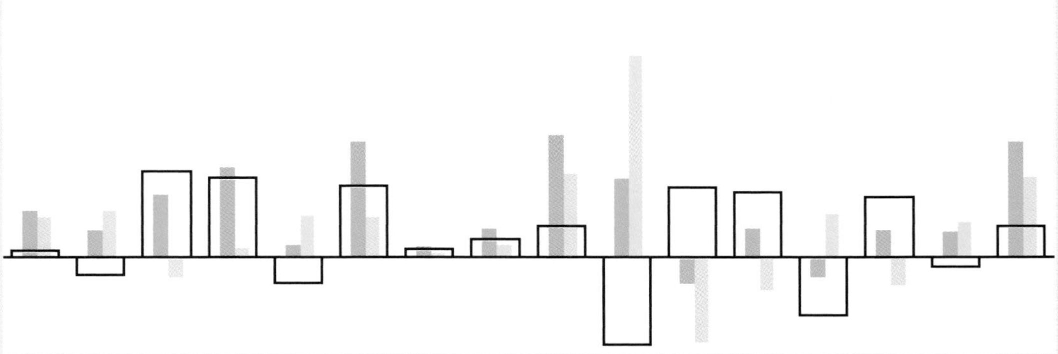

	EU-15	EUR-11	B	DK	D	EL	E	F	IRL	I	L	NL	A	P	FIN	S
Remuneration	109	106	113	118	103	123	102	106	125	116	95	106	96	106	105	123
Productivity	108	109	96	102	108	108	101	102	117	141	83	93	109	94	107	116
CLUP	101	96	117	116	95	114	101	103	106	82	114	113	88	112	98	106

Manufacturing

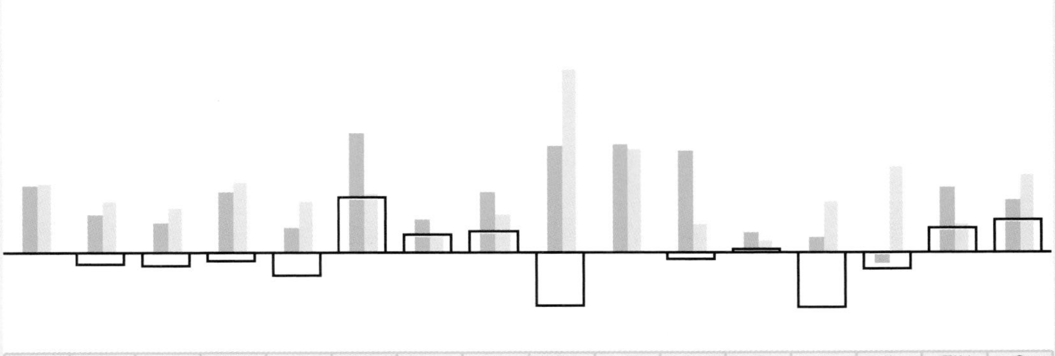

	EU-15	EUR-11	B	DK	D	EL	E	F	IRL	I	L	NL	A	P	FIN	S
Remuneration	114	108	106	112	105	124	107	112	122	122	121	104	103	98	113	111
Productivity	114	110	109	114	110	112	103	108	137	121	106	102	110	117	106	116
CLUP	100	98	97	98	95	111	103	104	89	100	98	101	89	97	105	106

Construction

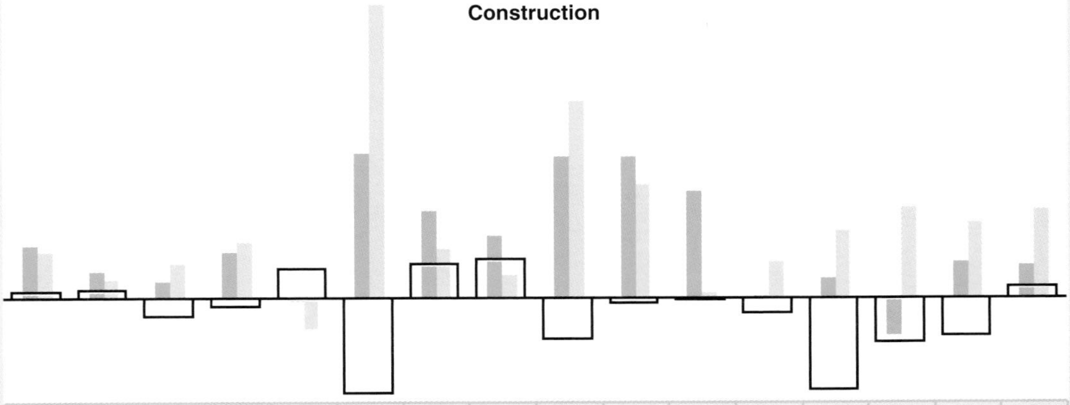

	EU-15	EUR-11	B	DK	D	EL	E	F	IRL	I	L	NL	A	P	FIN	S
Remuneration	111	105	103	109	100	128	117	112	128	128	121	101	104	93	107	107
Productivity	109	104	107	111	94	157	110	105	139	122	101	107	113	118	115	117
CLUP	101	102	97	98	106	81	107	107	92	99	100	97	82	91	93	102

Trade, transport and communication

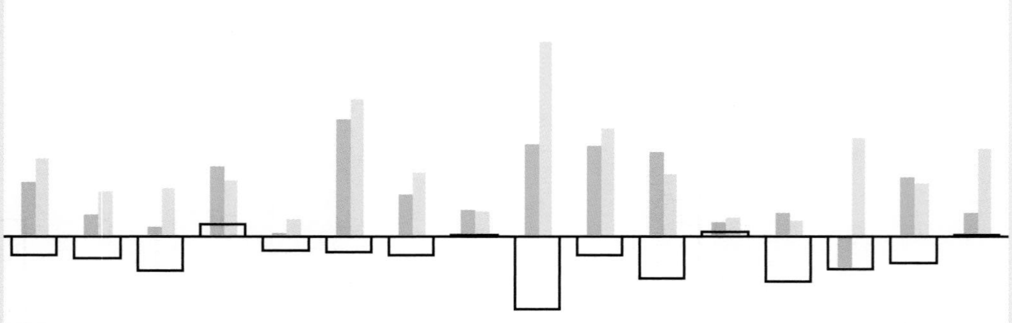

	EU-15	EUR-11	B	DK	D	EL	E	F	IRL	I	L	NL	A	P	FIN	S
Remuneration	111	104	102	115	101	124	109	105	119	119	118	103	105	93	112	105
Productivity	116	109	110	112	104	129	113	105	141	122	113	104	103	121	111	118
CLUP	96	95	93	103	97	97	96	100	85	96	91	101	90	93	94	100

Financial services and business activities

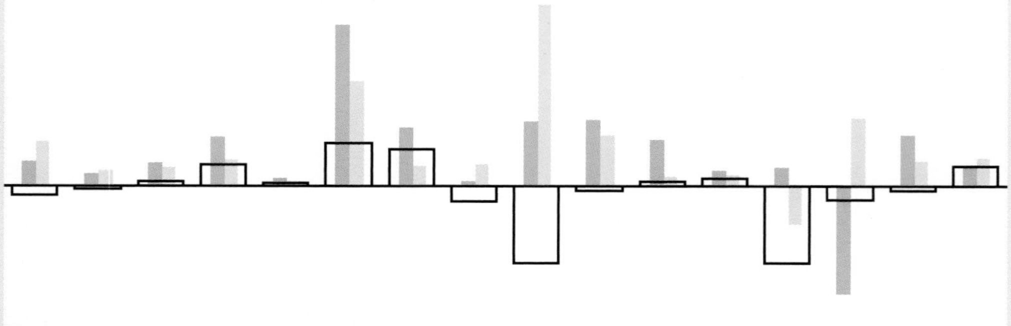

	EU-15	EUR-11	B	DK	D	EL	E	F	IRL	I	L	NL	A	P	FIN	S
Remuneration	107	104	107	114	102	144	116	102	118	118	113	104	105	71	114	106
Productivity	112	104	105	107	101	129	105	106	149	114	103	103	90	118	107	108
CLUP	98	99	101	106	101	112	110	96	79	99	102	102	79	96	99	105

Public services

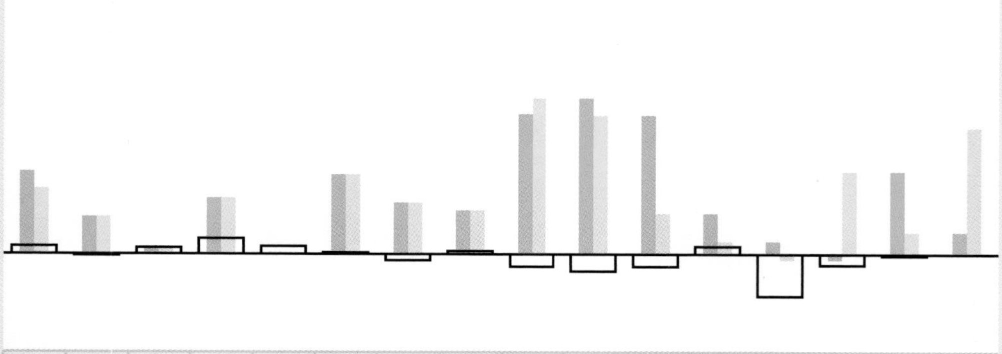

	EU-15	EUR-11	B	DK	D	EL	E	F	IRL	I	L	NL	A	P	FIN	S
Remuneration	117	108	101	111	100	116	110	109	128	132	128	108	103	99	117	104
Productivity	113	108	101	111	100	116	110	109	132	128	108	103	99	117	104	126
CLUP	102	100	101	103	102	100	99	101	97	97	98	101	92	98	100	100

NB: CLUP = cost of labour per unit of product, i.e. unit labour cost. No data available by branch for the United Kingdom.
Source: Eurostat.

4. PRIVATE HOUSEHOLDS IN THE UNION

4.1. The European consumer

The consumption habits of the European consumers vary substantially among the 15 Member States of the Union. Factors such as culture, traditions and degree of urbanisation influence the habits in every country. The family situation plays an important role for the consumption of the individual household.

Figure 4.1.1. Total consumer expenditure per adult equivalent in 1994

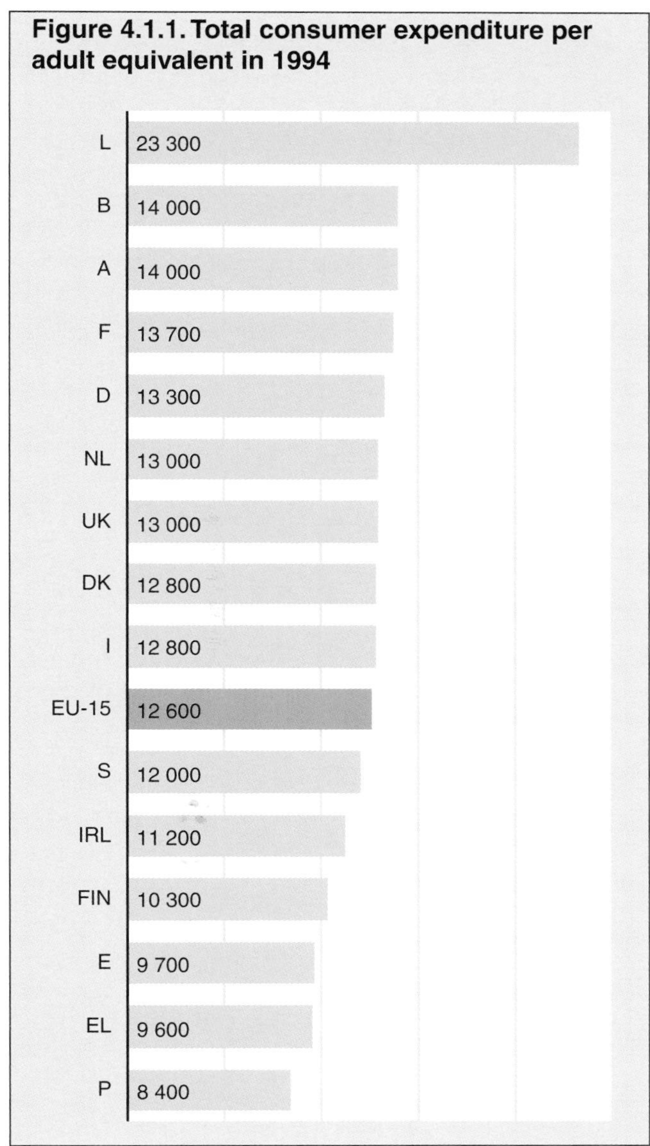

Source: Eurostat.

Around 144 000 households from the 15 Member States were surveyed in 1994 ([27]) on their consumption expenditure and income: the results are now available in Community format and allow to compare standards of living across Europe.

The national standards of living can be measured in terms of total consumption expenditure. Figure 4.1.1 shows that a large number of countries spent around 13 000 PPS per adult equivalent ([28]) in 1994. They are mainly located in the centre of the European Union. For those at the 'periphery' (Portugal, Greece, Spain, Finland, Ireland and Sweden), total consumption expenditure per adult equivalent varied between 8 400 and 11 900 PPS. These results are presented in 'purchasing power standards per adult equivalent' to take into account the differences in purchasing power and size of household between the countries.

Concept of expenditure

The categories of consumption used here correspond to the Coicop — 'HBS' (classification of individual consumption by purpose — household budget survey). In addition to households' traditional expenditure (purchases in shops, payment of invoices, etc.) 'consumption' in household budget survey includes the own production of households and benefits in kind received. Notional rents are also imputed to owner–occupiers and households accommodated free of charge. Eurostat has done this imputation for Ireland, France and the United Kingdom only using Eurostat information.

This definition of expenditure is close to that of the national accounts but any comparisons with final household consumption data from national accounts should take into account that:

- household budget surveys cover only national 'private households' excluding institutional households (hospital, etc.) and foreign tourist consumption;
- household budget surveys collect individual data from a representative sample through individual questionnaires. National accounts may use other statistical sources (retail sales for instance) to build the final consumption aggregates;
- country specific systems affect the comparability of data regarding the items of consumption such as 'health' and 'education'.

([27]) Eurostat experience year. For the individual countries the survey year may differ, see the household budget surveys in box.

([28]) To take account of economies of scale, an equivalence scale is applied to adjust consumption expenditure for the varying size and composition of households. A coefficient of 1 is attributed to the first adult, 0.5 to other persons over 13 years of age and 0.3 to children aged 13 years or under (OECD modified scale).

The average European household spent 3 960 PPS ([29]) of their total budget, 18.9 % of 20 915 PPS, on food and beverages (including own production but excluding catering) in 1994. The average amount spent on recreation, culture, hotels and restaurants was 3 300 PPS, which is 15.8 % of the budget, and the amount on transport and communication was almost as great. The average expenditures for housing and other services including health, education, insurance and financial services, etc. are more difficult to estimate across the EU, since the conditions are so different in the countries.

The largest expenditure item in the EU was housing ([30]) which accounted for nearly a quarter of all household expenditure in 1994 (Figure 4.1.2). The second largest expenditure item in 1994 was food ([31]). The share of the budget devoted to food was 18.9 %. Expenditure on recreation, culture and hotels/restaurants came third with around 16 % of the budgets. In the EU, 6.4 % of the budgets were spent in hotels, restaurants and cafes, 9.4 % on recreation and culture.

Figure 4.1.2. Structure of the total consumer expenditure in EU-15, 1994 (as a %)

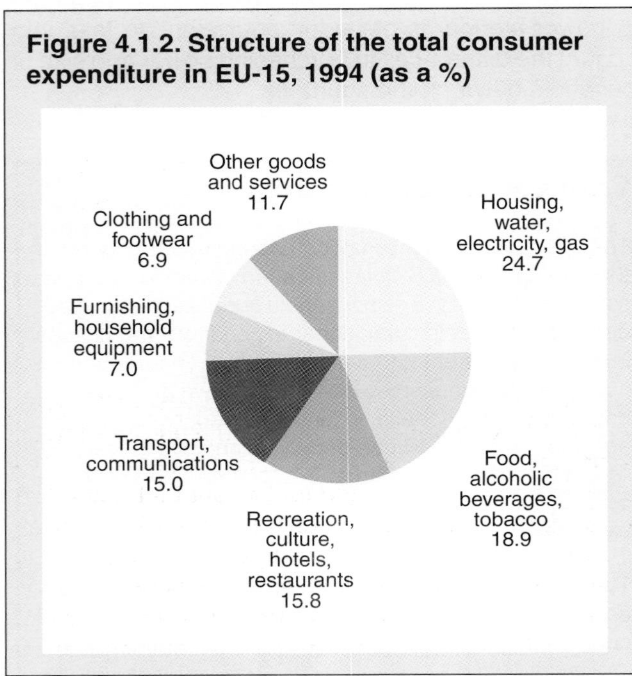

Source: Eurostat.

Recreation and culture includes ([32]):

- services such as package holidays, museum, cinema, concert, hire of videocassettes and sport facilities (3.6 % of the EU total average expenditure);
- video, musical and sport equipment and accessories (4 % in the EU);
- books, newspapers and stationery (1.9 % in the EU).

Transport and communication represented almost the same share as recreation, culture and hotels/restaurants, with 15 % of the average household expenditure. The expenditure on transport includes:

- purchase of vehicles (5.1 % in the EU, from 3 % in Italy to 7.8 % in Luxembourg and 8.3 % in Austria);
- equipment, fuels, maintenance and repair of vehicles (6.5 % in the EU, from 4.6 % in Greece and the Netherlands to 9.3 % in Italy);
- purchase of transport services (passenger transport by railway, road, air or sea excluding package holidays) accounted for 1.5 % of the budgets. Countries spending proportionally more on transport services are Denmark, France and the United Kingdom (1.9 %).

The expenditure on communications (postal services, telephone equipment and services) represented about 2 % for all countries.

([29]) See Section 7.4 for the definition of purchasing power standards (PPS).

([30]) Housing includes water, electricity, fuels, rent paid by tenants as well as imputed rents of owner–occupiers and households accomodated free of charge.

([31]) Food includes beverages and tobacco.

([32]) Austria has not done this subdivision.

Table 4.1.1. Consumption expenditure by item in 1994 (as a %)

	Housing, water, electricity, gas	Food, alcoholic beverages, tobacco	Recreation, culture, hotels, restaurants	Transport, communication	Furnishings, household equipment	Clothing and footwear	Other goods and services
EU-15	**24.7**	**18.9**	**15.8**	**15.0**	**7.0**	**6.9**	**11.7**
B	29.0	14.0	16.7	12.7	6.7	6.2	14.7
DK	27.9	17.8	14.1	17.5	6.3	5.7	10.7
D	24.8	16.0	17.0	16.5	6.8	7.3	11.7
EL	24.0	21.2	9.0	10.9	6.7	12.9	15.3
E	23.5	25.3	15.3	13.0	6.2	8.0	8.7
F	23.2	18.9	14.5	16.5	7.6	5.6	13.8
IRL	21.6	26.3	13.5	15.2	4.8	6.5	12.2
I	24.1	23.5	13.0	15.0	6.2	7.3	10.9
L	27.4	14.5	15.7	15.2	9.3	8.5	9.4
NL	27.2	14.4	15.5	11.2	7.1	6.0	18.7
A	21.6	18.1	13.0	18.8	10.6	8.8	9.2
P	19.9	24.1	12.9	17.7	6.7	6.3	12.4
FIN	27.2	19.1	15.7	15.6	4.6	4.6	13.3
S	26.0	21.0	16.0	15.1	5.3	6.1	10.5
UK	25.9	17.0	19.9	13.6	7.9	6.3	9.5

Source: Eurostat.

The largest expenditure items: housing and food

Housing: one fourth of the budgets

As noted, housing is the largest expenditure item, and in 1994 it accounted for 24.7 % of the average household expenditure. Housing includes actual rents for tenants (tenants are the households that pay full rent) and imputed rents for owner–occupiers and households with rent free or reduced rent.

In order to compare consumption on housing between tenants and owner–occupiers, expenditure was imputed for owner–occupiers. This is a calculated value that in theory should correspond to the rent that should be paid for a similar housing rented on the market. The imputed rent accounts for more than two thirds of the housing expenditure for the owner–occupiers and the actual rents accounted for around the same share for tenants. Regular maintenance is slightly higher for owner–occupiers while electricity, gas and other fuels is slightly higher for tenants. Housing expenditure is difficult to compare between countries since the type of

Table 4.1.2. Housing expenditure in the EU, 1994 (as a %)

Housing components	Owner–occupiers	Tenants	Total households
Actual rentals for housing	1.7	68.2	22.5
Imputed rentals for housing	65.0	1.8	45.7
Regular maintenance and repair of dwelling	7.7	4.4	6.5
Other services relating to the dwelling	6.5	6.1	6.3
Electricity, gas and other fuels	19.1	19.4	19.1
Total	*100.0*	*100.0*	*100.0*

Source: Eurostat.

'ownership' varies considerably across the EU. In Spain, Greece and Ireland about four out of five dwellings are owned while in the Netherlands and in Austria this share is less than 50 %.

Food, beverages and restaurants

For the item food, beverages and restaurants, in 1994, European households spent 4 765 PPS (or 22.4 % of the budget) on food and beverages whether consumed at home, in a restaurant, a cafe or a canteen (see Figure 4.1.3). In Luxembourg, households consumed 6 954 PPS on food, being the highest amount in Europe. However, food expenditures made up only 18 % of the budget in this country. With more than 6 000 PPS, households in Spain, Ireland and Italy also spent relatively much on food but at a much higher share of the budget than in Luxembourg (more than a quarter). The high number of persons per household in these countries should be noted. In the Netherlands, household expenditure on food was the lowest in Europe, not only in PPS (3 480 PPS), but also in terms of the budget (17.1 %).

Table 4.1.3. Expenditure on food, 1994

	Number of persons per household	Expenditure on food, beverages and catering per household	
		PPS per head	Share on total expenditure (%)
EU-15	**2.5**	**4 765**	**22.4**
B	2.5	4 245	18.7
DK	2.1	3 577	18.6
D	2.3	4 023	19.5
EL	2.9	4 176	23.6
E	3.3	6 213	31.7
F	2.5	4 846	21.7
IRL	3.3	6 180	27.8
I	2.8	6 052	26.5
L	2.6	6 954	18.0
NL	2.3	3 480	17.1
A	2.7	5 209	21.5
P	3.0	5 141	31.5
FIN	2.2	3 559	25.7
S	2.2	4 124	22.9
UK	2.4	4 645	20.1

Source: Eurostat.

Table 4.1.4. Expenditure on food by items in the EU, 1994 (as a % of total food expenditure)

	Bread and cereals	Meat	Fish	Milk, cheese and eggs	Oils and fats	Fruit	Vegetables	Sugar, jam, honey	Other food products
EU-15	18.1	27.3	6.3	15.0	4.1	8.0	10.9	6.2	4.0
B	14.5	21.3	8.6	15.6	3.9	9.2	12.8	9.2	5.0
DK	17.7	27.3	4.3	15.4	3.5	6.2	9.8	13.3	2.6
D	18.3	26.8	4.3	13.4	4.5	8.6	10.2	8.9	5.0
EL	12.5	29.0	7.4	21.3	9.3	9.1	8.3	3.1	0.0
E	14.8	29.8	13.1	14.0	4.8	8.8	9.4	3.6	1.6
F	18.6	29.6	6.4	14.6	2.6	7.4	11.8	5.1	4.1
IRL	14.2	30.0	2.6	17.2	3.9	5.1	12.4	9.3	5.3
I	21.4	28.2	7.7	16.0	5.8	8.2	8.6	4.0	0.0
L	16.0	33.8	4.4	14.0	3.7	7.4	8.2	6.5	5.9
NL	18.6	24.3	2.3	18.0	2.9	8.7	11.8	7.3	6.1
A	:	:	:	:	:	:	:	:	:
P	15.6	30.2	15.8	12.1	5.8	7.6	9.8	2.6	0.5
FIN	16.8	24.5	4.1	19.4	3.6	6.9	9.1	9.3	6.2
S	:	:	:	:	:	:	:	:	:
UK	18.2	25.4	4.4	15.7	2.7	7.0	14.2	5.3	7.1

NB: Vegetables including potatoes and other tubers; sugar, jam, honey, syrup, chocolate and confectionery.
Source: Eurostat.

Figure 4.1.3. Expenditure on catering in 1994 (as a % of total food, beverages and catering)

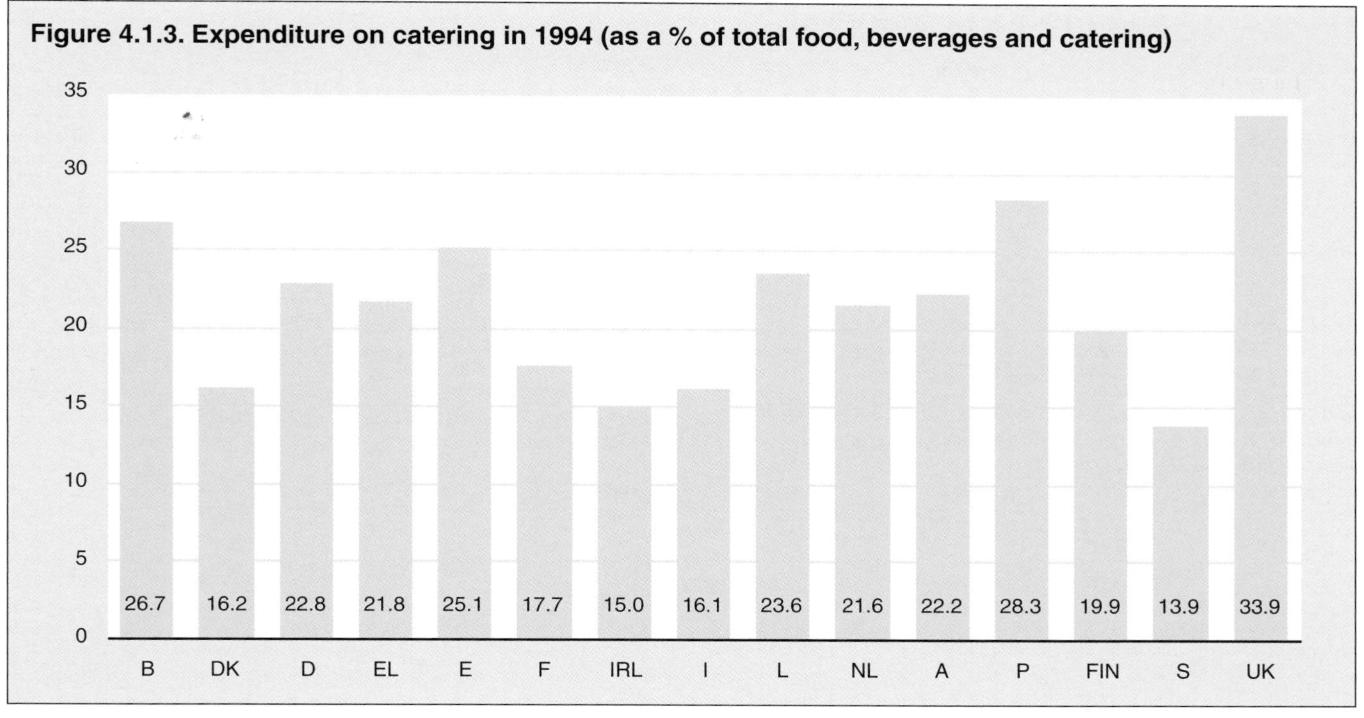

NB: Catering includes restaurants, cafes and canteens.
Source: Eurostat.

Within Europe, households in Belgium, the United Kingdom and Portugal spent the largest share of food in restaurants, cafes or canteens (more than a quarter) in 1994 (see Figure 4.1.3). Households in these countries also belonged to the highest spenders on food in PPS 'outside home'. In Greece, Finland, France and Italy, around 85 % of this type of expenditures were spent 'at home'. High-income households devoted a much higher share of food expenditures 'outside home' (30 %) than the least well-off households (12 %).

Food consumed at home (including own production) has been subdivided into food categories by all countries except Sweden and Austria. Expenditure on meat was the largest among all food items in Europe (27.3 %), followed by 'bread and cereals' and 'milk, cheese and eggs' with 18.1 % and 15.0 %. With 33.8 % of the food budget spent on meat, households in Luxembourg were highest in Europe. Belgium was lowest with 21.3 %. In Italy the 'bread and cereals' share ranked highest compared with other countries and in Ireland the lowest with 14.2 %.

Different households ... different patterns

Consumption by type of household

Each household is classified into one of the following four types of households:

1. Retired household/one person or couple aged 65 years or more;
2. Household without children/one person or couple (less than 65 years) without children;
3. Household with children/couple or single parent (less than 65 years) with children;
4. Other household.

There are notable differences in the structure of consumption expenditure between different types of households. For instance, housing is a larger part (32 %) for retired households than for other types of households. To a certain extent this depends on the imputation of rents for owner–occupiers. Recreation, culture, hotels/restaurants is a comparatively smaller item for retired households. Transport and communication is a small part for retired households (10 %), while for other types of households is a large part (15 %).

Figure 4.1.4. Household consumption expenditure by item and type of household, 1994 (as a % of total consumption)

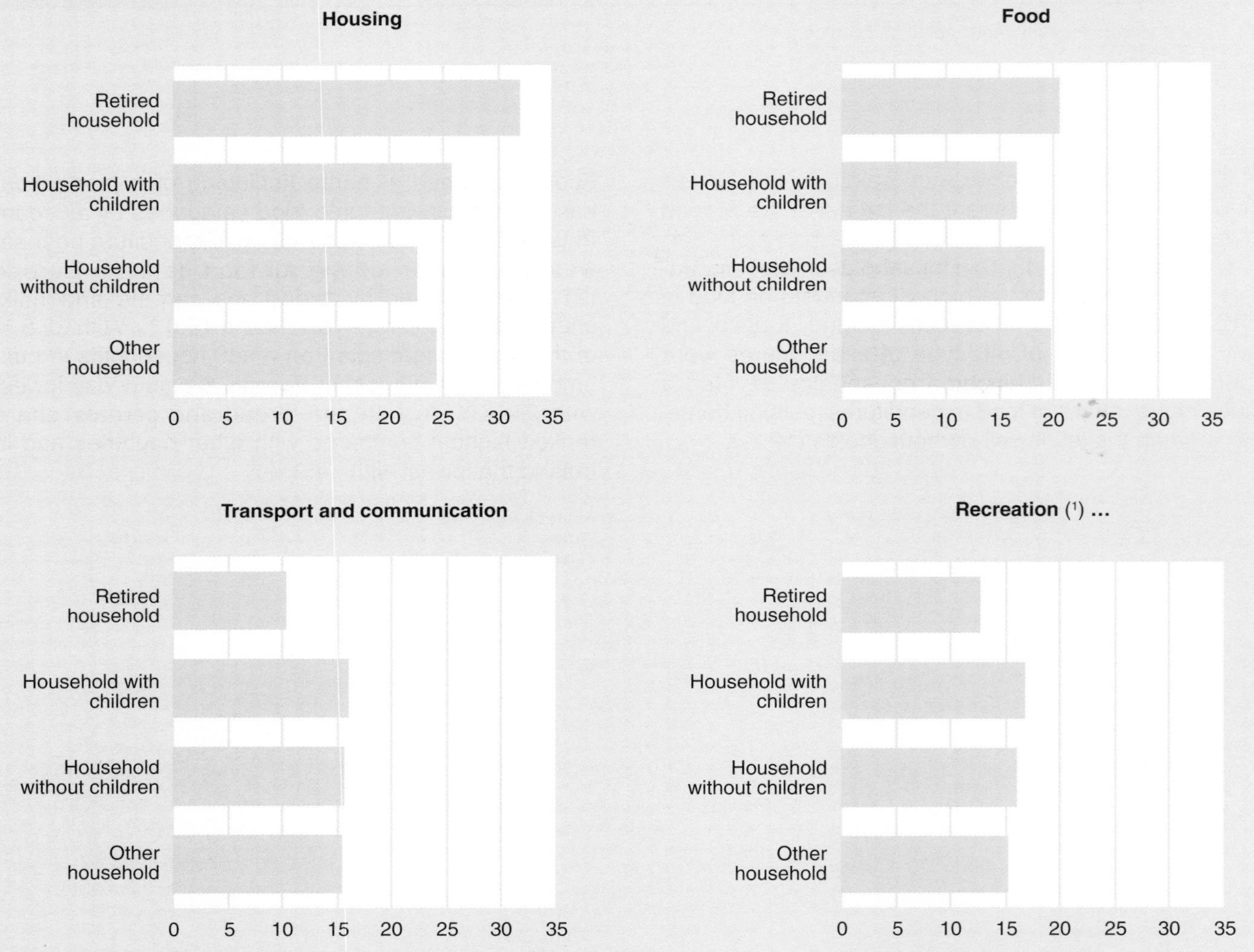

Housing

Retired household
Household with children
Household without children
Other household

0 5 10 15 20 25 30 35

Food

Retired household
Household with children
Household without children
Other household

0 5 10 15 20 25 30 35

Transport and communication

Retired household
Household with children
Household without children
Other household

0 5 10 15 20 25 30 35

Recreation (1) ...

Retired household
Household with children
Household without children
Other household

0 5 10 15 20 25 30 35

(1) Recreation, culture, hotels and restaurants.
Source: Eurostat.

Consumption by socioeconomic category

The structure of expenditure is somewhat different between households in different socioeconomic categories:

- manual worker;
- non-manual worker;
- self-employed (33);
- unemployed;
- retired;
- other inactive households.

Housing is a substantially smaller part of the expenditure for households headed by manual and non-manual workers and the self-employed compared to the unemployed, retired and other inactive households. The smallest part for food is spent by non-manual worker households while the unemployed and the other inactive households spent relatively more. For the category transport and communication and the category recreation, culture, hotels/restaurants, the spending patterns are very similar for the five socioeconomic groups.

Figure 4.1.5. Household consumption expenditure by item and socioeconomic category, 1994 (as a % of total consumption)

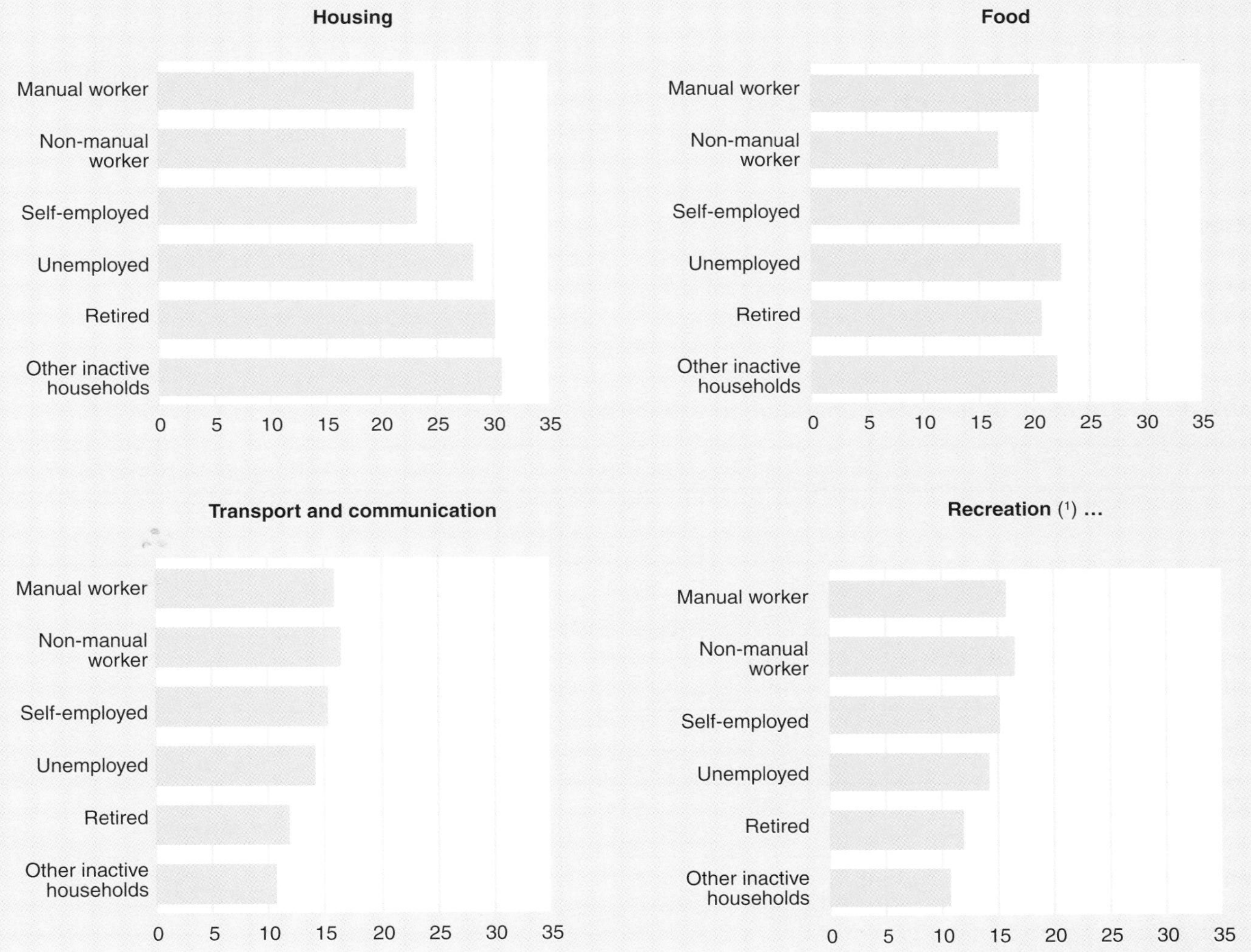

(1) Recreation, culture, hotels and restaurants.
Source: Eurostat.

(33) The category self-employed includes the self-employed, farmers and agricultural workers. For some expenditure items, for example for food, this is a heterogeneous group.

4.2. Consumption trend

For nine EU countries, Belgium, Germany, Greece, Spain, Italy, Luxembourg, the Netherlands, Portugal and Finland, data on 1988 consumption are available; in the following paragraph it has therefore been possible to carry out a comparison of private households' consumption by goods and services categories and expenditure classes in 1988 and 1994. For the other six countries, comparable data are not yet available for both years.

In the period 1988–94, the average final household consumption in the nine EU countries ([34]) increased on average almost 2 % a year. The yearly pattern is marked by steadily decreasing growth rates between 1988 and 1992, with even a fall back in the level of consumption in 1993. In 1994, household consumption increased again.

A glance over time: changes in consumption structure

Stronger importance of housing

Housing accounted for 25.3 % of the household expenditure in 1994. The corresponding share in 1988 was 20.6 %. The share devoted to food decreased on average 3.2 points from 22.9 % in 1988 to 19.7 % in 1994 (see Table 4.2.1). The gap between housing and food increased in all considered countries. In Belgium for instance, housing and food accounted for 29.0 % and 14.0 % of the budgets in 1994. In 1988, it was 23.9 % and 18.5 %. Not in each country, expenditure on housing was higher than on food in 1994: Spain and Portugal still had larger shares on food.

Expenditure on recreation and hotels/restaurants remained third with around 15.2 % of the budgets of the nine countries as a whole. By country, the difference between 1988 and 1994 was about +/– 1.5 points except in Greece (– 3.2 points) and Luxembourg (+ 4.2 points).

Transport and communication had about the same share as recreation, hotels/restaurants, 15.2 % on average. It had increased by 1.4 points since 1988. The increase was larger in Germany (+ 3.1 points), Luxembourg (+ 2.4 points) and Portugal (+ 1.8 points). Only Italy and Finland noted decreases, – 0.4 and – 2.3 points respectively.

Expenditure on clothing and footwear decreased by about 2 points in Spain, Italy and Portugal as well as in the Netherlands and Finland. In the other four countries, the share did not change significantly.

Table 4.2.1. Structure of the total consumption expenditure in nine countries, 1988 and 1994 (as a %)

	Year	EU-9	Lowest		Highest	
Housing, water, electricity, gas	**1988**	20.6	12.2	P	24.3	L
	1994	25.3	19.9	P	29.0	B
Food, alcoholic beverages, tobacco	**1988**	22.9	15.7	NL	33.3	P
	1994	19.7	14.0	B	25.3	E
Recreation, culture, hotels, restaurants	**1988**	14.9	11.5	L	16.9	NL
	1994	15.2	9.0	EL	17.1	D
Transport, communication	**1988**	13.8	10.2	EL	17.7	FIN
	1994	15.2	10.9	EL	17.7	P
Clothing and footwear	**1988**	8.5	6.0	FIN	12.6	EL
	1994	7.6	4.6	FIN	12.9	EL
Furnishings, household equipment	**1988**	7.2	5.5	FIN	8.2	L
	1994	6.6	4.6	FIN	9.3	L
Other goods and services	**1988**	12.2	8.3	I	21.2	NL
	1994	10.3	7.6	D	18.7	NL

NB: Provisional 1994 data for Finland and Germany.
Source: Eurostat.

([34]) Weighted average for nine countries.

4.3. Elderly consumption

In the 50-year period 1960–2010, the 65-plus proportion in the European Union is projected to increase from 11 to 18 %. When referring to elderly household's the reference person is aged 65 and over.

Elderly households consume much less than younger counterparts

EU-wide, an elderly household's consumption expenditure is about 11 000 PPS per adult equivalent. This figure is about 15 % lower than for the 'younger' households. Compared to households with a reference person aged 45–64 years, the difference is almost 20 %; the gap is particularly wide in Portugal (34 %) and the United Kingdom, Finland, Ireland, Greece and Denmark (around 25 %). In Belgium, the elderly households almost have the same level of expenditures as the 45–64 years counterparts (see Table 4.3.1).

Table 4.3.1. Consumer expenditure of households by age of the reference person per adult equivalent, 1994 (PPS)

	Age of reference person			
	18–44 years	45–64 years	≥ 65 years	Total
EU-15	12 700	13 700	11 100	12 600
P	9 900	9 200	6 100	8 400
EL	10 800	9 900	7 500	9 600
E	10 500	10 000	8 400	9 700
FIN	10 500	11 200	8 400	10 300
IRL	11 700	12 100	9 100	11 200
UK	12 900	14 200	10 300	12 700
I	13 500	13 200	10 700	12 800
S	11 600	13 300	10 800	12 000
DK	12 600	14 300	11 000	12 800
NL	12 900	14 300	11 700	13 000
D	12 800	14 700	12 300	13 300
F	13 400	15 100	12 600	13 700
A	13 900	14 800	12 800	14 000
B	13 900	14 400	13 800	14 000
L	23 400	24 000	21 300	23 300

NB: The order of the countries in the table is based on the level of expenditures of the elderly households (orange column). This order is kept in all the tables of the report.
Source: Eurostat, HBS.

Consumption expenditure

It is important to note that household consumption expenditures on goods and services are looked upon from the perspective of (material) welfare in this report, i.e. used for the direct satisfaction of needs and wants of the household. This means that non-monetary consumption of, for instance, own-produced crops, a company car, or a self-owned dwelling are included and have been given a monetary imputed value. As a result, welfare conditions between different groups of people can be compared properly (for instance between owner–occupiers and tenants).

Housing, food and transport heading the expenditure list

EU-wide, nearly one third of elderly household's consumption is taken up by housing; for the younger households, it is just a quarter of the budget (see Figure 4.3.1). There are significant differences between the Member States. The elderly households in Portugal use only somewhat less than 25 % of their budget on housing, whereas the percentage in Denmark is almost 40. The majority of elderly households rent their accommodation in Denmark.

Consumption expenditures on food are in second place with almost a fifth of the budget. The figure for retired households is marginally higher than for the younger counterparts. Elderly households in Belgium, Denmark, Germany, Luxembourg and the Netherlands consume relatively less of their budget on food (around 14 %).

Transport expenditures take nearly one tenth of the budget of the elderly households. For the younger households it is higher (almost 15 %). Between the Member States, proportions of transport expenditures hardly differ.

Figure 4.3.1. Consumer expenditure of households in the EU by item and age of the reference person, 1994 (as a %)

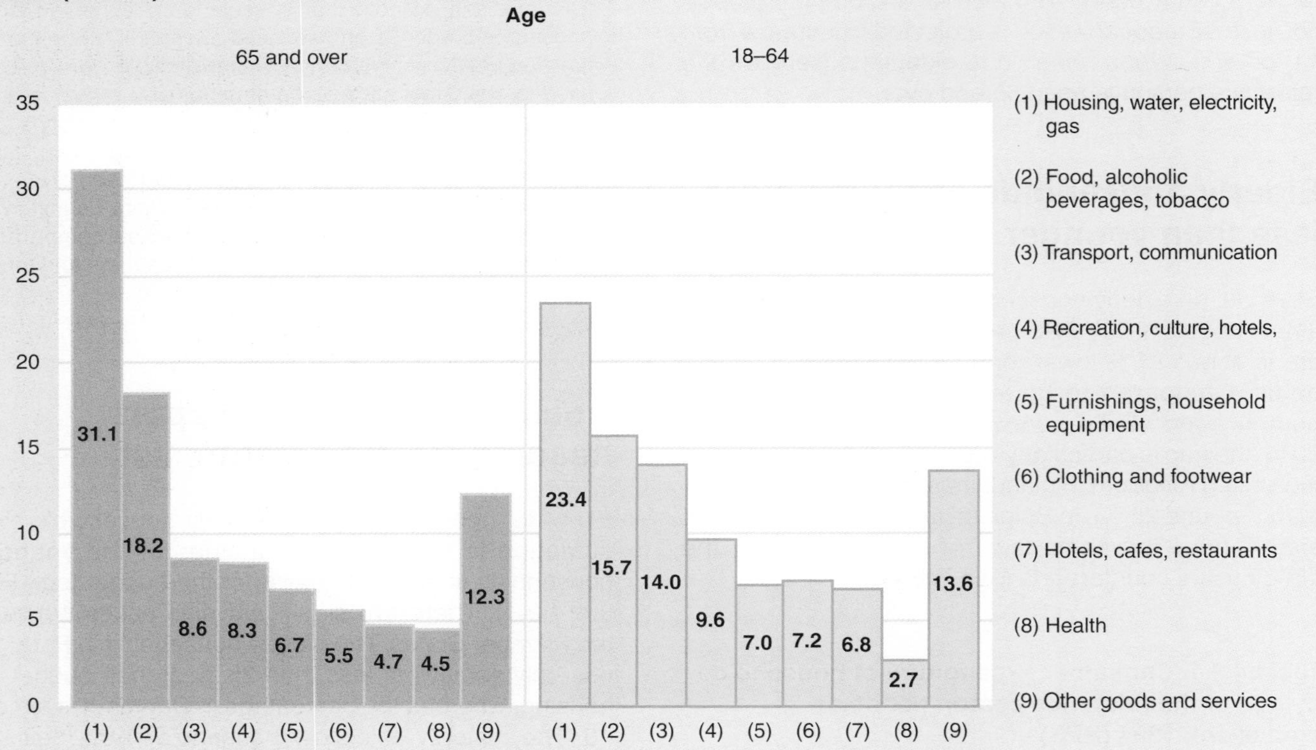

Item	65 and over	18–64
(1) Housing, water, electricity, gas	31.1	23.4
(2) Food, alcoholic beverages, tobacco	18.2	15.7
(3) Transport, communication	8.6	14.0
(4) Recreation, culture, hotels,	8.3	9.6
(5) Furnishings, household equipment	6.7	7.0
(6) Clothing and footwear	5.5	7.2
(7) Hotels, cafes, restaurants	4.7	6.8
(8) Health	4.5	2.7
(9) Other goods and services	12.3	13.6

Source: Eurostat, HBS.

The household budget surveys

This section draws data from the household budget surveys (HBS). The household budget surveys are conducted in all the Member States of the European Union. They can be used to estimate some items of the final consumption of households for the national accounts but their objective is not strictly an accounting one.

The household budget surveys collect microdata on the expenditure, income and socioeconomic characteristics of private households. They use a detailed product classification (derived, as in the case of the national accounts, from the 'Coicop' — classification of individual consumption by purpose). In addition they are used:

- to fix the weightings used to calculate the consumer price index;
- to make socioeconomic analyses of the living conditions of households (patterns of consumption, poverty, etc.).

The data of the household budget surveys are collected by each Member State and harmonised by Eurostat as part of a process to convert national data files to the Community format. Unfortunately, the survey years do not always coincide with the reference year fixed by Eurostat. When this is the case, the data are deflated using the general consumer price index. The size of the samples varies substantially according to various factors, which include budget constraints and the desired accuracy of the estimate.

Survey years and size of samples

	Collection year	Size of sample	Total household population (1 000)(1)
EU-15	—	144 187	145 634
B	1995–96	2 724	4 044
DK	1993–95	2 936	2 274
D	1993	40 009	36 309
EL	1993–94	6 756	3 709
E	1994	2 876	12 007
F	1994–95	9 634	22 807
IRL	1994	7 877	1 127
I	1994	33 928	20 411
L	1993	3 012	152
NL	1994	2 050	6 421
A	1993–94	6 604	3 013
P	1994–95	10 554	3 243
FIN	1994–95	4 493	2 037
S	1992	3 806	3 830
UK	1994	6 928	24 250

(1) Labour force survey, 1994. European census programme, 1990–91.
Source: Eurostat.

5. GENERAL GOVERNMENT IN THE UNION

This section sets out to provide an overview of the size and structure of the public sector in the various Member States (see box entitled 'Definition of general government'). After outlining the importance of general government in national economies with the help of the major aggregates in the national accounts, it will first consider the expenditure and revenue of general government and then the difference between the two that amounts to public deficit which has to be covered by borrowing, which in turn makes up public debt.

Definition of general government

According to the 'European system of national and regional accounts in the Community' (ESA 95), the general government sector includes 'all institutional units which are other non-market producers whose output is intended for individual and collective consumption, and mainly financed by compulsory payments made by units belonging to other sectors, and/or all institutional units principally engaged in the redistribution of national income and wealth'. General government is divided into four subsectors: central government, State government, local government and social security funds.

5.1. Major aggregates of general government

In the Union and in the euro zone, general government output accounts for slightly more than a fifth of GDP (see Table 5.1.1). If intermediate consumption — 8.5 % of GDP in the Union, on average — is disregarded, the gross value added of the sector amounted to 12.4 % of GDP in the Union, and 12.7 % in the euro zone, in 1998. It ranged in the Member States between 9.2 % and 19.8 %.

General government compensation of employees in the Union and the euro zone amounted to 10.5 % and 10.8 % of GDP respectively in 1998, with figures in individual Member States ranging from 7.5 % in the United Kingdom to 16.9 % in Sweden and 17.4 % in Denmark.

Table 5.1.1. Main aggregates of general government, 1998 (as a % of GDP)

	P1	P2	D1	P3	P51
	Productivity	Intermediate consumption	Compensation of employees	Final consumption expenditure	GFCF
EU-15	20.9	8.5	10.5	20.3	2.2
EUR-11	20.5	7.8	10.8	20.5	2.4
B	16.3	2.8	11.7	21.1	1.6
DK	27.6	7.8	17.4	25.7	1.7
D	21.2	11.2	8.4	19	1.8
EL	16.2	4.7	11.3	14.8	3.6
E	16.2	4	10.7	17.4	3.2
F	21.9	5.5	13.7	23.7	3
IRL	14.8	5	9	14.6	2.4
I	19.5	6.9	10.7	18	2.4
L	15.6	3.4	9.2	17.2	4.6
NL	18.9	6.2	10.2	23	2.8
A	23	10.6	11.3	19.8	1.9
P	21.4	4.8	14.4	19.7	4.2
FIN	25.8	9.3	14	21.7	2.9
S	30.6	10.9	16.9	26.4	2.6
UK	20.2	11	7.5	18.2	1.3

Source: Eurostat.

Final consumption expenditure of general government in the Member States ranged between 14.6 % (Ireland) and 26.4 % (Sweden) of GDP in 1998, the Community average being 20.3 %. As for gross fixed capital formation, it accounted for between 1.3 % (United Kingdom) and 4.6 % (Luxembourg) of GDP in 1998. The average for the Union as a whole was 2.2 %, and for the euro zone 2.4 %.

5.2. General government revenue and expenditure

On 10 July 2000, the European Commission adopted Regulation (EC) No 1500/2000 implementing Council Regulation (EC) No 2223/96 (the 'ESA 95 regulation') with respect to general government expenditure and revenue.

The culmination of the work of a task force that brought together Eurostat, the 15 Member States, the European Central Bank and the ECFIN Directorate-General, the regulation offers for the first time a common definition of total general government revenue and expenditure and provides one of the first components of a complete and consistent set of harmonised accounts relating to the public sector in Europe.

Since this report was written before all the required data had to be submitted by the Member States, comments on this year will be restricted to those aggregates that are available.

General government revenue

Taxes and social security contributions account for about 90 % of general government revenue in the Union. Other sources (property income, other current transfers, capital transfers) are of minor importance (see Figure 5.2.1). It is worth noting that the Union's own resources (agricultural levies, customs duties, VAT revenue) appear in the accounts according to the ESA as direct payments to the rest of the world and are not therefore included under either revenue or expenditure of general government.

Figure 5.2.1. Main categories of general government revenue, 1998 (as a % of total)

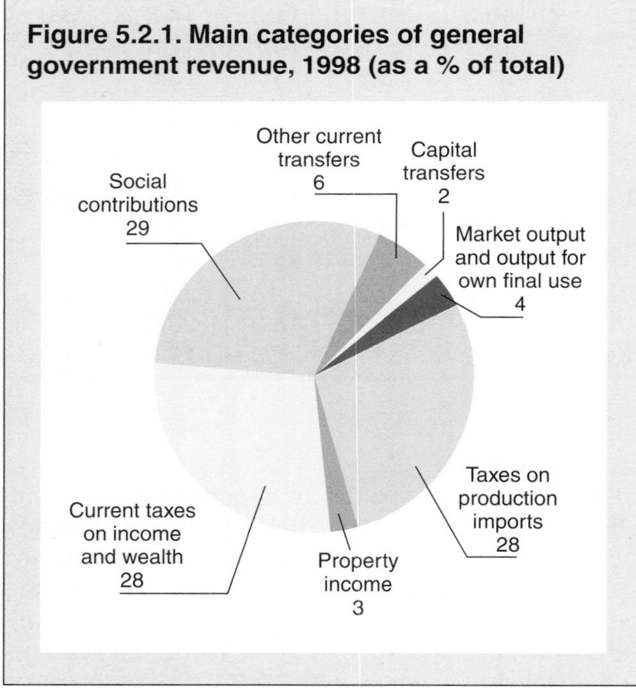

Source: Eurostat.

Total general government revenue varies between 35 % and 60 % of GDP, depending on the Member State. By way of comparison, the overall figure for government revenue in the United States and Japan varies between 33 % and 35 % of GDP.

Taxes and social security contributions are thus the main source of general government revenue in the Union.

Taxes on production and imports in the Union reached 13.4 % of GDP in 1998, with taxes on income and wealth accounting for 13.6 % (see Table 5.2.1). The figures for the euro zone were 13.1 % and 12.0 % respectively. The range for taxes on production and imports (from 11.1 % in Spain to 18.0 % in Denmark) was narrower than for taxes on income and wealth (from 8.5 % in Greece to 29.5 % in Denmark).

Table 5.2.1. Main categories of taxes and social contributions, 1998 (as a % of GDP)

	D2	D5	D91	D611	D612	
	T.P.I.	C.T.I.W.	C.T.	A.S.C.	I.S.C.	Total [1]
EU-15	13.4	13.6	0.3	13.8	1.2	42.3
EUR-11	13.1	12.0	0.3	16.1	1.3	42.8
B	12.9	17.6	0.4	14.5	2.1	47.5
DK	18.0	29.5	0.2	1.6	1.0	50.3
D	11.6	11.5	0.1	18.1	1.1	42.4
EL	14.6	8.5	0.4	10.9	2.0	36.4
E	11.1	10.3	0.4	12.3	0.9	35.0
F	16.1	11.6	0.5	16.5	1.8	46.5
IRL	13.4	13.8	0.2	4.3	1.5	33.2
I	15.3	14.4	0.4	12.5	0.4	43.0
L	13.4	17.0	0.1	10.6	1.0	42.1
NL	11.6	12.2	0.3	15.3	1.1	40.5
A	15.0	13.8	0.1	15.1	2.0	46.0
P	15.0	10.4	0.1	11.6	0.9	38.0
FIN	14.1	18.9	0.2	13.0	0.1	46.3
S	15.5	22.8	0.1	14.5	0.3	53.2
UK	13.6	16.4	0.2	7.0	0.7	37.9

(1) The rate of compulsory levies ('fiscal burden') cannot be calculated directly from the data in this table as internal consolidation would first be required.
Source: Eurostat.

Social security contributions accounted for a significant percentage of GDP in 1998: 13.8 % in the Union and 16.1 % in the euro zone. Here, too, there were big differences between Member States, since actual social contributions as a percentage of GDP ranged from 1.6 % in Denmark to 18.1 % in Germany.

Because of the recent changeover from ESA 79 to ESA 95, it is again hard this year to calculate the compulsory levy ratio (total taxes and social security contributions in relation to gross domestic product). On account of the discrepancies observed among the Member States with regard to the format of data and the length of series concerning GDP, taxes and social security contributions, together with the lack of any harmonised methodology incorporating the changes in concepts that came with ESA 95 (new classifications and definitions of taxes and social security contributions, recording on an accruals basis), it was felt that it would be better to forgo this traditional exercise so that there would be no risk of misinterpreting the results.

Functional taxation approach

In order to be able to compare countries, tax revenue is usually expressed as a percentage of GDP. It may also be expressed as a percentage of total deductions. However, there is a third indicator that proves particularly useful: the statistical tax ratio (see box entitled 'Implicit tax rates').

Table 5.2.2. Implicit tax rates

	1970	1975	1980	1985	1990	1991	1992	1993	1994	1995	1996	1997
Consumption	17.6	15.5	16.0	15.6	16.2	16.2	16.2	16.1	16.5	16.7	16.7	16.8
Labour employed	28.9	32.2	35.1	37.1	37.5	38.3	39.0	39.7	40.2	41.7	42.0	41.9
Other factors of production	26.2	34.7	36.6	32.3	31.5	31.9	32.2	32.2	30.3	29.4	30.5	31.1

Source: Eurostat/Taxations and Customs Union DG (provisional estimates).

Since 1970, tax on consumption (as measured by the implicit tax rate) has remained fairly stable, at around 16–17 % (see Table 5.2.2). Taxes on the other factors of production (capital, energy, etc.) rose until 1980 (36.6 % of GDP) but subsequently declined to settle at just over 30 % of GDP. Taxes on employed labour have steadily increased, however, with the implicit tax rate rising from less than 30 % in the early 1970s to 35 % at the beginning of the 1980s and edging over 40 % from the mid 1990s.

More and more tax on employed labour

Taxes on labour (non-wage labour costs) are defined as taxes and social contributions which in some way or other discriminate against the use of the labour factor in the official (visible) sector of the economy. More specifically, taxes on employed labour primarily include social security contributions payable by employers and employees as well as income tax, i.e. taxes which discourage an employee from working more or an unemployed person from accepting a job instead of receiving social benefits or moonlighting.

Table 5.2.3. Taxes on employed labour

	As a % of GDP					As a % of total taxes				
	1980	1985	1990	1995	1997	1980	1985	1990	1995	1997
EU-15	19.7	20.1	20.1	21.4	21.2	51.3	49.8	49.5	51.1	49.9
EUR-11	19.9	20.8	20.5	22.1	22.1	51.7	51.6	50.8	52.2	51.3
B	22.2	23.9	22.4	23.2	22.8	50.3	50.6	50.5	50.4	48.9
DK	21.3	23.8	24.1	25.0	24.6	46.8	48.4	49.4	48.8	47.6
D	21.4	22.1	20.9	24.0	23.2	51.4	53.2	52.9	56.0	55.5
EL	3.9	7.7	12.1	15.2	16.0	34.5	31.7	41.2	45.4	46.1
E	14.7	14.7	16.1	16.8	17.2	57.4	49.0	46.5	49.1	48.4
F	20.8	22.2	21.9	23.2	23.5	50.0	50.0	50.0	51.7	50.6
IRL	14.0	16.3	14.6	13.3	12.9	40.3	42.0	41.0	39.5	38.0
I	16.0	17.8	19.2	18.8	20.9	52.1	51.3	49.5	45.9	47.4
L	21.7	18.1	16.6	16.2	16.3	46.8	39.2	39.8	37.4	37.3
NL	26.7	26.5	25.8	25.0	23.9	58.1	58.3	57.1	55.4	52.2
A	19.0	19.9	19.3	22.1	22.3	46.4	46.4	46.7	51.2	49.7
P	9.4	10.6	12.6	14.5	15.4	36.7	36.1	39.0	40.8	41.4
FIN	21.4	23.8	26.5	27.2	26.6	58.1	58.3	58.4	58.8	56.6
S	33.2	31.5	35.8	31.9	34.7	67.6	63.0	64.1	63.7	63.9
UK	16.7	14.8	14.3	14.9	14.5	45.5	38.3	37.8	40.4	39.0

Source: Eurostat/Taxation and Customs Union DG (provisional estimates).

In 1998, taxes and social contributions in relation to employed labour accounted for a half (49.9 %) of all levies in the Union and just over a fifth (21.2 %) of GDP (see Table 5.2.3). While a greater tax burden on employed labour has been a fairly common feature of virtually every tax system in the Union over the last three decades, there have been some slight exceptions to the general pattern in the last 20 years.

Between 1980 et 1990 deductions increased as a percentage of GDP in 11 countries, but as a percentage of all levies in only eight. Between 1990 and 1997 there were 10 countries that were increasing taxation on employed labour. Of the four Member States — Luxembourg, Netherlands, United Kingdom and Germany — that had set out to reduce taxation on employed labour in the 1980s, only the first two have maintained the policy until now. When deductions are considered as a percentage of all levies, the lower figures recorded by eight Member States between 1990 and 1997 can be explained in the case of six of them by an increase in total levies, rather than by the emergence of any real trend.

It is possible to give a little more detail to the analysis by dividing deductions on employed labour between those borne by employers and those paid by employees. At the beginning of the 1970s the figure for both types of contributor was 7.3 % of GDP. Since 1973, employees have had to bear almost the full brunt of increased taxation on employed labour. The gap between employers and employees has steadily widened, with the result that the former now provide only two fifths of deductions while employees account for three fifths.

Figure 5.2.2. Taxes on employed labour (as a % of GDP)

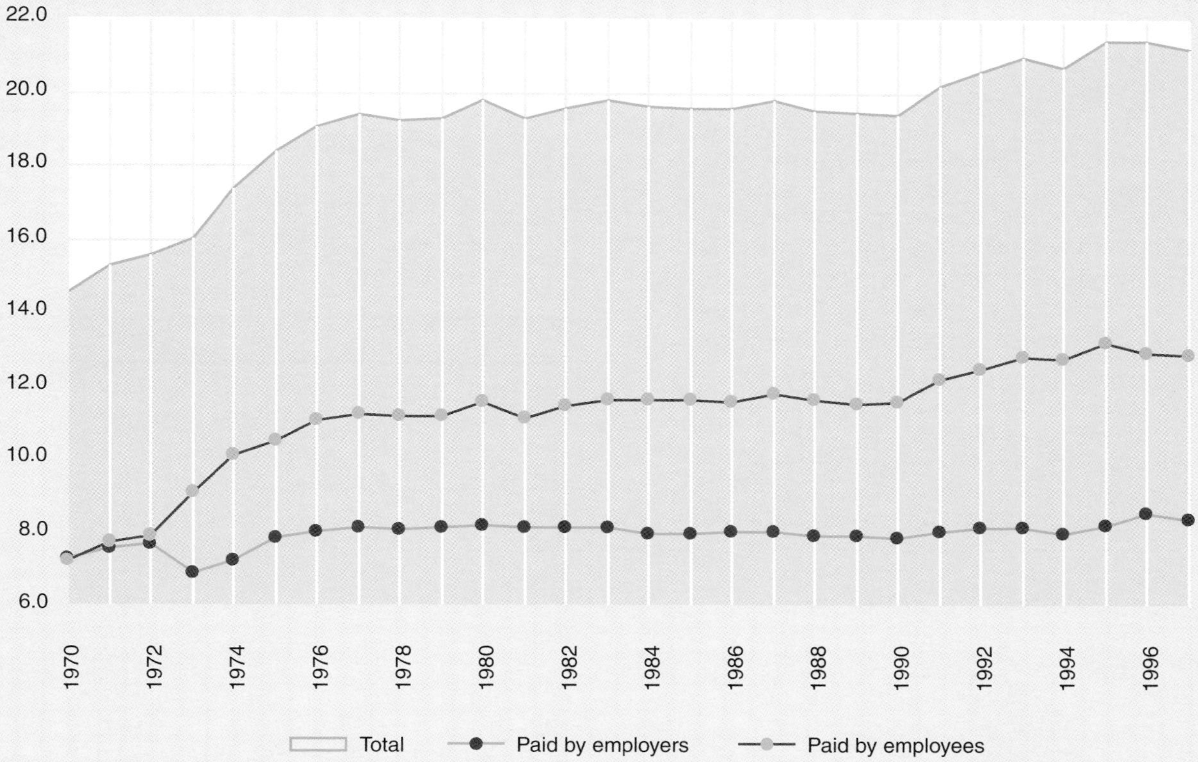

22.0
20.0
18.0
16.0
14.0
12.0
10.0
8.0
6.0

1970 1972 1974 1976 1978 1980 1982 1984 1986 1988 1990 1992 1994 1996

Total — Paid by employers — Paid by employees

Source: Eurostat/Taxation and Customs Union DG (provisional estimates).

Implicit tax rates

There are two main methods that are used to calculate tax rates. The microeconomic method compares the internal rate of an activity with and without taxation, thereby giving the actual marginal tax rate. The main aim of this method is to construct a specimen operator (household, investor, etc.) using data from household surveys, business statistics or other sources and to apply the tax rules (rates, rules governing tax relief, etc.) in order to work out the tax burden normally borne by the economic operator that has been defined. The advantage of the microeconomic model is that it reveals the actual tax burden on the economic operator and not *ex post* results. The method is hampered, however, by major problems in connection with the availability of data.

In macroeconomic terms, it is possible to calculate a tax rate by dividing the taxes imposed on a specific activity or good by a suitable matching tax base. This gives an average tax rate or implicit tax rate (ITR). Determining this kind of rate requires fewer statistical data and less complicated calculations. However, it provides very reliable results, that are often very similar to those obtained using the microeconomic method.

In collaboration with the TAXUD (Customs and Indirect Taxation) Directorate-General, Eurostat has for some years published various implicit tax rates defined as follows:

— implicit tax rate on consumption = taxes on consumption divided by private consumption in the economic territory (excluding general government compensation of employees);
— implicit tax rate on employed labour = taxes on employed labour divided by compensation of employees;
— implicit tax rate on other factors of production = taxes on self-employed persons plus taxes on capital divided by the net operating surplus of the economy plus consolidated government interest payments.

General government expenditure

General government expenditure in the Union accounts on average for about 47 % of GDP, although the range of figures is fairly wide, from about 35.0 % to 60.0 %. By way of comparison, overall government spending accounts for about 34–35 % of GDP in the United States and 37–38 % in Japan.

There is clearly a strong correlation between the overall amount of public spending — which goes hand-in-hand with a high level of revenue — and the general degree of economic development, which is normally matched by wider social benefits (see Table 5.2.4).

Figure 5.2.3. Main categories of general government expenditure, 1998 (as a % of total)

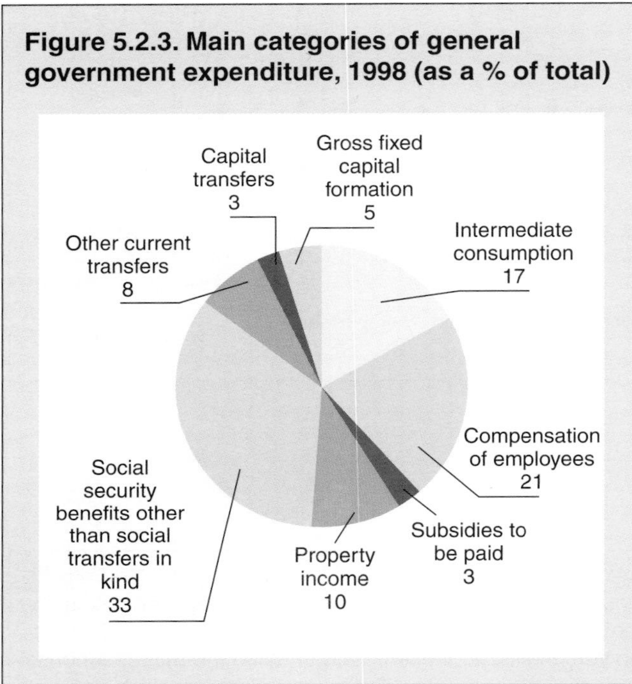

Source: Eurostat.

The main component by far of general government expenditure (see Figure 5.2.3) comprises social benefits other than social transfers in kind (about 35 % of all expenditure). This is followed by compensation of employees in the public sector (just over 20 %), intermediate consumption (17 %) and income from property (10 %). Finally, gross fixed capital formation accounts for 4.6 % of general government expenditure in the Member States.

Some important functions

Among the main items accounting for government expenditure, there are some that merit special attention. Accounting for just over a fifth of GDP in 1998, social benefits (excluding social transfers in kind) — which include pensions, health care, unemployment benefits, etc. — represent the main item of expenditure (see Table 5.2.4). Depending on the Member State, they range between 10.4 % and 19.5 % of GDP. Topping the table in this are Sweden, France and Finland. The countries where such expenditure is proportionally the lowest are Ireland, Spain and the Netherlands.

Table 5.2.4. Social benefits paid by general government — other than social transfers in kind (as a % of GDP)

	1995	1996	1997	1998
EU-15	17.3	17.5	17.2	16.7
EUR-11	17.4	17.9	17.7	17.3
B	16.6	16.7	16.3	16.0
DK	20.4	19.8	18.9	18.2
D	18.1	19.2	19.2	18.8
EL	15.1	15.4	15.5	15.5
E	13.9	13.8	13.4	13.0
F	18.5	18.8	18.8	18.5
IRL	11.5	11.2	10.7	10.4
I	16.7	16.9	17.3	16.9
L	16.5	16.4	15.7	15.5
NL	15.3	14.8	13.9	13.0
A	19.5	19.4	18.8	18.4
P	11.7	11.9	13.2	13.3
FIN	22.2	21.5	19.9	18.5
S	21.3	20.3	19.7	19.5
UK	15.4	14.9	14.5	13.8

Source: Eurostat.

While the provision of social benefits to households represents a traditional function of allocation among the various categories of the population (active population, pensioners, unemployed, sick, etc.), general government of course provides a whole range of other functions for the benefit of the community, e.g. national defence and public security, education, transport, communications, cultural and leisure facilities.

By virtue of the production and consumption activities that these entail, general government has an influence on the economy that varies from country to country but which is never insignificant. While compensation of employees and intermediate consumption are the major items of general government expenditure, subsidies paid to businesses and gross fixed capital formation also figure strongly.

Production subsidies provided by general government in 1998 amounted to 1.4 % of GDP in the Union. The countries that provide most help to businesses are Sweden, Denmark and Austria; those that provide the least help are Greece, the United Kingdom and Ireland.

Table 5.2.5. Subsidies paid by general government (as a % of GDP)

	1995	1996	1997	1998
EU-15	1.7	1.6	1.5	1.4
EUR-11	1.8	1.7	1.6	1.6
B	1.5	1.6	1.5	1.5
DK	2.5	2.6	2.5	2.3
D	2.1	2.0	1.8	1.8
EL	0.4	0.5	0.1	0.2
E	1.1	1.0	0.9	1.2
F	1.5	1.5	1.5	1.4
IRL	1.1	1.2	1.3	1.1
I	1.5	1.5	1.2	1.3
L	1.7	2.0	1.8	1.8
NL	1.1	1.2	1.5	1.5
A	2.9	2.6	2.6	2.7
P	1.4	1.2	1.3	1.4
FIN	2.8	2.1	1.9	1.8
S	3.7	3.1	2.6	2.1
UK	0.7	0.8	0.6	0.5

Source: Eurostat.

Table 5.2.6. General government gross fixed capital formation (as a % of GDP)

	1995	1996	1997	1998
EU-15	2.7	2.5	2.3	2.2
EUR-11	2.8	2.7	2.5	2.4
B	1.8	1.6	1.6	1.6
DK	1.8	2.0	1.9	1.7
D	2.3	2.1	1.9	1.8
EL	3.2	3.2	3.4	3.6
E	3.7	3.1	3.1	3.2
F	3.3	3.2	3.0	3.0
IRL	2.3	2.4	2.5	2.4
I	2.1	2.2	2.3	2.4
L	4.6	4.7	4.2	4.6
NL	3.0	3.1	2.9	2.8
A	2.9	2.8	1.9	1.9
P	3.8	4.2	4.3	4.2
FIN	2.8	2.9	3.2	2.9
S	3.4	3.0	2.6	2.6
UK	2.0	1.5	1.2	1.3

Source: Eurostat.

On average, government investment in fixed capital goods amounts to 2.2 % of GDP in the Union. The figures differ widely, however, ranging from 1.3 % in Belgium to 4.6 % in Luxembourg. While countries such as Germany, Austria and Sweden have steadily reduced government investment in recent years, the trend in many other Member States has fluctuated up and down.

5.3. Public debt and deficit

Depending on whether or not a country's revenue covers its expenditure, there will be a surplus or a deficit in its budget. If there is a shortfall in revenue, the government is obliged to borrow. Expressed as a percentage of GDP, a country's annual (deficit) and cumulative (debt) financing requirements are significant indicators of the burden that government borrowing places on the national economy. These are in fact two of the criteria used to assess the government finances of the Member States that are referred to in the Maastricht Treaty in connection with qualifying for the single currency (see box).

Fairly general reduction of public deficit ...

Public deficit (see Table 5.3.1) is defined in the Maastricht Treaty as general government's net borrowing according to the European system of accounts (see box). In 1999, seven Member States achieved a surplus in the budget (net lending), while in all the others the deficit was less than 2 % of GDP. Apart from Ireland and Luxembourg — which have been recording a surplus for several years — every country reduced its deficit or increased its surplus. The general improvement is thus continuing. The budget restrictions introduced in recent years are clearly bearing fruit.

Table 5.3.1. General government deficit (as a % of GDP)

	1996	1997	1998	1999
EU-15	– 4.2	– 2.4	– 1.5	– 0.7
EUR-11	– 4.2	– 2.6	– 2.0	– 1.2
B	– 3.7	– 2.0	– 1.0	– 0.9
DK	– 1.0	0.1	1.2	3.0
D	– 3.4	– 2.6	– 1.7	– 1.2
EL	– 7.4	– 3.9	– 2.5	– 1.6
E	– 5.0	– 3.2	– 2.6	– 1.1
F	– 4.2	– 3.0	– 2.7	– 1.8
IRL	– 0.6	0.8	2.1	2.0
I	– 7.1	– 2.7	– 2.8	– 1.9
L	2.7	3.6	3.2	2.4
NL	– 1.8	– 1.2	– 0.8	0.5
A	– 3.8	– 1.9	– 2.5	– 2.0
P	– 3.8	– 2.6	– 2.1	– 2.0
FIN	– 3.2	– 1.5	1.3	2.3
S	– 3.4	– 2.0	1.9	1.9
UK	– 4.4	– 2.0	0.3	1.2

Source: Eurostat.

The average figures for the Union and the euro zone declined steadily throughout the four years under review, and at the end of 1999 they were – 0.7 % and – 1.2 % of GDP respectively. In 1996 they had both been – 4.2 %.

... and public debt

Public debt (see Table 5.3.2) is defined in the Maastricht Treaty as total general government gross, nominal and consolidated debt outstanding at the end of the year.

At the end of 1999, seven countries had a level of public debt below the 60 % threshold, and five others were in the 60–70 % range. Three Member States (Italy, Belgium and Greece) were still above 100 %, but the figure has been dropping every year since 1995. In the case of Germany, Austria and Portugal, however, public debt increased between 1998 and 1999.

Table 5.3.2. General government debt (as a % of GDP)

	1996	1997	1998	1999
EU-15	72.5	70.9	68.9	68.1
EUR-11	74.4	74.0	73.4	72.2
B	128.3	123.0	117.4	114.4
DK	65.0	61.3	55.6	52.6
D	59.8	60.9	60.7	61.1
EL	111.3	108.5	105.4	104.4
E	68.0	66.7	64.9	63.5
F	57.1	59.0	59.3	58.6
IRL	74.1	65.3	55.6	52.4
I	122.1	119.8	116.3	114.9
L	6.2	6.0	6.4	6.2
NL	75.3	70.3	67.0	63.8
A	68.3	63.9	63.5	64.9
P	63.6	60.3	56.5	56.8
FIN	57.1	54.1	49.0	47.1
S	76.0	75.0	72.4	65.5
UK	52.6	50.8	48.4	46.0

Source: Eurostat.

At the end of 1999, the average debt ratio for the 15 Member States stood at 68.1 %, with a figure of 72.2 % for the countries in the euro zone.

Budgetary discipline and notification of public debt and deficit

The Maastricht Treaty states that the Member States are required to avoid excessive public deficits. To this end, they must fulfil two conditions. Firstly, the ratio of government deficit to GDP must not exceed a reference value (3 %), unless the ratio has declined substantially and continuously and reached a level close to the reference value, or that the reference value has been exceeded only exceptionally and temporarily and the ratio is close to the reference value. Secondly, the ratio of government debt to GDP must not exceed a reference value (60 %), unless the ratio is diminishing sufficiently and approaching the reference value at a satisfactory pace.

At the Madrid Summit in December 1995, the European Council stressed the need for budgetary discipline both before the introduction of monetary union and after the start of stage three on 1 January 1999. This determination was reflected in the Growth and Stability Pact, which is intended to prevent any country, no longer able to rely on exchange rates and interest rates, to resort to budgetary policy to revive its economy, since such a solution could very quickly have a negative effect on its public deficit, thereby prompting a rise in interest rates which would be detrimental to all the participants in EMU.

Starting with the notification of March 2000, government debt and deficit figures must be compiled in accordance with the methodology of the European system of national and regional accounts in the Community (ESA 95).

6. POPULATION, LABOUR MARKET AND SOCIAL PROTECTION IN THE UNION

6.1. Population

The EU, the world's third most populous economic area

Having 376 million inhabitants on 1 January 2000, the European Union is the third most populous economic area after China (1 253 million) and India (1 009 million), which reached its first billion well before the millennium change. Indeed, after these two giants, its population is almost as large as those of the United States (274 million) and Japan (126 million) together.

The European Union currently covers nearly 80 % of the population of the whole of Europe (excluding most of the former Soviet Union, parts of the former Republic of Yugoslavia and Turkey). The 10 central European countries plus Cyprus and Malta, which are potential future Member States of the Union have a total population of about 110 million people. Poland is the largest of those countries with a population of 38.6 million. Romania (22.7 million), the Czech Republic and Hungary (both 10 million) rank in the medium-size group of countries and the remainder have less than 10 million inhabitants.

The six largest EU countries by area (France, Spain, Sweden, Germany, Finland and Italy) occupy nearly 80 % of the total EU territory. The five countries with the highest populations i.e. Germany, the United Kingdom, France, Italy and Spain, represent 80 % of the whole population of the Union. Population density ranges from just 15 per km^2 in Finland to nearly 400 per km^2 in the Netherlands. The population is most dense in a belt running from northern Italy through south and west Germany and the Benelux countries to southern England. Border regions in all directions tend to be less densely populated. In 1991, more than half of the population of the EU countries lived in urban settlements (defined as compact areas with a population density of at least 500 persons per km^2). This percentage ranges however from a low of 21 % in Sweden to a high of 77 % in the United Kingdom.

Slow population growth as compared with the United States

Population growth in the EU slowed in the 1970s and 1980s but accelerated in the early 1990s. This was due to a temporary increase in immigration. The long-term trend points to a decline in the growth rate, even though there was a peak last year in Kosovo. The United States' population has grown steadily since the 1970s until recently. In Japan, population growth diminished substantially during the same period.

Table 6.1.1 shows the recent development of the components of the population change in 1995–99. The population of the EU increased in 1999 by 0.26 %, a rate a little higher than that of Japan (+ 0.19 %), and much slower than that of the United States (+ 0.94 %). Net migration is still the most important source of population growth in the Union. Its share of total population increase was 72 %. The Kosovo crisis increased net migration last year, which has almost doubled from the previous year. In the United States, net migration is also important but the natural increase is the major driving force of the relatively strong population growth. Japan faces a situation of near zero net migration, thus migration having no role in the population growth.

Table 6.1.1. Components of population change, 1995–99 (as a %)

	Natural increase	and	Net migration	=	Population change
EU-15					
1999	0.07		0.19		0.26
1998	0.08		0.14		0.22
1997	0.09		0.14		0.23
1996	0.08		0.20		0.28
1995	0.07		0.22		0.29
EUR-11					
1999	0.07		0.17		0.24
1998	0.07		0.10		0.17
1997	0.09		0.13		0.22
1996	0.07		0.20		0.27
1995	0.06		0.22		0.28
US					
1999	0.59		0.35		0.94
1998	0.59		0.36		0.95
1997	0.59		0.32		0.91
1996	0.60		0.33		0.93
1995	0.61		0.34		0.95
JP					
1999	0.19		0.0		0.19
1998	0.20		– 0.04		0.20
1997	0.23		– 0.04		0.19
1996	0.22		– 0.04		0.18
1995	0.21		0.02		0.23

Source: Eurostat.

Increasing share of non-EU nationals

The European Union has witnessed a slow but steady growth in the share of the non-national population during recent decades. The total number of non-nationals has increased from 13.6 million in 1985 to 19.1 million in 1998. In 1998 the share of the non-nationals from other EU countries was 31.4 % and the share of those from outside the Union was 68.6 %. The share of the non-EU nationals has been growing until recently even when the net migration decreased almost continuously from 1992 to 1998.

Non-EU nationals account for a greater share of the total population in Austria (estimated about 8 %) and Germany (6.7 %) than in any of the other Member States where the equivalent figures range from 1 % and 4 %. As a proportion of the total population, EU nationals of other Member States are most significant in Luxembourg (31 %) and Belgium (5.5 %), the figures in other countries of the Union varying between 0 % and 2 %.

In 1997, 47 % of immigrants to EU countries were citizens of some EU country. They were either returning to their own country or moving to another EU country. Some 30 % of immigrants are nationals of more developed non-EU countries and 23 % are nationals of less developed non-EU countries

Ageing population and labour force

Figure 6.1.1 shows the age and sex structure of the European Union in 1998 in the form of a population pyramid. The pyramid has a broad waist and narrow shoulders. But things will change. The waist will rise upwards and the shoulders will broaden in the coming years. This is because the low fertility continues to decrease the younger age classes and expanding life expectancy tends further to increase the share of the older age classes.

Figure 6.1.1. Age pyramid for the European Union on 1 January 1998

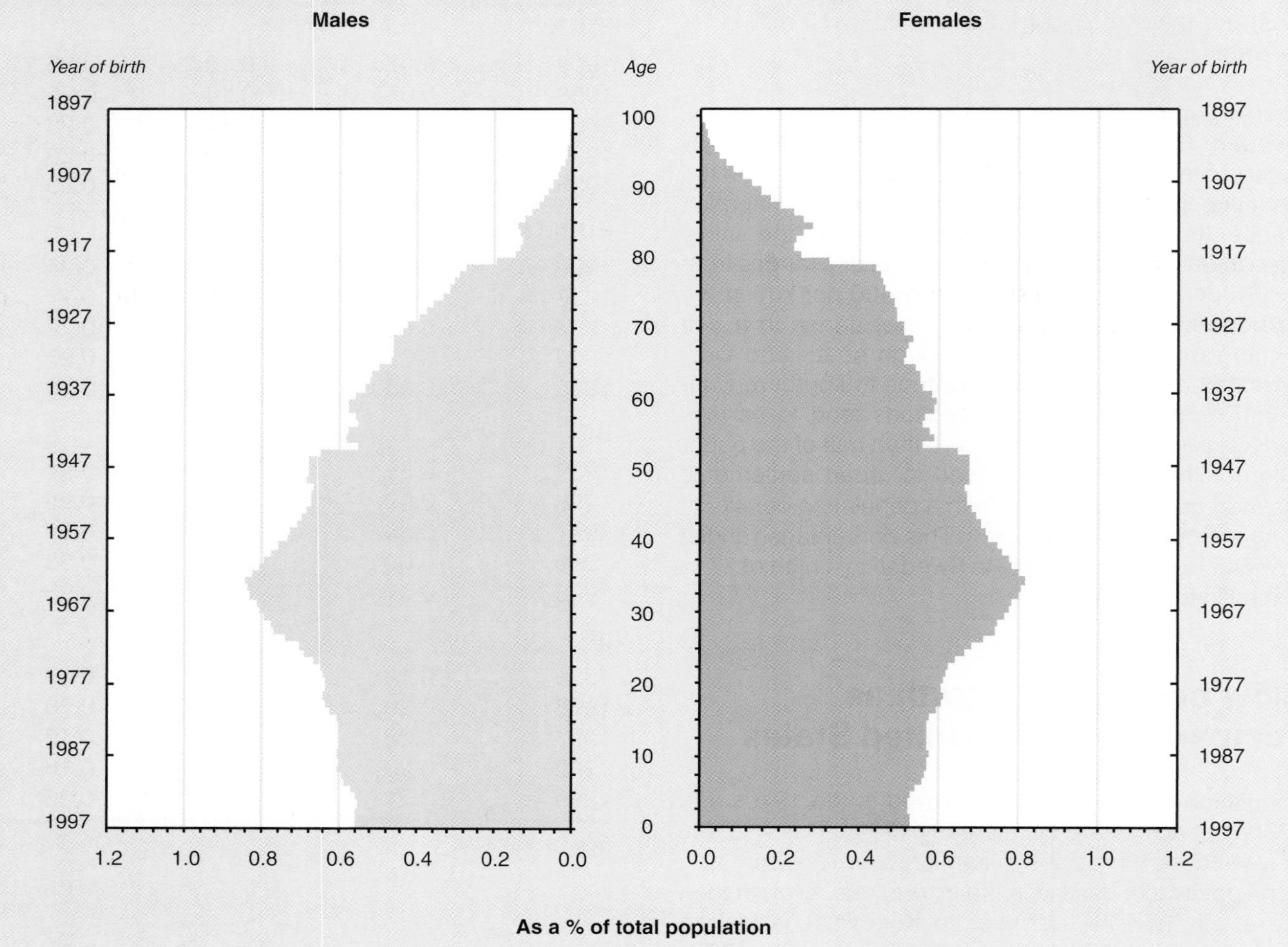

Males | Females

Year of birth | Age | Year of birth

As a % of total population

Source: Eurostat.

Long-term changes in fertility changes of the EU and Japan have been remarkably similar. In 1970, both had total fertility higher than 2 (EU 2.38 and Japan 2.09). After a rapid decrease in the 1970s there was a steady downward slope to levels 1.45 and 1.40 in 1998, which are well below the level of reproduction. The United States, on the other hand, had the highest level in 1970 (2.48) dropping to nearly 1.7 in the mid of 1970s, but turning up again and staying just over 2 in the whole 1990s (2.07 in 1998).

Since 1945, life expectancy at birth in the EU has increased almost continuously. Following an interruption in 1995, the upward trend was resumed in 1996. For the Union as a whole, and based on mortality rates measured in 1998, it is estimated that life expectancy is now at an all-time high: at birth, girls can now expect to live an average of 80.9 years and boys 74.6 years, well over 10 years more than in 1945.

The corresponding figures for the United States were 74.1 for men and 79.7 for women and for Japan 78.8 and 83.9. In most other developed countries, average life spans are shorter than in the EU: the most extreme case appears to be the Russian Federation, where the average man now lives 14.8 years less than his EU counterpart.

In Table 6.1.2 the population is split into several age groups for 1970 and 1995–98. In all three areas the proportion of young persons (0–14) has declined in the last 25 years. However, in the United States the share of this group remains much higher than in the Union or Japan. Within the European Union, the southern Member States Spain, Italy and Portugal have experienced the greatest fall in share of young people and this trend is expected to continue. In all three economic areas and especially in Japan, the proportion of elderly people (65 +) increased considerably.

The population of 15–64 year-olds is a good indicator of the actual and potential labour force. In the European Union and United States, this age group accounted for a substantially higher percentage of the population in 1997 than in 1970. In Japan, although there was virtually no change over the same period, the 15–64 cohort remained a larger component of the Japanese population than that in the EU or United States. In recent years (1995–98), the share of this age group has been almost constant in all three countries. However, the internal structure has been changing in all three countries during the 1990s. The share of the older part of the potential labour force (40 to 64 years) increased from 1990 to 1998 in the EU from 44.1 % to 46 %, in Japan from 49 % to 50.3 % and in the United States from 38.9 % to 44.5 %. This indicates ageing of the labour force, which will also continue in the coming years.

The old age dependency ratio (65 +/15–64) increased in all three areas with a doubling in Japan. However, the ratio is still highest in the EU.

The total age dependency ratio (the number of people aged 0–14 and 65 and over related to the number of people aged 15–64) has dropped substantially since 1970 in the EU and in the United States with the EU being most affected. In Japan, a fall in the proportion of young people was counterbalanced by a rise in that of the elderly. However, during the recent years (1995–98) the ratio has been almost constant in all three economic areas.

Table 6.1.2. Population shares (as a %) in major age groups and age dependency ratios 1995–97

	Population shares				Age dependency ratios
	0–14	15–64	65 +	65 +/15–64	(0–14 and 65 +) /15–64
EU-15					
1998	17.1	67.0	15.9	23.7	49.3
1997	17.3	67.0	15.7	23.6	49.3
1996	17.4	67.0	15.6	23.3	49.3
1995	17.6	67.0	15.4	23.0	49.2
1970	24.7	63.1	12.2	19.3	58.5
US					
1998	21.5	65.8	12.7	19.3	52.0
1997	21.6	65.7	12.7	19.3	52.2
1996	21.7	65.6	12.7	19.3	52.5
1995	21.8	65.4	12.8	19.6	52.9
1970	28.3	61.9	9.8	15.8	61.2
JP					
1998	15.2	68.8	16.0	23.3	45.3
1997	15.4	69.1	15.5	22.4	44.8
1996	15.7	69.3	15.0	21.6	44.3
1995	16.2	69.6	14.2	20.4	43.7
1970	24.0	69.0	7.0	10.1	44.9

Source: Eurostat.

6.2. Employment

Employment continued to increase by 1.4 %

Employment continued to increase in the European Union by 1.4 % in 1999 compared with 1998, the same rate of increase as one year before. In the euro zone, the employment growth was slightly higher (1.5 %). Ireland continues to have by far the highest employment growth. In Spain, Luxembourg, the Netherlands and Finland employment growth was at least as rapid as it was a year before (2 % or more). In Sweden, employment growth was also more than 2 %. In all other Member States, the growth in employment was within a range of 0.9 and 1.8 % except in Germany and Greece. In Germany, the growth in employment of 0.3 % was practically the same as the year before whereas Greece was the only Member State where employment decreased.

Table 6.2.1. Annual employment growth

	In 1 000			%	
	1997	1998	1999	1998–97	1999–98
EU-15	155 853	158 088	160 304	1.4	1.4
EUR-11	118 457	120 150	121 936	1.4	1.5
B	3 808	3 855	3 888	1.2	0.9
DK	2 654	2 707	2 736	2.0	1.1
D	35 802	35 935	36 041	0.4	0.3
EL	3 792	3 921	3 891	3.4	- 0.8
E	14 124	14 628	15 112	3.6	3.3
F	23 095	23 418	23 784	1.4	1.6
IRL	1 432	1 531	1 624	6.9	6.1
I	21 793	21 991	22 283	0.9	1.3
L	171	174	181	2.1	4.2
NL	7 537	7 724	7 924	2.5	2.6
A	3 926	3 962	4 018	0.9	1.4
P	4 632	4 752	4 825	2.6	1.5
FIN	2 137	2 179	2 255	2.0	3.5
S	4 034	4 081	4 178	1.2	2.4
UK	26 916	27 229	27 563	1.2	1.2

Source: Eurostat, national accounts (ESA 95).

62 % of the population aged 15–64 is employed

The EU employment rate (% of employed persons in the population aged 15–64) is 62 %. This rate is 2 percentage points more than the employment rate for the euro zone. The reason is that in three of the four Member States outside the EMU (Denmark, Sweden and the United Kingdom), the employment rates are 70 % and over, which are among the highest in the EU. The Netherlands also has a rate of more than 70 %. In Austria, Portugal and Finland, the employment rate is 67 % or more. Compared with 1998, the employment rate increased the most in Finland (4 points). In three of the Member States, Denmark, Austria and Portugal, the employment rate for full-time employed persons is also far above the EU average of 50 %. In Spain, Italy, Greece and Belgium, employment rates are below the EU average. In Ireland, the employment rate increased by almost 3 points and is above the EU average while it was below the EU average in 1998.

Table 6.2.2. Employment rates (15–64 years) by full-time/part-time, 1999 (as a % of the total population of the same age)

	Total	Full-time	Part-time
EU-15	62.0	51.3	10.8
EUR-11	60.1	50.6	9.6
B	58.9	47.3	11.6
DK	76.5	60.6	15.7
D	64.8	52.7	12.1
EL	55.4	52.2	3.2
E	52.3	48.0	4.3
F	60.4	50.1	10.4
IRL	62.5	52.1	10.3
I	52.5	48.4	4.1
L	61.6	55.0	6.6
NL	70.9	43.1	27.7
A	68.2	57.0	11.2
P	67.4	61.6	5.9
FIN	67.4	59.3	8.0
S	70.6	53.9	16.6
UK	70.4	53.5	16.9

Source: Eurostat, labour force survey (LFS).

Part-time employment rate in the Member States between 4 % and 28 %

Standard full-time wage employment seems to be less prevalent in the EU. Part-time employment, a reduction and sometimes a polarisation of working hours — when employed persons move away from the standard working week into both short and long hours — and fixed-term contracts are now common structural characteristics of employment in the EU.

Part-time employment is prevalent in the Netherlands, Denmark, Sweden and the United Kingdom. In the Netherlands, in sharp contrast with Denmark, the employment rate for full-time employed persons is the lowest rate of all Member States. Part-time employment is relatively uncommon in Spain, Italy, Greece and Portugal. In these countries, apart from Portugal, employment rates are also low. Other Member States with relatively few part-time employed persons are Luxembourg and Finland.

Table 6.2.3. Employment rates (15–64 years) by sex and full-time/part-time, 1999 (as a % of the population of the same age and sex)

	Male			Female		
	Total	Full-time	Part-time	Total	Full-time	Part-time
EU-15	71.5	67.5	4.0	52.6	35.1	17.5
EUR-11	70.3	66.7	3.6	50.0	34.5	15.5
B	67.5	64.4	3.1	50.2	30.2	20.0
DK	81.2	73.5	7.6	71.6	47.4	24.1
D	72.4	69.2	3.2	57.1	36.0	21.1
EL	70.9	68.6	2.3	40.7	36.7	4.0
E	67.8	65.9	2.0	37.3	30.8	6.5
F	67.5	63.9	3.6	53.5	36.6	16.9
IRL	73.6	68.4	5.1	51.4	35.7	15.6
I	67.1	64.9	2.2	38.1	32.1	6.0
L	74.4	73.2	1.2	48.5	36.5	12.0
NL	80.3	66.3	13.9	61.3	19.2	41.8
A	76.7	73.6	3.1	59.7	40.4	19.3
P	75.7	72.5	3.1	59.6	51.1	8.5
FIN	70.2	64.9	5.2	64.6	53.7	10.9
S	72.1	65.9	6.3	68.9	41.3	27.7
UK	76.9	70.9	6.0	63.7	35.8	27.9

Source: Eurostat, LFS.

Not all employed people choose to work part-time. Every sixth employed person in the EU are working part-time because (s)he can not find a full-time job. In Finland, Greece, Italy, Portugal and Sweden, involuntary part-time is above the EU average. On the other hand, in Denmark, the Netherlands and the United Kingdom, where there is a lot of part-time employment, involuntary part-time is below the EU average. The situation is clearly different for men and women. Relatively more men work part-time because they could not find a full-time job in all Member States except in Denmark and Finland where relatively more women are involuntary part-time workers.

Table 6.2.4. Involuntary part-time by sex, 1999 (as a % of part-time employment)

	Total	Male	Female
EU-15	17.3	26.6	15.2
EUR-11	18.7	26.8	16.9
B	20.3	31.8	18.6
DK	15.4	12.6	16.3
D	13.3	19.9	12.3
EL	47.0	54.2	43.0
E	25.6	27.5	25.1
F	27.8	42.7	24.6
IRL	13.1	28.1	8.1
I	37.4	48.3	33.5
L	9.9	9.4	9.9
NL	4.4	6.9	3.5
A	11.3	23.0	9.4
P	30.5	29.1	31.0
FIN	38.9	34.3	41.2
S	30.2	36.8	28.7
UK	10.7	24.2	7.7

Source: Eurostat, LFS.

A gender gap in employment rates of 19 points

The female employment rate is 19 percentage points less than the male employment rate in the EU. Compared with 1998, the gender gap narrowed from almost 20 points to 19 points. In Greece, Spain, Luxembourg and Italy, this gender gap is much wider, the low female employment rate being related to a low part-time employment rates. On the other hand, the gender gap is much smaller in Sweden, Finland and Denmark where similar employment rates for men and women are related in a different way to part-time employment. In Sweden and Denmark, the female part-time employment rate is high, but in Finland, the female full-time employment rate is the highest of all Member States.

This gender gap is also obvious in part-time work. The female part-time employment rate in the EU is almost 18 % in contrast to the male part-time employment rate of only 4 %. In the Netherlands, female part-time employment is particularly high, with 2 in 3 women working part-time. Other Member States with a high female part-time employment are Denmark, Germany, Sweden and the United Kingdom.

6.3. Unemployment

In 1999, the total number of unemployed in the EU averaged 15.7 million or 9 % of the labour force, excluding collective households. The unemployment rate for the euro zone is higher than for the entire EU because the unemployment rate in Denmark, Sweden and the United Kingdom is below the EU average. The decrease of 7 decimal points between 1998 and 1999 confirmed the steady annual decrease since 1996. The unemployment rate decreased in all Member States except in Greece and in Denmark where it remained at 5.2 %. It decreased most in Spain and Ireland. Although unemployment decreased in Spain, it remains the highest of the Member States. In contrast, the unemployment rate is 5 % or less in Luxembourg, Denmark, the Netherlands, Austria and Portugal.

Table 6.3.1. Unemployment rate, yearly average (as a %)

	1998	1999
EU-15	9.9	9.2
EUR-11	10.9	9.9
B	9.5	9.0
DK	5.2	5.2
D	9.4	8.7
EL	10.7	:
E	18.8	15.8
F	11.8	11.3
IRL	7.6	5.7
I	11.9	11.3
L	2.7	2.3
NL	4.0	3.3
A	4.5	3.7
P	5.2	4.5
FIN	11.4	10.2
S	8.3	7.2
UK	6.3	6.1

NB: Harmonised unemployment rate.
Source: Eurostat.

Definition of unemployment

Harmonised unemployment rate

Eurostat harmonised unemployment rates are calculated according to the recommendations of the 13th International Conference of Labour Statisticians (1982). According to these recommendations, the unemployed comprise persons aged 15 and over who are without work; are currently available for work and (iii) have been actively looking for work or have already found a job to start later.

Counts of the number of persons registered at public employment offices are not suitable for international comparison because of effects of changes in national administrative rules and procedures.

Long-term unemployment

The summit in Luxembourg in November 1997 agreed on a coordinated European employment strategy. On the basis of these conclusions, a set of employment guidelines were adopted by the Council in February 1999. The first two guidelines concern youth unemployment and the prevention of long-term unemployment.

Table 6.3.2. Long-term unemployment rate, yearly average (as a % of the labour force)

	1998	1999
EU-15	4.7	4.2
EUR-11	5.4	4.8
B	5.7	5.0
DK	1.3	1.1
D	4.8	4.4
EL	:	:
E	9.4	7.2
F	4.8	4.4
IRL	3.2	2.3
I	7.2	6.9
L	0.9	0.8
NL	1.7	1.2
A	1.3	1.2
P	2.2	1.7
FIN	3.9	2.9
S	2.9	2.1
UK	2.1	1.8

NB: Harmonised unemployment rate.
Source: Eurostat.

The long-term unemployment rate (unemployed persons without a job for one year or longer) has also decreased along with the overall unemployment rate. Nevertheless, the relatively high long-term unemployment rate remains endemic in several Member States. In Spain and Italy, it is 7 % and in Belgium, Germany, France, it remains above the EU average.

The long-term unemployment rate for people under 25 is higher than the overall long-term unemployment rate in the EU. In Italy, the youth long-term unemployment rate is the highest of all Member States. In Spain and Belgium it also exceeds the EU average.

Table 6.3.3. Youth long-term unemployment rate (15–24 years), yearly average (as a % of the labour force of the same age)

	1998	1999
EU-15	6.7	5.6
EUR-11	7.9	6.5
B	9.4	7.4
DK	0.6	0.6
D	2.7	2.3
EL	:	:
E	13.5	9.8
F	5.8	4.8
IRL	4.0	2.9
I	19.3	18.8
L	1.9	1.3
NL	1.4	0.9
A	0.9	0.8
P	2.8	1.7
FIN	2.5	1.6
S	2.2	1.3
UK	2.3	1.8

NB: Harmonised unemployment rate.
Source: Eurostat.

Higher unemployment among women and young people

The female unemployment rate in the EU is almost 3 points higher than the male unemployment rate. This less favourable situation for women occurs in all Member States except Ireland, Sweden and the United Kingdom. The situation is particularly unfavourable to women in Greece, Spain and Italy, where the female unemployment rate is twice the male unemployment rate.

Table 6.3.4. Unemployment rate by sex, yearly average 1999 (as a %)

	Males	Females
EU-15	7.9	10.8
EUR-11	8.3	12.2
B	7.8	10.7
DK	4.5	6.0
D	8.3	9.3
EL	7.0	16.5
E	11.2	23.0
F	9.6	13.3
IRL	5.8	5.5
I	8.7	15.6
L	1.7	3.3
NL	2.3	4.7
A	3.1	4.5
P	3.9	5.2
FIN	9.8	10.7
S	7.2	7.1
UK	6.7	5.3

NB: Harmonised unemployment rate. 1998 for Greece.
Source: Eurostat.

When the unemployment rates are compared by age, the youth unemployment rate in the EU and in most Member States is more than twice the rate of those aged 25 and over. Half of the young people are looking for their first job. In Belgium, Greece and Italy, the youth unemployment rate is more than three times the rate of those aged 25 and over. Belgium, Italy and Denmark were the only Member States where the youth unemployment rate increased. The large difference between the youth unemployment rate and the rate of those aged 25 and over is partly due to a low labour participation.

Table 6.3.5. Unemployment rate by age, yearly average 1999 (as a % of the labour force of the same age)

	Less than 25 years	25 years and over
EU-15	17.7	7.9
EUR-11	19.0	8.7
B	24.7	7.3
DK	9.7	4.3
D	9.0	8.6
EL	29.8	7.9
E	29.5	13.4
F	23.6	10.0
IRL	8.3	5.1
I	32.7	8.6
L	6.6	1.9
NL	7.2	2.6
A	5.0	3.5
P	8.9	3.7
FIN	21.4	8.6
S	13.6	6.5
UK	13.0	4.8

NB: Harmonised unemployment rate. 1998 for Greece.
Source: Eurostat.

Table 6.3.6. Youth unemployment population ratio (15–24 years), yearly average 1999, as a % of the total population of the same age

EU-15	8.4
EUR-11	8.3
B	8.4
DK	7.1
D	4.6
EL	11.9
E	12.5
F	8.2
IRL	4.2
I	12.4
L	2.3
NL	4.8
A	2.9
P	4.3
FIN	10.9
S	6.2
UK	8.6

NB: 1998 for Greece.
Source: Eurostat.

A youth unemployment population ratio does not depend on the participation rates in the Member States because the basis is the total youth population instead of the labour force. In the EU, the youth unemployment population ratio is 8.5 %. In Luxembourg, Ireland and Austria, the youth unemployment ratio is less than half the EU average while in Greece, Spain and Italy, the youth unemployment ratio is the highest.

Higher unemployment among those with a lower level of education

The risk of unemployment is higher among those aged 25-64 with an educational level below upper secondary education. It shows the importance of further education and training in a period of employment growth, job vacancies and decreasing unemployment. In Luxembourg, the Netherlands and the United Kingdom, the unemployment rate for those with less than upper secondary education is twice the unemployment rate for those with an upper secondary education. The odds to be unemployed for those with less than upper secondary education (compared with upper secondary education) are also high in Belgium, Germany and Austria.

Table 6.3.7. Adult unemployment rates (25–64 years) by educational attainment, spring 1999 (as a % of labour force of the same age and level of education)

	Third level	Upper secondary	Less than upper secondary
EU-15	5.2	7.6	11.8
EUR-11	5.8	8.2	12.2
B	3.1	6.6	12.0
DK	3.0	4.1	7.0
D	5.0	8.8	15.5
EL	7.3	10.9	8.5
E	10.8	13.2	14.5
F	6.2	9.3	15.2
IRL	:	:	:
I	6.9	8.1	10.2
L	1.0	1.1	3.7
NL	1.7	2.4	4.9
A	1.9	4.1	7.8
P	2.5	5.1	4.2
FIN	4.7	9.5	13.1
S	4.0	7.1	10.0
UK	2.8	4.8	9.7

Source: Eurostat, LFS.

6.4. Social protection and pensions

Social protection

The data on expenditure and receipts of social protection schemes presented here are drawn up according to the 'Esspros Manual 1996'. Esspros stands for European system of integrated social protection statistics, a harmonised system providing a means of analysing and comparing social protection financial flows.

In this manual, social protection is defined as follows: 'Social protection encompasses all interventions from public or private bodies intended to relieve households and individuals of the burden of a defined set of risks or needs, provided that there is neither a simultaneous reciprocal nor an individual arrangement involved.

The list of risks or needs that may give rise to social protection is fixed by convention as follows:

- sickness/health care;
- disability;
- old age;
- survivors;
- family/children;
- unemployment;
- housing;
- social exclusion not elsewhere classified.'

Social benefits are recorded without any deduction of taxes or other compulsory levies payable on them by beneficiaries.

'Tax benefits' (tax reductions granted to households for social protection purposes) are generally excluded.

The functions of social protections

Sickness/health care: includes, *inter alia*, paid sick leave, medical care and the supply of pharmaceutical products.

Disability: includes, *inter alia*, disability pensions and the provision of goods and services (other than medical care) to the disabled.

Old-age: includes, *inter alia*, old-age pensions and the provision of goods and services (other than medical care) to the elderly.

Survivors: income maintenance and support in connection with the death of a family member (e.g. survivors' pensions).

Family/children: includes support (other than medical care) in connection with pregnancy, childbirth, maternity and the care of children and other dependent family members.

Unemployment: includes, *inter alia*, unemployment benefits and vocational training financed by public agencies.

Housing: includes interventions by public authorities to help households meet the cost of housing.

Social exclusion not elsewhere classified (n.e.c.): includes income-support benefits, rehabilitation of alcoholics and drug addicts, and various other benefits (other than medical care).

Expenditure on social protection

Between 1996 and 1997, expenditure on social protection in EU-15 as a percentage of GDP fell by 0.5 points from 28.7 % to 28.2 %. In contrast, it rose by almost three points compared with 1990, when the figure was 25.4 %. The trend in expenditure on social protection was not regular during the period 1990–97. Between 1990 and 1993, there was a considerable increase, which peaked at 29.0 % in 1993. This was due mainly to the slower rate of growth of GDP and the increasing unemployment level.

Figure 6.4.1. Expenditure on social protection in EU-15 (as a % of GDP)

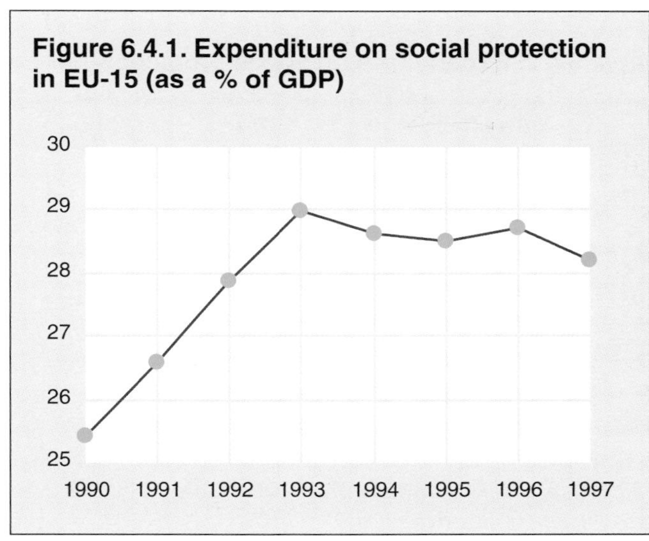

Source: Eurostat, Esspros.

Between 1993 and 1996, expenditure on social protection as a percentage of GDP showed a slight downward trend, which continued in 1997 and was due partly to renewed growth in GDP but also to a slowdown in the growth of social protection expenditure (in particular a decrease in unemployment benefits).

Table 6.4.1. Expenditure on social protection (as a % of GDP)

	1990	1993	1996	1997
EU-15	**25.4**	**29.0**	**28.7**	**28.2**
EUR-11	**25.4**	**28.7**	**28.7**	**28.3**
B	26.7	29.4	28.8	28.5
DK	29.7	33.0	32.5	31.4
D	25.4	29.1	30.6	29.9
EL	23.2	22.3	23.1	23.6
E	19.9	24.0	21.9	21.4
F	27.7	31.0	31.0	30.8
IRL	19.1	20.7	18.5	17.5
I	24.1	26.0	25.3	25.9
L	22.6	24.5	25.2	24.8
NL	32.5	33.6	30.8	30.3
A	26.7	29.0	29.6	28.8
P	15.6	21.0	21.6	22.5
FIN	25.5	35.3	32.3	29.9
S	33.1	38.6	34.6	33.7
UK	23.2	28.9	27.7	26.8
IS	:	18.9	18.6	18.3
NO	26.4	28.8	26.1	25.7
EEA	**:**	**29.0**	**28.6**	**28.1**

Source: Eurostat, Esspros.

Between 1996 and 1997, the decrease was most marked in Finland (– 2.4 points), Denmark (– 1.1 points) and Sweden (– 0.9 points), countries in which the level of expenditure was among the highest in EU-15 in 1996. Ireland also saw a noticeable reduction (about 1 point). The rate increased, however, in Portugal, Italy and Greece.

Slowdown in growth of expenditure

Expenditure on social protection per capita increased in real terms by about 4.1 % per year during the period 1990–93 in EU-15. The increase was particularly marked in Portugal (13 % per year). Only Greece reduced its per capita expenditure in real terms during this period.

In contrast, during the period 1993–96 there was an average increase of 1.6 % per year for EU-15 as a whole. The growth rate then fell to 0.6 % in 1997. In Austria, Sweden and the United Kingdom, per capita expenditure in real terms stabilised in 1997.There was a distinct decrease in Germany, Denmark and Finland, while Portugal, Greece, Ireland and Italy had growth rates well above the average in 1997.

Table 6.4.2. Expenditure on social protection per capita at constant prices (1990 = 100)

	1991	1992	1993	1994	1995	1996	1997
EU-15	**103**	**109**	**113**	**114**	**116**	**118**	**119**
EUR-11	**103**	**108**	**111**	**112**	**114**	**117**	**118**
B	104	106	113	114	114	116	118
DK	105	108	113	122	122	122	121
D	96	103	104	106	110	114	112
EL	96	94	96	97	101	104	111
E	110	117	124	119	119	120	121
F	103	107	111	112	116	117	118
IRL	106	112	119	123	131	133	139
I	105	109	109	109	109	112	116
L	108	112	120	124	129	134	138
NL	101	103	104	102	101	100	102
A	104	107	110	115	117	118	118
P	112	128	143	147	151	162	176
FIN	108	115	116	119	119	122	121
S	100	105	107	108	106	106	106
UK	108	118	127	127	128	131	131
IS	:	:	:	:	:	:	:
NO	106	110	113	114	115	119	121
EEA (1)	**103**	**109**	**113**	**114**	**116**	**118**	**119**

(1) Data for Iceland not included.
Source: Eurostat, Esspros.

Expenditure on social protection: major differences between countries

The EU average for social protection expenditure as a percentage of GDP (28.2 % in 1997) conceals major differences between Member States. Ireland (17.5 %), Spain (21.4 %) and Portugal (22.5 %) had the lowest rates, while Sweden (33.7 %), Denmark (31.4 %) and France (30.8 %) had the highest. Expressed in PPS (purchasing power standards) per capita, the differences between countries are even more marked. Luxembourg spends the most (8 837 PPS per capita) and Portugal and Greece the least (under 3 000 PPS per capita). The ratio between the country which spends the most and the one which spends the least was thus 3.1:1 in 1997 (compared with 3.7:1 in 1990). The differences between the countries reflect the differences in social protection systems, demographic changes, unemployment rates and other social, institutional and economic factors.

Figure 6.4.2. Expenditure on social protection in PPS per capita, 1997

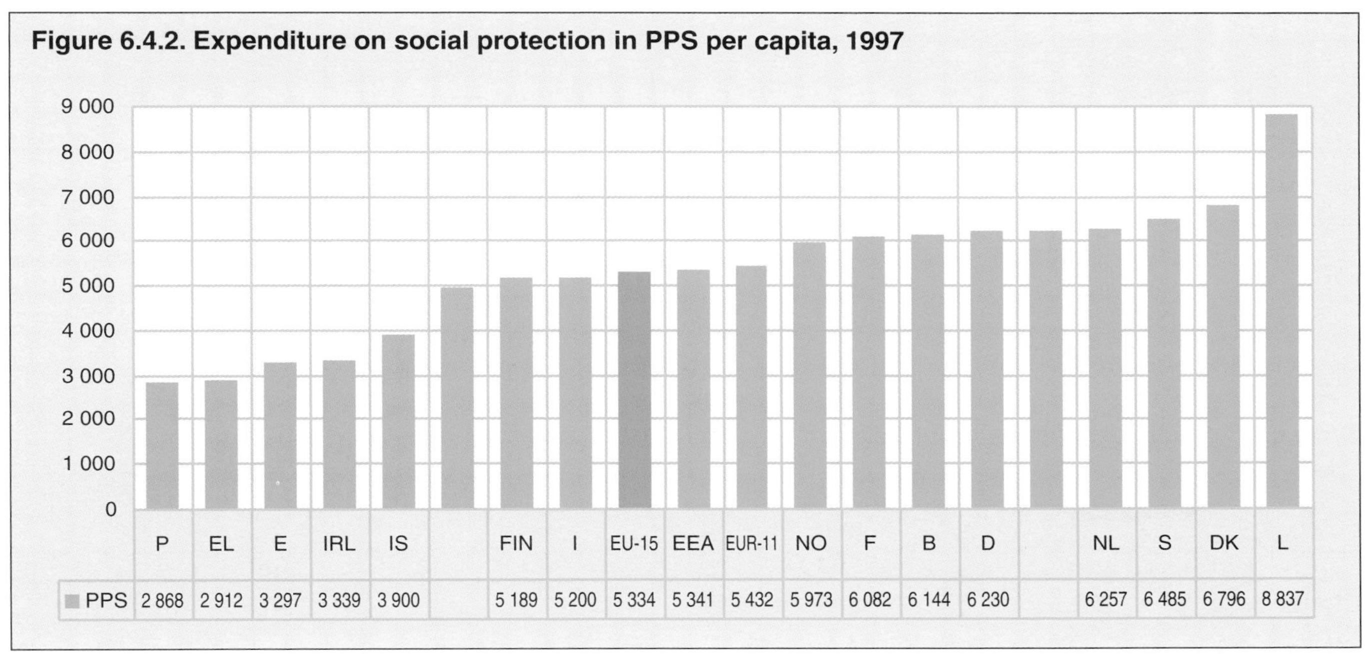

	P	EL	E	IRL	IS		FIN	I	EU-15	EEA	EUR-11	NO	F	B	D		NL	S	DK	L
PPS	2 868	2 912	3 297	3 339	3 900		5 189	5 200	5 334	5 341	5 432	5 973	6 082	6 144	6 230		6 257	6 485	6 796	8 837

Source: Eurostat, Esspros.

Social benefits

The old-age and survivors' functions account for the major part of total benefits

In 1997, in most of the Member States, benefits under the old-age and survivors' functions took the lion's share of expenditure on social protection: 45.2 % of total benefits in EU-15 as a whole, or 12.2 % of GDP. This was particularly true for Italy, where over 65 % of total benefits was accounted for by these functions. One of the reasons for this was that the proportion of the population in the over-65 age group (17.3 % compared with an EU-15 average of 15.8 %). In Ireland, on the other hand, benefits in respect of the old-age and survivors' functions represented well under 30 %.

Figure 6.4.3. Social benefits by group of functions EU-15, 1997 (as a % of total benefits and as a % of GDP)

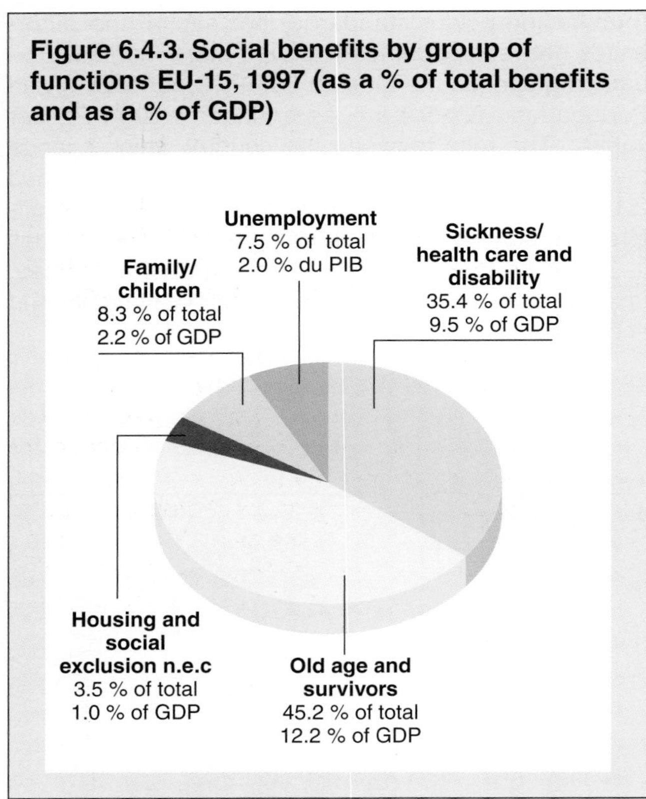

NB: Data for Sweden are not included.
Source: Eurostat, Esspros.

In Portugal, the Netherlands, Ireland and Finland, the sickness/health care and disability group of functions had the largest share of total benefits. This was also true for Iceland (almost 50 %) and Norway. The family/children function accounted for 8.3 % of total benefits in EU-15, or 2.2 % of GDP. The figure was over 12 % in Luxembourg, Ireland, Finland and Denmark, and under 5 % in Spain, Italy and the Netherlands. In the European Economic Area, Norway was the country which spent the most in family-related benefits: 13.7 % of the total. There are considerable differences between the Member States in the share of unemployment-related benefits in the total. They represented over 14 % of total benefits in Ireland and Spain and under 2 % in Italy. It is important to note that the amount of 'unemployment' benefits is not always explained by the level of unemployment in the country, since considerable differences remain regarding the cover and the amount of unemployment benefits.

Table 6.4.3. Social benefits by group of functions, 1997 (as a % of total social benefits)

	Old age and survivors	Sickness/ health care and disability	Family/ children	Unemployment	Housing and social exclusion n.e.c.
EU-15 (1)	**45.2**	**35.4**	**8.3**	**7.5**	**3.5**
EUR-11	**46.2**	**35.1**	**8.0**	**8.1**	**2.6**
B	43.0	32.8	8.8	12.7	2.7
DK	39.4	28.9	12.6	12.6	6.5
D	41.8	36.1	10.1	9.1	2.9
EL	51.4	31.4	8.2	4.6	4.5
E	46.1	36.6	2.0	14.1	1.1
F	43.6	34.0	10.0	7.8	4.6
IRL	24.9	40.7	13.2	15.7	5.5
I	65.1	29.5	3.5	1.8	0.1
L	43.6	38.0	13.2	3.7	1.5
NL	37.7	45.9	3.7	11.0	1.7
A	48.5	34.1	10.5	5.5	1.4
P	42.8	45.9	5.3	5.0	0.9
FIN	33.8	36.6	12.6	13.3	3.7
S	39.6	34.2	10.8	9.5	5.8
UK	40.7	38.2	9.1	4.0	7.9
IS	31.2	49.9	12.5	3.2	3.1
NO	34.3	44.3	13.7	4.3	3.4
EEA (2)	**45.0**	**35.6**	**8.4**	**7.5**	**3.5**

(1) Data for Sweden not included.
(2) Data for Sweden and Iceland not included.
Source: Eurostat, Esspros.

The structure of expenditure on social benefits changes over time

Between 1990 and 1997, the structure of social benefits showed different rates of growth for the various functions. The variations resulted from evolving needs and changes in social protection legislation.

Table 6.4.4. Social benefits per capita at constant prices in EU-15 (1990 = 100)

	1991	1992	1993	1994	1995	1996	1997
Old age and survivors	101	107	109	112	115	117	119
Sickness/health care and disability	103	109	110	111	114	116	116
Family/children	103	111	114	112	115	127	130
Unemployment	122	136	151	143	133	136	129
Housing and social exclusion n.e.c.	100	111	122	127	129	129	131
Total benefits	**104**	**110**	**113**	**114**	**116**	**119**	**120**

NB: Data for Sweden not included.
Source: Eurostat, ESSPROS.

Between 1990 and 1997, per capita expenditure in EU-15 under the old-age and survivors' functions increased very steadily by 19 % in real terms. In the same period the percentage of the population in the over-65 age group rose from 14.6 % in 1990 to 15.8 % in 1997.

Expenditure under the sickness/health care and disability group of functions grew at a lower rate than the average increase of 20 % in total benefits. This reflects, *inter alia*, the Member States' efforts to control costs.

In contrast, family-related expenditure increased at a higher rate than the average. This increase (+ 30 % between 1990 and 1997) was particularly marked in 1996, when Germany introduced reforms and extended the system of family benefits. The trend in unemployment-related expenditure calls for more thorough analysis. Between 1990 and 1997, it rose by 29 % in EU-15, but it was not a steady increase, since the total level of these benefits depends broadly on the trend in unemployment.

Table 6.4.5. Expenditure on unemployment function (as a % of total social benefits)

	1990	1991	1992	1993	1994	1995	1996	1997
EU-15 (1)	**7.0**	**8.2**	**8.7**	**9.5**	**8.9**	**8.2**	**8.2**	**7.5**
EUR-11	**7.1**	**8.2**	**8.8**	**9.7**	**9.1**	**8.5**	**8.6**	**8.1**
B	13.3	13.3	12.9	13.4	13.4	13.0	12.9	12.7
DK	15.4	15.9	16.8	17.9	16.3	14.7	13.8	12.6
D	5.9	8.6	9.7	10.6	9.7	9.1	9.6	9.1
EL	4.1	4.8	4.5	3.7	3.5	4.5	4.2	4.6
E	18.0	19.4	19.7	21.7	19.1	16.6	14.8	14.1
F	8.3	8.7	8.9	9.3	8.9	7.8	7.9	7.8
IRL	14.6	15.6	16.5	17.0	17.2	17.3	17.4	15.7
I	1.7	1.8	1.9	2.3	2.3	2.1	1.9	1.8
L	2.6	2.6	2.4	2.7	3.1	3.1	3.5	3.7
NL	8.3	8.3	8.4	9.3	10.3	10.0	12.0	11.0
A	4.6	5.1	5.0	5.6	5.5	5.6	5.7	5.5
P	3.0	3.3	3.9	5.3	5.7	5.7	5.9	5.0
FIN	6.1	8.8	13.2	16.0	15.7	14.4	14.0	13.3
S	:	:	:	10.8	11.0	10.4	9.8	9.5
UK	5.7	7.3	7.3	7.1	6.4	5.6	4.9	4.0
IS	:	1.5	2.7	3.8	4.2	4.3	3.7	3.2
NO	6.9	7.0	7.7	8.6	7.9	6.7	5.7	4.3
EEA (2)	**7.0**	**8.2**	**8.7**	**9.5**	**8.9**	**8.2**	**8.1**	**7.5**

(1) Data for Sweden not included.
(2) Data for Sweden and Iceland not included.
Source: Eurostat, Esspros.

Between 1990 and 1993, these benefits increased very rapidly in EU-15. Their share of total benefits rose from 7.0 % in 1990 to 9.5 % in 1993.

The corresponding figures for unemployment-related expenditure during this period increased in all the countries except Greece. The increase was particularly marked in Finland (from 6.1 % in 1990 to 16.0 % in 1993), where there was a steeper rise in unemployment than elsewhere.

From 1993 on, there was a decrease in unemployment-related benefits in EU-15, resulting partly from a gradual improvement in the economic situation and partly from reforms of the payment system (e.g. limitation of the period during which benefits are payable, changes in the conditions of entitlement to benefits) in some countries. Between 1993 and 1997, the share of unemployment-related expenditure in total benefits fell from 9.5 to 7.5 % in EU-15. The decrease was more marked in Spain (from 21.7 to 14.1 %), Denmark (from 17.9 to 12.6 %), the United Kingdom (from 7.1 to 4.0 %) and Finland (from 16.0 to 13.3 %). There was also a significant decrease in Norway.

Figure 6.4.4. Receipts of social protection by type, EU-15, 1997 (as a % of total receipts)

General government contributions 32.4
Other receipts 5.2
Employers' social contributions 38.4
Social contributions of protected persons 24.0

NB: Data for Sweden are not included.
Source: Eurostat, Esspros.

The financing of social protection

The systems for funding social protection vary considerably between countries

In 1997 for EU-15 as a whole, the main sources of funding for the social protection system were social contributions, which accounted for 62.4 % of total receipts (68.2 % for the euro zone: EUR-11), followed by tax-funded general government contributions (32.4 % for EU-15 and 28.2 % for EUR-11). Social contributions are paid partly by employers and partly by the protected persons (employees, self-employed, pensioners and others).

The European average conceals considerable differences between the countries in the structure of social protection funding (Table 6.4.7). The proportion derived from social contributions is greater in France, Belgium, Spain, the Netherlands, Germany and Italy, where this type of funding accounts for over 65 % of total receipts.

In contrast, Denmark, Ireland and Norway finance their social protection systems mainly through taxes, which account for over 60 % of total receipts. The United Kingdom, Luxembourg, Sweden and Iceland are also heavily dependent on general government contributions.

Financing social protection: during the 1990s the proportion of general government contributions increased while that of employers' social contributions decreased

During the economic slowdown from 1990 to 1993, general government contributions per capita increased in real terms (+ 24 %) in EU-15 more rapidly than the other sources of funding (+ 9 % for total receipts). In contrast, employers' social contributions showed very little increase (+ 2 %). Between 1993 and 1997, when GDP recovered, general government contributions increased at a lower rate and employers' contributions began to rise again.

Overall, between 1990 and 1997 general government contributions as a proportion of total receipts increased by 3.6 points in EU-15 (Table 6.4.7). Particularly in Portugal and the United Kingdom, these contributions increased more rapidly than in the other countries. On the other hand, they accounted for considerably less of the total receipts in Denmark and the Netherlands. In 1997, only 15.6 % of social protection in the Netherlands was funded by general government contributions.

Table 6.4.6. Receipts of social protection per capita at constant prices in EU-15 (¹) (1990 = 100)

	1991	1992	1993	1994	1995	1996	1997
General government contributions	106	114	124	127	125	130	131
Social contributions	101	104	104	107	108	111	112
— by employers	100	102	102	103	105	107	108
— by protected persons (²)	103	106	109	113	115	118	120
Other receipts	93	93	93	90	92	95	94
Total receipts	**102**	**106**	**109**	**111**	**112**	**115**	**117**

(¹) Data for Sweden not included.
(²) Employees, self-employed, pensioners and others.
Source: Eurostat, Esspros.

Between 1990 and 1997, the share of employers' social contributions fell by 3.6 points in EU-15, decreasing in all the countries except Belgium, the Netherlands and Denmark. There were particularly large reductions in Portugal and Finland.

In contrast, the share of social contributions by protected persons increased by about one point in EU-15 as a whole. In Denmark, in particular, a new contribution called the 'labour market contribution' was introduced in 1994 to finance sickness, unemployment and vocational training insurance. France, Belgium, Ireland, Portugal and the United Kingdom, on the other hand, saw a decrease in their share of social contributions by protected persons.

Table 6.4.7. Receipts of social protection by type (as a % of total receipts)

	General government contributions		Social contributions						Other receipts	
			Total		Employers		Protected persons (¹)			
	1990	1997	1990	1997	1990	1997	1990	1997	1990	1997
EU-15 (²)	**28.8**	**32.4**	**65.0**	**62.4**	**42.0**	**38.4**	**23.0**	**24.0**	**6.2**	**5.2**
EUR-11	**25.0**	**28.2**	**70.8**	**68.1**	**46.0**	**42.2**	**24.8**	**26.0**	**4.2**	**3.6**
B	24.7	24.9	66.0	72.3	40.9	49.2	25.2	23.1	9.3	2.8
DK	80.1	67.8	13.1	26.0	7.8	8.5	5.3	17.5	6.8	6.2
D	25.3	30.1	72.0	67.5	43.6	38.6	28.4	28.9	2.8	2.4
EL	33.0	29.6	59.0	60.8	39.4	37.6	19.6	23.2	8.0	9.6
E	26.2	27.1	71.3	69.7	54.4	52.2	16.9	17.5	2.5	3.3
F	16.7	24.0	80.8	72.8	52.0	46.4	28.8	26.4	2.5	3.2
IRL	59.0	63.9	40.0	35.3	24.4	21.4	15.6	13.8	1.0	0.9
I	29.0	30.5	67.9	67.4	52.9	50.3	15.0	17.1	3.1	2.1
L	40.6	47.2	51.5	48.7	28.9	25.1	22.6	23.6	7.9	4.1
NL	25.0	15.6	59.0	69.1	20.0	22.6	39.1	46.4	15.9	15.3
A	35.9	34.6	63.1	64.8	38.1	37.7	25.1	27.1	0.9	0.6
P	33.7	43.3	57.1	46.7	37.1	28.6	20.0	18.1	9.2	10.1
FIN	40.6	44.8	52.1	48.4	44.1	35.1	8.0	13.3	7.3	6.8
S	:	46.2	:	47.0	:	39.2	:	7.8	:	6.8
UK	39.9	47.3	43.5	40.4	27.2	25.2	16.3	15.3	16.6	12.3
IS	:	56.2	:	43.8	:	35.4	:	8.4	:	0.0
NO	63.0	60.8	36.4	38.3	24.0	23.9	12.4	14.4	0.5	1.0
EEA (³)	**29.4**	**32.9**	**64.5**	**62.0**	**41.7**	**38.2**	**22.8**	**23.8**	**6.1**	**5.1**

(¹) Employees, self-employed, pensioners and others.
(²) Data for Sweden not included.
(³) Data for Sweden and Iceland not included.
Source: Eurostat, Esspros.

Notes on the data

Data on benefits and receipts are not available for Sweden for the period 1990–92. Data for Iceland are not available for 1990. The figures for EU-15 and the EEA have been calculated, wherever necessary, without Sweden and Iceland either to enable the results to be compared over time or to maintain consistency with other results presented in this publication. No data are available for Liechtenstein. France and Ireland record disability pensions paid to persons of retirement age as benefits under the disability function (instead of the old-age function).

For France (from 1995) and Sweden (from 1993), the figures are calculated according to the new national accounts methodology ESA 95.

The 1997 data are provisional for Belgium, Germany, Spain, Italy, the Netherlands, Portugal, Finland and the United Kingdom.

Expenditure on pensions

The Esspros methodology distinguishes between cash benefits and benefits in kind. Cash benefits can be periodic or lump sum. The 'pensions' aggregate only includes some periodic cash benefits in the disability, old age, survivors' and unemployment functions. More specifically, the 'pensions' aggregate is defined in this publication as the sum of the following social benefits (with the function to which the category of benefit belongs in brackets):

- disability pensions (disability function);
- early retirement benefits due to reduced capacity to work (disability function);
- old age pensions (old age function);
- anticipated old age pensions (old age function);
- partial pensions (old age function);
- survivors' pensions (survivors' function);
- early retirement benefits for labour market reasons (unemployment function).

These benefits are divided into means-tested and non-means-tested benefits. The value of the 'pensions' aggregate was calculated for all countries in accordance with the above definition, regardless of national differences in the institutional organisation of social protection systems. Some of the benefits which make up the 'pensions' aggregate (for example disability pensions) are paid to people who have not reached the standard retirement age.

The definitions of the different categories of social benefits can be found in the Esspros manual 1996. In accordance with Esspros, pensions are recorded without any deduction of taxes or other compulsory levies payable on them by beneficiaries. On the other hand, the values of pensions do not include the social contributions which pension schemes pay on behalf of their pensioners to other social protection schemes (e.g. health schemes). Esspros records these payments under the heading 're-routed social contributions'.

In 1997, expenditure on pensions in EU-15 accounted for 13.0 % of GDP. In Italy, expenditure represented approximately 16 % of GDP, followed by Austria and the Netherlands where the ratio was higher than 14 %. In contrast, Ireland spent less than 5 % of GDP on pensions and Iceland less than 6 %.

Between 1990 and 1997, expenditure on pensions in EU-15 as a percentage of GDP increased by 1.2 % from 11.8 % to 13.0 %. This was a general trend in EU-15, with the exception of Ireland, the Netherlands and Greece where there was a decrease in expenditure. The ratio also decreased in Norway between 1990 and 1997. The increase was particularly pronounced in Portugal and Italy (more than 2 % as a percentage of GDP).

The differences between countries can be partly explained by the proportion of the population in the age group 65 and over. In 1997, more than 17 % of Italy's population was in this age group as opposed to less than 12 % in Ireland and compared to an EU-15 average of 15.8 %. In 1997, old age pensions accounted for approximately 75 % of expenditure on pensions in EU-15.

The different regulations concerning early retirement and disability benefits partly explain these results.

For example, in Ireland and Austria expenditure on early retirement benefits ([35]) accounted for more than 12 % of total expenditure on pensions compared to an EU-15 average of approximately 5 %. In contrast expenditure was less than 1 % in Sweden. In Ireland and Austria more than 40 % of the population in the 50–59 age group was inactive compared to an EU-15 average of 36 % in 1997. In Sweden, on the other hand, the rate was less than 15 %.

In 1997, for example, in the Netherlands, Portugal and Finland, disability pensions accounted for more than 20 % of total expenditure on pensions compared to an EU-15 average of approximately 10 %. This was also the case in Iceland and Norway. In France, on the other hand, disability pensions accounted for less than 5 % of total expenditure on pensions.

Figure 6.4.5. Expenditure on pensions, 1997 (as a % of GDP)

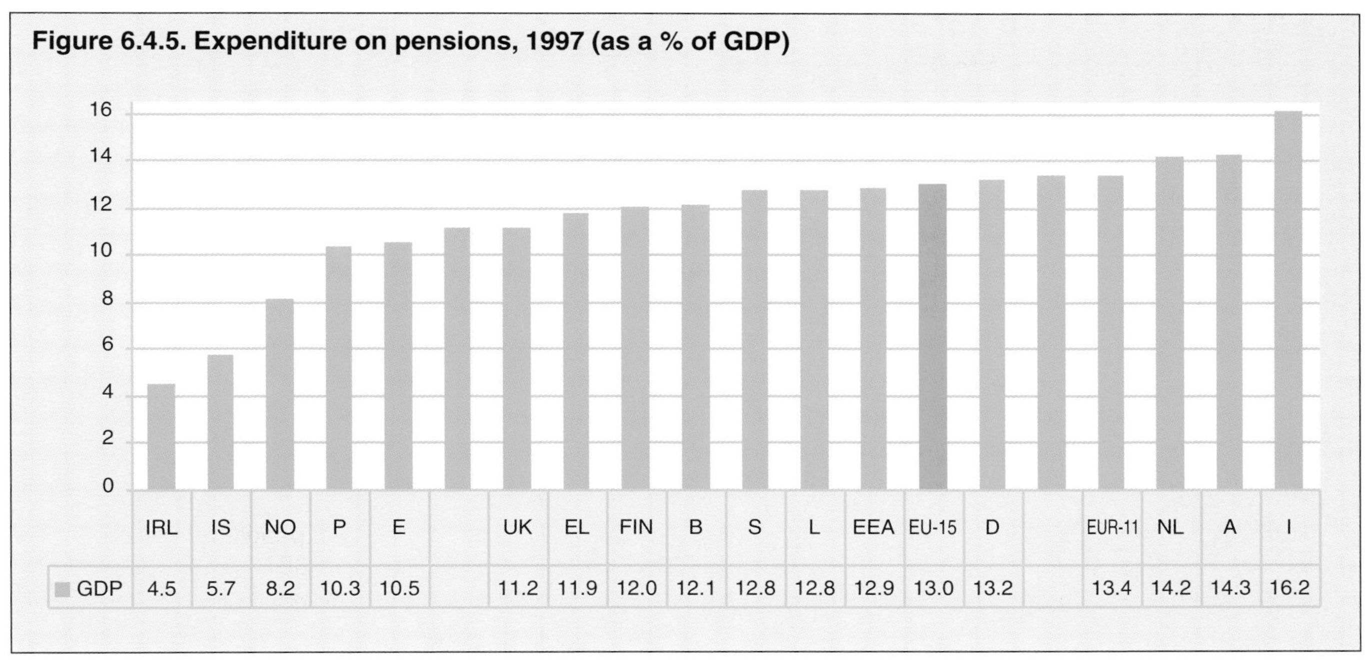

	IRL	IS	NO	P	E	UK	EL	FIN	B	S	L	EEA	EU-15	D	EUR-11	NL	A	I
GDP	4.5	5.7	8.2	10.3	10.5	11.2	11.9	12.0	12.1	12.8	12.8	12.9	13.0	13.2	13.4	14.2	14.3	16.2

Source: Eurostat, Esspros.

Expenditure on pensions represents almost half of total social benefits

In 1997, in the majority of Member States, expenditure on pensions took the largest share of expenditure on social protection, namely 48 % of total expenditure. This was particularly true for Italy, where pensions accounted for over 64 % of total benefits. In Portugal, Greece, Austria and Spain, expenditure on pensions was more than 50 % of total social benefits.

In contrast, in Ireland and Sweden, expenditure on benefits in kind ([36]) was higher than expenditure on pensions. This was also true in Iceland and Norway. In Denmark the proportion of benefits in kind was almost the same as pensions i.e. more than 36 % of the total. In Italy, on the other hand, benefits in kind only represented 5.7 % of GDP compared to an EU-15 average of 8.3 %.

Other cash benefits i.e. cash benefits excluding pensions ([37]) represented 22 % of total benefits in EU-15 or 5.9 % of GDP in 1997. In contrast, they represented more than 30 % of the total in Ireland and less than 15 % of the total in Portugal, Italy and Greece.

Figure 6.4.6. Expenditure in EU-15 in 1997 (as % of total benefits and of GDP)

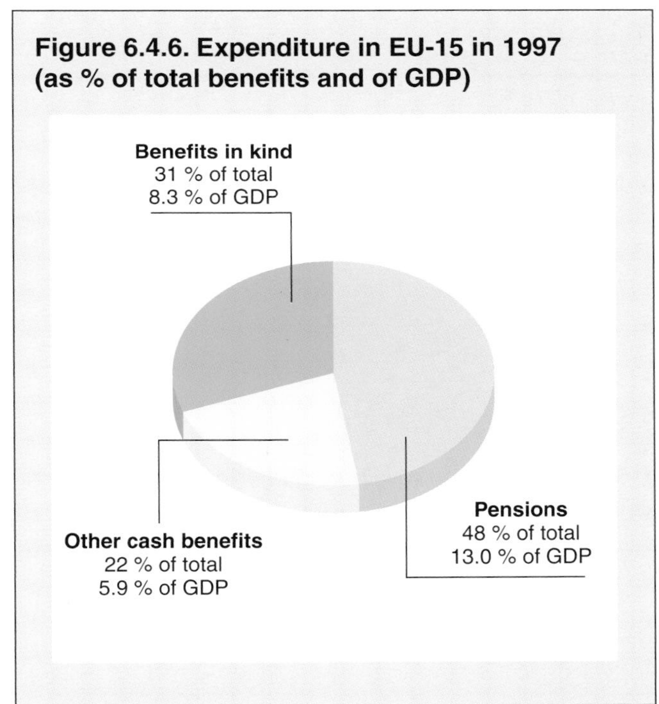

Source: Eurostat, Esspros.

([35]) Early retirement benefits due to reduced capacity to work, anticipated old age pensions, partial pensions and early retirement benefits for labour market reasons.

([36]) Benefits in kind: for example hospital and out-patient treatment, accommodation for elderly and disabled people, child day care, etc.

([37]) Other cash benefits: for example family allowances, birth grants, death grants, unemployment and vocational training benefits, paid sick leave and maternity leave, etc.

Table 6.4.8. Expenditure as a % of GDP, 1997

	Pensions	Other cash benefits	Benefits in kind	Total benefits
EU-15	13.0	5.9	8.3	27.2
EUR-11	13.4	5.8	7.9	27.1
B	12.1	7.9	6.7	26.7
DK	11.2	7.8	10.7	29.6
D	13.2	6.8	8.8	28.8
EL	11.8	3.3	7.5	22.7
E	10.5	4.5	5.8	20.9
F	13.4	6.4	9.5	29.3
IRL	4.5	5.8	6.5	16.8
I	16.2	3.2	5.7	25.1
L	12.8	:	:	23.9
NL	14.2	6.8	7.9	28.9
A	14.3	5.6	8.0	27.9
P	10.3	2.4	7.1	19.8
FIN	12.0	7.5	8.9	28.5
S	12.8	6.8	13.4	32.9
UK	11.2	6.5	9.1	26.9
IS	5.7	3.4	8.6	17.8
NO	8.2	6.5	10.5	25.1
EEA	12.9	6.0	8.4	27.2

Source: Eurostat, Esspros.

7. MONEY, INTEREST RATES AND PRICES IN THE UNION

7.1. Exchange rates, the euro and EMU

The third stage of economic and monetary union (EMU) began with the introduction of the single currency, the euro, on 1 January 1999. In May 1998, the European Council announced the 11 countries that would be part of EMU from the outset: Austria, Belgium, Finland, France, Germany, Ireland, Italy, Luxembourg, Netherlands, Portugal and Spain. Since 1 January 1999, the currencies of these countries have been fixed against the euro at an irrevocable conversion rate (see Table 7.1.1) and they have thus become non-decimal subdivisions of the euro. On that date the euro also replaced the ecu at a rate of 1 to 1. Rounding rules apply for the conversion of currencies (see box).

Rounding rules (summary)

Conversion from national currency to euro

The official euro conversion rates are always to six figures. In order to ensure accuracy, these rates must not be shortened or rounded off during conversion. To convert a national currency amount into euro, the amount must be multiplied by the appropriate conversion rate. An amount in euro can be converted to national currency by dividing by the conversion rate.

Conversion of two euro zone currencies

Conversion must always be via the euro, using the conversion rates.

Conversion of euro zone currency and third currency

Conversion must also be via the euro, but using the third currency's current exchange rate against the euro.

Milestones in EMU

1 January 1999

- Introduction of the euro and its use in non-cash form
- Entry into force of the legislation (principle of 'neither obligation nor prohibition', the rounding rules)
- Definition and implementation of monetary policy by the ECB and the ESCB
- Exchange transactions in euro
- Public debt issuance in euro
- Introduction of Target settlement system

1 January 2002

- Introduction of euro notes and coins
- All accounting in euro
- Gradual withdrawal of national currency notes and coins

1 July 2002

- National currencies no longer legal tender

In June 2000, the European Council agreed that Greece would join the list of euro zone countries with effect from 1 January 2001. Euro notes and coins will be introduced in cash form throughout the euro zone in January 2002, and national currency denominations will disappear by July 2002.

ERM and ERM II

Between March 1979 and the end of 1998 the exchange rate mechanism (ERM) linked the currencies that were part of the European monetary system (EMS). From August 1993 their exchange rates were obliged to remain within fluctuation bands of 15 % around the bilateral central rates. In March 1998, when the Greek drachma joined the ERM, the central rates were adjusted for the last time, with the Irish pound being revalued by 3 %. For the last 10 months of its existence, the ERM included 13 Member State currencies: only the pound sterling and the Swedish krona (a 'notional' central rate applied to the former) were not part of the system.

ERM II came into existence on 1 January 1999, linking to the euro the Greek drachma and the Danish krone, the currencies of two Member States that did not join the euro zone from the outset. (The other two currencies, the pound sterling and the Swedish krona, are not members of ERM II). The aim of ERM II is to prepare the second-wave countries for eventual participation in the euro zone, while helping to ensure exchange rate stability within the EU. The two currencies have a central rate against the euro of 340.75 in the case of the Greek drachma and 7.46038 for the Danish krone. Their fluctuation bands are ± 15 % for the Greek drachma and ± 2.25 % for the Danish krone. The fluctuation band is supported at the margins by unlimited intervention, with short-term financing available. However, the ECB (European Central Bank), as well as the national central banks not participating in the euro can suspend intervention if the main purpose — maintaining price stability — can no longer be guaranteed.

Greece will enter the euro zone in January 2001: its conversion rate against the euro will be the same as its central rate in ERM II.

Exchange rates

The official exchange rates for the ecu, as it existed until 31 December 1998, against its constituent currencies and other currencies were calculated every day by the European Commission on the basis of the composition of the ecu basket (see *The economic accounts of the European Union — 1997*).

Since 1 January 1999, the exchange rates of the countries which formed the euro zone have been fixed to the euro. Every day the ECB provides the official reference rates for the main international currencies against the euro.

Table 7.1.1 shows the exchange rates of the ecu (until 1998) and the euro (from 1999) against the national currencies of the EU Member States, the US dollar and the Japanese yen since 1990. The figures indicate the value of an ecu or euro in national currency. For the countries belonging to the euro zone from 1 January 1999, the exchange rates shown in 1999 are the fixed conversion rates to the euro.

Table 7.1.1. Ecu/euro exchange rates, annual average

	BEF/LUF	DKK	DEM	GRD	ESP	FRF	IEP	ITL
1990	42.4257	7.85652	2.05209	201.412	129.411	6.91412	0.767768	1 521.98
1991	42.2233	7.90859	2.05076	225.216	128.469	6.97332	0.767809	1 533.24
1992	41.5932	7.80925	2.02031	247.026	132.526	6.84839	0.760718	1 595.52
1993	40.4713	7.59359	1.93639	268.568	149.124	6.63368	0.799952	1 841.23
1994	39.6565	7.54328	1.92453	288.026	158.918	6.58262	0.793618	1 915.06
1995	38.5519	7.32804	1.87375	302.989	163.000	6.52506	0.815525	2 130.14
1996	39.2986	7.35934	1.90954	305.546	160.748	6.49300	0.793448	1 958.96
1997	40.5332	7.48361	1.96438	309.355	165.887	6.61260	0.747516	1 929.30
1998	40.6207	7.4993	1.96913	330.731	167.184	6.60141	0.786245	1 943.65
1999	40.3399	7.43556	1.95583	325.763	166.386	6.55957	0.787564	1 936.27

	NLG	ATS	PTE	FIM	SEK	GBP	USD	JPY
1990	2.31212	14.4399	181.109	4.85496	7.52051	0.713851	1.27343	183.66
1991	2.31098	14.4309	178.614	5.00211	7.47927	0.701012	1.23916	166.493
1992	2.27482	14.2169	174.714	5.80703	7.53295	0.737650	1.29810	164.223
1993	2.17521	13.6238	188.37	6.69628	9.12151	0.779988	1.17100	130.148
1994	2.15827	13.5396	196.896	6.19077	9.16308	0.775903	1.18952	121.322
1995	2.09891	13.1824	196.105	5.70855	9.33192	0.828789	1.30801	123.012
1996	2.13973	13.4345	195.761	5.82817	8.51472	0.813798	1.26975	138.084
1997	2.21081	13.824	198.589	5.88064	8.65117	0.692304	1.13404	137.077
1998	2.21967	13.8545	201.695	5.98251	8.91593	0.676434	1.12109	146.415
1999	2.20371	13.7603	200.482	5.94573	8.80752	0.658735	1.06578	121.317

NB: for 1999 the following currencies are fixed against the euro at the rates shown: BEF, LUF, DEM, ESP, FRF, IEP, ITL, NLG, ATS, PTE, FIM.
Source: Eurostat.

Table 7.1.2. Ecu/euro exchange rate indices, annual average (1996 = 100)

	BEF/ LUF	DKK	DEM	GRD	ESP	FRF	IEP	ITL	NLG	ATS	PTE	FIM	SEK	GBP	USD	JPY
1990	92.6	93.7	93.1	151.8	124.2	93.9	103.3	128.7	92.5	93.0	108.1	120.0	113.2	113.9	100.0	75.2
1991	93.1	93.1	93.1	135.7	125.1	93.1	103.3	127.7	92.6	93.1	109.6	116.7	113.8	116.0	102.8	83.1
1992	94.5	94.3	94.5	123.8	121.4	94.8	104.3	123.0	94.1	94.5	112.1	100.7	113.2	110.5	98.0	84.2
1993	97.1	96.9	98.6	113.8	108.1	97.9	99.2	106.4	98.4	98.6	104.1	87.1	93.4	104.3	108.5	106.6
1994	99.1	97.6	99.2	106.1	101.1	98.6	99.9	102.3	99.1	99.2	99.4	94.2	92.9	104.8	106.9	113.8
1995	101.9	100.4	101.9	100.9	98.6	99.5	97.3	92.1	101.9	101.9	99.8	102.1	91.4	98.1	97.1	112.7
1996	100.0	100.0	100.0	100.0	100.0	100.0	100.0	100.0	100.0	100.0	100.0	100.0	100.0	100.0	100.0	100.0
1997	96.9	98.3	97.2	98.8	96.9	98.2	106.1	101.5	96.8	97.2	98.6	99.1	98.4	117.5	112.1	100.9
1998	96.7	98.1	97.0	92.5	96.1	98.4	100.9	100.7	96.4	97.0	97.1	97.4	95.6	120.2	113.4	94.5
1999	97.4	99.0	97.6	93.8	96.6	99.0	100.7	101.1	97.1	97.6	97.6	98.0	96.7	123.5	119.3	114.5

NB: Euro for 1999.
Source: Eurostat.

Table 7.1.2 shows the exchange rates of EU currencies, the US dollar and the Japanese yen against the ecu (until 1998) and euro (from 1999) in index terms. It shows the value in ecu/euro of one unit of national currency, the base year being 1996.

A comparison of the data for 1990 and 1998 reveals that 7 of the 13 currencies in the ERM in 1998 appreciated against the ecu, with increases ranging between 4 % and 6 %. Four other ERM currencies lost between 2 % and 22 % of their value against the ecu. The Greek drachma, which entered the system in March 1998, lost about 39 % in eight years. As a rule, the countries that were in the ERM for several years had fairly stable currencies. The ERM currencies converged more and more until, in the second half of 1998, there were hardly any fluctuations between the currencies which formed the euro zone in January 1999. Compared with 1990, the US dollar and the Japanese yen had appreciated by 13 % and 25 % respectively against the ECU by 1998.

In 1999, between 1 January and 31 December, the following fluctuations against the euro took place:

- the ERM II member currencies were very stable: the Danish krone (DKK) rose by 0.1 % and Greek drachma (GRD) depreciated by 0.2 %;
- the pound sterling (GBP) gained 13.4 % and the Swedish krona (SEK) 10.8 % respectively;
- the US dollar (USD) and Japanese yen (JPY) appreciated by 16.1 % and 29.3 % respectively.

7.2. Interest rates

Government bond yields are a good indicator of long-term interest rates, since the government securities market generally attracts a large proportion of available capital. They also provide a fairly good reflection of a country's financial situation and of expectations in terms of economic policy.

The significance of government bond yields as a measure of economic and monetary convergence is recognised in the Treaty on European Union, where it appears as one of the criteria for moving to stage three of monetary union, which got under way on 1 January 1999.

Table 7.2.1 shows the yield on 10-year government bonds, as defined in the Maastricht Treaty. After the economic recession in 1993 and in response to the recovery that occurred in the following year, government bond yields rose in most European countries to peak in the second half of 1994, or in the first quarter of 1995 for countries such as Spain, Portugal, Italy and Sweden. At that time there was still a considerable yield differential between these four countries and other EU countries.

Since then, apart from a slight rise in yields in a number of European countries at the beginning of 1996, the situation has been marked by two interesting features: a general fall in yields in every Member State until the end of 1998, when they reached record lows, and a degree of convergence that had never been attained before.

At the start of 1999, when the third phase of monetary union became effective, the interest differential on 10-year bonds among the various countries involved in monetary union had practically disappeared. The rate differential had been as much as 510 basis points in the case of Germany and Italy at the end of 1995, and 388 between Germany and Spain at the same time.

It is also interesting to note that at the start of 1999 the interest differential on 10-year bonds between the 11 countries — apart from Greece — in the euro zone and the countries not involved in EMU was only 40 basis points.

There was a slight rise in long-term interest rates in the EU Member States in 1999, with 10-year bonds reaching 5.3 % at the end of December 1999 for EUR-11 and EU-15, compared with 4.0 % and 4.1 % respectively one year earlier.

Long-term interest rates in the United States and Japan also bottomed out in the last quarter of 1998, before beginning a rise that continued throughout 1999. The rise in yields was more marked in the United States than Japan, however.

Short-term interest rates have also tended to show remarkable convergence in recent years (see Table 7.2.2).

One of the major factors in this convergence was of course the third phase of monetary union that began on 1 January 1999. In this regard, it is obvious that the countries planning to take part in EMU needed to have the same official rates on 31 December 1998.

For the 11 countries making up the euro zone, the pattern of convergence was as follows: on the one hand, there was a group of countries — Belgium, Germany, France, Luxembourg, the Netherlands, Austria and Finland — where official interest rates had been fairly low for some years and where the rates had remained unchanged, apart from a slight rise in the third quarter of 1997, followed by an equivalent cut in December 1998. There was a second group of countries — Spain, Italy and Portugal — where official rates had recently been higher and where efforts had been made to lower them steadily to bring them in line with the rates in the other countries.

Lastly, Ireland had put up its official rates, which peaked at 6.75 % in May 1997 before being reduced several times in the last two months of 1998.

Since all 11 countries had identical rates on 31 December 1998, it was possible to launch EMU with a main key rate of 3 %.

During 1999, the European Central Bank (ECB) cut the repo rate to 2.5 % in April, before raising it to 3 % again in November.

The situation was less settled in the four other Member States that are not part of EMU. Denmark and Sweden lowered their official rates several times in 1999, before the central banks in the two countries raised them again in November. At the end of 1999, the repo rate was 3.3 % in Denmark and 3.25 % in Sweden.

Like its counterparts in Denmark and Sweden, the Bank of England cut its key rate several times in the first half of 1999. The difference with regard to the two other countries was that the official rates in the United Kingdom started to rise again in September. They went up again in November and stood at 5.5 % at the end of the year.

For its part, Greece cut its official rates three times during 1999, with the repo rate falling from 12.25 to 10.75 %. By the end of May 2000 the rate had been cut to 8.75 %.

Table 7.2.1. Long-term interest rates, monthly average (as a %)

	Jan. 1994	Jan. 1995	Jan. 1996	Jan. 1997	Jan. 1998	Jan. 1999	Feb. 1999	March 1999	April 1999
EU-15	6.9	9.5	7.5	6.6	5.5	3.9	4.1	4.3	4.1
EUR-11	6.7	9.3	7.4	6.2	5.2	3.8	4.0	4.2	4.0
B	6.5	8.5	6.4	5.9	5.2	3.9	4.0	4.3	4.1
DK	6.0	9.1	7.0	6.5	5.4	4.0	4.2	4.4	4.2
D	5.8	7.6	5.9	5.8	5.1	3.7	3.9	4.0	3.9
EL	22.0	19.0	15.4	12.3	11.0	6.3	6.0	6.0	5.9
E	8.0	11.9	9.5	6.8	5.4	3.9	4.0	4.3	4.1
F	5.7	8.2	6.4	5.7	5.1	3.8	3.9	4.1	4.0
IRL	6.2	8.8	7.2	6.6	5.4	3.9	4.0	4.2	4.0
I	8.7	12.4	10.4	7.4	5.4	3.9	4.1	4.3	4.1
L	6.3	7.8	6.4	5.7	5.2	3.9	3.9	4.2	4.0
NL	5.6	7.7	5.9	5.7	5.1	3.8	3.9	4.1	4.0
A	5.8	7.7	6.2	5.8	5.2	3.8	4.0	4.2	4.0
P	8.9	11.8	9.4	6.7	5.4	3.9	4.0	4.2	4.1
FIN	6.5	10.2	7.0	6.1	5.3	3.9	4.0	4.3	4.1
S	7.0	11.0	8.2	6.7	5.7	4.0	4.2	4.4	4.2
UK	6.3	8.8	7.6	7.7	6.2	4.2	4.4	4.6	4.5
US	5.8	7.9	5.7	6.7	5.6	4.8	5.0	5.2	5.2
JP	3.3	4.7	3.0	2.5	1.7	2.1	2.1	1.7	1.6

	May 1999	June 1999	July 1999	Aug. 1999	Sept. 1999	Oct. 1999	Nov. 1999	Dec. 1999
EU-15	4.3	4.6	4.9	5.1	5.3	5.5	5.2	5.3
EUR-11	4.2	4.5	4.9	5.1	5.2	5.5	5.2	5.3
B	4.3	4.6	4.9	5.2	5.3	5.6	5.3	5.4
DK	4.5	4.8	5.1	5.4	5.6	5.8	5.5	5.5
D	4.0	4.4	4.7	4.9	5.0	5.3	5.0	5.2
EL	5.8	6.0	6.4	6.7	6.6	7.0	6.6	6.4
E	4.3	4.6	4.9	5.2	5.3	5.6	5.3	5.4
F	4.2	4.5	4.8	5.0	5.2	5.4	5.2	5.3
IRL	4.2	4.6	4.9	5.2	5.3	5.6	5.3	5.4
I	4.3	4.6	4.9	5.1	5.3	5.5	5.3	5.4
L	4.2	4.4	4.9	5.2	5.3	5.5	5.3	5.3
NL	4.2	4.5	4.8	5.0	5.2	5.5	5.2	5.3
A	4.2	4.5	4.9	5.1	5.3	5.5	5.3	5.4
P	4.3	4.6	5.0	5.3	5.4	5.6	5.4	5.5
FIN	4.2	4.6	4.9	5.2	5.3	5.6	5.3	5.4
S	4.5	4.9	5.3	5.5	5.7	5.9	5.6	5.6
UK	4.8	5.1	5.3	5.3	5.6	5.8	5.2	5.4
US	5.5	5.9	5.8	5.9	5.9	6.1	6.0	6.3
JP	1.4	1.6	1.7	1.9	1.8	1.8	1.8	1.7

NB: Ten-year government bond yield, except for the US (10 years or more).
Source: Eurostat.

In the United States the Federal Reserve put rates up three times in 1999. At the end of the year, the rate for federal funds was 5.5 %, compared with 4.75 % a year earlier. This trend continued in the first few months of 2000.

In Japan, the discount rate has been fixed at a record low of 0.5 % since September 1995.

Table 7.2.2. Short-term interest rates, monthly average (as a %)

	Jan. 1994	Jan. 1995	Jan. 1996	Jan. 1997	Jan. 1998	Jan. 1999	Feb. 1999	March 1999	April 1999
EUR-11	6.8	5.9	5.3	4.4	3.9	3.1	3.1	2.9	2.7
B	7.2	5.0	3.7	3.0	3.4	:	:	:	:
DK	6.8	5.5	4.7	3.5	3.7	3.8	3.6	3.4	3.0
D	6.2	5.0	3.6	3.1	3.4	:	:	:	:
EL	19.5	16.9	13.9	12.4	15.1	11.4	10.2	10.2	10.2
E	9.0	8.0	9.0	6.1	4.8	:	:	:	:
F	6.5	5.4	4.5	3.3	3.4	:	:	:	:
IRL	5.9	5.1	5.0	5.5	6.3	:	:	:	:
I	8.7	8.4	10.2	7.7	6.3	:	:	:	:
L	:	:	:	:	:	:	:	:	:
NL	5.5	5.0	3.3	2.7	3.3	:	:	:	:
A	5.5	4.8	3.7	3.2	3.4	:	:	:	:
P	10.6	8.8	8.1	6.4	5.0	:	:	:	:
FIN	5.6	4.4	4.3	2.7	2.8	:	:	:	:
S	7.9	7.6	8.8	4.2	4.5	3.5	3.4	3.2	3.0
UK	5.5	5.6	6.3	5.9	7.3	5.9	5.8	5.6	5.4
US	3.1	5.3	5.6	5.3	5.6	4.6	4.8	4.8	4.7
JP	2.30	2.30	0.50	0.50	0.40	0.20	0.20	0.04	0.03

	May 1999	June 1999	July 1999	Aug. 1999	Sept. 1999	Oct. 1999	Nov. 1999	Dec. 1999
EUR-11	2.6	2.6	2.5	2.4	2.4	2.5	2.9	3.0
B	:	:	:	:	:	:	:	:
DK	2.9	2.9	2.9	2.8	2.9	2.9	3.2	3.1
D	:	:	:	:	:	:	:	:
EL	10.4	10.4	10.3	10.3	10.3	10.6	10.8	9.8
E	:	:	:	:	:	:	:	:
F	:	:	:	:	:	:	:	:
IRL	:	:	:	:	:	:	:	:
I	:	:	:	:	:	:	:	:
L	:	:	:	:	:	:	:	:
NL	:	:	:	:	:	:	:	:
A	:	:	:	:	:	:	:	:
P	:	:	:	:	:	:	:	:
FIN	:	:	:	:	:	:	:	:
S	3.0	3.0	3.0	3.0	3.0	3.0	3.2	3.4
UK	5.3	4.9	5.0	4.9	5.1	5.3	5.3	5.6
US	4.7	4.8	5.0	5.1	5.2	5.2	5.4	5.3
JP	0.03	0.03	0.03	0.03	0.03	0.02	0.03	0.02

Source: Eurostat.

7.3. Consumer prices

Consumer price inflation (CPI) is best compared at international level by the 'harmonised index of consumer prices' (HICP). They are calculated in each Member State of the European Union, Iceland and Norway. HICPs form the basis of the monetary union index of consumer prices (MUICP), the EICP and the EEAICP. HICPs are not intended to replace national CPIs. Member States have continued so far their existing CPIs for domestic purposes.

HICPs and the MUICP are used by, among others, the European Central Bank (ECB) for monitoring inflation in the economic and monetary union and the assessment of inflation convergence. As required by the treaty, the maintenance of price stability is the primary objective of the ECB which defined price stability 'as a year-on-year increase in the harmonised index of consumer prices for the euro zone of below 2 %'. Strictly speaking this definition applies to the MUICP.

The MUICP was published for the first time for the 11 countries going to participate in the third stage of EMU with the release of the index for April 1998.

Trends in consumer price inflation 1997–2000

The annual rate of change (m/(m–12)) is commonly used for analysing inflation trends. This measure is appropriate for short-term analysis, although it suffers from variability due to one-off effects (such as tax changes). Table 7.3.1 and Figure 7.3.1 show the annual rates of change in the HICPs, the MUICP and the EICP for every third month between January 1997 and June 2000.

The annual rates of change of the EICP illustrate an overall falling trend from 2.2 % in January 1997 to 1.0 % in December 1998. This trend reversed from June 1999 and led to an annual rate of change of 2.1 % in June 2000. With the index for March 2000 the annual rates of change of the MUICP have passed beyond the 2.0 % stability threshold defined by the ECB with the exception of a 1.9 % rate in May 2000. It should also be noted that since October 1999 the annual rates of change of the MUICP have become generally higher than those of the EICP.

A more stable measure — the 12-month average change — is the average index for the latest 12 months compared with the average index for the previous 12 months. It is less sensitive to transient changes in prices but it requires a longer time series of indices. Nevertheless, similar trends to those described above may be noted, as shown in Table 2. In June 2000, however, the 12-month average rate of change is at 1.7 % for the MUICP and at 1.6 % for the EICP. Both rates are indeed much lower than 2.0 %, seen as a medium-term price stability threshold.

The protocol on convergence criteria relating to Article 109(j)(1) of the treaty requires that a Member State's rate of inflation 'does not exceed by more than 1½ percentage points that of, at most, the three best performing Member States'. Table 7.3.2 shows some summary data based on 12-month average changes. The reference values have been calculated using a simple arithmetic mean of 'the three best performing Member States' and 'the three best performing Member States of the euro zone'.

Since the launch of the euro in January 1999, Austria, France, Germany, and Luxembourg have been, as shown in Table 7.3.2 among the three best performing Member States in the euro zone. Austria, France, Germany, Luxembourg and Sweden were among the three best performing Member States in the EU. From March 1999 to April 2000, Austria, France and Sweden have permanently been among the three best performing EU Member States. In May and June, the United Kingdom replaced Austria.

Table 7.3.1. Harmonised Indices of consumer prices (1997–2000), annual rates of change m/m–12 (as a %)

	1997					1998				1999				2000	
	Jan.	March	June	Sept.	Dec.	March	June	Sept.	Dec.	March	June	Sept.	Dec.	March	June
B	2.1	1.3	1.6	1.6	0.9	1.0	1.2	0.8	0.7	1.3	0.7	1.3	2.1	2.5	3.0
D	1.8	1.4	1.5	1.5	1.4	0.5	0.8	0.5	0.2	0.5	0.4	0.8	1.4	2.1	2.0
E	2.8	2.2	1.4	1.9	1.9	1.7	2.0	1.6	1.4	2.1	2.1	2.5	2.8	3.0	3.5
F	1.8	1.1	1.0	1.5	1.2	0.8	1.1	0.5	0.3	0.4	0.3	0.6	1.4	1.7	1.9
IRL	1.8	1.3	1.5	0.6	1.0	1.5	2.6	2.8	2.2	2.0	2.1	2.6	3.9	5.0	5.4
I	2.6	2.2	1.6	1.6	1.8	2.1	2.1	2.1	1.7	1.4	1.4	1.9	2.1	2.6	2.7
L	1.3	1.3	1.2	1.7	1.5	1.3	1.2	0.7	0.4	0.6	1.2	1.6	2.3	3.0	4.4
NL	1.7	1.2	1.5	2.5	2.2	2.2	2.2	1.3	1.5	2.0	2.1	2.0	1.9	1.6	2.5
A	1.2	1.2	1.0	1.2	1.0	1.0	0.8	0.6	0.5	0.2	0.2	0.6	1.7	2.0	2.4
P	2.8	2.3	1.6	1.5	2.1	1.5	2.7	2.2	2.8	2.8	2.1	1.9	1.7	1.4	2.8
FIN	0.9	0.7	1.1	1.6	1.6	1.6	1.6	1.4	0.8	0.9	1.2	1.4	2.2	3.2	3.1
MUICP	**2**	**1.6**	**1.4**	**1.6**	**1.5**	**1.1**	**1.4**	**1.0**	**0.8**	**1.0**	**0.9**	**1.2**	**1.7**	**2.1**	**2.4**
DK	2.3	1.8	2.4	1.9	1.6	1.6	1.2	1.1	1.1	1.7	1.9	2.4	3.1	3.0	2.9
EL	6.6	5.9	5.6	4.9	4.5	4.3	4.9	5.0	3.7	3.0	1.5	1.3	2.3	2.8	2.2
S	1.3	1.0	1.7	2.6	2.7	1.7	1.4	– 0.1	0.0	0.5	0.4	1.1	1.2	1.4	1.4
UK	2.1	1.7	1.7	1.8	1.7	1.6	1.7	1.5	1.6	1.7	1.4	1.2	1.2	0.7	0.8
EICP	**2.2**	**1.7**	**1.6**	**1.7**	**1.6**	**1.3**	**1.5**	**1.2**	**1.0**	**1.2**	**1.0**	**1.2**	**1.7**	**1.9**	**2.1**
US	3.0	2.8	2.3	2.2	1.7	1.4	1.7	1.5	1.6	1.7	2.0	2.6	2.7	3.7	3.7
JP	0.6	0.5	2.2	2.4	1.8	2.2	0.1	– 0.2	0.6	– 0.4	– 0.3	– 0.2	– 1.1	– 0.5	– 0.7

NB: m/m–12 is the price change between the current month and the same month in the previous year. Please note that for the US and Japan the national CPIs are given which are not strictly comparable with the HICPs.
Source: Eurostat.

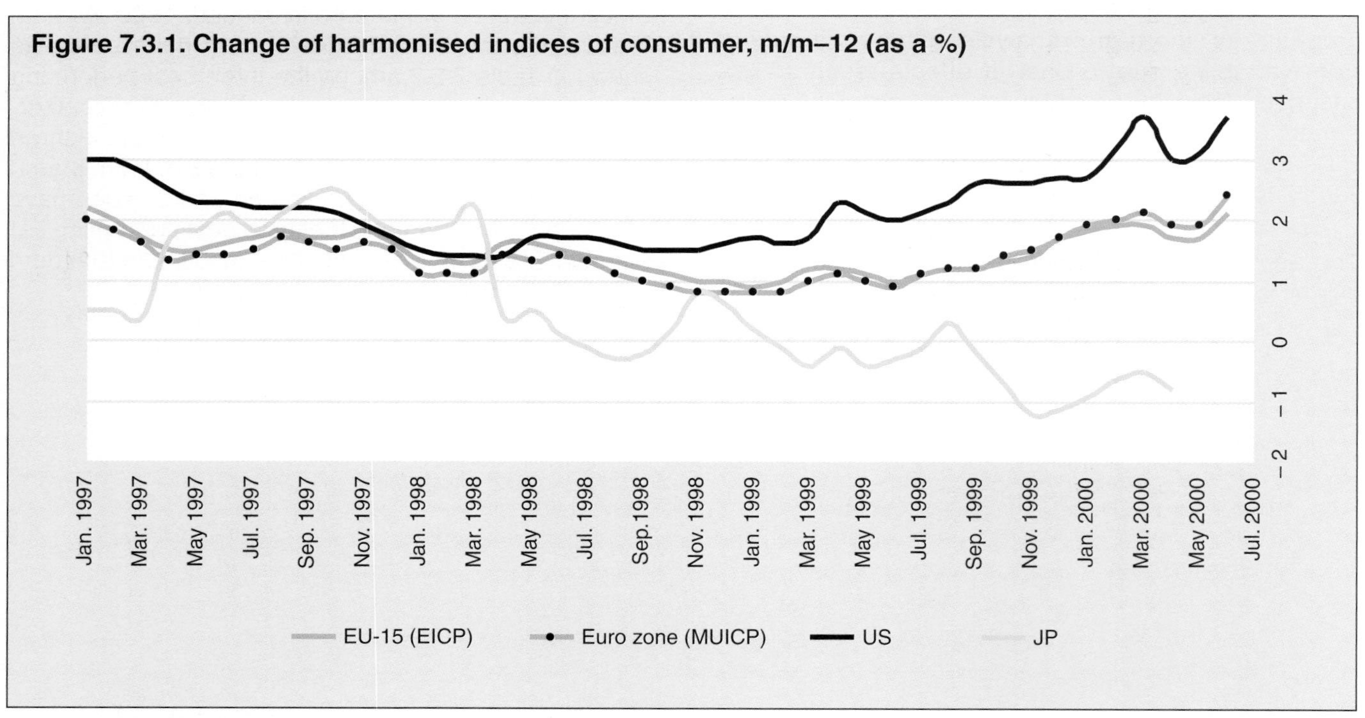

Figure 7.3.1. Change of harmonised indices of consumer, m/m–12 (as a %)

NB: As before, price change between the current month and the same month in the previous year.
Source: Eurostat.

Table 7.3.2. Harmonised indices of consumer prices, 12-month average rate (¹)

1999																	
Jan.		Feb.		March		April		May		June		July		Aug.		Sept.	
D	0.6	D	0.5	D	0.5	D	0.5	S	0.4	S	0.3	S	0.2	S	0.2	S	0.3
F	0.6	F	0.6	F	0.6	F	0.5	A	0.5	D	0.4	D	0.4	D	0.4	D	0.4
L	0.7	L	0.7	L	0.6	A	0.5	D	0.5	F	0.4	F	0.4	F	0.4	F	0.4
A	0.7	A	0.7	A	0.6	S	0.5	F	0.5	A	0.4	A	0.4	A	0.4	A	0.4
S	0.8	S	0.7	S	0.6	L	0.6	L	0.6	L	0.6	L	0.5	L	0.6	L	0.6
B	1.0	B	1.0	B	1.0	B	1.0	B	0.9	B	0.9	B	0.8	B	0.8	B	0.9
MUICP	1.1	MUICP	1.0	MUICP	1.0	MUICP	1.0	MUICP	1.0	MUICP	0.9	MUICP	0.9	MUICP	0.9	MUICP	0.9
FIN	1.2	DK	1.2	FIN	1.1	FIN	1.1	EICP	1.1	FIN	1.0	EICP	1.1	EICP	1.1	EICP	1.1
DK	1.3	EICP	1.2	EICP	1.2	EICP	1.2	FIN	1.1	EICP	1.1	FIN	1.1	FIN	1.1	FIN	1.1
EICP	1.3	FIN	1.2	FIN	1.2	DK	1.3	DK	1.3	DK	1.3	DK	1.4	UK	1.4	UK	1.4
UK	1.6	UK	1.6	UK	1.6	UK	1.5	UK	1.5	UK	1.5	UK	1.4	DK	1.5	DK	1.6
E	1.7	E	1.7	E	1.8	I	1.7	I	1.7	I	1.7	I	1.6	I	1.6	I	1.6
NL	1.8	NL	1.8	I	1.8	E	1.8	E	1.8	E	1.8	E	1.8	RV (EU)	1.8	E	1.9
I	1.9	I	1.9	NL	1.8	NL	1.8	NL	1.8	NL	1.8	NL	1.8	E	1.9	NL	1.9
RV (EU)	2.1	RV (EU)	2.1	RV (EU)	2.1	RV (EU)	2.0	RV (EU)	2.0	RV (EU)	1.9	RV (EU)	1.8	NL	1.9	RV (EU)	1.9
RV (EMU)	2.1	RV (EMU)	2.1	RV (EMU)	2.1	RV (EMU)	2.0	RV (EMU)	2.0	RV (EMU)	1.9	RV (EMU)	1.9	RV (EMU)	1.9	RV (EMU)	1.9
IRL	2.2	IRL	2.3	IRL	2.4	IRL	2.4	IRL	2.4	IRL	2.3	IRL	2.3	IRL	2.2	IRL	2.2
P	2.3	P	2.4	P	2.5	P	2.6	P	2.6	P	2.5	P	2.4	P	2.4	P	2.4
EL	4.4	EL	4.3	EL	4.2	EL	4.0	EL	3.8	EL	3.5	EL	3.2	EL	2.9	EL	2.6

1999						2000											
Oct.		Nov.		Dec.		Jan.		Feb.		March		April		May		July	
F	0.4	A	0.4	A	0.5	A	0.6	A	0.7	S	0.8	S	0.9	S	0.9	S	1.0
A	0.4	D	0.5	D	0.6	S	0.6	S	0.7	F	0.9	F	1.0	UK	1.0	UK	1.0
S	0.4	F	0.5	F	0.6	F	0.7	F	0.8	A	0.9	A	1.0	F	1.1	F	1.2
D	0.5	S	0.5	S	0.6	D	0.8	D	0.9	D	1.1	D	1.1	A	1.1	A	1.3
L	0.7	L	0.9	L	1.0	B	1.2	UK	1.2	UK	1.2	UK	1.1	D	1.2	D	1.4
B	0.9	B	1.0	B	1.1	MUICP	1.2	B	1.3	B	1.4	EICP	1.4	EICP	1.5	EICP	1.6
MUICP	1.0	MUICP	1.0	MUICP	1.1	UK	1.3	EICP	1.3	EICP	1.4	B	1.5	B	1.6	MUICP	1.7
EICP	1.1	EICP	1.1	EICP	1.2	EICP	1.3	MUICP	1.3	MUICP	1.4	MUICP	1.5	MUICP	1.6	B	1.8
FIN	1.1	FIN	1.2	FIN	1.3	L	1.4	L	1.6	L	1.8	P	1.8	NL	1.9	NL	1.9
UK	1.4	UK	1.4	UK	1.3	FIN	1.5	FIN	1.6	FIN	1.8	NL	1.9	P	1.9	P	1.9
I	1.6	I	1.6	I	1.7	I	1.7	I	1.8	I	1.9	FIN	1.9	EL	2.0	EL	2.1
DK	1.8	DK	1.9	NL	2.0	NL	2.0	EL	2.0	NL	1.9	EL	2.0	FIN	2.0	I	2.2
RV (EU)	1.9	NL	2.0	DK	2.1	EL	2.1	NL	2.0	P	1.9	I	2.0	I	2.1	FIN	2.2
RV (EMU)	1.9	RV (EU)	2.0	EL	2.1	P	2.1	P	2.0	EL	2.0	L	2.0	L	2.1	L	2.4
E	2.0	RV (EMU)	2.0	RV (EU)	2.1	RV (EU)	2.1	RV (EU)	2.2	DK	2.4	DK	2.5	RV(EU)	2.5	RV(EU)	2.6
NL	2.0	E	2.1	RV (EMU)	2.1	DK	2.2	DK	2.3	RV (EU)	2.4	RV(EU)	2.5	DK	2.6	DK	2.7
IRL	2.2	EL	2.3	E	2.2	RV (EMU)	2.2	RV (EMU)	2.3	E	2.5	RV(EMU)	2.5	RV (EMU)	2.6	E	2.8
P	2.3	IRL	2.3	P	2.2	E	2.4	E	2.4	RV (EMU)	2.5	E	2.6	E	2.7	RV(EMU)	2.8
EL	2.4	P	2.3	IRL	2.5	IRL	2.7	IRL	2.9	IRL	3.1	IRL	3.3	IRL	3.6	IRL	3.9

(¹) Average of the latest 12 months compared to the average of the previous 12 months.
NB: RV (EU) = reference value defined as unweighted arithmetic mean of the three best-performing countries in the EU.
RV (EMU) = reference value defined as unweighted arithmetic mean of the three best-performing countries in the EMU.
Source: Eurostat.

Table 7.3.2 also shows which Member States are above or below the reference values in each month. Ireland, Portugal, Greece, Spain have been above both reference values up to November 1999. Greece, since December 1999, and Portugal, since January 2000, have been comfortably below both reference values. Since October 1999, Spain also fell below both reference values, although in March 2000 the rate coincided with the euro zone reference value. In May 2000, Spain was above the EU reference value but met the euro zone reference value. Denmark was above the EU reference value and below the euro zone reference value in January and February 2000. In March 2000 it was, with 2.4 %, exactly on the EU reference value and below the euro zone reference value. In April 2000, Denmark met both reference values with 2.5 %, while it met the euro zone reference value and was above the EU reference value in May 2000. In June 2000, Denmark was above the EU reference value but below the euro zone reference value. In just one month, August 1999, the Netherlands were above the EU reference value, although they met exactly the euro zone reference value of 1.9 %. Ireland is the only Member State of the euro zone which, at varying magnitudes, remains above both reference values since the launch of the euro in January 1999.

The average spread of inflation rates provides a useful tool for illustrating price convergence since the early stages of the EMU. Graph 7.3.2 illustrates both price stability and the average spread of inflation rates (inflation convergence aspects). The central line shows annual rates of change of the EICP, while the upper and lower lines mark the spread of the HICPs. The spread is calculated as the standard deviation of annual inflation rates of HICPs from the EICP taking into account country weights.

Figure 7.3.2. Average spread of inflation rates (1996–2000)

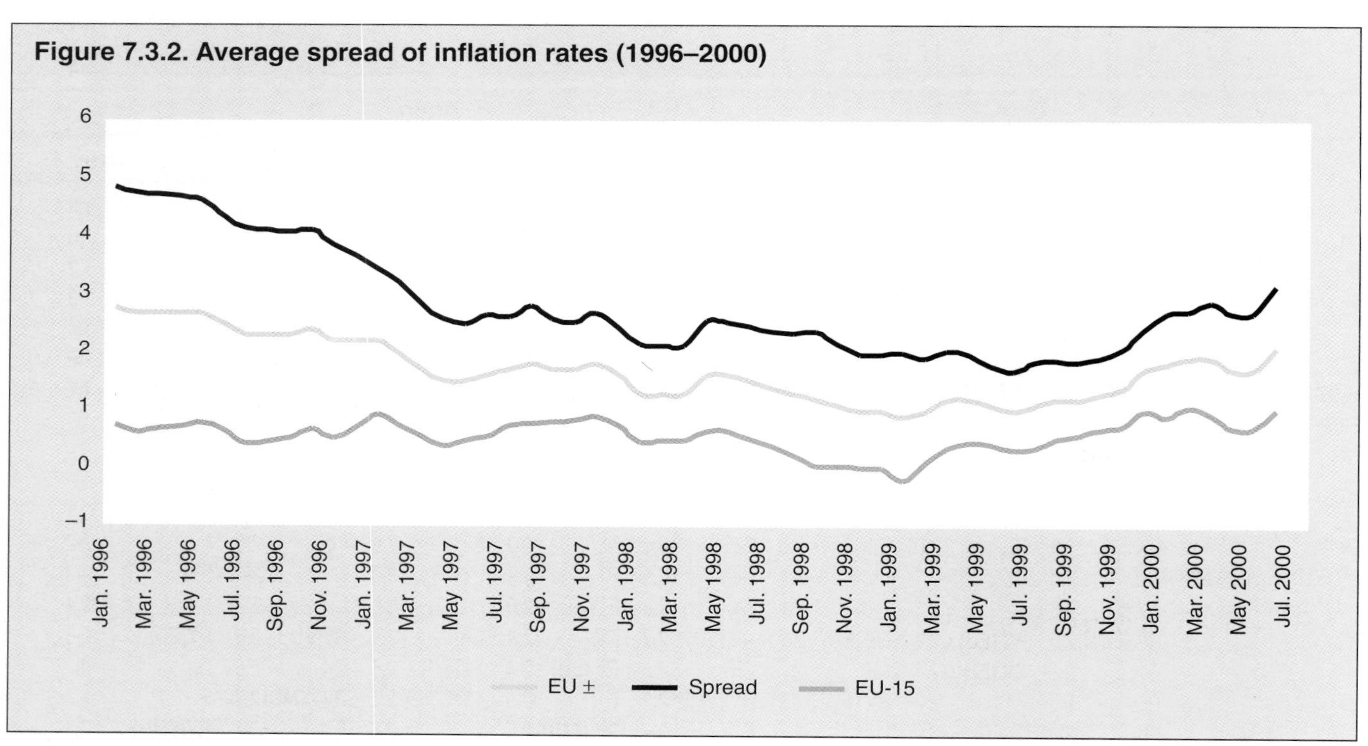

Source: Eurostat.

Household consumption patterns

The consumption patterns of households determine the relative importance ('weight') of household monetary expenditure that is attached to each of the categories of goods and services covered by the HICP. The impact on the all-items index of any price change is proportional to the size of the corresponding weight. There is no uniform basket applying to all Member States. The structure of the weights may vary considerably between the HICPs for individual Member States as well as between the HICP for an individual Member State and the average weighting structure according to the EICP or the MUICP. The index is computed as an annual chain-index allowing for weights to change each year.

Table 7.3.3. Consumption weights in the EU, the EMU and the 15 Member States, as used in 2000 (%)

	EICP	MUICP	B	DK	D	EL	E	F
Food (and non-alcoholic beverages)	136	167	183	162	140	211	244	170
Alcoholic beverages, tobacco and narcotics	56	42	34	60	48	50	34	41
Clothing and footwear	75	80	78	63	75	123	107	59
Housing (including water, electricity, gas and other fuels)	126	158	150	183	208	99	105	151
Furnishings (household equipment and routine maintenance of the house)	76	81	81	71	77	81	59	72
Health	19	32	32	26	34	48	23	32
Transport	158	156	149	165	154	128	137	180
Communications	26	23	23	19	21	27	14	27
Recreation and culture	134	97	111	119	115	43	65	93
Education	13	9	5	9	7	22	16	5
Restaurants and hotels	123	85	83	54	51	112	152	84
Miscellaneous goods and services	58	70	71	71	70	57	46	86

	IRL	I	L	NL	A	P	FIN	S	UK
Food (and non-alcoholic beverages)	190	174	120	158	131	216	173	157	121
Alcoholic beverages, tobacco and narcotics	90	29	101	50	40	33	73	53	57
Clothing and footwear	53	111	76	67	83	70	54	73	70
Housing (including water, electricity, gas and other fuels)	80	101	110	194	139	93	158	195	118
Furnishings (household equipment and routine maintenance of the house)	45	110	108	92	90	79	51	58	78
Health	20	34	14	22	19	57	45	30	14
Transport	118	150	192	135	145	205	163	158	161
Communications	16	28	13	20	32	21	24	36	25
Recreation and culture	114	74	110	121	116	39	115	114	149
Education	20	11	1	16	7	18	2	4	13
Restaurants and hotels	197	102	96	72	143	131	94	64	137
Miscellaneous goods and services	56	76	59	53	54	39	47	60	57

Source: Eurostat.

Table 7.3.3 gives an overview about the weights used in the 15 Member States, the euro zone (MUICP) and for the EU (EICP) in 2000.

For 2000, according to the weighting pattern for the MUICP the divisions food, housing and transport are the three categories with the largest weights when calculated as averages for the country groupings concerned. For the EICP, the divisions transport, food and recreation and culture are the categories with the largest weights. Recreation and culture has replaced housing compared to last year's consumption pattern of the EICP. A weight of approximately 17 % for the MUICP and 14 % for the EICP is attached to food, a weight of approximately 16 % for both indices is attached to transport. A weight of approximately 13 % for the EICP and 10 % for the MUICP is attached to recreation and culture, while a weight of approximately 13 % for the EICP and 16 % for the MUICP is attached to housing.

In individual HICPs the weight for food varies between 12–14 % (Luxembourg, the United Kingdom, Austria and Germany) and 19–24 % (Ireland, Greece, Portugal and Spain). For transport the weight varies between 12–14 % (Ireland, Greece, the Netherlands and Spain) and 16–21 % (Denmark, France, Luxembourg and Portugal). In contrast, the weight for recreation and culture ranges between 4–7 % (Denmark, Belgium, Italy and Sweden) and 12–15 % (Spain, the United Kingdom, Ireland and Portugal), and the weight for housing varies between 8–10 % (Ireland, Portugal, Greece, Italy and Spain) and 18–21 % (Denmark, the Netherlands, Sweden and Germany). It should, however, be noted that HICPs capture only monetary expenditure and unlike national accounts or household budget surveys do not impute costs for the shelter service provided by owner-occupied dwellings. This means that countries in which a larger proportion of the population live in rented dwellings tend to have a larger weight for housing than countries in which a larger proportion of households live in their own dwellings.

Table 7.3.4. Country weights (%) for 2000, price updated to December 1999 prices

	MUICP	EICP	EEAICP
B	39.90		
D	346.51		
E	90.83		
F	209.07		
IRL	9.80		
I	183.08		
L	1.99		
NL	56.54		
A	29.10		
P	18.13		
FIN	15.07		
MUICP	1 000.00	783.49	775.92
DK		13.50	13.37
EL		21.87	21.66
S		17.80	17.63
UK		163.34	161.76
EICP		1 000.00	
IS			0.82
NO			8.84
EEAICP			1 000.00

NB: Due to rounding effects, the weights may not add up exactly to 1 000.
Source: Eurostat.

The weight of a Member State in the EMU total and in the EU is its share of household final monetary consumption expenditure in the EMU or in the EU. The country weights used in 2000 are national accounts data for 1998 updated to December 1999 prices. For the EMU, weights in national currencies are converted into euro using the irrevocably locked exchange rates. For the EU, weights in national currencies are converted into purchasing power standard (PPS). The euro zone country weight reflects its share in the EU.

7.4. Purchasing power parities

As noted in Section 1, in order to compare the size of different economies, it is useful to consider purchasing power parities (PPP) instead of exchange rates for the conversion. The reason for the euro (38) not being used as a conversion rate is that official exchange rates are mainly determined on the one hand by the supply of and demand for currencies necessary to effect commercial flows and on the other hand by a series of factors like capital flows, speculation and others such as a country's perceived political and economic situation.

In other words they do not necessarily reflect price level differences. Consequently, their use for conversion of economic aggregates expressed in nominal values does not allow real comparison of the volume of goods and services produced and consumed. The disadvantages of conversion using exchange rates may be eliminated by using purchasing power parities as conversion rates.

How are PPP's calculated?

The parities represent the relationship between the amounts of national currency needed to purchase a comparable, representative basket of goods in the countries concerned. The ratio between the prices of the individual products is aggregated in accordance with well-defined criteria, so as to obtain a parity for the main aggregates and the global parity of GDP itself. These parities are expressed relative to the value for the Union as a whole, and the unit in which the values are expressed is known as the purchasing power standard (PPS), which is, in fact, the euro in real terms.

Exchange rates and purchasing power parities

Table 7.4.1 gives the PPS figures established every year by Eurostat (39). The comparison of these figures with the exchange rates of the euro shown in Table 7.4.2, provides an interesting information. For example, on the basis of the official exchange rate fixed at the beginning of 1999, EUR 1 was worth PTE 200.482, whereas on the basis of purchasing power parities, PTE 31.098 was sufficient to purchase the volume of goods and services corresponding to one PPS. In 1999 therefore, the real purchasing power of the Portuguese escudo was much higher (+ 53 %) than a comparison based on the official exchange rate would suggest.

Table 7.4.1. The purchasing power parities of GDP, 1 PPS = ... national currency

	1990	1995	1996	1997	1998	1999
EU-15	1.0	1.0	1.0	1.0	1.0	1.0
EUR-11	1.0	1.0	1.0	1.0	1.0	1.0
B	42.5	40.5	40.1	39.3	39.5	39.2
DK	10.2	9.3	9.2	9.1	9.5	9.1
D	2.3	2.2	2.2	2.2	2.1	2.1
EL	151.5	223.8	231.5	236.4	255.2	256.1
E	117.7	134.5	134.0	133.7	135.9	136.4
F	7.1	7.1	7.1	7.0	7.1	7.0
IRL	0.7	0.7	0.7	0.7	0.8	0.8
I	1 527.0	1 708.2	1 735.0	1 710.6	1 751.0	1 745.6
L	42.7	42.8	42.9	42.7	43.6	43.3
NL	2.3	2.2	2.3	2.2	2.1	2.2
A	15.2	15.1	14.7	14.5	14.3	14.1
P	111.6	131.2	133.6	131.7	136.9	131.1
FIN	6.9	6.5	6.5	6.5	6.4	6.6
S	10.1	10.7	10.6	10.4	10.6	10.3
UK	0.7	0.7	0.7	0.7	0.7	0.7
US	1.1	1.1	1.1	1.1	1.0	1.0
JP	211.0	190.1	183.2	179.5	164.0	170.9

NB: Estimation by the Commission services for 1999.
Source: Eurostat.

In Section 1, particularly, PPS has been used for inter-country comparison of GDP per head and component expenditure.

Table 7.4.2 shows the values of GDP per capita in euro and PPS, expressed as the ratio between GDP per head of population in each country and average per capita GDP in the Union (EU-15 = 100). It is interesting to note how each country's figure varies depending on whether it is calculated in euro or PPS.

Considering the four biggest EU countries in 1999, Germany's GDP per head in euro was by 14.3 % higher than the EU average, but the distance reduces to 7.5 % when figures are expressed in PPS. For France the gap is even more evident: calculated in euro the French GDP per capita is by 4.9 % higher than the EU figure, but in PPS is lower by 1.3 %. A symmetrical situation is recorded in Italy: the euro figure is by 9.7 % lower than the average, but when considering PPS data are almost the same. In the United Kingdom, both in euro and PPS, GDP per head is above the EU figure, but in euro by 7.7 % and in PPS by only 2.2 %.

(38) As a convention, when referring to euro, we consider that in reality the euro exists only for 1999; for the previous years we refer to ecu (1 EUR = 1 ECU).

(39) 1999 years figures have been estimated by the services of the Commission.

As a general rule, the higher the nominal index figure (in euro) is, the lower the volume index figure (in PPS) is relative to it. Luxembourg is an exception, and the two index figures are fairly similar. In Denmark, Portugal and Greece the differences between figures expressed in euro and in PPS are the widest, but opposite: this gives for Denmark a per capita index figure in euro 45.4 % above the Union's average; compared with only + 18.6 % in PPS terms. At the opposite end, Portugal's GDP per head in euro is by 50 % below the EU average and when considered in PPS the gap is reduced to 23.5 %. For Greece the gap to the EU figure is 47.2 % when GDP per head is calculated in euro, but the gap reduces to 32.8 % when in PPS. Although figures are very similar, it is interesting to note that in euro the lowest GDP per capita among the 15 EU countries is recorded for Portugal, but when referring to PPS the lowest figure is for Greece.

Table 7.4.2. GDP per head, 1999 (EU-15 = 100)

	EUR	PPS
EUR-11	98.7	100.3
B	108.0	110.9
DK	145.4	118.6
D	114.3	107.5
EL	52.8	67.2
E	67.2	81.9
F	104.9	98.7
IRL	110.8	114.6
I	90.3	100.1
L	197.1	183.4
NL	110.6	112.8
A	114.3	111.7
P	50.0	76.5
FIN	111.5	100.9
S	119.6	102.3
UK	107.7	102.2

Source: Eurostat.

Figure 7.4.1. Price level index of GDP (EU-15 = 100)

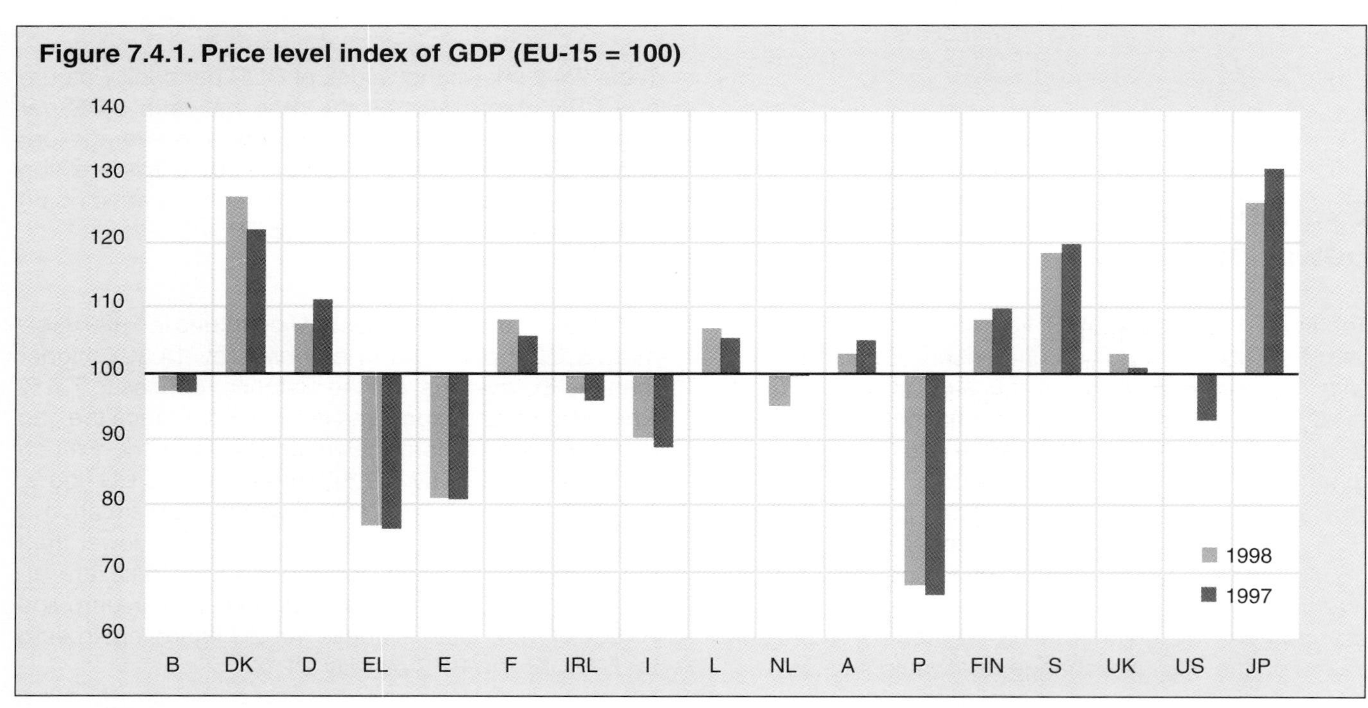

Source: Eurostat.

Price level index

The ratio between the value of a PPS and that of the euro allows us to calculate the price level index, which measures the difference between the general price level in a given country and the Union average (EU-15 = 100). It also permits direct comparisons between one country and another.

Table 7.4.3 shows that, in 1999, Portugal had the lowest prices in the Union (34.6 percentage points below the Union average) and Denmark the highest (22.7 percentage points above this average). The United States comes out at 2.7 percentage points below the EU average, while Japan exceeds it by 40.9 percentage points.

Table 7.4.3. Price level index of GDP (EU-15 = 100)

	1990	1995	1996	1997	1998	1999
B	100.4	105.0	101.9	98.1	97.4	97.3
DK	129.1	126.6	124.4	121.2	121.8	122.7
D	109.9	118.5	113.1	108.5	107.5	106.3
EL	75.5	73.9	75.8	79.8	77.5	78.6
E	91.3	82.5	83.4	81.2	81.1	82.0
F	103.3	109.1	109.1	107.9	107.4	106.3
IRL	97.1	85.8	91.3	95.9	95.2	96.6
I	100.8	80.2	88.6	90.4	90.5	90.2
L	101.0	111.1	109.3	108.0	107.5	107.4
NL	101.1	106.4	105.8	97.7	97.9	98.1
A	105.0	114.8	109.7	104.4	103.3	102.4
P	61.8	66.9	68.3	65.3	65.0	65.4
FIN	142.0	113.2	111.2	109.1	108.8	110.5
S	134.1	114.9	124.4	120.1	116.6	116.9
UK	91.1	86.9	86.9	99.8	103.0	105.4
US	84.8	82.2	83.7	92.8	93.4	97.3
JP	114.8	153.8	131.7	130.4	120.8	140.9

Source: Eurostat.

Another way of interpreting Table 7.4.2 is to say that, in 1999, a given basket of goods and services could be purchased for EUR 65 in Portugal and EUR 123, nearly twice as much, in Denmark.

KEY INDICATORS FOR EU COUNTRIES

Euro-SICS

The following technical sheets give a selected set of key indicators for the Union, the euro zone and the 15 Member States.

A more comprehensive set of indicators is available under 'Euro-SICS' whose aim is to supply institutional users with a wide range of short-term indicators and which is in fact an extension of the 'Euro-indicators' website developed by Eurostat in 1998 and currently available to the public.

The series included in Euro-SICS were selected according to economic and statistical criteria in order to give an accurate picture of the short-term economic situation. Particular attention in the choice of the series was given to their cyclical features (leading–lagging structure) and to their importance for the construction of key macroeconomic aggregates. Quarterly national accounts were considered to be the centre of this exercise and the usefulness of other short-term indicators in explaining the evolution of quarterly account aggregates has been evaluated.

The indicators included in Euro-SICS have been classified into three main categories:

- fully harmonised;
- national, generally available;
- country specific.

The first two categories are under the responsibility of Eurostat, the third one is under the responsibility of Member States NSIs. Fully harmonised data and national data are available on Euro-SICS; country-specific indicators have not yet been defined by Member States. Euro-SICS is organised into 14 domains and until now composed of 56 main indicators. Taking into account the different breakdown and presentation of each main indicator, the total number of indicators is 600. In total, Euro-SICS contains about 8 000 series due to the fact that not all Member States compile all the required indicators.

In order to be really of interest for short-term analysts and policy-makers, Euro-SICS must achieve progressively the following objectives, which are judged by Eurostat a *condicio sine qua non* for the success of the project:

- to be quasi real-time updated;
- to contain long time-series;
- to be fully documented;
- to be continuously improved.

Starting from this year, Eurostat is periodically monitoring the state of Euro-SICS in order to have a useful instrument for improving the quality and reliability of this site, which external users judge (the ECB in particular) as being of crucial importance for their activity. In this context, it is also possible to follow up the process of achievement for the objectives listed above.

Euro-SICS is actually opened to a restricted number of privileged users (+ /– 200) including NSIs, NCBs, the ECB, DG-ECFIN of the European Commission and other institutional users agreed by Member States, as well as some international organisations such as the IMF and OECD.

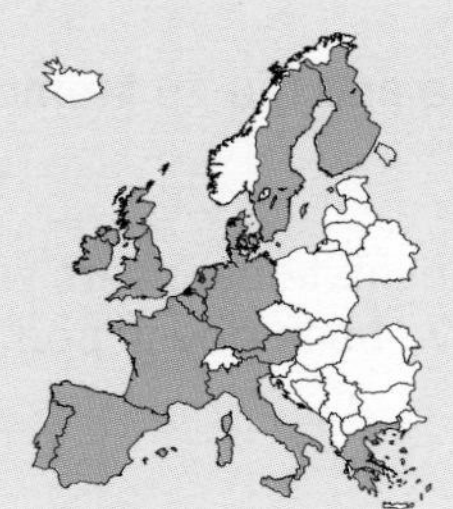

EU-15

		1999	2000 q1
GDP	% growth	2.4	0.8
Consumption	% growth	2.7	0.7
Investments	% growth	4.9	1.6
Consumer prices	% growth	1.2	0.2
Unemployment	% growth	– 6.8	– 7.3
Industrial production	% growth	1.6	1.1

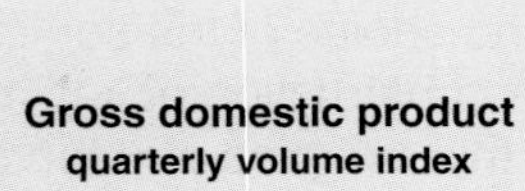

Gross domestic product
quarterly volume index

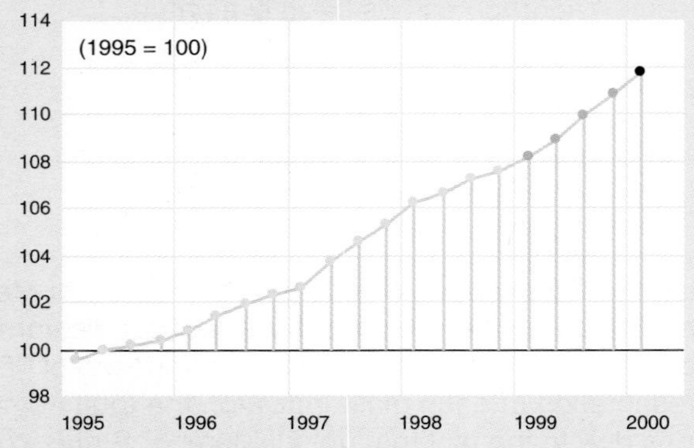

Gross domestic product
quarterly volume rates

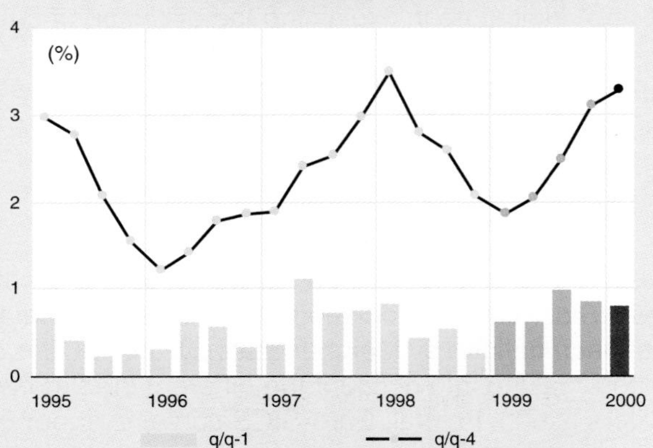

Consumption and investments
quarterly growth rates

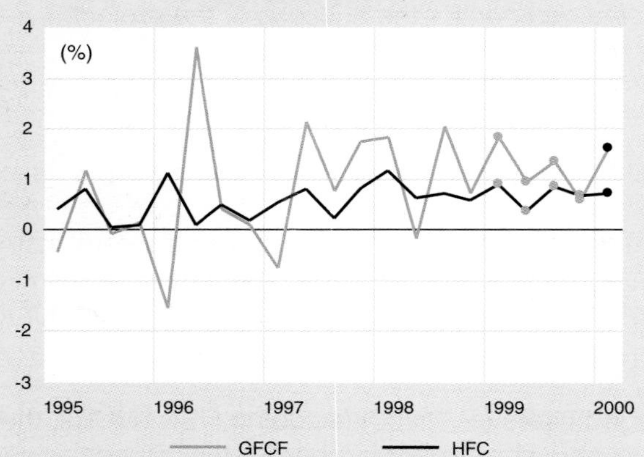

Harmonised index of consumer prices
monthly

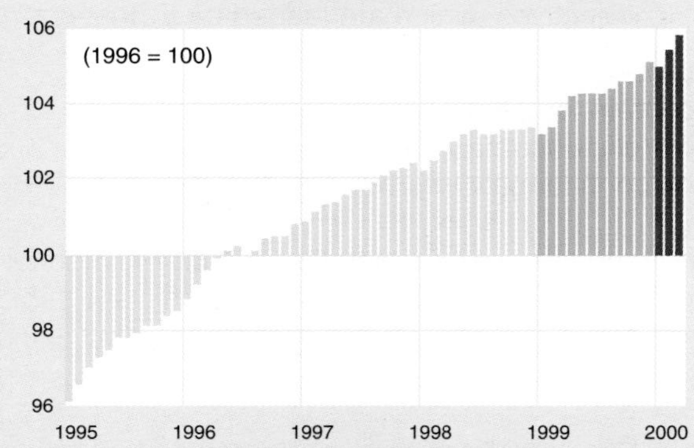

Unemployment
monthly

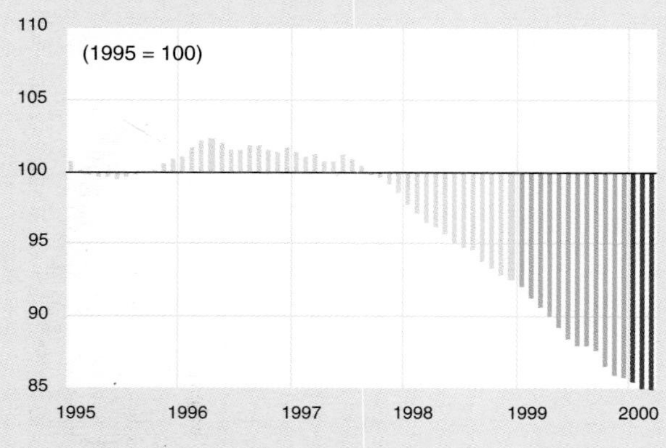

Industrial production
monthly

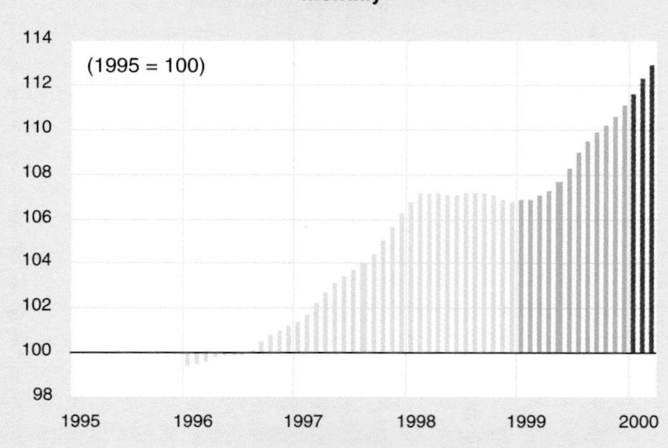

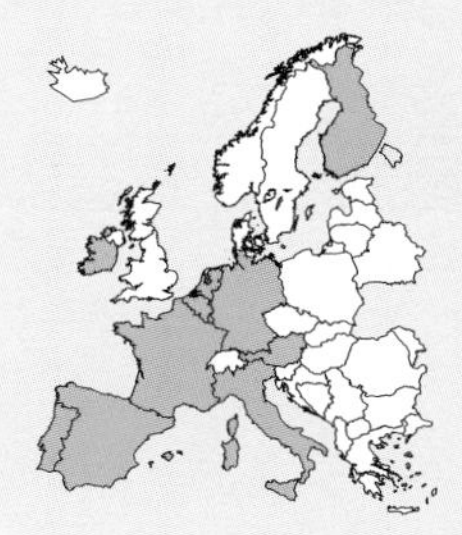

Euro zone

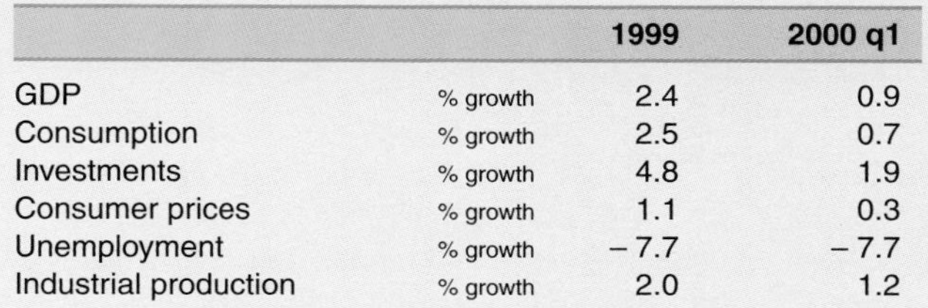

		1999	2000 q1
GDP	% growth	2.4	0.9
Consumption	% growth	2.5	0.7
Investments	% growth	4.8	1.9
Consumer prices	% growth	1.1	0.3
Unemployment	% growth	− 7.7	− 7.7
Industrial production	% growth	2.0	1.2

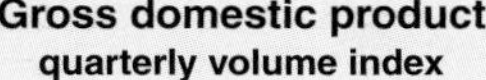

Gross domestic product
quarterly volume index

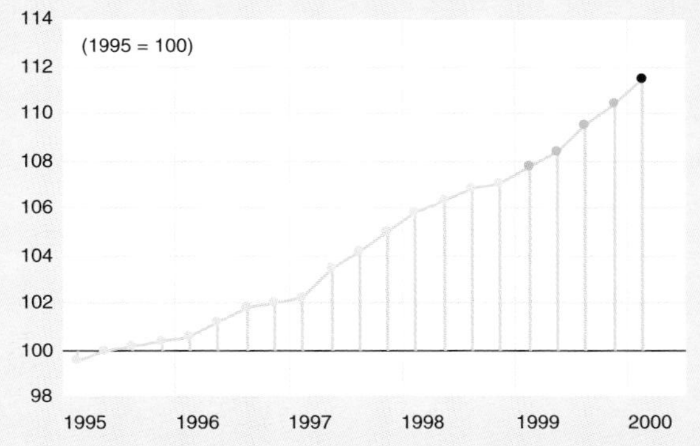

Gross domestic product
quarterly volume rates

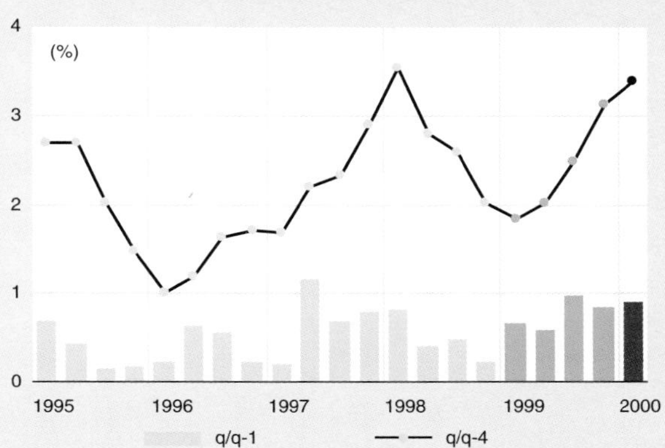

Consumption and investments
quarterly growth rates

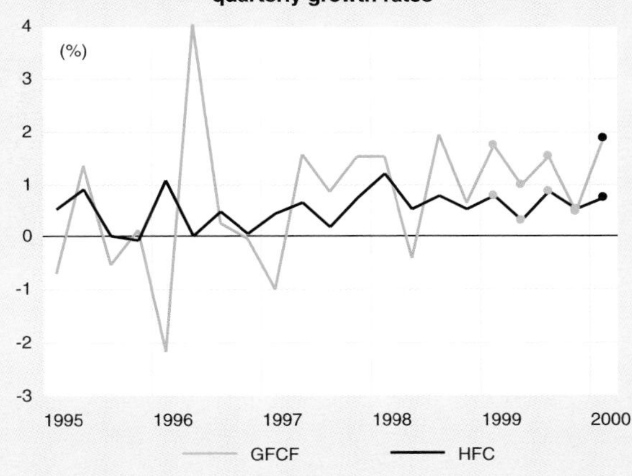

Harmonised index of consumer prices
monthly

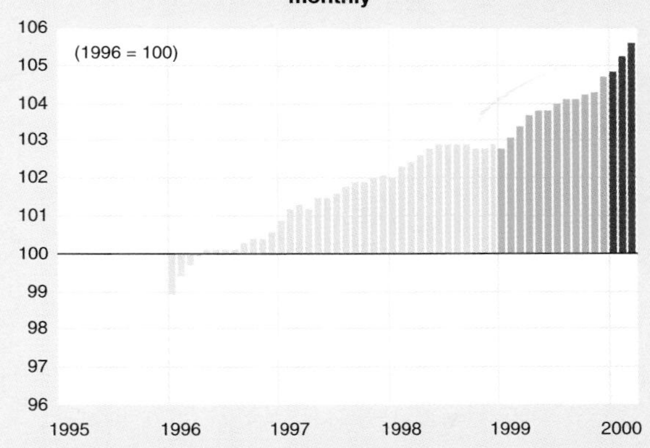

Unemployment
monthly

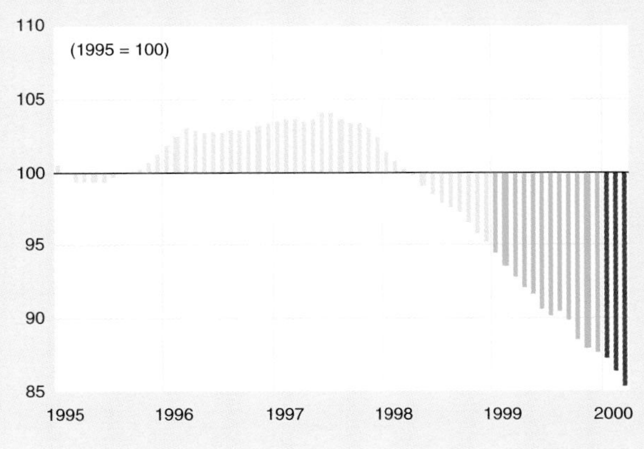

Industrial production
monthly

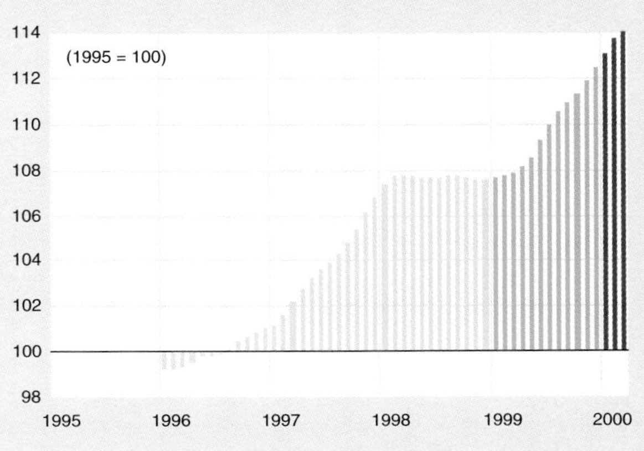

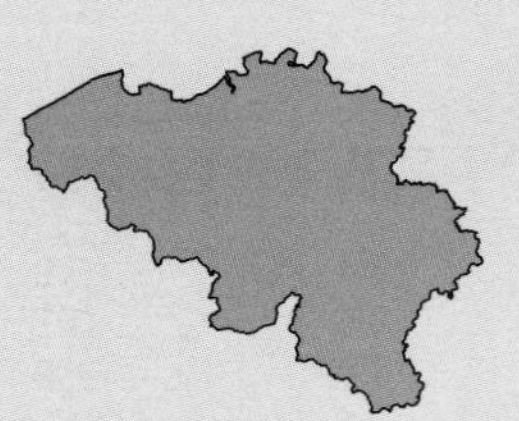

Belgium

		1999	2000 q1
GDP	% growth	2.5	1.3
Consumption	% growth	2.0	1.3
Investments	% growth	5.4	3.1
Consumer prices	% growth	1.1	0.4
Unemployment	% growth	– 2.9	– 6.3
Industrial production	% growth	1.4	0.8

Gross domestic product
quarterly volume index

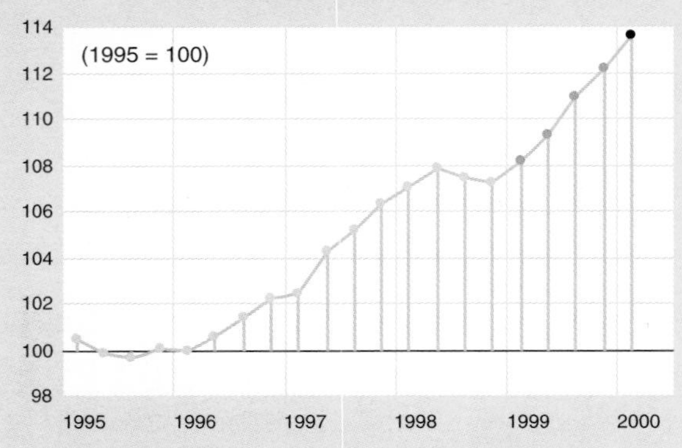

Gross domestic product
quarterly volume rates

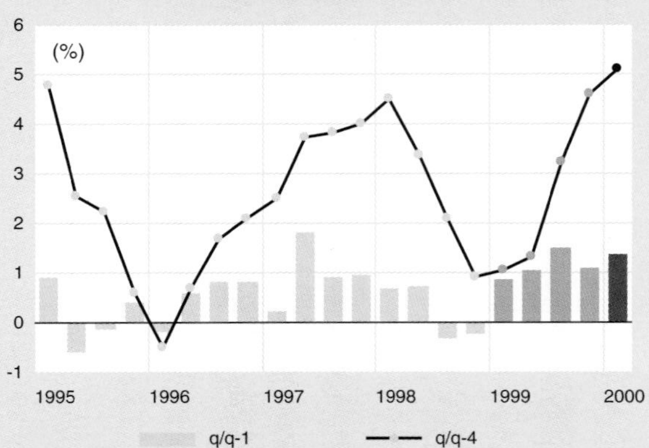

Consumption and investments
quarterly growth rates

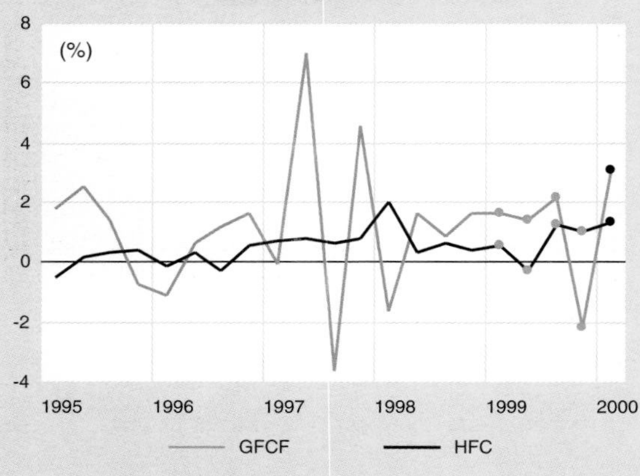

Harmonised index of consumer prices
monthly

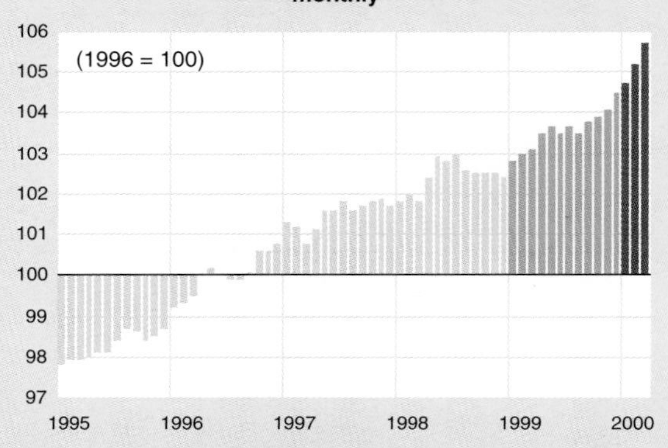

Unemployment
monthly

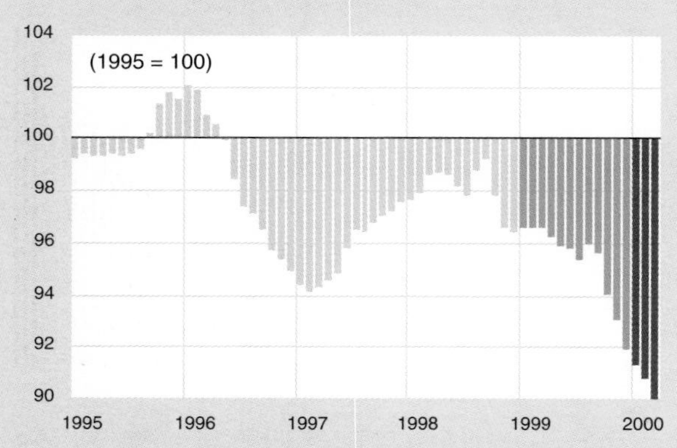

Industrial production
monthly

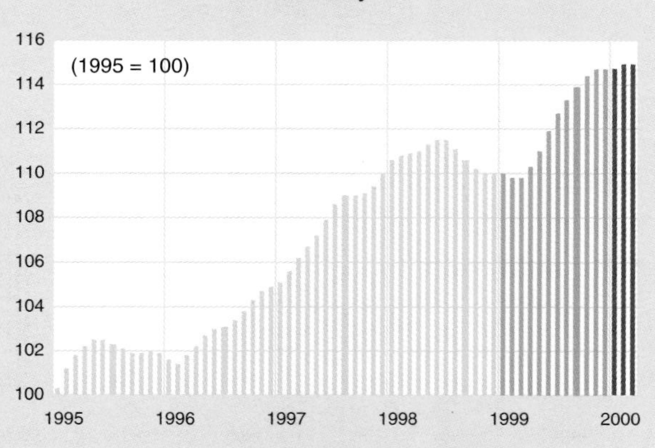

Denmark

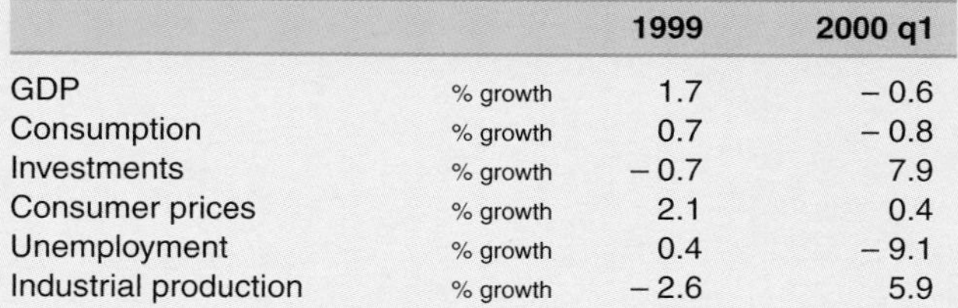

		1999	2000 q1
GDP	% growth	1.7	– 0.6
Consumption	% growth	0.7	– 0.8
Investments	% growth	– 0.7	7.9
Consumer prices	% growth	2.1	0.4
Unemployment	% growth	0.4	– 9.1
Industrial production	% growth	– 2.6	5.9

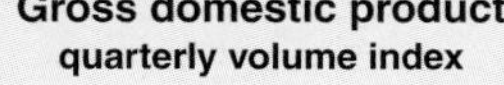

Gross domestic product
quarterly volume index

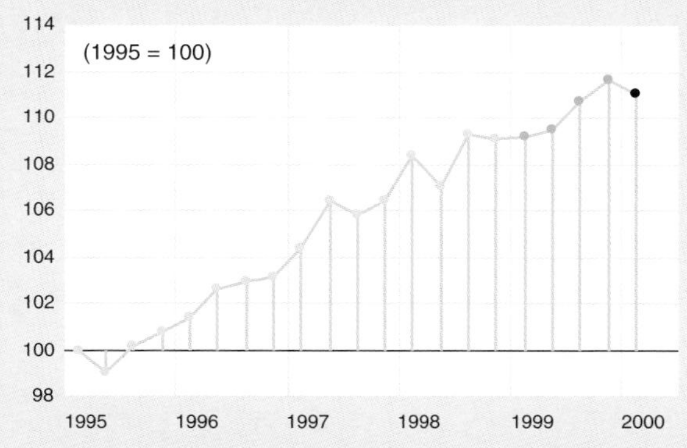

Gross domestic product
quarterly volume rates

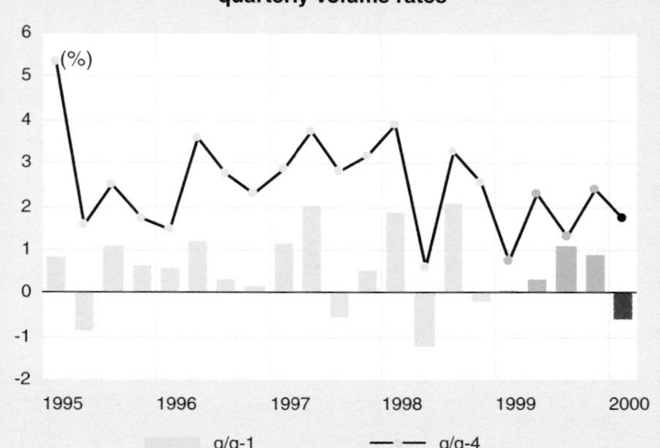

Consumption and investments
quarterly growth rates

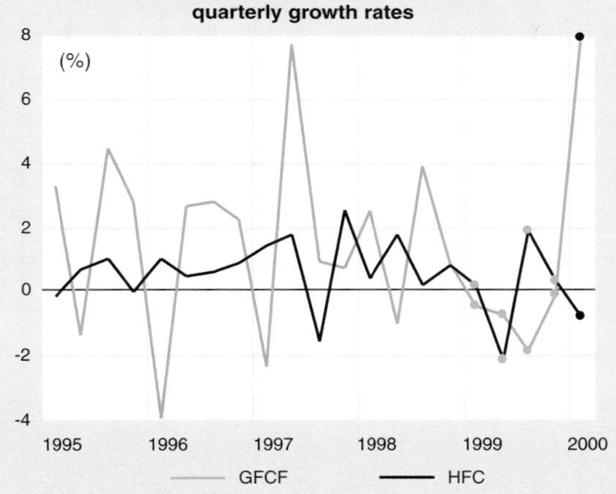

Harmonised index of consumer prices
monthly

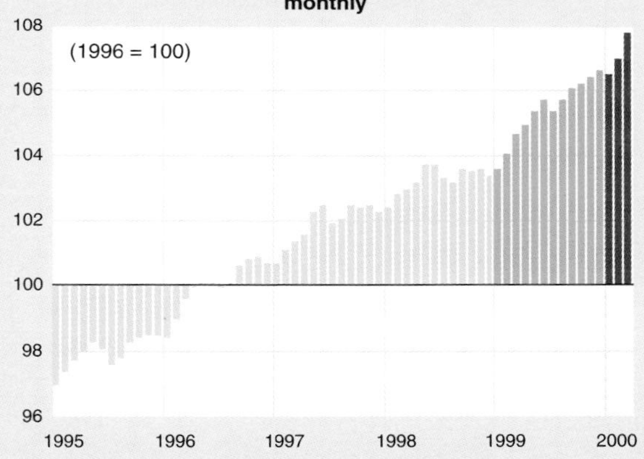

Unemployment
monthly

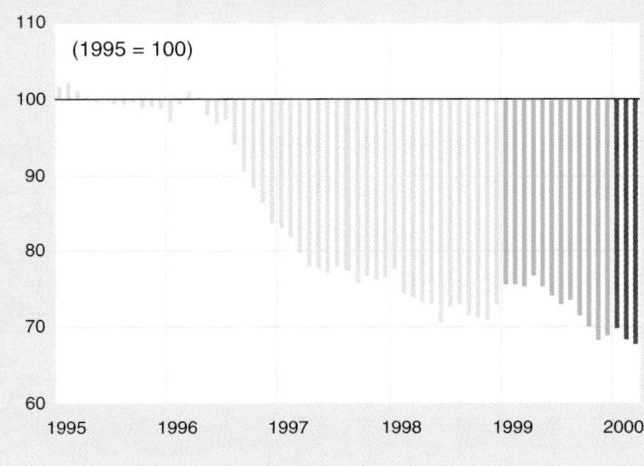

Industrial production
monthly

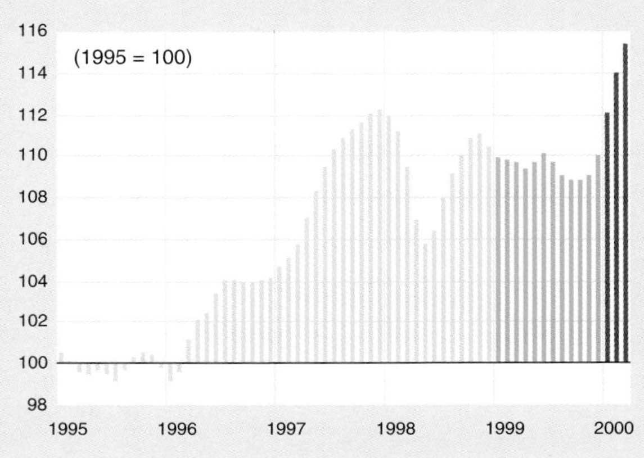

Germany

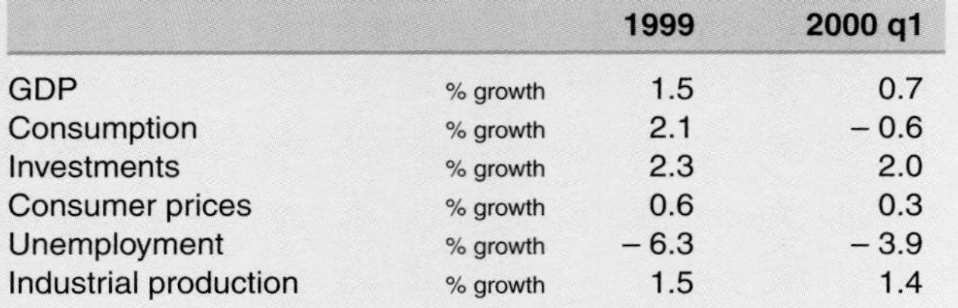

		1999	2000 q1
GDP	% growth	1.5	0.7
Consumption	% growth	2.1	− 0.6
Investments	% growth	2.3	2.0
Consumer prices	% growth	0.6	0.3
Unemployment	% growth	− 6.3	− 3.9
Industrial production	% growth	1.5	1.4

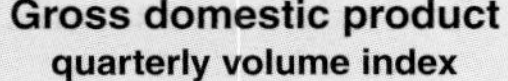

Gross domestic product
quarterly volume index

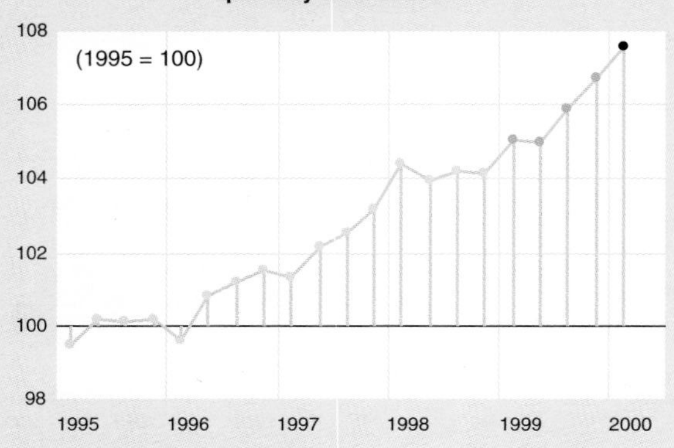

Gross domestic product
quarterly volume rates

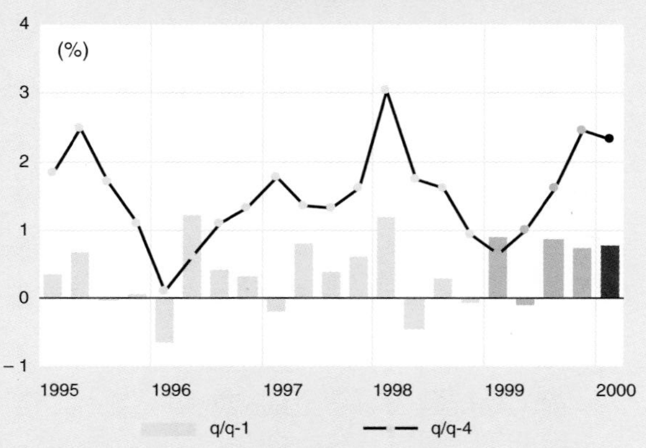

Consumption and investments
quarterly growth rates

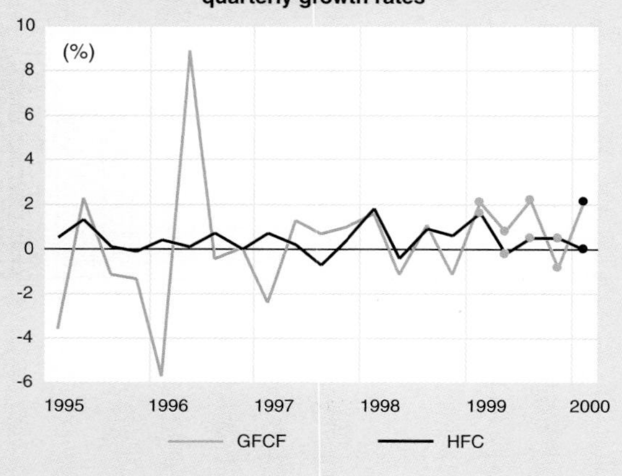

Harmonised index of consumer prices
monthly

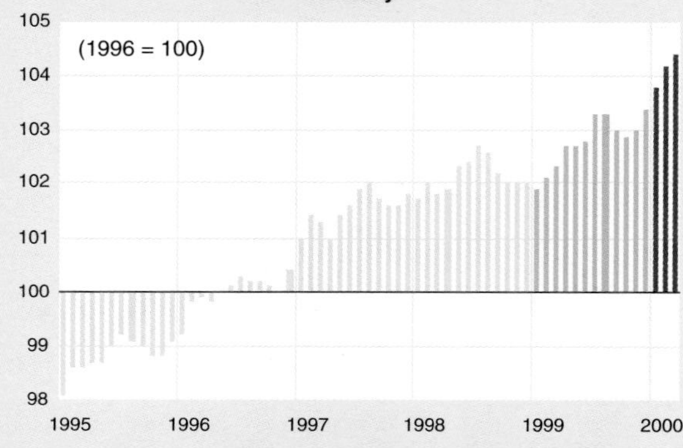

Unemployment
monthly

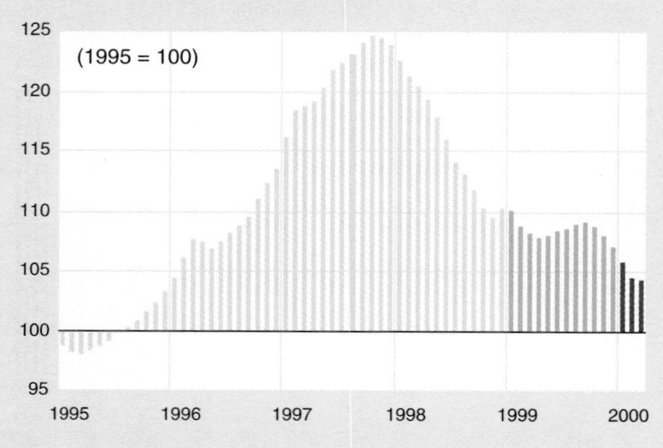

Industrial production
monthly

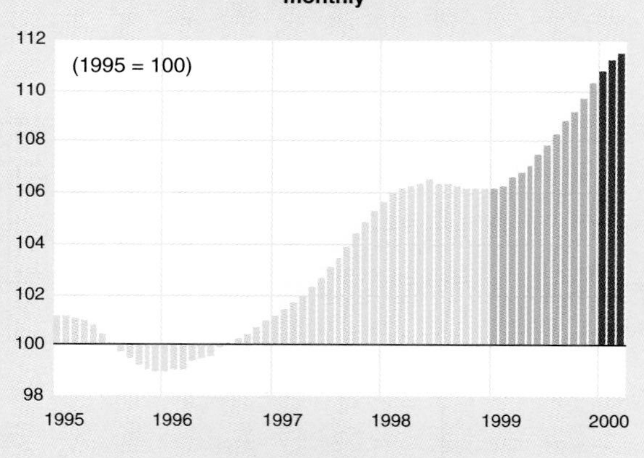

Greece

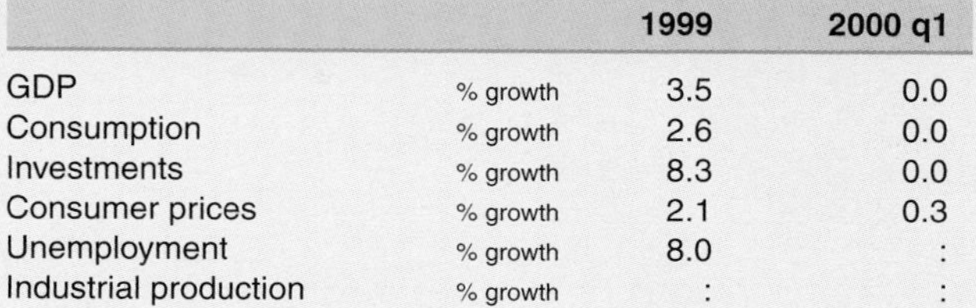

		1999	2000 q1
GDP	% growth	3.5	0.0
Consumption	% growth	2.6	0.0
Investments	% growth	8.3	0.0
Consumer prices	% growth	2.1	0.3
Unemployment	% growth	8.0	:
Industrial production	% growth	:	:

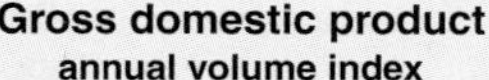

Gross domestic product
annual volume index

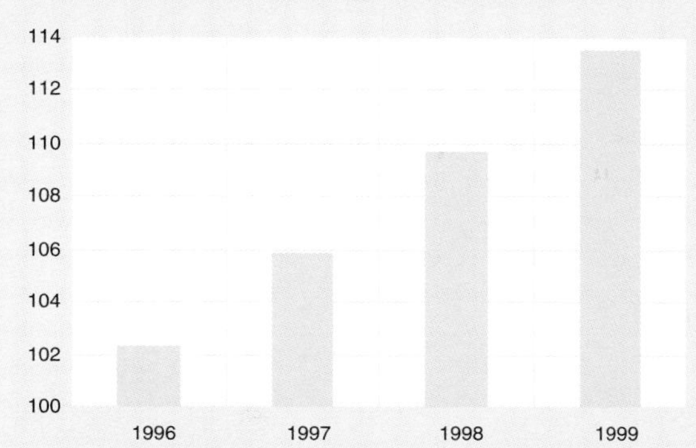

Gross domestic product
annual growth rates

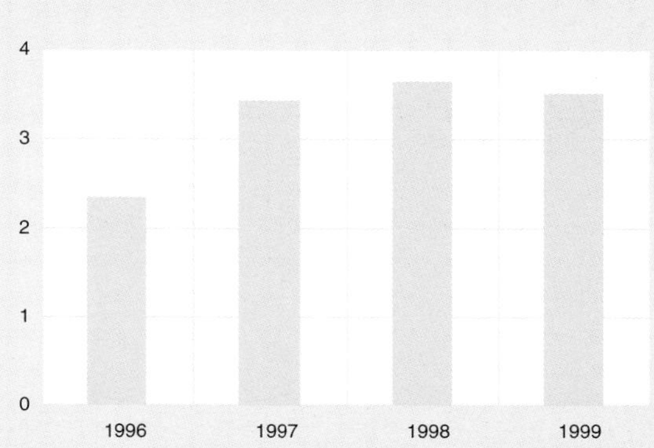

Consumption and investments
annual growth rates

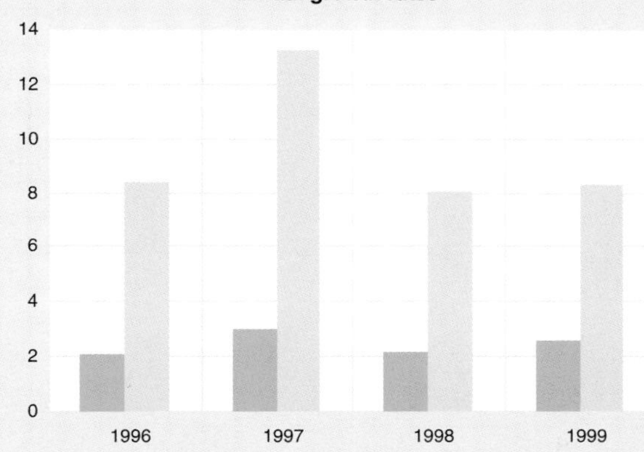

Harmonised index of consumer prices
monthly

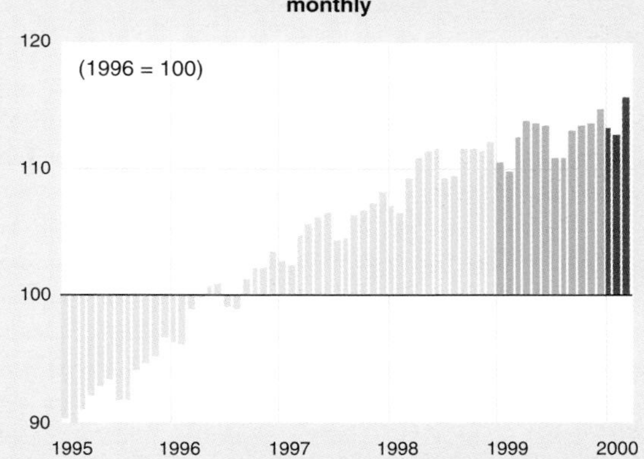

Unemployment
monthly

Industrial production
monthly

Spain

		1999	2000 q1
GDP	% growth	3.7	1.4
Consumption	% growth	4.4	3.0
Investments	% growth	8.3	1.8
Consumer prices	% growth	2.2	0.4
Unemployment	% growth	– 14.7	– 9.1
Industrial production	% growth	4.0	1.7

Gross domestic product
quarterly volume index

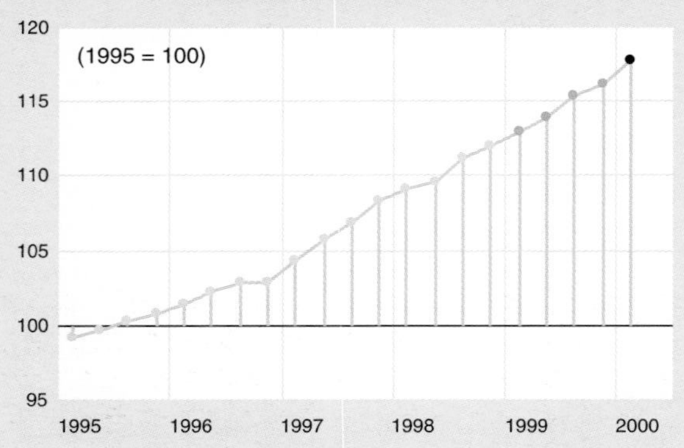

Gross domestic product
quarterly volume rates

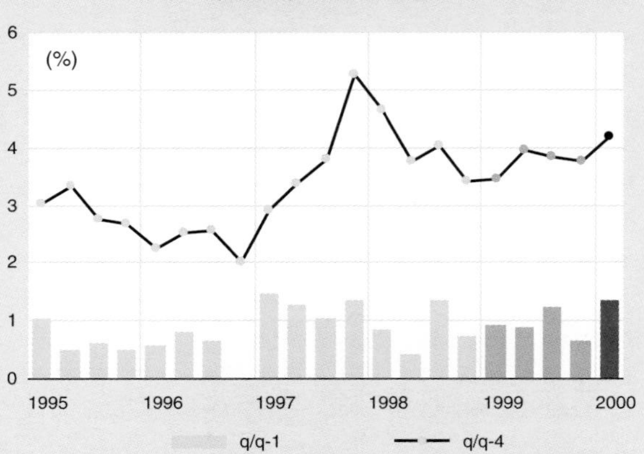

Consumption and investments
quarterly growth rates

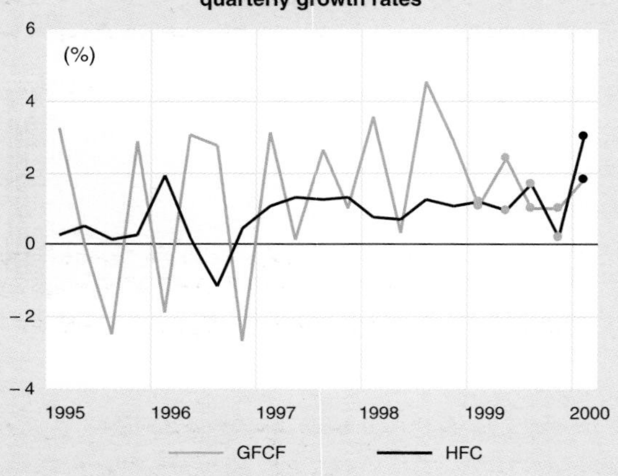

Harmonised index of consumer prices
monthly

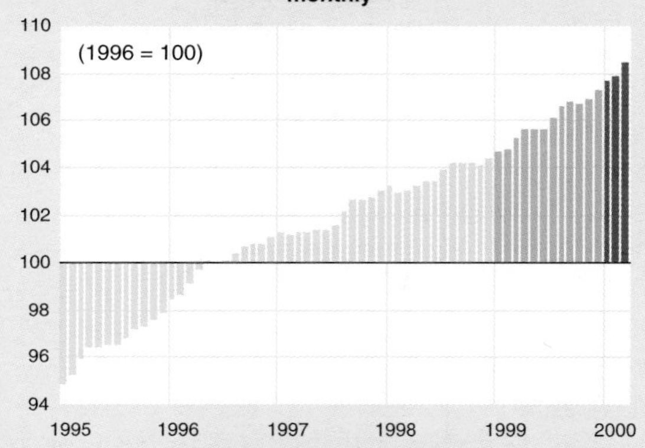

Unemployment
monthly

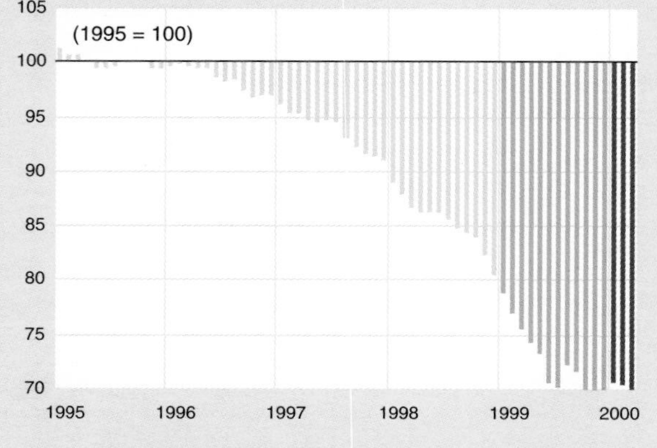

Industrial production index
monthly

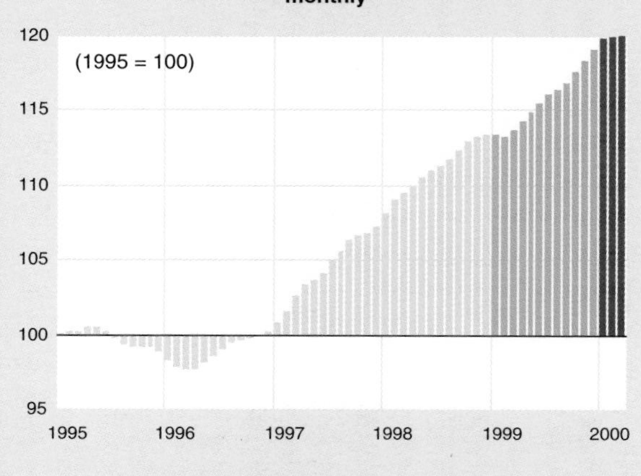

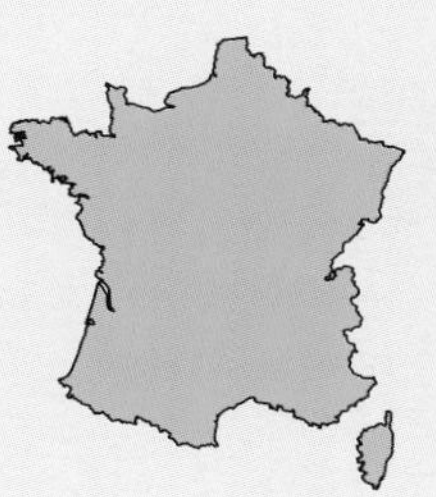

France

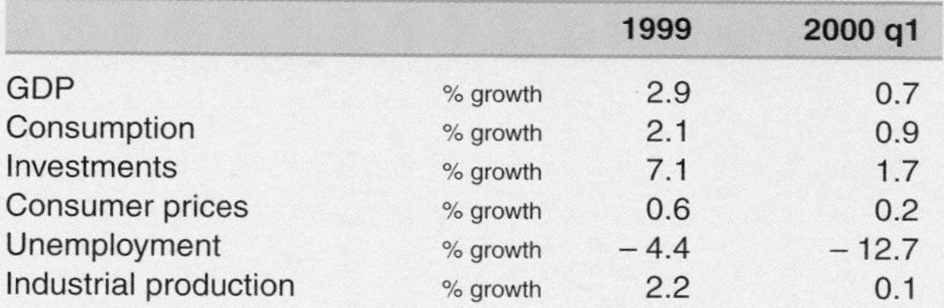

		1999	2000 q1
GDP	% growth	2.9	0.7
Consumption	% growth	2.1	0.9
Investments	% growth	7.1	1.7
Consumer prices	% growth	0.6	0.2
Unemployment	% growth	– 4.4	– 12.7
Industrial production	% growth	2.2	0.1

Gross domestic product
quarterly volume index

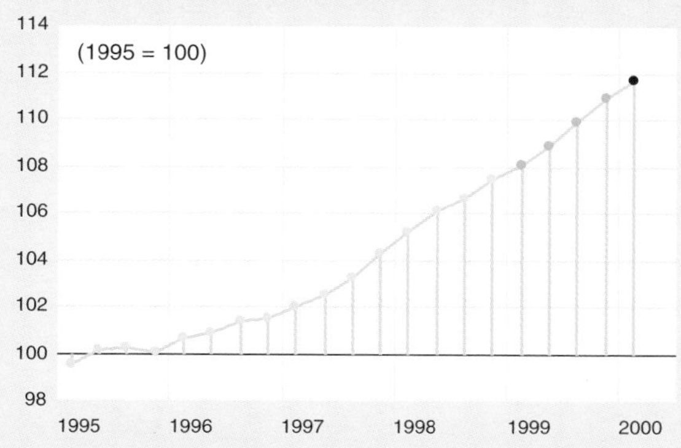

Gross domestic product
quarterly volume rates

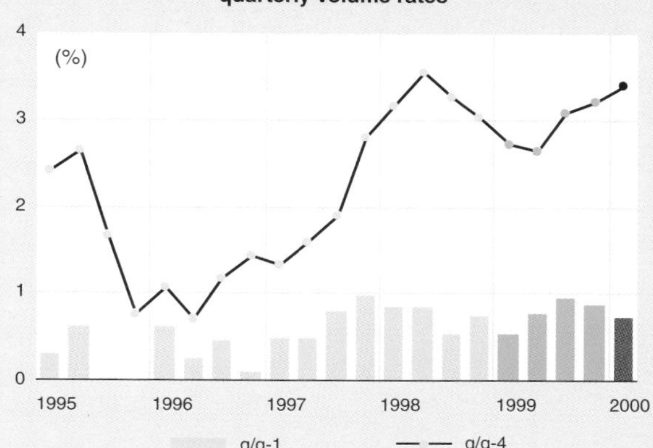

Consumption and investments
quarterly growth rates

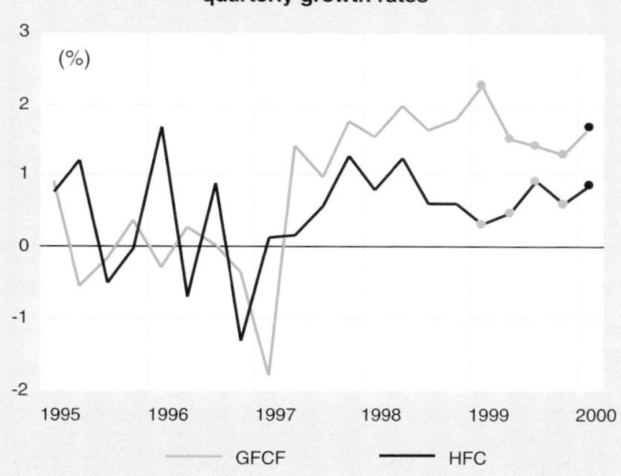

Harmonised index of consumer prices
monthly

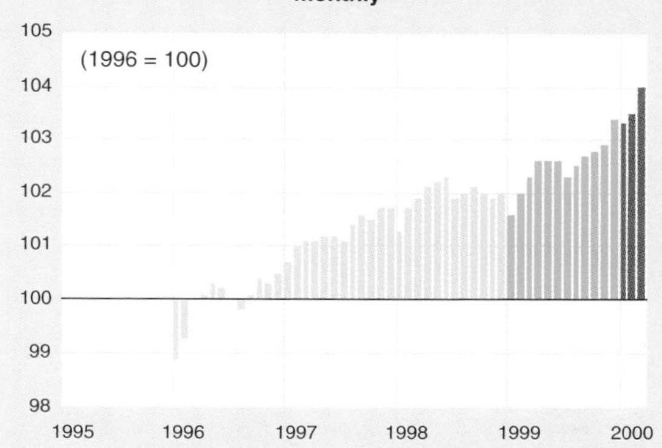

Unemployment rate
monthly

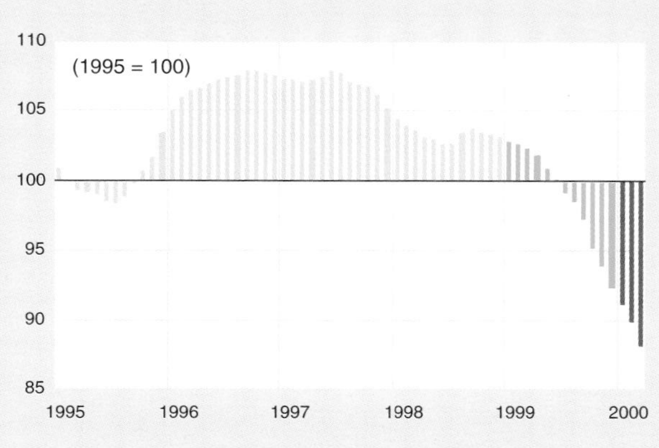

Industrial production
monthly

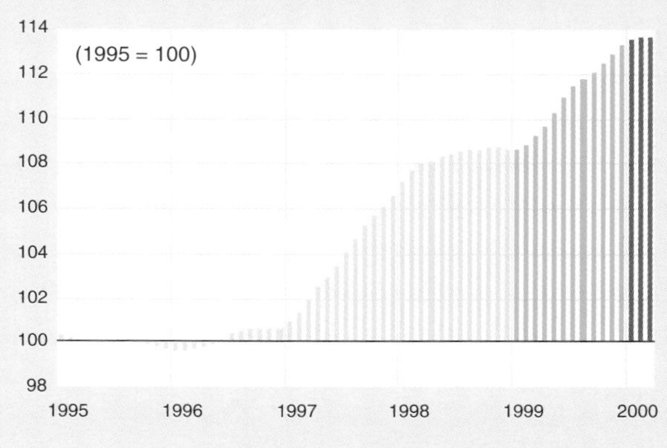

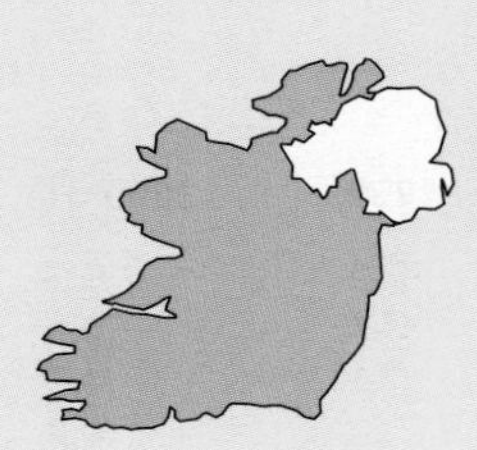

Ireland

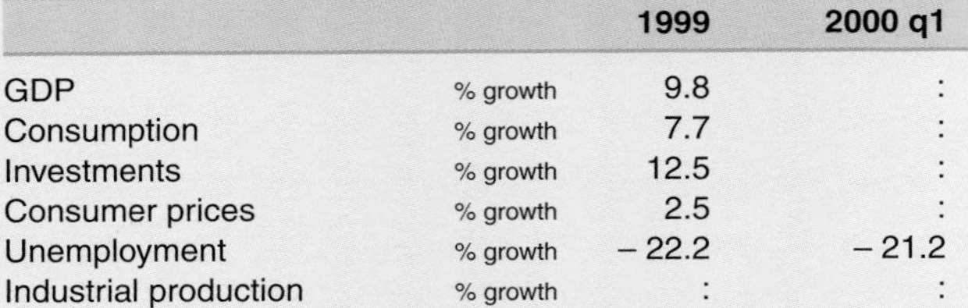

		1999	2000 q1
GDP	% growth	9.8	:
Consumption	% growth	7.7	:
Investments	% growth	12.5	:
Consumer prices	% growth	2.5	:
Unemployment	% growth	– 22.2	– 21.2
Industrial production	% growth	:	:

Gross domestic product
annual volume index

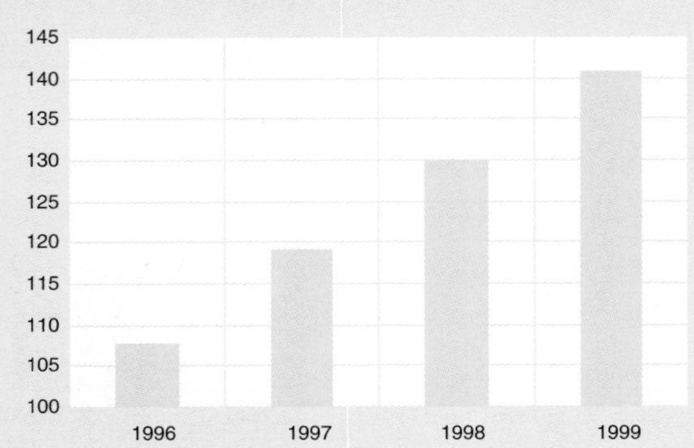

Gross domestic product
annual growth rates

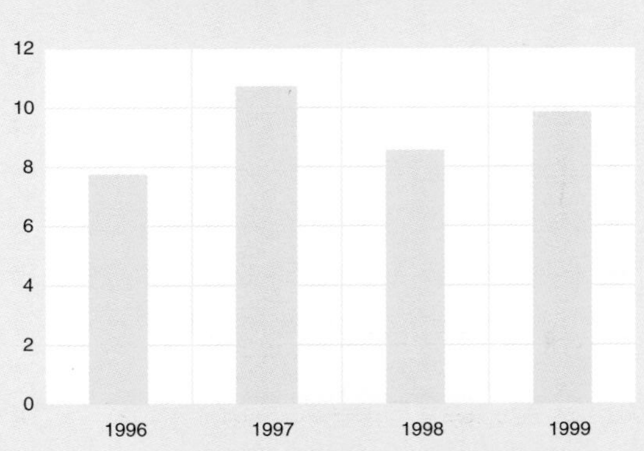

Consumption and investments
annual growth rates

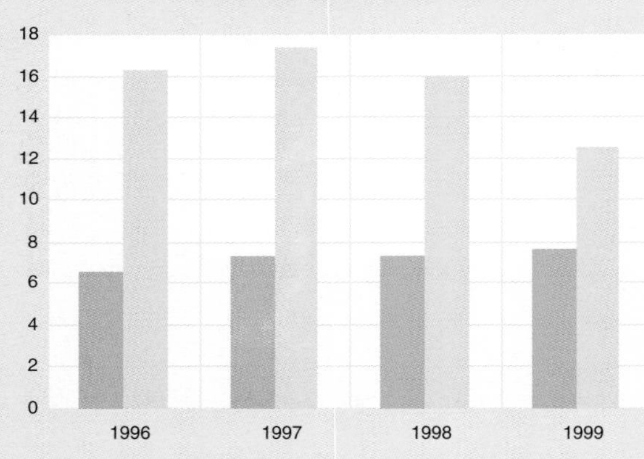

Harmonised index of consumer prices
monthly

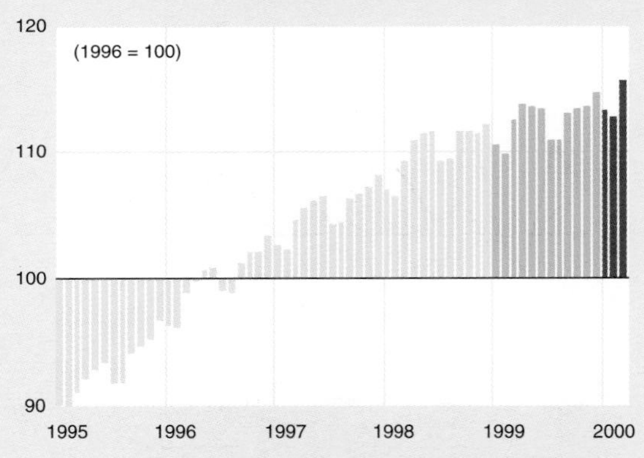

Unemployment
monthly

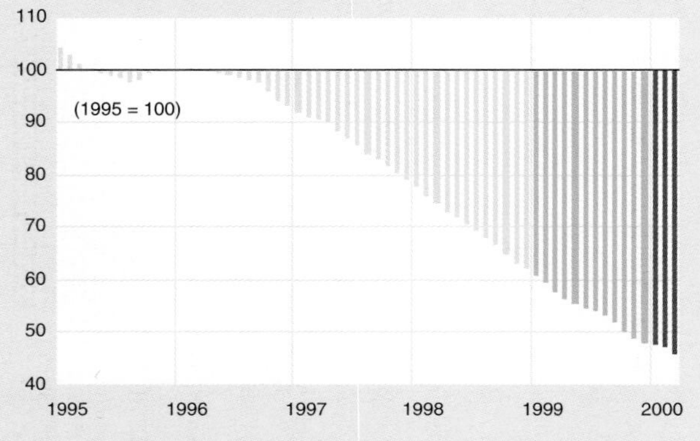

Industrial production
monthly

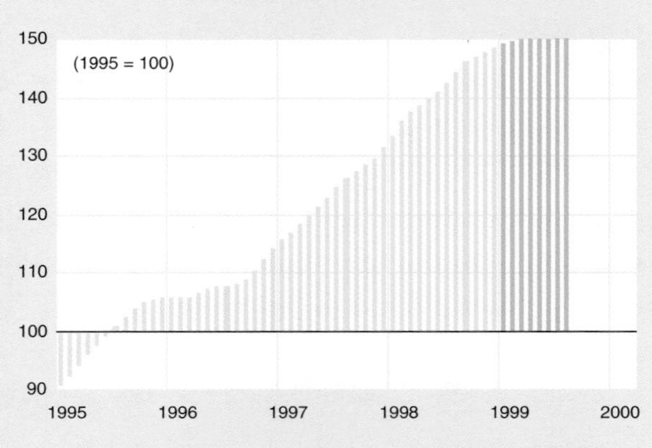

Italy

		1999	2000 q1
GDP	% growth	2.5	1.3
Consumption	% growth	2.0	1.3
Investments	% growth	5.4	3.1
Consumer prices	% growth	1.1	0.4
Unemployment	% growth	– 2.9	– 6.3
Industrial production	% growth	1.4	0.8

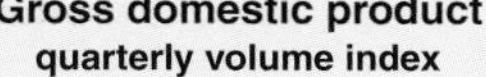

Gross domestic product
quarterly volume index

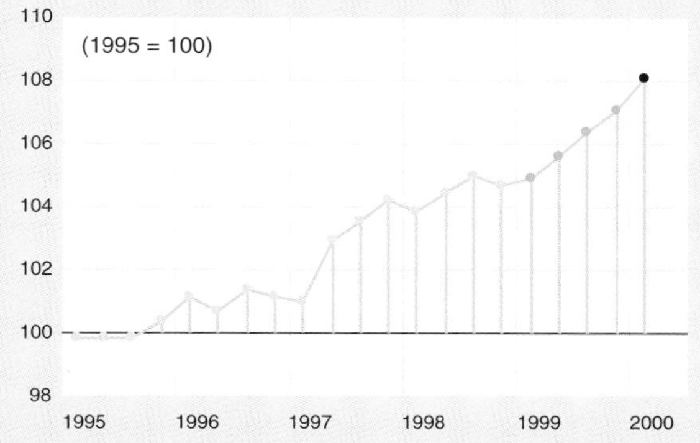

Gross domestic product
quarterly volume rates

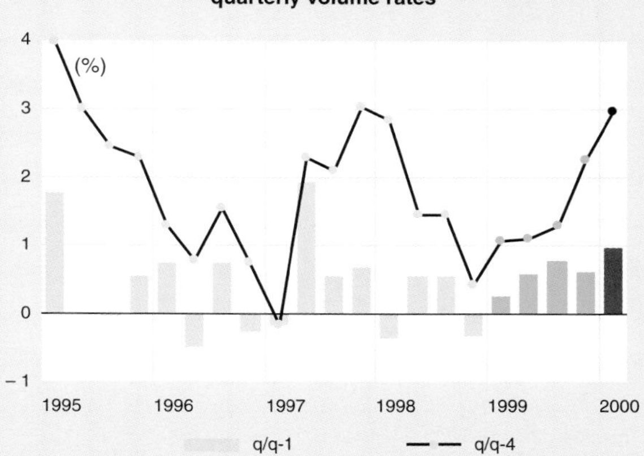

Consumption and investments
quarterly growth rates

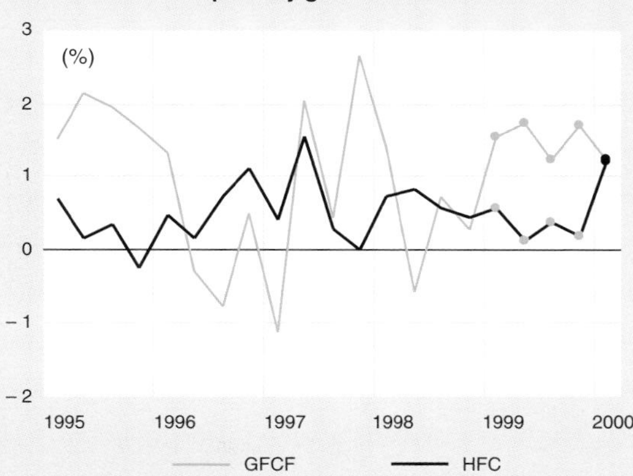

Harmonised index of consumer prices
monthly

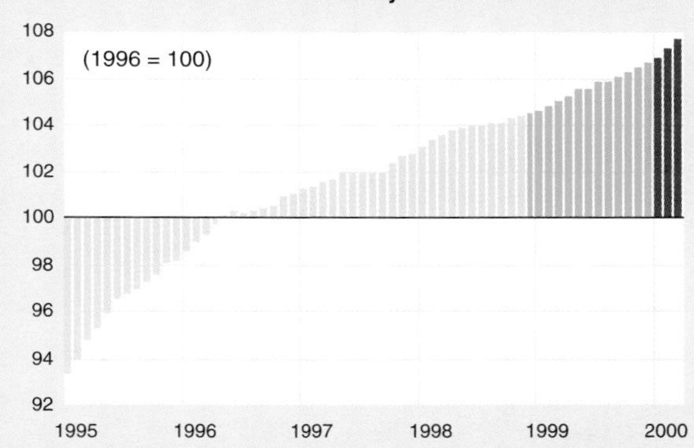

Unemployment
monthly

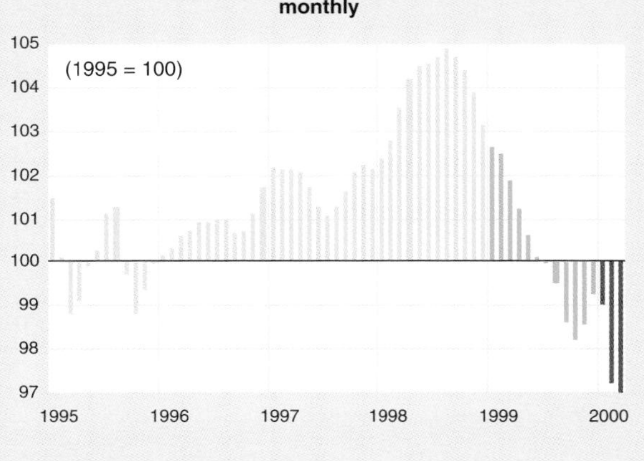

Industrial production
monthly

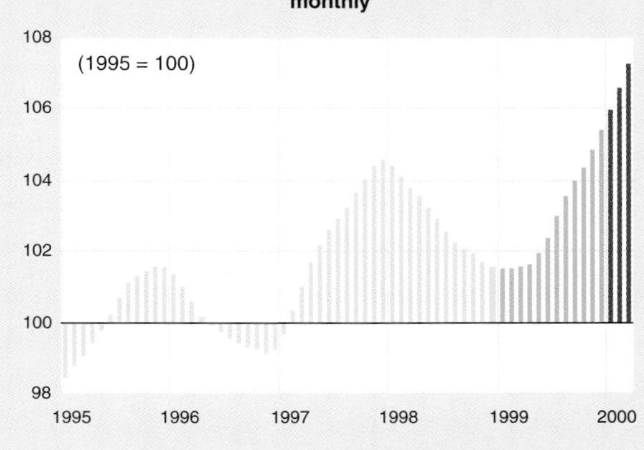

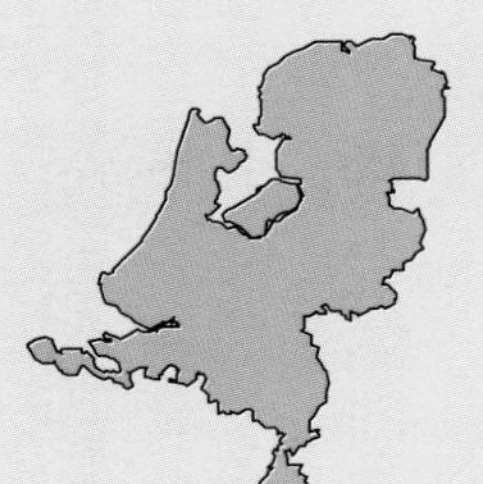

Netherlands

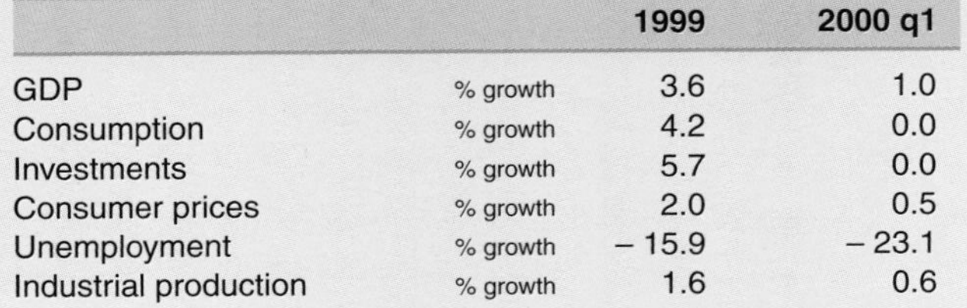

		1999	2000 q1
GDP	% growth	3.6	1.0
Consumption	% growth	4.2	0.0
Investments	% growth	5.7	0.0
Consumer prices	% growth	2.0	0.5
Unemployment	% growth	– 15.9	– 23.1
Industrial production	% growth	1.6	0.6

Gross domestic product
quarterly volume index

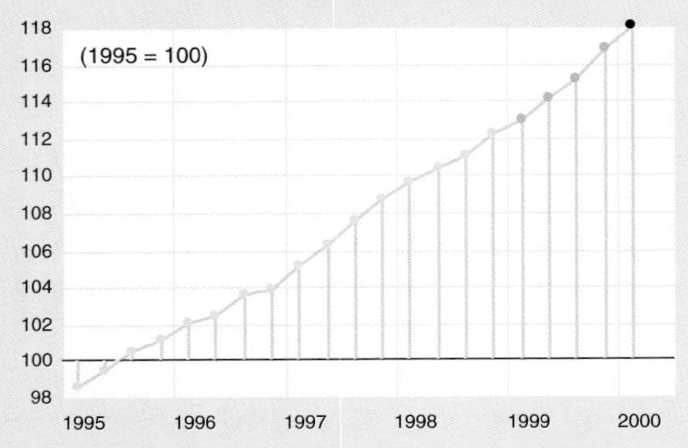

Gross domestic product
quarterly volume rates

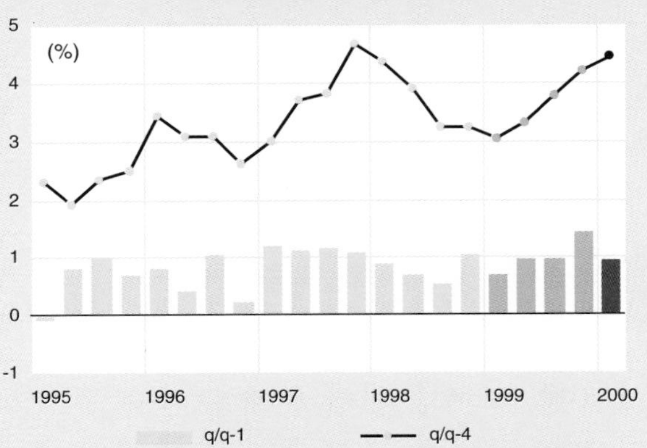

Consumption and investments
quarterly growth rates

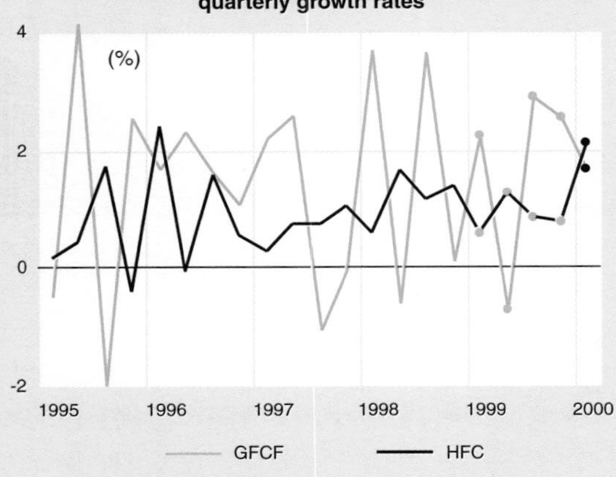

Harmonised index of consumer prices
monthly

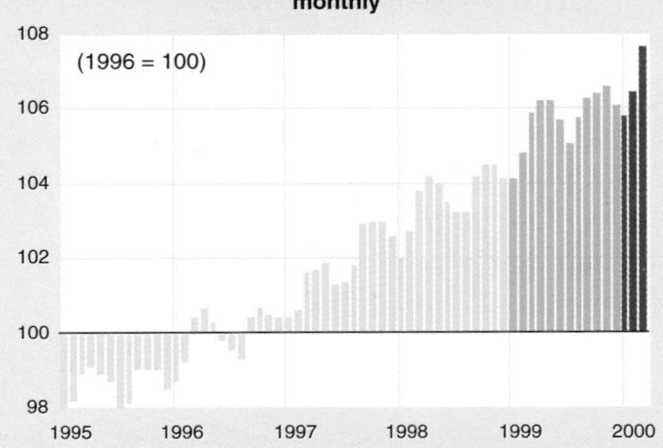

Unemployment
monthly

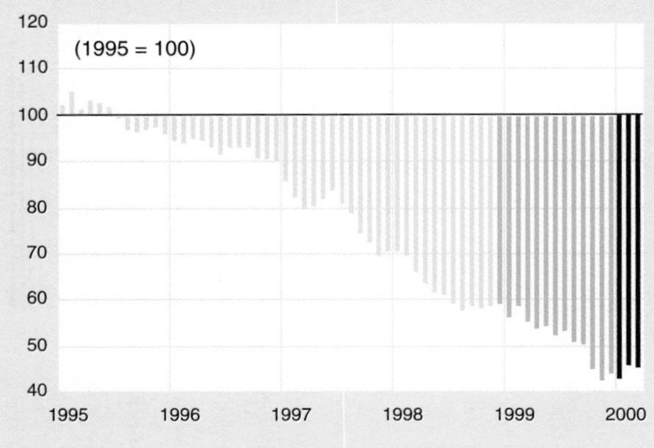

Industrial production
monthly

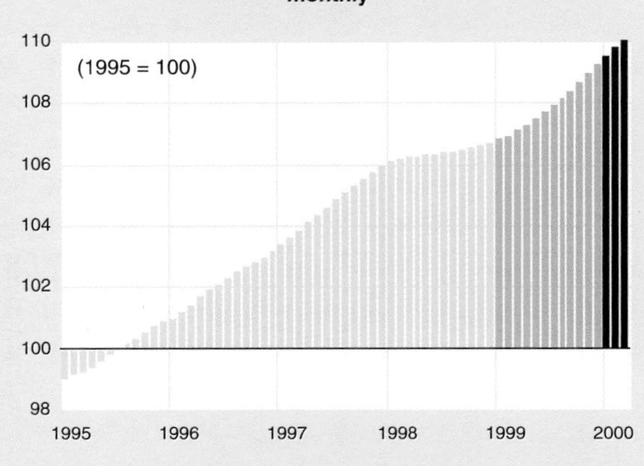

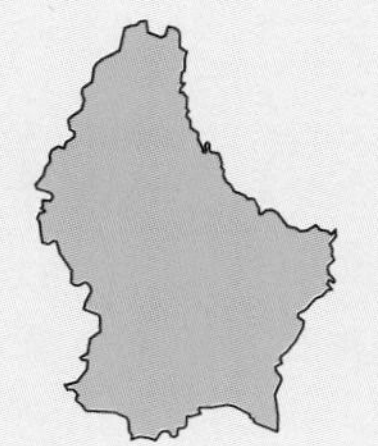

Luxembourg

		1999	2000 q1
GDP	% growth	7.5	0.0
Consumption	% growth	4.1	2.1
Investments	% growth	10.1	1.6
Consumer prices	% growth	1.0	0.3
Unemployment	% growth	– 12.2	– 10.3
Industrial production	% growth	3.6	– 3.0

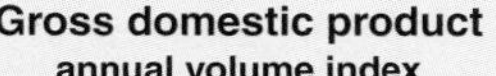

Gross domestic product
annual volume index

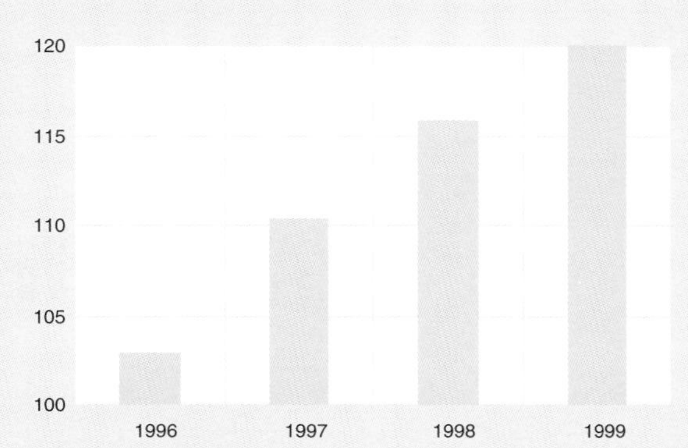

Gross domestic product
annual growth rates

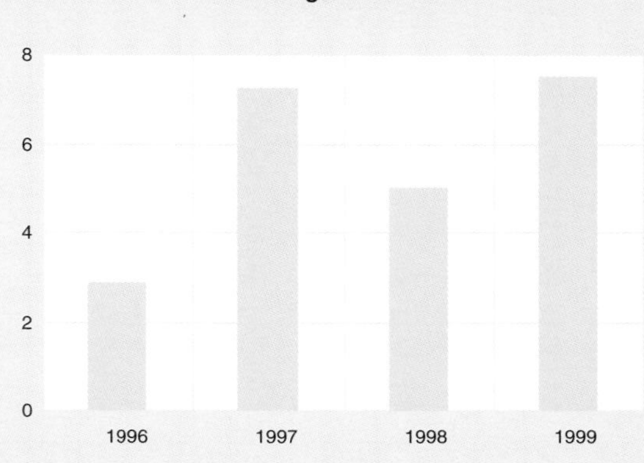

Consumption and investments
annual growth rates

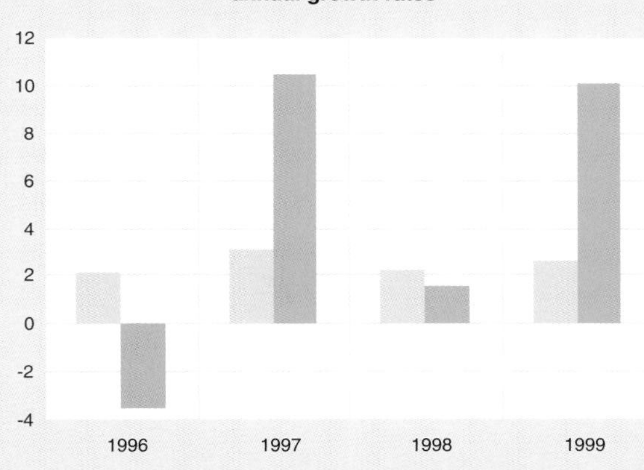

Harmonised index of consumer prices
monthly

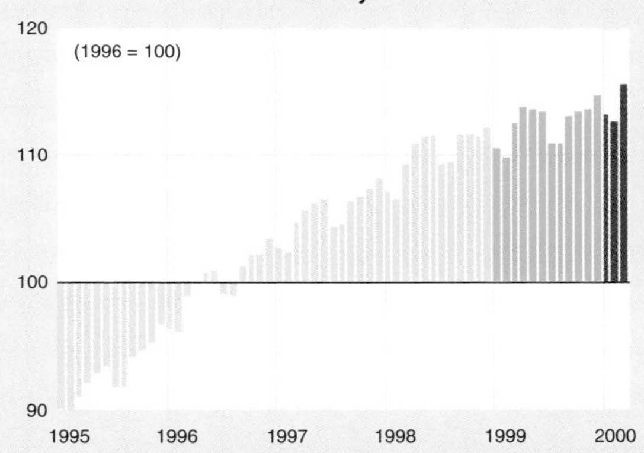

Unemployment
monthly

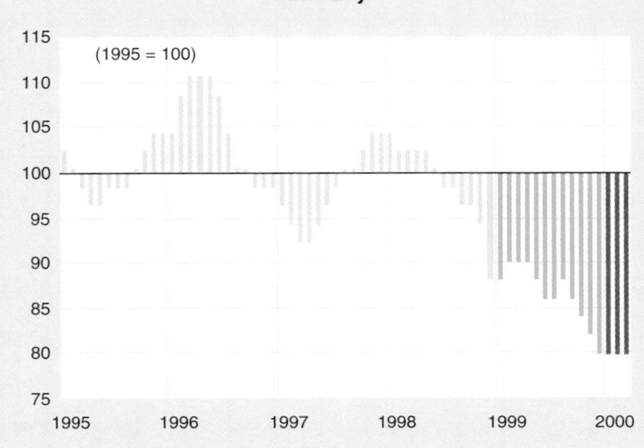

Industrial production
monthly

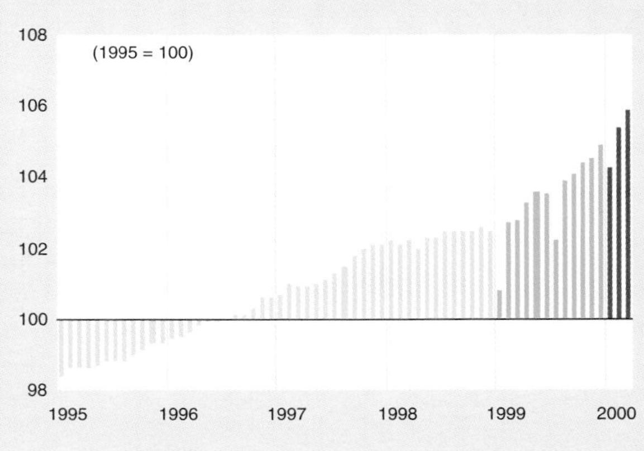

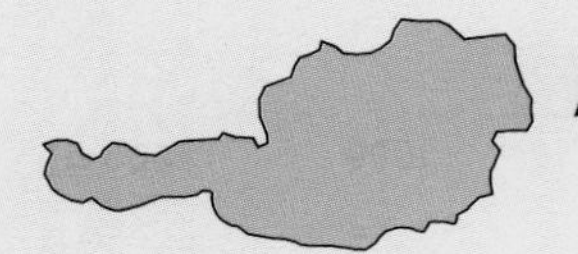

Austria

		1999	2000 q1
GDP	% growth	2.1	1.0
Consumption	% growth	2.4	1.2
Investments	% growth	3.5	1.2
Consumer prices	% growth	0.5	0.3
Unemployment	% growth	– 14.5	– 4.8
Industrial production	% growth	4.7	0.5

Gross domestic product
quarterly volume index

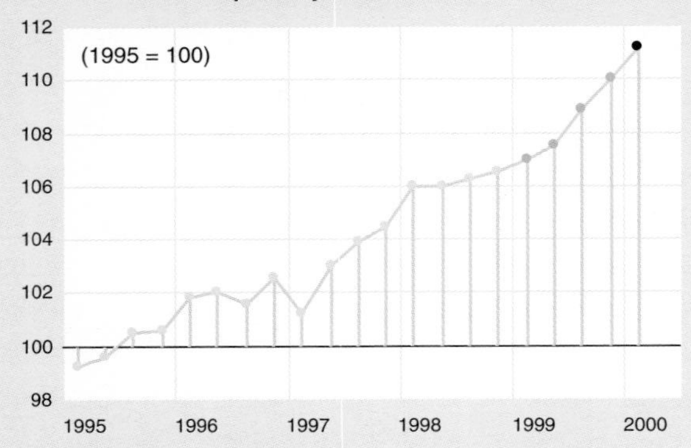

Gross domestic product
quarterly volume rates

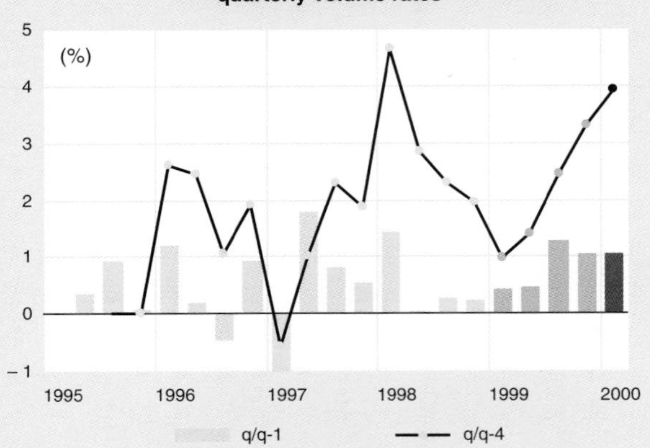

Consumption and investments
quarterly growth rates

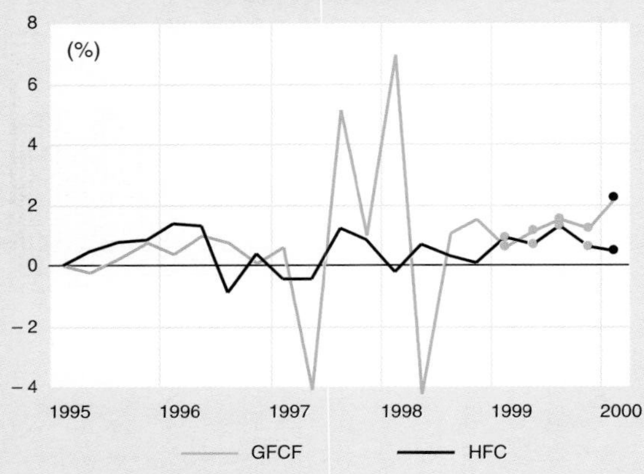

Harmonised index of consumer prices
monthly

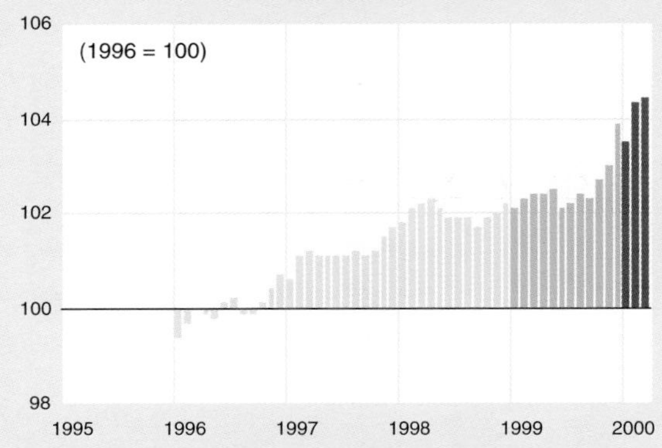

Unemployment
monthly

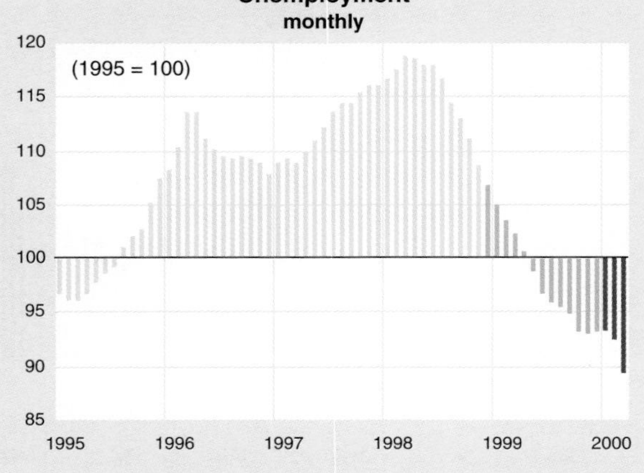

Industrial production
monthly

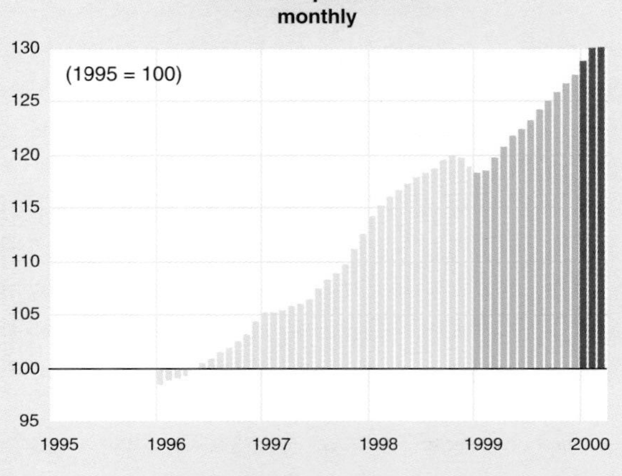

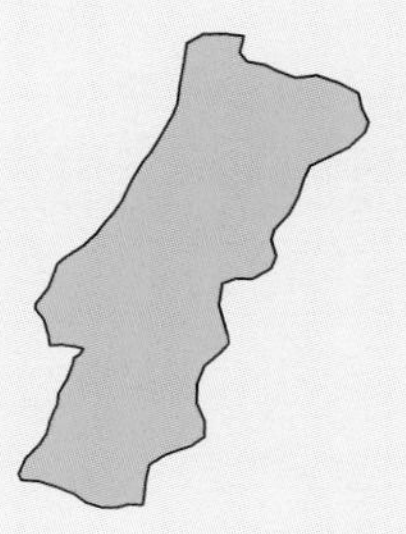

Portugal

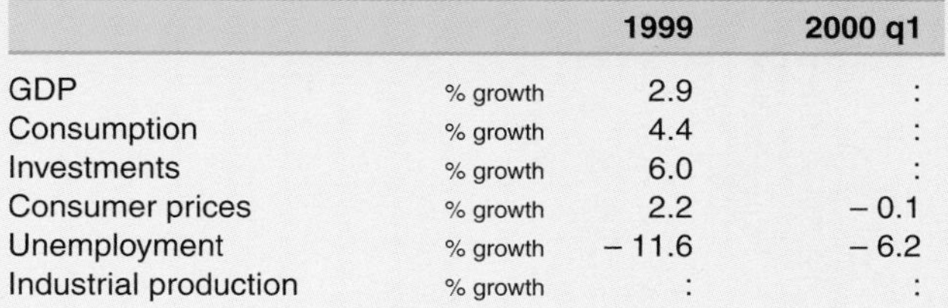

		1999	2000 q1
GDP	% growth	2.9	:
Consumption	% growth	4.4	:
Investments	% growth	6.0	:
Consumer prices	% growth	2.2	– 0.1
Unemployment	% growth	– 11.6	– 6.2
Industrial production	% growth	:	:

Gross domestic product
quarterly volume index

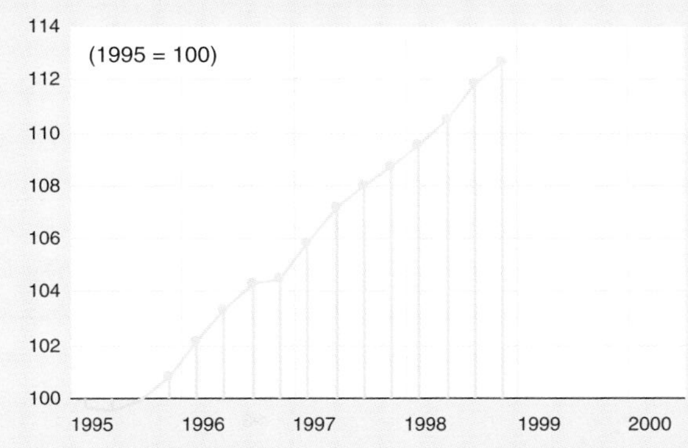

Gross domestic product
quarterly volume rates

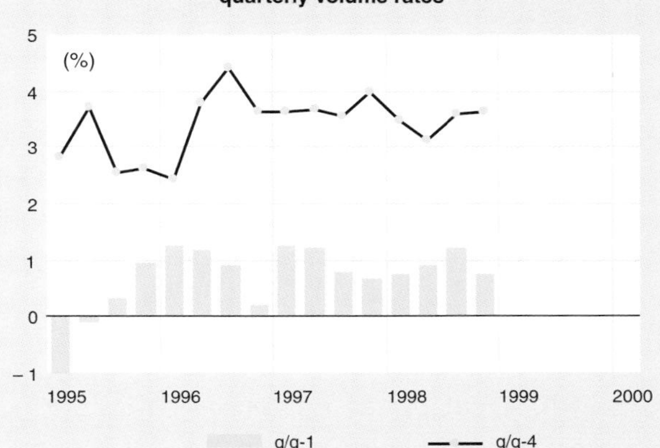

Consumption and investments
quarterly growth rates

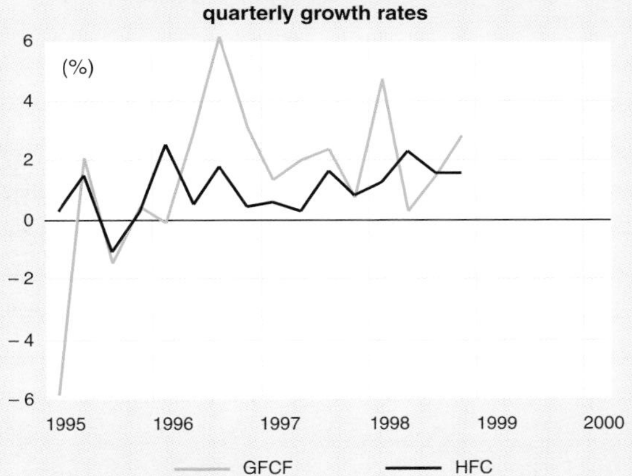

Harmonised index of consumer prices
monthly

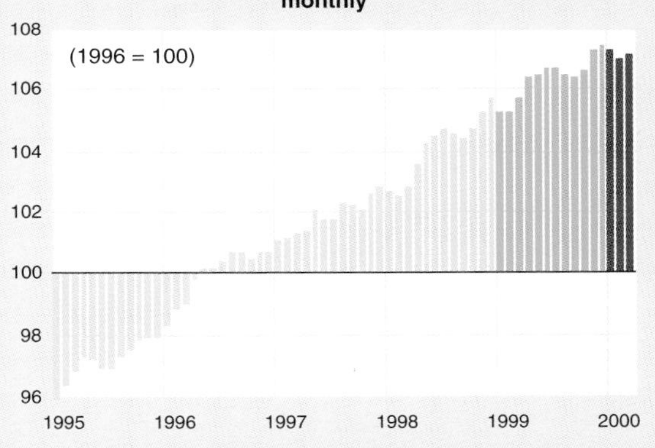

Unemployment
monthly

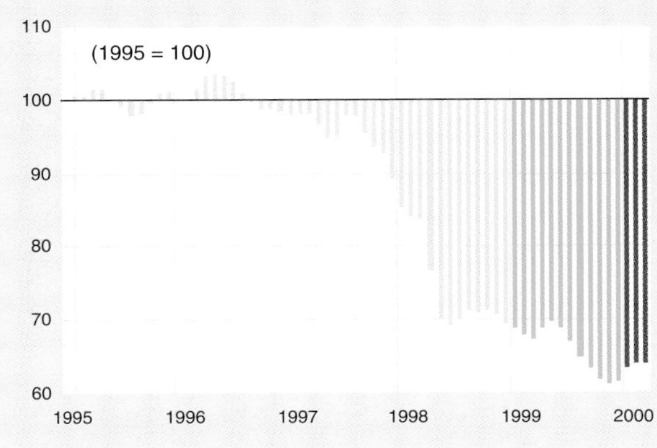

Industrial production
monthly

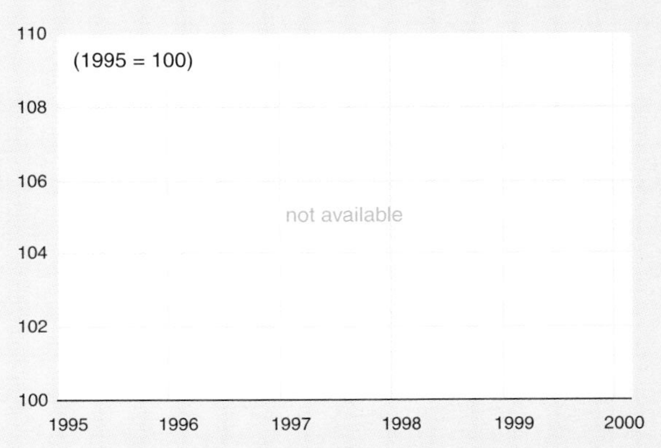

Finland

		1999	2000 q1
GDP	% growth	4.0	1.6
Consumption	% growth	2.9	1.2
Investments	% growth	4.8	0.8
Consumer prices	% growth	1.3	0.5
Unemployment	% growth	– 8.5	2.4
Industrial production	% growth	5.4	2.7

Gross domestic product
quarterly volume index

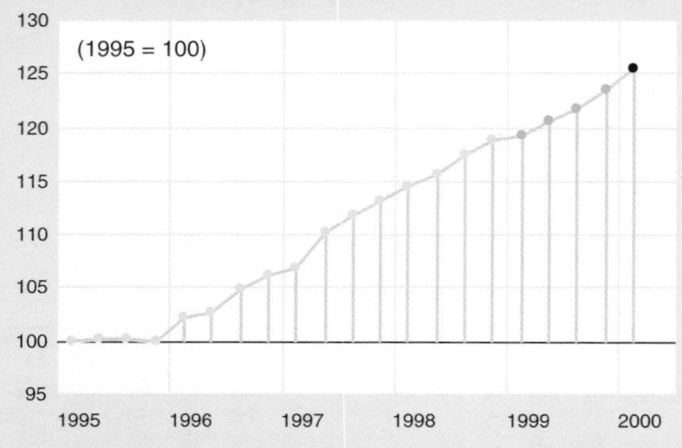

Gross domestic product
quarterly volume rates

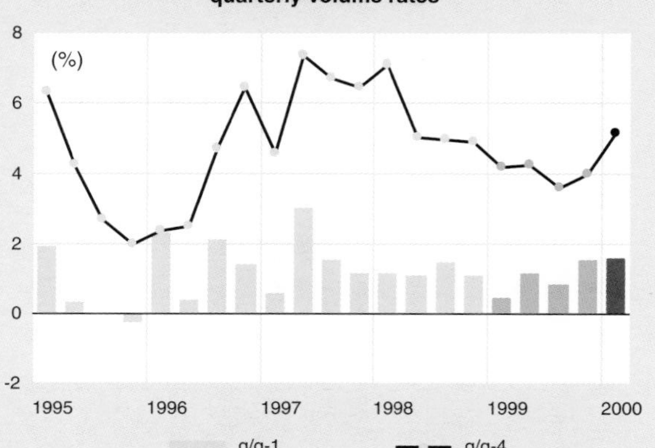

Consumption and investments
quarterly growth rates

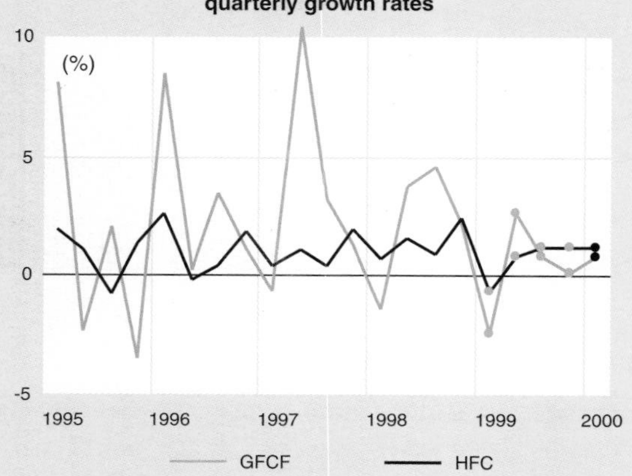

Harmonised index of consumer prices
monthly

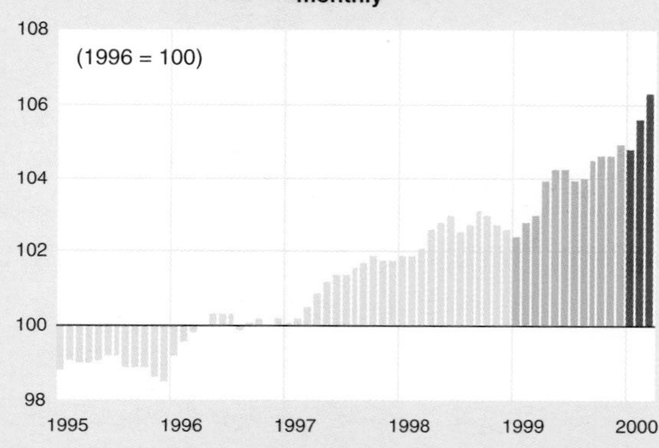

Unemployment
monthly

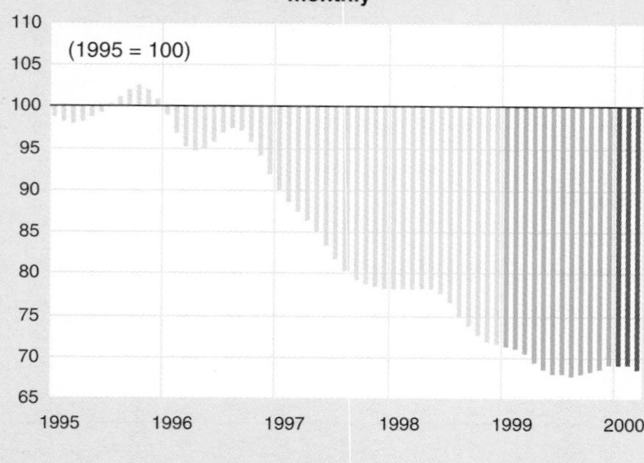

Industrial production
monthly

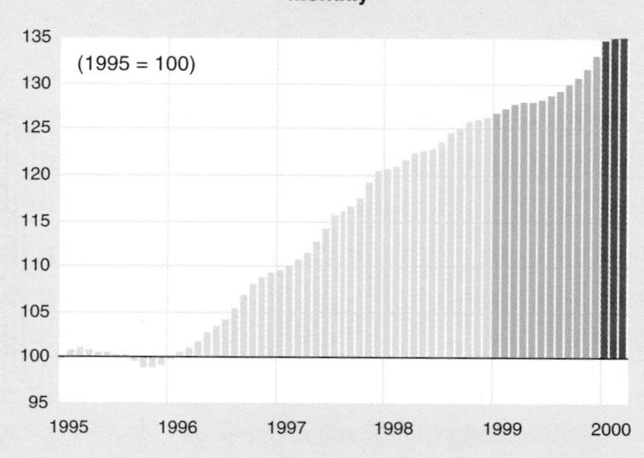

Sweden

		1999	2000 q1
GDP	% growth	3.8	0.7
Consumption	% growth	4.1	1.1
Investments	% growth	8.1	0.6
Consumer prices	% growth	0.6	0.2
Unemployment	% growth	– 13.2	– 13.9
Industrial production	% growth	:	:

Gross domestic product
quarterly volume index

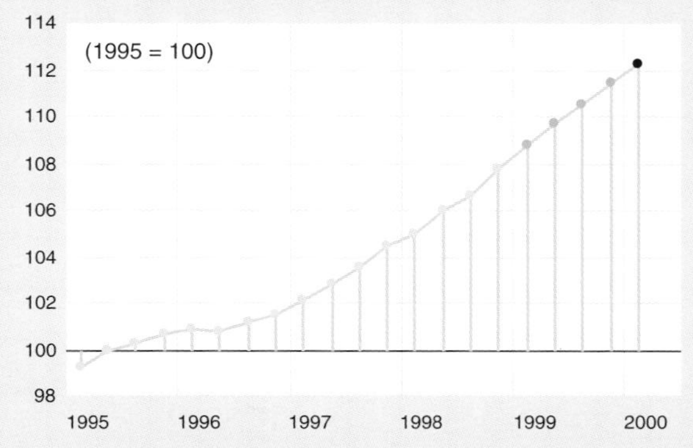

Gross domestic product
quarterly volume rates

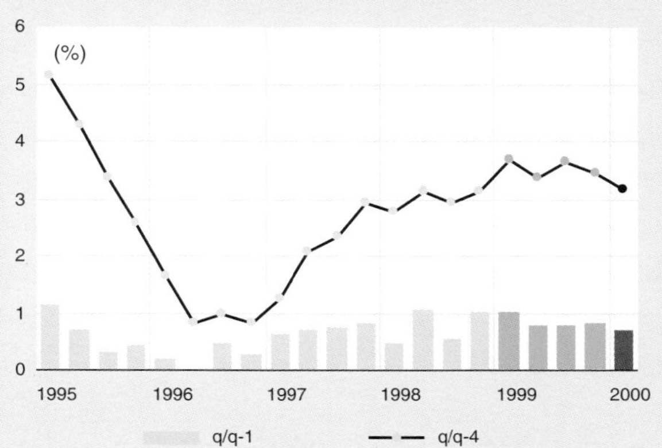

Consumption and investments
quarterly growth rates

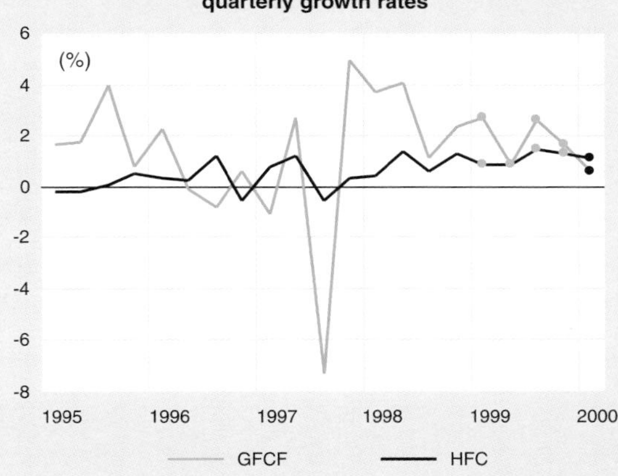

Harmonised index of consumer prices
monthly

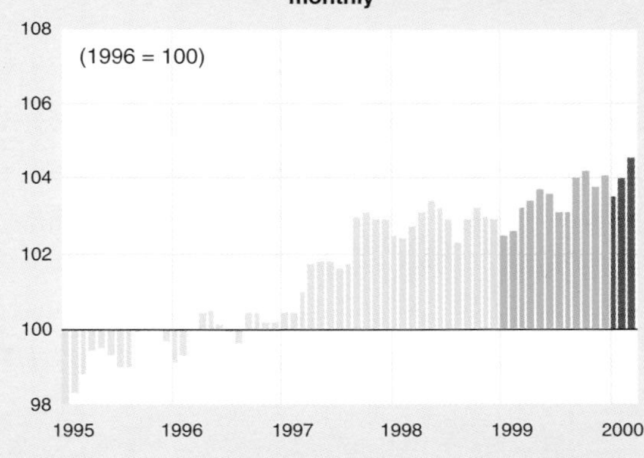

Unemployment
monthly

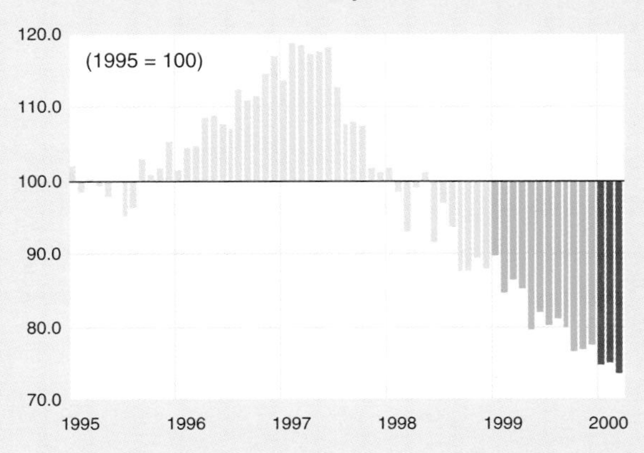

Industrial production
monthly

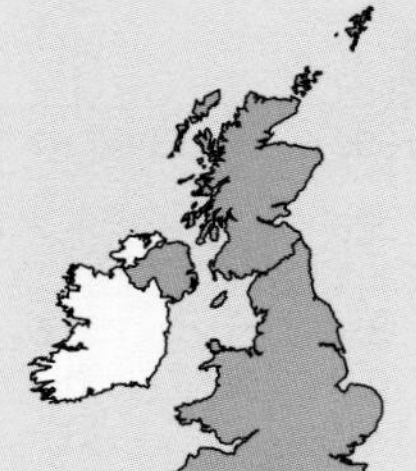

United Kingdom

		1999	2000 q1
GDP	% growth	2.1	0.5
Consumption	% growth	3.9	0.7
Investments	% growth	5.2	– 1.1
Consumer prices	% growth	1.3	– 0.1
Unemployment	% growth	– 3.5	– 5.7
Industrial production	% growth	0.1	0.3

Gross domestic product
quarterly volume index

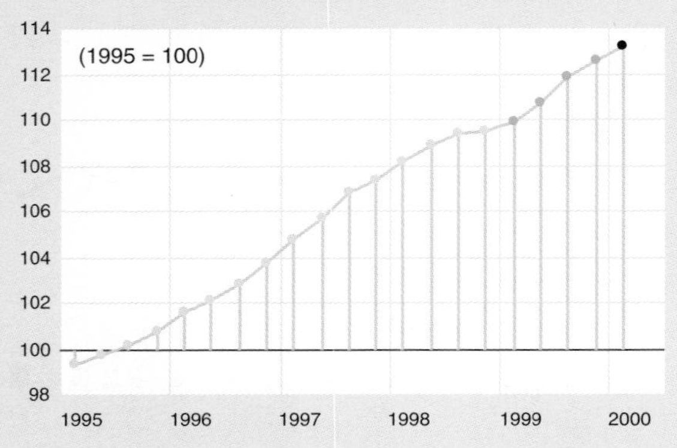

Gross domestic product
quarterly volume rates

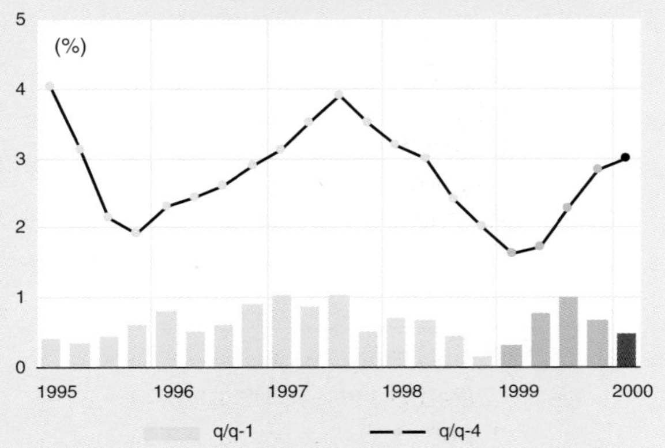

Consumption and investments
quarterly growth rates

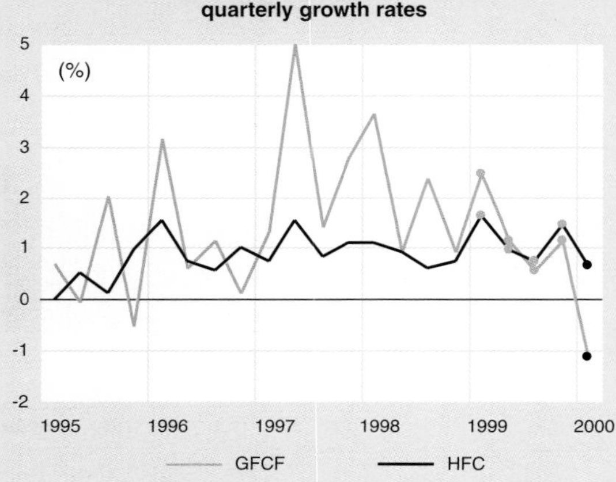

Harmonised index of consumer prices
monthly

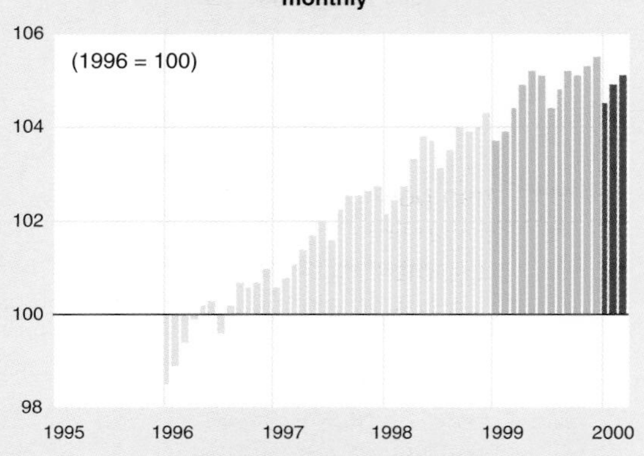

Unemployment
monthly

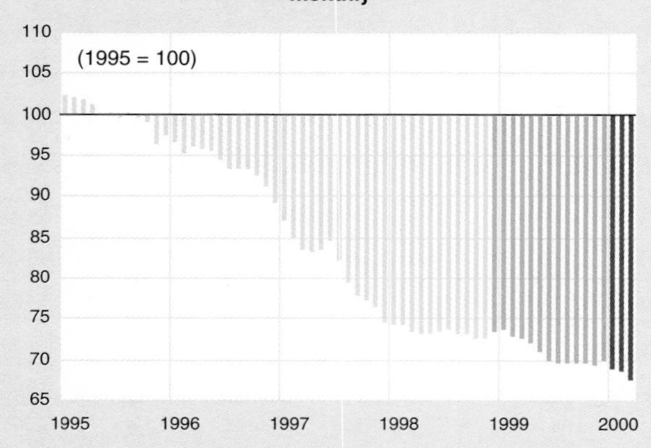

Industrial production
monthly

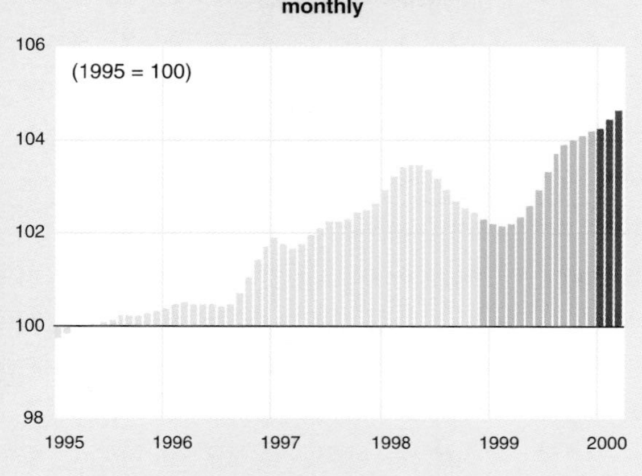

Symbols and abbreviations

EU	European Union
EUR-11	euro zone (Belgium, Germany, Spain, France, Ireland, Italy, Luxembourg, Netherlands, Austria, Portugal and Finland)
EU-15	European Union of 15 Member States
B	Belgium
DK	Denmark
D	Germany (former FRG and West Berlin until 1990, Unified Germany since 1991)
EL	Greece
E	Spain
F	France
IRL	Ireland
I	Italy
L	Luxembourg
NL	Netherlands
A	Austria
P	Portugal
FIN	Finland
S	Sweden
UK	United Kingdom
US	United States of America
JP	Japan
BEF	Belgian franc
DKK	Danish crown
DEM	German mark
GRD	Greek drachma
ESP	Spanish peseta
FRF	French franc
IEP	Irish pound
ITL	Italian lira
LUF	Luxembourgish franc
NLG	Dutch guilder
ATS	Austrian schilling
PTE	Portuguese escudo
FIM	Finnish mark
SEK	Swedish crown
GBP	Pound Sterling
USD	United States dollar
YEN	Japanese yen
billion	billion (thousand million)
:	data not available

European Commission

Economic portrait of the European Union — 1999

Luxembourg: Office for Official Publications of the European Communities

2000 — 195 pp. — 21 x 29.7 cm

Theme 2: Economy and finance
Collection: Panorama of the European Union

ISBN 92-828-9913-6

Price (excluding VAT) in Luxembourg: EUR 30

.... Eurostat Data Shops

BELGIQUE/BELGIË

Eurostat Data Shop
Bruxelles/Brussel
Planistat Belgique
Rue du Commerce 124
Handelsstraat 124
B-1000 Bruxelles/Brussel
Tél. (32-2) 234 67 50
Fax (32-2) 234 67 51
E-mail: datashop@planistat.be

DANMARK

DANMARKS STATISTIK
Bibliotek og Information
Eurostat Data Shop
Sejrøgade 11
DK-2100 København Ø
Tlf. (45) 39 17 30 30
Fax (45) 39 17 30 03
E-mail: bib@dst.dk

DEUTSCHLAND

Statistisches Bundesamt
Eurostat Data Shop Berlin
Otto-Braun-Straße 70-72
(Eingang: Karl-Marx-Allee)
D-10178 Berlin
Tel. (49) 1888-644 94 27/28
Fax (49) 1888-644 94 30
E-Mail:
datashop@statistik-bund.de

ESPAÑA

INE
Eurostat Data Shop
Paseo de la Castellana, 183
Oficina 009
Entrada por Estébanez
Calderón
E-28046 Madrid
Tel. (34) 91 583 91 67
Fax (34) 91 579 71 20
E-mail:
datashop.eurostat@ine.es
Member of the MIDAS Net

FRANCE

INSEE Info service
Eurostat Data Shop
195, rue de Bercy
Tour Gamma A
F-75582 Paris Cedex 12
Tél. (33) 1 53 17 88 44
Fax (33) 1 53 17 88 22
E-mail: datashop@insee.fr
Member of the MIDAS Net

ITALIA - ROMA

ISTAT
Centro di informazione statistica — Sede di Roma
Eurostat Data Shop
Via Cesare Balbo, 11a
I-00184 Roma
Tel. (39) 06 46 73 31 02/06
Fax (39) 06 46 73 31 01/07
E-mail: dipdiff@istat.it
Member of the MIDAS Net

ITALIA - MILANO

ISTAT
Ufficio regionale per la Lombardia
Eurostat Data Shop
Via Fieno, 3
I-20123 Milano
Tel. (39) 02 80 61 32 460
Fax (39) 02 80 61 32 304
E-mail: mileuro@tin.it
Member of the MIDAS Net

LUXEMBOURG

Eurostat Data Shop Luxembourg
BP 453
L-2014 Luxembourg
4, rue Alphonse Weicker
L-2721 Luxembourg
Tél. (352) 43 35-2251
Fax (352) 43 35-22221
E-mail:
dslux@eurostat.datashop.lu
Member of the MIDAS Net

NEDERLAND

STATISTICS NETHERLANDS
Eurostat Data Shop — Voorburg
Postbus 4000
2270 JM Voorburg
Nederland
Tel. (31-70) 337 49 00
Fax (31-70) 337 59 84
E-mail: datashop@cbs.nl

PORTUGAL

Eurostat Data Shop Lisboa
INE/Serviço de Difusão
Av. António José de Almeida, 2
P-1000-043 Lisboa
Tel. (351) 21 842 61 00
Fax (351) 21 842 63 64
E-mail: data.shop@ine.pt

SUOMI/FINLAND

STATISTICS FINLAND
Eurostat DataShop Helsinki
Tilastokirjasto
PL 2B
FIN-00022 Tilastokeskus
Työpajakatu 13 B, 2. Kerros,
Helsinki
P. (358-9) 17 34 22 21
F. (358-9) 17 34 22 79
Sähköposti:
datashop.tilastokeskus@
tilastokeskus.fi
URL:
http://www.tilastokeskus.fi/tk/kk/datashop.html

SVERIGE

STATISTICS SWEDEN
Information service
Eurostat Data Shop
Karlavägen 100
Box 24 300
S-104 51 Stockholm
Tfn (46-8) 50 69 48 01
Fax (46-8) 50 69 48 99
E-post: infoservice@scb.se
Internet:
http://www.scb.se/info/
datashop/eudatashop.asp

UNITED KINGDOM

Eurostat Data Shop
Enquiries & advice and publications
Office for National Statistics
Customers & Electronic
Services Unit B1/05
1 Drummond Gate
London SW1V 2QQ
United Kingdom
Tel. (44-20) 75 33 56 76
Fax (44-1633) 81 27 62
E-mail:
eurostat.datashop@ons.gov.uk
Member of the MIDAS Net

Eurostat Data Shop
Electronic Data Extractions, enquiries & advice r.cade
1L Mountjoy Research Centre
University of Durham
Durham DH1 3SW
United Kingdom
Tel. (44-191) 374 73 50
Fax (44-191) 384 49 71
E-mail: r-cade@dur.ac.uk
Internet:
http://www-rcade.dur.ac.uk

NORWAY

Statistics Norway
Library and Information Centre
Eurostat Data Shop
Kongens gate 6
Boks 8131 Dep.
N-0033 Oslo
Tel. (47) 22 86 46 43
Fax (47) 22 86 45 04
E-mail: Datashop@ssb.no

SCHWEIZ/SUISSE/SVIZZERA

Statistisches Amt des Kantons Zürich
Eurostat Data Shop
Bleicherweg 5
CH-8090 Zürich
Tel. (41-1) 225 12 12
Fax (41-1) 225 12 99
E-mail: datashop@zh.ch
Internet:
http://www.zh.ch/statistik

USA

HAVER ANALYTICS
Eurostat Data Shop
60 East 42nd Street
Suite 3310
New York, NY 10165
Tel. (1-212) 986 93 00
Fax (1-212) 986 69 81
E-mail: eurodata@haver.com

EUROSTAT HOME PAGE
www.europa.eu.int/comm/eurostat/

MEDIA SUPPORT EUROSTAT
(only for professional journalists)
Postal address:
Jean Monnet building
L-2920 Luxembourg
Office: BECH A3/48 —
5, rue Alphonse Weicker
L-2721 Luxembourg
Tel. (352) 43 01-33408
Fax (352) 43 01-32649
E-mail:
Eurostat-mediasupport@cec.eu.int